Challenging Orthodoxies

Studies in the
Postmodern Theory of Education

Joe L. Kincheloe and Shirley R. Steinberg
General Editors

Vol. 76

PETER LANG
New York • Washington, D.C./Baltimore • Boston
Bern • Frankfurt am Main • Berlin • Vienna • Paris

Sol Cohen

Challenging Orthodoxies

Toward a New Cultural History of Education

PETER LANG
New York • Washington, D.C./Baltimore • Boston
Bern • Frankfurt am Main • Berlin • Vienna • Paris

Library of Congress Cataloging-in-Publication Data

Cohen, Sol.
Challenging orthodoxies: toward a new cultural history of education / Sol Cohen.
p. cm. — (Counterpoints; v. 76)
Includes bibliographical references and index.
1. Education—United States—History—20th century. 2. Education—Social aspects—
United States—History—20th century. 3. Educational anthropology—United States—
History—20th century. I. Title. II. Series: Counterpoints (New York, N.Y.); vol. 76.
LA209.C635   370'.973—dc21   97-38331
ISBN 0-8204-3940-1
ISSN 1058-1634

Die Deutsche Bibliothek-CIP-Einheitsaufnahme

Cohen, Sol:
Challenging orthodoxies: toward a new cultural history of education / Sol Cohen.
–New York; Washington, D.C./Baltimore; Boston; Bern;
Frankfurt am Main; Berlin; Vienna; Paris: Lang.
(Counterpoints; Vol. 76)
ISBN 0-8204-3940-1

Cover design by David Gonzalez

The paper in this book meets the guidelines for permanence and durability
of the Committee on Production Guidelines for Book Longevity
of the Council of Library Resources.

Printed in the United States of America

Table of Contents

Preface

I.

The genesis of this book was the confluence of two developments. The first was an invitation in 1995 to co-edit a special issue of *Paedagogica Historica*, the international journal of the history of education, on "History of Education in the Postmodern Era." The editors, Marc Depaepe and Frank Simon, felt that postmodernism confronts historians of education with new challenges but that the ongoing discussion in general historiography seems to pass by at the fringes of our discipline. The question was how to address these challenges "within historical writing about education or in criticism or theory about historical writing in education or how they might affect the forms of historical expression." Since I had been teaching a seminar in postmodernism in history and the social sciences for several years, the invitation from *Paedagogica Historica* couldn't have been more timely. It unexpectedly confirmed the relevance and necessity of my recent historiographical pursuits.[1]

The second development was a joint conference of the Canadian History of Education Association (CHEA) and the (American) History of Education Society (HES) at the University of Toronto in 1996; the main theme was "Challenging Orthodoxies: New Perspectives in Histories of Education." The challenge set by CHEA/HES was to question the orthodoxies of what counts as historical research and historical knowledge, expand the boundaries of theory and method that currently define the practice of history of education, and debate recent theoretical challenges to history within and beyond education. This call also couldn't have been more timely; its subject has been the theme of my work for almost two decades. All of my projects, seemingly unconnected, began to fall in line, serving a coherent theme. The nexus of these two developments presented an opportunity for me to take stock not only of my own work as a historian of education, but of the historiography of education as well.

II.

My title is intended to give the feel of the book. I make no apologies for my use of "new" in the subtitle. I mean it as a point of departure, not as a point of arrival. (Note: I qualify "new" with the word "toward"; I haven't arrived yet). And something new is going on across a broad range of historical discourses.[2]

The new cultural history of education does not represent an absolute rupture with the past. The vogue of social history of education, which began in the late 1960s and which came at the expense of intellectual history of education, has lasted thirty years now. The perspectives of social history of education are today so well-known, and its achievements are so extensive, that it's hard to remember a time when social control and social conflict approaches, urban history, family history, black history, history of women, history of people of color, history of ethnic and religious minorities, and "history from the bottom up" were not part of the historiographical frame. I do not wish to deny the continued utility of class and class struggle, social stratification, and racial, ethnic, and gender discrimination as working concepts, but I would like to see history of education move forward or, less normatively, to bring history of ideas or intellectual history back into the frame. I think this can be done through the new cultural history without devaluing social history of education. The new cultural history, as I point out below, integrates social and intellectual history, two fields usually studied in isolation from one another; I might say the new cultural history is a continuation of intellectual and social history by other means.

What exactly is the new cultural history? It is quite clear that there is no more agreement over what constitutes the new cultural history than there is agreement over what constitutes culture.[3] The new cultural history is a broad, complex, and seemingly all-encompassing rubric.[4] I would like to avoid debate over the problem of definition—the boundaries of the various branches of history are flags of convenience, arbitrary and conventional, not names of essences—and to simply mark out a sphere of interest in a different approach to doing history of education. In general, the new cultural history offers an opportunity for historians of education to cross disciplinary boundaries, multiply the "forms of curiosity," and "wander in every field."[5] As Clifford Geertz, whose influence on the new cultural history has been immense, observes, the cultural approach has induced a blurring of genres and of disciplines.[6] The new cultural history encourages the recognition that cultural meaning can be carried by a variety of texts. The new cultural history creates new possibilities for reading history into any cultural artifact, "elite" or "popular," academic tome or cartoon, and vice versa, for interpreting any cultural artifact as text in history.

Specifically, I am mainly concerned with connecting the historiography of education to those developments which go under a synoptic label—the "linguistic turn"—and which stress the socially constructed nature of reality and the importance of language and rhetorical structures in the production of historical knowledge and historical understanding. The linguistic turn suggests an approach to doing history which, while obligating us to challenge (but not necessarily negate or reject) inherited orthodoxies, will make us more self-reflective about our practices as we enlarge our repertoire of reading, writing, and teaching strategies. The linguistic turn has led some historians to language not simply as a methodological tool, but to language as itself the object of historical investigation. The new cultural history, as I understand it, however, does not imply textual imperialism or pantextualism. The linguistic turn does not textualize the whole of reality. On the contrary, the linguistic turn can't help making us more sensitive to Michel Foucault's question: "Whom does discourse serve and what are its effects?," to the supremely political nature of language, and to the relations between language, discourse, and power.

III.

The dominant concern of *Challenging Orthodoxies* is to explore the implications of the linguistic turn for historians of education. Two aspects of the many-faceted linguistic turn are of special interest to me. One has to do with the implications of literary theory for the writing, reading, and interpretation of historical narratives. As Lloyd S. Kramer observes: "The one truly distinguishing feature of the new cultural approach to history is the pervasive influence of recent literary theory, which has taught historians to recognize the active role of language, texts, and narrative structures in the creation and description of historical reality."[8] The new cultural history privileges the literary and rhetorical properties of historical narratives and the linguistic structures and genres that operate in the construction of meaning in historical narratives and consequently adds an important dimension to our interpretive project. The other aspect of the linguistic turn that interests me has to do with considering language as a historical source— as material or empirical as any other historical source—and making language itself both a basic object of and a methodology for historical investigation.

One virtue of the new cultural history is that it highlights neglected approaches to historical inquiry without necessarily excluding any. The new cultural approach to history of education may be perceived as challenging the hegemony of social history of education, but I perceive the cultural approach as an attempt to right an imbalance. In fact, the new cultural history embraces social and intellectual history. There is no conflict between them; they cannot be divorced from each other. Ideas and language are themselves social events and forms of social action, instruments that are used to attempt to influence, persuade, and control. And, vice versa, every social action possesses an essential linguistic or symbolic dimension.[9] The new cultural approach assumes that all historians must be concerned with problems of meaning and interpretation of "text," inclusively defined. In fact, the new cultural history expands the terrain of both social and intellectual history by opening up a whole new world of social facts, a new family of social acts or social events: language. All social historians must deal with language, discourse, and textual sources. They must be concerned with the hermeneutics of texts, with problems of language, meaning, and interpretation. And intellectual historians must be concerned with the performative function of language and texts. The cultural approach makes these concerns explicit and subject to scrutiny while expanding our repertoire of writing, reading, and interpretive methodologies. In this sense, the new cultural history deals with issues relevant to all historians of education.

IV.

It is no doubt true that all my writing projects in the last fifteen or twenty years have been motivated by a fascination with "challenging orthodoxies" and "new perspectives" in history of education. But my work and this book go beyond any personal interest. My primary concern is with the fortunes of the history of education, not with the fortunes of the new cultural history of education. I think we must be concerned with the state of the discipline of history of education in the United States, if not elsewhere. Certainly, given the problems of contemporary education in general in the United States, we cannot relax in the comfort and security of a well-established, thriving discipline. At any rate, as we approach the millennium, I sense not the end of history but a resurgence of interest in history. How will historians of education respond? History of education as a field of study in the professional education program has been able to survive for a century because it has always redefined or reinvented itself as needed. I cannot put the matter much better than Joan Burstyn did a decade ago in connection with her plea for the incorporation of women's studies into the historiography of education:

> We in the history of education have narrowed our impact by becoming too set in our ways. If we expanded our repertoire of techniques, broadened our set of subjects, and projected our work to a wider audience, we would rejuvenate not only ourselves but the whole historical enterprise.[10]

The new cultural history points to a way in which we may renew our vocation as well as our specialty.

V.

Now for some more detailed description of the book's contents. In each chapter, I try to incorporate the new cultural approach to history of education. Themes of language, rhetoric, and representation are interwoven throughout the book. For the reader's convenience I divide the book into two parts. The essays in both parts of the book deal with historiographical and theoretical as well as empirical issues.

Part I

Historians of American education, like other academics, devote little time to studying their own discipline. The result is a paucity of studies concerning the internal politics of the field, the relation between history of education and the general discipline of history, the relation between history of education and the other components of the curriculum in the professional program, or the relation of education schools to arts and science faculties.

Throughout its existence as a field of study, history of American education has offered different meanings to different historians. Chap-

ters 1 and 2 reconstruct the history of the history of American education, a past that is a living component of the personal and community
identity of historians of education in the present. They consider a
fundamental and long-standing problem all historians of education face:
the degree to which they should be engaged with the educational or
social problems of the day, that is, questions about the "function" or
usefulness of history of education in a college, school, or department
of education—liberal, professional or technical, or social
reconstructionist. There is no dispute about historians of education
being useful to the professional program. But how, for whom, and for
what interest, aim, or purpose? This issue, debated from the turn of
the century to the present, remains unresolved, and the passage of
time hasn't diminished it.

It has often been said that history is written by the victors. It might
also be said that history is forgotten by the victors, who think they can
afford to forget. The received wisdom of even the most recent histories of American education begins with an account of the ways in
which Elwood P. Cubberley or the Cubberley historiographical tradition of the early twentieth century stymied the development of the
field. Indeed, the inherited wisdom suggests that the Cubberley tradition was the only obstacle to the progressive development of history
of American education until the pathbreaking contributions of Bernard Bailyn and Lawrence Cremin in the late 1950s and early 1960s.
In Chapter 1, I point out that the Cubberley tradition was challenged
long before the late 1950s, and that a rich and controversial chapter
in the history of American education was suppressed in the zeal to get
on with their new history of education. I reevaluate the received interpretation of Cubberley, advance a new interpretation of Bailyn's and
Cremin's rejection of the Cubberley tradition, and place their new
history of education in the broader context of the debate over and the
assault upon history of education that came from both inside and
outside the field in the 1950s. After tracing the development of this
controversy, I note certain continuities between the past and present
in the history of education as a field of study. I suggest that our problems today are not so very different from those experienced in the
past, and suggest ways by which we may resume the conversation
with the past where it was broken off, or perhaps change the conversation in preparation for the new century.

Chapter 2 provides a new perspective on the emergence of a "radical revisionist" movement in educational historiography in the late
1960s, and on its foremost practitioner, Michael B. Katz. It locates

the radical revisionist controversy which polarized historians of education in the 1970s in the context of that tumultuous decade. Chapter 2
also explores the role of Diane Ravitch and Lawrence Cremin in the
revisionist affair. Revisiting this controversy, I argue that it was not so
much the issue of the radical revisionists' conflict approach to the
historiography of American education that was at stake, but which of
the two contending interpretive frames—romance and tragedy or satire—would have control over the interpretation of the American educational past. In the end, no one historiographical genre, neither romance nor satire, was to achieve hegemony. There was to be no single
authorized mode of investigating the past of American education. I
make the point that the revisionist controversy did result in a subtler
and more complex social history of urban education, and I reassess
the contribution of David B. Tyack's organizational interpretation of
urban educational historiography in this context. I go on to argue that
a new radical revisionism in the form of counternarratives, of which
cinema provides an obvious example, may be appropriate for our
time.

Chapters 1 and 2 both stress that historians of American education
(and their students and anyone interested in the history of education
as a field of study) have to be reminded of this past because their
published work is situated within the context of this body of preexisting debates, its participants, and its canon of texts. Additionally, the
debates of the past anticipate to a great extent the terms and debates
of the present. But as the past recedes, so does memory. These chapters are written against forgetting.

Historians of education have paid scant attention to the role of
rhetoric in the production of their histories or in constituting our discipline. Rhetoric is ordinarily deemed mere adornment or decoration
on the substantive historical content. Chapter 3 argues that rhetoric is
mixed right into the content. Drawing mainly on Hayden White's poetics of history, I attempt to demonstrate how literary and rhetorical
devices operate in the construction of historians' texts and in our
critical reception of them. I raise the rhetorical question of how historical texts do what they do. This perspective allows me to focus on
the rhetorical strategies historians employ to establish the reality of
their version of the past of American education and to persuade readers that their version is a true and authoritative reconstruction of that
past. I argue that the attention paid to texts and narrative by literary
theorists (and philosophers) is something that historians of education
could well learn from and that a rhetorical reading—in contrast to a

referential (or what Dominick LaCapra calls a "documentary") reading—can yield new insights, help us discover meaning in unexpected
places, make us aware of unexpected aspects of the writing of history,
and enable us to read histories in ways we have not done before.

Chapters 4 and 5 argue that the core ideas of the linguistic turn and
some of its leading theorists and practitioners—Ferdinand de Saussure,
J. L. Austin, John G. A. Pocock, Michel Foucault, Richard Rorty, and
Hayden White—can shed new light on one of the central, persistent,
and seemingly intractable historiographical problems of the past thirty-
five years: that of "progressive education."

Lawrence Cremin's *The Transformation of the School: Progressivism in American Education, 1876–1957* (1961) is the founding
metanarrative of progressive education. However, Cremin's interpretation of the history of progressive education is strongly contested.
Among the issues are these: Was there a "progressive education"? If
yes, how should "progressive education" be understood? How far-
reaching was its influence on the "transformation" of American education in the twentieth century, if there was a "transformation"at all?
This problem remains a preoccupation of the historiography of American education. In Chapters 4 and 5, I redescribe progressive education and the transformation of the school solely in terms of language
and argue that with this move, we can preserve both terms as meaningful entities while creating new possibilities for moving the historiographical debate onto fresh and more fertile ground.

In Chapter 6, I propose that we extend the range of what counts as
evidence or historical source for understanding the world of education, past and present, to include film. The historians Robert
Rosenstone, Robert Toplin, and Michael Wood, among others I cite,
have persuasively made the case that film is an important cultural text,
a legitimate source for research in history and a subject for textual
study (as well as a potent teaching device). The theories of Raymond
Williams, Mikhail Bakhtin, Bill Nichols, and Jacques Derrida become
the means for a deconstructive and intertextual reading of *Dead Poets Society* (1989) and for a meditation on the enduring and vital
tension between traditionalism and progressivism, self and community, and freedom and order in American education. Since cinema
raises in exemplary form all the historical discipline's anxieties about
representation, reality, objectivity, and truth, Chapter 6 also becomes
a vehicle for reflection on the epistemological and literary status of
written history and historical knowledge.

Part II

In the 1950s, there were two massive shifts in the discursive landscape of American education—one, about which we know something, is associated with progressive education; the other, about which we know very little, has to do with the mental hygiene movement and what I call the "medicalization" of American education. Chapters 7 through 11 treat different facets of this development.

Chapter 7 provides an account of the history of the movement to create a psychoanalytic pedagogy that would prevent neurosis. It describes the movement's core Freudian terminology and concepts, its main participants—central European child analysts led by Anna Freud—and several long-overlooked experiments in psychoanalytic pedagogy on the continent in school settings. I go on to describe the movement's demise and its linguistic and rhetorical legacy, by way of the mental hygiene movement in American education. I consider this essay an attempt to retrieve an important chapter in the history of progressive education, with important ramifications for understanding contemporary American culture as well as education.

Chapters 8 through 11 deal with the origins of the "mental hygiene point of view" as a belief system and describe the dissemination of psychiatric or therapeutic and essentially psychoanalytic norms, concepts, and language of discourse throughout American educational theory and practice. I identify the major actors and the main textual and linguistic channels used to diffuse the mental hygiene point of view. These chapters retain their critical pertinence today. The ramifications of the mental hygiene movement and the medicalization of American education include the assumption by the school of a therapeutic function and of responsibilities formerly borne by parents, the family, and other social agencies—one of the major themes of the American educational experience of the twentieth century. Moreover, the mental hygiene point of view embodies a fundamental linguistic and rhetorical shift, a reformulated sense of human nature, how we teach, and what education is or should be about. The medicalization of American education is another marker in the shift in American culture in the twentieth century from a controlling ethic to an expressive ethic, a shift, in Warren Susman's phrase, from a "culture of character" to a "culture of personality." These chapters not only fill in a gap in the historical record, but enlarge our understanding of American education after World War II. The medicalization of education

casts a long shadow over the present, yet it remains, so far as public
debate is concerned, in almost total abeyance. Thus, my mini-narrative
may have some direct usefulness for the present educational situation
and current efforts at school reform, not for action but for perspective
and reflection, a necessary preliminary to effective action.

VI.

Here, I want to briefly describe an approach to the problem of change
that I employ throughout the book. All historians of education have to
wrestle with the problem of influence and change in education. But
the question of how and in what form ideas are diffused and become
influential and how to document change is a question historians of
education, with all their preoccupation with reform movements in education, have yet to engage seriously. I argue the insufficiency of social
class as the primary determinant of meaningful change in education. I
argue that language is crucially involved in change and the redistribution of power and that moving language and its production, dissemination, and consumption over time into the forefront of historical inquiry into change provides another tool for the historical study of reform
movements in education and sheds new light on the nature of change
in education.

Following an approach influenced by J. L. Austin, Thomas Kuhn,
and Michel Foucault, and marked out by the historians J. G. A. Pocock
and Keith M. Baker, among others, I argue that a critical evidentiary
source for the historical investigation of change in education is language or language systems. The chapters on progressive education
and on the mental hygiene movement and the medicalization of American education employ language theory to illuminate the problem of
how and in what form ideas about education are disseminated and of
how to gauge their influence. Defining use of language as an historical
event or act, I isolate language as the primary datum in tracking the
diffusion and appropriation of educational ideas, and I prefigure the
field of educational thought as consisting of alternative and competing
systems of language. I assume that fundamental change in the field of
education can be gauged by change in the language of educational
discourse, that is, when a previously marginal language or language
system displaces a previously dominant one. While privileging language or language systems, I try always to keep in mind Foucault's
insight into the relation between language, discourse, and power. Education is a site of struggle; control of the language of educational dis-

course is one of the stakes of the struggle. Here, clearly, the new cultural history can bring together historians of education who call themselves intellectual historians and those who call themselves social historians; all share an interest in tracing the complex process of the dissemination of ideas in society and the interactions between text and agency, between ideas, language, and behavior.

VII.

My Epilogue is a reflection on the career of Lawrence Cremin, generally recognized as the most important American historian of education of the post-World War II era, who died of a heart attack on 4 September 1990. His shockingly sudden death at the age of sixty-four caught everyone who knew him off guard. Cremin left no memoir or autobiography. He gave only a few interviews. The obituaries written by historians of education closest to him are suited to the occasion; eulogies observing decorum and a certain privacy. The rest is silence. It's been almost a decade since Cremin's death. I think it is time to start a conversation.

The Epilogue started out as another homage to Cremin. Instead it became a reflection on the academic life and the privileges and perils of being a professional historian, more perils than privileges in the case of Cremin. That's the way it seems to me, anyway. The Epilogue is personal, subjective, and partly autobiographical. I have been at the center of a few events about which I write and on the margins of others. Some things I learned only in the course of writing this memoir. I am primarily concerned with Cremin's career as a historian but this memoir inevitably involves his career as an administrator; Cremin was president of Teachers College, Columbia University, and then of the Spencer Foundation while working on the trilogy, *American Education*. It is remarkable how little is known about the paths academics choose to follow in the course of their careers. There may be something to be learned from Cremin's career about our own professional lives and the historian's vocation.

VIII.

Most of the issues addressed and positions taken in this book have been aired (again and again) in my seminars in history of education in recent years. My teaching reflects my intense interest in language, textuality, and narrative structures and how they shroud the practices of history and historiography. The new cultural history has caused me to reflect on the relation of meaning to the words we speak and write, and it has turned my attention to the nature of the rhetorical instruments we use to shape our histories of education. My once confident belief in the givenness of the past and in the historian's claims to the attainability of certain historical knowledge of the past has been replaced by a more circumspect belief in the reality of a past that is accessible only through historical construction or reconstruction. While the constructed nature of our histories is inescapable, still I believe it is possible to attain truths about, and reach at least truer understandings of, the past; I believe it is possible for historiography to be a continual work in progress, both corrective and, at least sometimes, cumulative. As difficult as this new approach to history was to articulate, my students seemed to understand what I was trying to get at. Their questions and criticisms ensured that my ideas would never become precious truths; orthodoxies to be memorized; too frozen or rigid to be saved.

This book brings together eleven previously published essays and one new essay, the Epilogue. Preparing the earlier essays for this volume has been full of surprises. My new cultural and rhetorical approach to the historian's project forced me to revisit this past with a completely changed interpretive perspective on what was worth investigating and writing about and how to write about it. I began to see things through a different lens, so that not only did new data come to light, but old data seemed either outdated or in need of serious redescription and reinterpretation. I felt like the scientist in Thomas Kuhn's famous chapter on "Revolutions as Changes of World View" in *The Structure of Scientific Revolutions*. I could not simply reprint previously published essays; I have substantially revised all of them. Bringing to bear on these essays a new set of perspectives and critical approaches not available to me when they were first published has made them virtually new essays. Although they have been rethought and revised, I have tried to retain the flavor of the specific historical milieu in which they were originally written without imposing on them too anachronistic an interpretive burden.

Although I embrace the freedom the new cultural history provides—no longer having to get the one right description—writing this preface, after I've finally finished revising the text, I'm haunted by the feeling that in trying to make sense of such problematic topics as education, culture, and history, we never can say precisely what we wish to say or mean precisely what we say. Well, explanations for and explications of what I've done can be interminable. It's time to get on with the project.

Notes

1   Sol Cohen and Marc Depaepe, eds., "History of Education in the Postmodern Era," *Paedagogica Historica*, 32 (1996).

2   E.g., Lynn Hunt, ed., *The New Cultural History* (Berkeley, 1989); Peter Burke, ed., *New Perspectives on Historical Writing* (Cambridge, England, 1991); H. Aram Veeser, ed., *The New Historicism* (New York, 1989); Jacques LeGoff, *La Nouvelle Histoire* (Paris, 1988); Frank Ankersmit and Hans Kellner, eds., *A New Philosophy of History* (London, 1995); and Philippe Carrard, *Poetics of the New History* (Baltimore, 1992).

3   Hunt, *The New Cultural History*; Roger Chartier, *Cultural History: Between Practices and Representations* (London, 1988); Peter Burke, *Varieties of Cultural History* (Ithaca, N. Y., 1997).

4   Robert W. Fox and T. J. Jackson Lears, eds., *The Power of Culture: Critical Essays in American History* (Chicago, 1993), pp. 1–3.

5   François Furet, quoted in Agustín Escolano, "Postmodernity or High Modernity? Emerging Approaches in the History of Education," *Paedagogica Historica*, 32 (1996): 329–330.

6   There is just "culture," conceived as a "network of meanings," and the analysis of culture as "an interpretive [science] in search of meaning." *The Interpretation of Culture: Selected Essays* (New York, 1973), p. 5. Clifford Geertz, "Blurred Genres: The Refiguration of Social Thought," in *Local Knowledge: Further Essays in Interpretive Anthropology* (New York, 1983).

7   Colin Gordon, ed., *Michel Foucault: Power/Knowledge* (New York, 1980), p. 115.

8   "Literature, Criticism, and Historical Imagination: The Literary Challenge of Hayden White and Dominick LaCapra," in Hunt, *The New Cultural History*, pp. 97–98.

9   "Social history and intellectual history are inseparable. Because man is a symbol–making, language–using animal who gives meaning to everything he does, culture and society, beliefs and behavior, are really of a piece with one another." Gordon S. Wood, "Intellectual History and the Social Sciences," in John Higham and Paul K. Conkin, eds., *New Directions in American Intellectual History* (Baltimore, 1979), pp. 32ff; William J. Bouwsma, "Intellectual History in the 1980s: From History of Ideas to History of Meaning," *Journal of Interdisciplinary History*, 12 (1981): 283–289. And in general, Dominick LaCapra and Steven L. Kaplan, eds., *Modern European Intellectual History: Reappraisals and New Perspectives* (Ithaca, N.Y., 1982).

10   "History as Image: Changing the Lens," *History of Education Quarterly*, 27 (1987): 180.

Acknowledgments

For their encouragement, there are many individuals I have to thank. Among the friends and colleagues to whom I am indebted are Carlos Alberto Torres, who first suggested that my work warranted publication in a single volume; and Eva Baker, Peter McLaren, and Wellford "Buzz" Wilms, who goaded me, gently but persistently, to pursue the project. I would also like to take this occasion to acknowledge my debt to Richard Angelo, Linda Rennie Forcey, Arif Amlani, and J. Donald Wilson, who supported and nurtured the course that my reading has taken over the past decade, though they are not responsible for the course my writing has taken. Cara Walker's assistance was invaluable in the preparation of this book. Claudia Ramirez Wiedeman and Jamiel Filer assisted whenever I called upon them. At the end, a pencil was useless. I owe a very special debt to Cathy Dawson, Robert Hodapp, Cary Whitcup, and the staff of the Educational Technology Unit of the UCLA Graduate School of Education & Information Studies for their aid in helping this Luddite get out the final draft.

I would also like to express my gratitude to a number of institutions that provided an indispensable forum for me while my ideas were still in a formative stage: Center for Studies in Higher Education, University of California, Berkeley; Boys Town Center, Stanford University; Rockefeller Archive Center, Pocantico Hills, New York; University of London Institute of Education; Institute for the Medical Humanities, University of Texas Medical School, Galveston, Texas; and Max Planck Institute for Educational Research, University of Berlin. I would also like to thank the following professional associations whose conferences allowed me to try out my ideas, and that led to conversations which have greatly helped me to see my way: Division F (History and Historiography of Education), American Educational Research Association, (American) History of Education Society, and Canadian History of Education Association. I am grateful to the Rockefeller Archive Center for access to their archives. Finally, I want to acknowledge the Committee on Research of the UCLA Academic Senate, which provided the financial assistance needed to do the research for this book.

Versions of Chapters 1 through 11 have appeared elsewhere and are reprinted by permission as indicated; the Epilogue is published here for the first time.

"The History of the History of American Education: The Uses of the Past" is a revised version of "The History of the History of American Education, 1900–1976: The Uses of the Past," *Harvard Educational Review*, 46:3 (August 1976), pp. 298–330. Copyright © 1976 by the President and Fellows of Harvard College. All rights reserved.

"Revisiting the History of Urban Education: Historiographical Reflections" is a revised version of "Reconstructing the History of Urban Education in America," in Gerald Grace, ed., *Education and the City: Theory, History, and Contemporary Practice* (London: Routledge, 1984), pp. 115–138. Permission by Routledge to reprint is gratefully acknowledged.

"Representations of History in the Linguistic Turn" combines the following: "Representations of History," *History of Education*, 20 (1991): 131–141; and "The Linguistic Turn: The Absent Text of American Educational Historiography," *Historical Studies in Education/Revue d'histoire de l'éducation*, 3 (1991): 237–246. Permission to reprint granted by Taylor & Francis Group, Ltd., and *HSE/RHE*, respectively.

"Language and History: A Perspective on School Reform Movements and Change in Education" is a revised version of "Language and History: A Perspective on School Reform Movements," *International Perspectives on Education and Society*, 4 (1994): 23–42. Permission to reprint has been granted by JAI Press, Inc. (Greenwich, Conn., and London).

"The Influence of Progressive Education on School Reform in the United States: Redescriptions" is a revised version of "The Influence of Progressive Education on School Reform in the U.S.A.," in Hermann Röhrs and Volker Lenhart, eds., *Progressive Education Across the*

Continents: A Handbook (Frankfurt am Main, New York, Wien: Peter Lang, 1995), pp. 359–371 (Heidelberger Studien zur Erziehungshrissenschaft, vol. 43). Permission granted by the publisher.

"Postmodernism, the New Cultural History, Film: Resisting Images of Education" is a revised version of an article which appeared originally in *Paedagogica Historica,* 32 (1996): 395–420. Reprinted by permission of the editor.

"In the Name of the Prevention of Neurosis: Psychoanalysis and Education in Europe, 1905–1938" is a revised version of "In the Name of the Prevention of Neurosis: The Search for a Psychoanalytic Pedagogy in Europe, 1905–1938," in Barbara Finkelstein, ed., *Regulated Children/Liberated Children: Education in Psychohistorical Perspective* (New York: Psychohistory Press, 1979), pp. 184–219. Reprinted by permission of the publisher.

"The Mental Hygiene Movement, the Commonwealth Fund, and Education, 1921–1933: 'Every School a Clinic'" is a revised version of "The Mental Hygiene Movement, the Commonwealth Fund, and Education, 1921–1933," in Gerald Benjamin, ed., *Private Philanthropy and Public Elementary and Secondary Education* (Pocantico Hills, N.Y.: Rockefeller Archive Center, 1980), pp. 33–46. Reprinted by permission of the Rockefeller Archive Center.

"Changing Conceptions of the American College and University, 1920–1940: The Mental Hygiene Movement and the 'Essentials of an Education'" is a revised version of an article that appeared originally under the title "The Mental Hygiene Movement and the Development of Personality: Changing Conceptions of the American College and University, 1920–1940," *History of Higher Education Annual,* 2 (1982): 65–101. Reprinted with permission of *History of Higher Education Annual.*

"The Mental Hygiene Movement, 'Personality,' and the Making of Twentieth-Century American Education" is a reconceived and rewritten version of "The School and Personality Development: Intellectual History," in John Hardin Best, ed., *Historical Inquiry in Education: A Research Agenda* (Washington, D.C.: American Educational Research Association, 1983), pp. 109–137. Original copyright 1983 by

American Educational Research Association. Reprinted by permission of the publisher.

"The Medicalization of American Education: The Social History of an Idea" combines the following: "The Mental Hygiene Movement, the Development of Personality, and the School: The Medicalization of American Education," *History of Education Quarterly*, 23 (1983): 123–149; and "Every School a Clinic: An Historical Perspective on Modern American Education" in Sol Cohen and Lewis C. Solmon, eds., *From the Campus: Perspectives on the School Reform Movement* (New York: Praeger, 1989), pp. 18–34. Reprinted with permission of *History of Education Quarterly* and Greenwood Publishing Group, Inc., Westport, Conn., respectively.

I am grateful to the editors and publishers of the journals and books involved for permission to reprint these essays here and in this form.

PART I

Chapter 1

The History of the History of American Education: The Uses of the Past

The past is never dead. It is not even past.

William Faulkner

I.

It is second nature for historians of education to take a historical view of everything except their own discipline. This essay was written in the conviction that the history of the history of American education as a specialty has been and still is profoundly influenced by its past. It may be true, metaphorically speaking, that, as David Lowenthal observes, "the past is a foreign country," and literally true to those who choose to forget it or never to visit it, or to those who, having been there, are afflicted by amnesia. But whether it is celebrated or rejected, whether we choose to remember it or forget it, attend to it or ignore it, the past is omnipresent.[1]

During its one hundred years as a discipline, history of education has offered many meanings to historians of education. The questions that have agitated our guild, that have caused the most rivalry and contentiousness, have been about the degree to which historians of education should be detached from or engaged in the educational or social problems of the day; that is, questions about what used to be called the "function" of history in a school or department of education.

In this essay, I consider this perennial controversy: the function of the historian of education on a faculty of education—"liberal," "technical" or "professional," or "social reconstructionist"—and of the history of education as a subject in the curriculum of the professional education program. All historians of education on education faculties want to be "useful" and practice "usable" history. There has never been any dispute about this. But the issue is: useful to whom and for what aim, interest, or purpose? This has been an issue from the turn of the twentieth century to the present. Our predecessors have raised issues that remain vital today; they exist wherever and whenever the history of education is taught within a school of education.[2]

Freud observed that "the whole progress of society rests upon the opposition between successive generations." That may be true, but opposition between generations is not the expunging of generations, something which has actually occurred in the history of the history of education. Generations struggle; and if they remember the struggles, they may learn something from each other. In this interaction, presumably, lies the progress of generations Freud refers to, and this applies to generations of historians of education as well. In the 1950s a critical chapter in the struggle among the generations of historians of education over the function of history of education in the professional program was suppressed in the haste to get on with a new history of education. A piece of our history is missing. Thus, our past—the history of the history of education—still remains, for too many historians of education, a "foreign country." To put all this under the sign of discourse theory, we do not do research or write our histories in a cognitive vacuum, but our projects are informed by a rich (or impoverished) network of texts, traditions of discourse, and debates. There are rival discourses within any tradition. The main intention of this essay is to reconstruct that network of texts, traditions of discourse, and debates of the past and reclaim it as part of the present conversation among historians of education.

What did the generations of historians of American education have to say about the "function" of history of education in the professional program? Walking awhile in the company of our predecessors may help us to formulate more clearly the situation of historians of education today. I make no claim of definiteness here. One has to make some choices—which is to say that there are other stories one might tell, other conversations one might pass on.

II.

In 1954, President Clarence H. Faust of the Ford Foundation's Fund for the Advancement of Education called a conference of leading

American scholars to explore the possibility of encouraging historical investigation of the role of education in the development of American society. Although American education as a field of historical study by that time had a long history, the conferees were unanimous in their conviction that it had been "shamefully neglected by American historians."[3] Although by the early 1950s the field of history of American education could boast perhaps a score of practitioners, none were invited to the conference. The Fund stressed that "no member of the group could be described as a specialist in the history of American education." That is, no member of the group—which included the historians Arthur Schlesinger, Sr., Merle Curti, Samuel Eliot Morison, Richard Hofstadter, Ralph Gabriel, Walter Metzger, Paul H. Buck, and Richard J. Storr, at least three of whom (Curti, Hofstadter, and Metzger) were deeply interested in the history of American education—was a member of an education faculty. The group held a second meeting in May 1956, at which time it became the Committee on the Role of Education in American History. In the spring of 1957, the committee issued a pamphlet announcing that financial assistance was available to faculty or graduate students in history departments who wished to pursue monographic study of the role of American education in American history. The committee assured historians that it aimed not at cutting them off from their departmental colleagues. It sought only to support studies calculated to bring "thorough knowledge of education immediately into the mainstream of historical scholarship and instruction."

The Fund, then, deliberately excluded "specialists" in the history of American education from its conferences and its offers of financial assistance. Why the snub? Part of the answer may be found in a famous critique of American educational historiography by the Harvard University history professor Bernard Bailyn, in the first section of his *Education in the Forming of American Society: Needs and Opportunities for Study,* a work initiated and sponsored in part by the Fund.[4] Bailyn repudiated turn-of-the-century "educational missionaries" like Ellwood P. Cubberley and Paul Monroe, who pioneered the history of education as a special field and wrote the most influential textbooks—particularly Cubberley's *Public Education in the United States: A Study and Interpretation of American Educational History.*[5] For more than three-quarters of a century the history of American education has had a promising future and a disappointing present as a subject of investigation. This is not to say, Bailyn continues, there is not a voluminous literature on the subject; there is. Unfortunately, too much of it is parochial, anachronistic, and out of touch with main currents of contemporary scholarship. Consequently, at a time of deep public concern over the schools, "the role of education in American history is obscure. We have almost no historical leverage on the problems of American education." Those who have taught the history of education—and written the textbooks—have viewed the subject not as an aspect of American history writ large but rather as a device for communicating an appropriate ideology to a newly self-conscious profession, education. Hence their scholarship proceeded in a special atmosphere of professional purpose, almost totally isolated "from the major influences and shaping minds of twentieth-century historiography." The facts, or at least a great quantity of them, are there, but they lie inert; they form no significant pattern.

Because Cubberley and his followers directed their attention almost exclusively to that part of the educational process carried on "in formal institutions of instruction," that is, the school, they lost the capacity to consider the history of education in the context of a host of other agencies engaged in education. Because they wrote history solely with an eye for relevance to contemporary problems of education, they "read present issues . . . back into the past [and] distortions and short-circuiting of thought" were inevitable. The result was a foreshortened chronicle of pedagogical institutions so caught up in anachronisms as to make historical explanation impossible.[6] With these preliminaries out of the way, Bailyn got on with the presentation of his new history of education. There were unlimited needs and opportunities for study in the history of education if historians were to think of education "not only as formal pedagogy but as the entire process by which a culture transmits itself across the generations, . . . in its elaborate, intricate involvements with the rest of society, and notes its shifting functions, meanings, and purposes."[7]

In 1961, in an article entitled "The New Historian of American Education," Wilson Smith, a professor of history at Johns Hopkins University, seconded Bailyn's critique of Cubberley and went on to describe the new historian of American education. Two traits, Smith suggested, would distinguish the new historians of education from their predecessors: "their use of broader historical references, and [their] wider, more humanistic, professional commitment." The new historians of education would look beyond the narrow professional goals of their predecessors. The historian of education would still be "useful" or "functional," but now as a "servant of intellect and disciplined thinking" and as a "representative of humane learning in our industrialized and specialized society."[8]

In 1965, in *The Wonderful World of Elwood Patterson Cubberley: An Essay on the Historiography of American Education*, the historian of education Lawrence A. Cremin of Teachers College, Columbia University, who had been invited to join the Committee on the Role of Education in American History in 1961, put the finishing touch on the hardening portrayal of Cubberley and the historiographical tradition that he purportedly founded. While acknowledging Cubberley's contributions to professional education, Cremin reconvicted Cubberley of the historiographical sins of anachronism, parochialism, evangelism, and isolation from the mainstream of American historiography.[9] Cremin's *The Transformation of the School: Progressivism in American Education, 1876–1957* had appeared in 1961 and won the Bancroft Prize for history in 1962; still, writing in 1965, Cremin inexplicably observed of Cubberley's *Public Education in the United States* that "the work is still read, . . . it has not been superseded. Its optimistic story of educational struggles waged and won, . . . of educational services extended and perfected, has influenced a vast literature . . . to the most recent scholarly text in American history."[10] Cremin reiterated that its portrayal of "the great [public school] battles as over and won had helped to produce a generation of schoolmen unable to comprehend—much less contend with—the great educational controversies following World War II."[11] A general reinterpretation of Cubberley, Cremin observed, was much needed: the "anachronism and parochialism of his work require correction, as do its evangelism and its isolation from the mainstream of American historiography." Cremin concluded by amplifying Bailyn's call for a new history of American education, one which would inquire into the impact of education broadly conceived, beyond the schools, to include a host of other institutions that educate, and which would ask: "What agencies, formal and informal, have shaped American thought, character, and sensibility over the years, and what have been the significant relationships between these agencies and the society that has sustained them?"[12]

The depiction by Bailyn and Cremin of Cubberley and the so-called Cubberley tradition has become the received wisdom of historians of education. This version has become a monument, so internalized by historians of education it has taken on the status of immutability. We all know Bailyn's and Cremin's version of Cubberley and the Cubberley tradition. We know it too well. Their interpretation has never been contested. Bailyn's and Cremin's reading of Cubberley was not only a misreading, but misdirected; Cubberley's influence was grossly exaggerated. A puzzling kind of overkill was at work here; several generations of historians of education between Cubberley and Bailyn and Cremin were ignored. Historians of education have inherited a distorted picture of their past.

I think it was necessary, by the late 1950s, to clear the way for a new comprehension of the role of education in American history and to put forward a new history of American education. But this could have been accomplished by remarking on the work of *contemporary* historians of education on education faculties—the "specialists"— emending *them,* and then presenting a new history of education and ignoring Cubberley altogether. Who exactly was reading Cubberley in the 1950s? It wasn't Cubberley who had to be exorcised from the history of American education. It is precisely the question of what was happening to and among historians of education in the 1940s and 1950s that is crucial, as we shall see below. As for the Fund's not including historians of education on school of education faculties—the "specialists"—in the deliberations of the Committee on the Role of Education in American History, given the situation in education of the mid-1950s, it is not too hard to understand. Recall the crisis in education in the late 1940s and 1950s. American public education was then equated with "progressive education," which was in turn being denounced as anti-intellectual and denigrated in press, pulpit, and academe. The leaders of the Fund, especially Clarence Faust, had a strong antipathy toward professors of education, the "educationists," an antipathy that American historians in general shared. The Fund's exclusion of the "specialists," the historians of education on school of education faculties, can be interpreted as another episode in the cold war between liberal arts and science schools and colleges of education.

But something else was involved here. What is particularly striking is that Cubberley's work was also isolated for obloquy by a historian of education like Lawrence Cremin, who knew the history of the history of education very well, indeed. It is as if there were no historians of education between Cubberley and Bailyn and himself. Cremin made the baffling claim in 1961 that, although history of education was a widely offered course in education schools, "in all but a few instances it is taught by persons who have not been trained as historians, and indeed who do not identify themselves as such."[13] But the domination of Cubberley had been challenged long before the 1950s. There were two whole generations of historians of education on education faculties between Cubberley and Cremin who were overlooked or erased, of whom some had a liberal or "humanistic" commitment to their specialty, and who were no more guilty of the sins of anachronism, parochialism, or evangelism, nor more isolated from the mainstream of American historiography, than Bailyn or Cremin, as well as other historians of education on education faculties who—shall I say it— could be so depicted. Why was Cubberly scapegoated? Several psychoanalytic concepts are helpful. One is displacement; the other is repression. Cubberley served as an object of displaced emotion; the real objects of discontent were repressed. Freud observed that "the whole progress of society rests upon the opposition between successive generations." In the case of historians of American education, there has not been such a generational confrontation: Cubberley and company were not Bailyn's and Cremin's "parents" and thus not the proper foci for their opposition. The new historians of education of the late 1950s and early 1960s, for what seemed like good reason at the time, decided to overlook or repress not only contemporary historians of education but the long conversation about the function of history of education—"liberal," "technical," or "social reconstructionist" —which had taken place in the three decades between Cubberley and themselves.

My intention here is not to defend or to blame but to restore the broken links between present historians of education and our predecessors, to fill in certain gaps in our memory. What follows represents an effort to restore to memory what the history of education as a field of study has forgotten or chosen to conceal as its repressed content. While I have no realistic expectation that it will be therapeutic, this history of the history of American education still provides, I think, a more comprehensive, unified, and intelligible past for historians of American education than was hitherto available. Walking awhile in the company of our predecessors may even provide a guide to our present embedded picture.

III.

In the late nineteenth century, history of education was one of the most widely offered courses in American teachers colleges and schools or departments of education. In its formative years, history of education as a special field of study shared the values and vicissitudes of the general field of history. But as a specialty in a professional school, the history of education also had problems uniquely its own: the skepticism of colleagues in history departments toward education as profession generally, the doubts of colleagues in schools of education as to the value of history of education in the professional program, and disagreement among the historians themselves as to the proper role or "function" of their specialty in the professional program.

Liberal arts faculties viewed the curricula of teachers colleges and departments or schools of education as devoid of scholarship—method without content, technical skills at best. When Cubberley was brought to Stanford University in 1898 as an assistant professor of education, he was given three years to make its education department "respectable."[14] In the professional education program, the history of education suffered from internal problems of staffing, teaching loads, and a paucity of monographs and textbooks. Few schools or departments of education had trained historians on the faculty, and faculty members who taught history of education could not devote themselves to the subject. Cubberley, for example, although not trained as a historian, found that his first teaching assignment at Stanford University included, among other responsibilities, history of education. The few textbooks in history of education were histories of European educational thought or of European educational philosophy.[15] Typically, a course in history of education treated the evolution of education from Greco-Roman antiquity to the modern European period; then, if time allowed, it treated educational developments in the United States. The major text around the turn of the century was Edwin Grant Dexter's *History of Education in the United States*, essentially a chronology, a compendium of facts about the evolution of formal institutions of schooling, school legislation, and administrative codes. Dexter's book, in the mode of the then-reigning scientific history, was 656 pages of densely packed facts.[16] Little surprise that history of education became an increasingly unpopular course, hard pressed to justify its presence in the curriculum.

Furthermore, and most crucial, a struggle between protagonists of the liberal and the technical or professional conception of history of education was waged not only between historians of education and their colleagues within college or school of education faculties, but between rival factions among historians of education themselves.[17] In 1908, at Teachers College, Columbia University, the historian of edu-

cation Henry Suzzallo dismissed Dexter's notion of history of education as irrelevant in the professional program and warned that if history of education wanted to continue to enjoy a place in the curriculum, it needed more professional content; that is, it needed to be tailored
to the professional education program. Suzzallo called upon historians of education to emphasize its "function," the key word, with relevance to present problems of education: "the most pertinent to an
understanding of the present educational system the better"[18] On the
other hand, Henry Johnson, his colleague at Teachers College, thought
the demand that history of education must "function"—that what is
taught in history of education must be of direct and immediate utility
to practitioners—"an abomination."[19] The demand that history of education be more directly relevant to the professional program was in-
tensified around the time of World War I by the rise of the scientific
movement in education. As this movement was expounded by Charles
Judd of the University of Chicago, the field of education was to be
divorced from theory and married to science in the form of scientific
psychology, statistics, tests, measurements, and quantitative methodology in general.[20] Here was a threat to history of education: history
of education was thought to be one of the humanities; no one claimed
that history of education was a science. Unless it could more clearly
demonstrate its utility in the professional program, perhaps history
of education as a specialty was faced with a problem of
survival.

This is the context in which Cubberley, as a historian of education,
should be appraised. In *Public Education in the United States*,
Cubberley broke with the educational historiography of Dexter as well
as Henry Johnson, while moving closer to Suzzalo's position. As
Cubberley noted in the preface to *Public Education in the United
States*, histories of education had been much criticized because they
had been "constructed on the old fact-theory-of-knowledge basis," had
"little relation to present-day problems in education," and "failed to
function in orienting the prospective teacher." Cubberley presented
his own history of education as an interpretation that would help teachers understand "the larger problems of present-day education in the
light of their historical development" and political and social bearings.
Of course Cubberley aimed to inspire and ennoble. He wanted prospective teachers "to see the educational service . . . as a great national institution evolved by democracy to help it solve its many perplexing problems." Thus Cubberley sought to secure a place for history
of American education in the professional program.

Public Education in the United States was an attempt to overcome the prejudice of colleagues on education faculties against history of education by shifting the emphasis from the history of European educational theory to the history of the development of American education, from the beginnings in the colonial period to the early twentieth century and then-contemporary problems of education, and placing those problems in the context of the social, industrial, and political changes that had taken place from the mid-nineteenth century on. When it is read today, *Public Education in the United States* seems no more anachronistic than Bailyn's interpretation of education in the colonial period in *Education in the Forming of American Society*; writing history is a constant struggle against anachronism. Narrowly institutional? Certainly the emphasis was on the school. But Cubberley was well aware of the elaborate involvement of school and society. Inspirational? No more so than any history written in the romance genre even today. Isolated from the mainstream of American historiography? *Public Education in the United States* had sections on the rise of the city, industrialization, immigration, the changing role of the family, and the school as a social welfare agency and vocational training center. Cubberley's bibliography was up-to-date, from Lewis Terman on intelligence testing to Charles Judd on the scientific movement in education and Randolph Bourne on the Gary school plan. In almost every respect, *Public Education in the United States* represented a terrific broadening of historical scholarship in American education.[21] *Public Education in the United States* was not a story of an inevitable rise and triumph of the public school movement. There were many school battles that had been fought and won, but for Cubberley the severest tests were yet to come. No leverage on problems facing post–World War II education? Why should anyone reasonably expect Cubberley in 1919 to provide leverage on the problems of a later era? Here is anachronism.

Public Education in the United States was extremely popular. It was, once the reader got through the colonial and early national periods, a lively, modern history of education. The first edition sold over 80,000 copies.[22] It dominated the field for more than a decade—until the late 1920s, when a new generation of historians of American education emerged on the scene and began to publish textbooks: Edgar Knight, *Education in the United States* (1929), Stuart Noble, *History of American Education* (1938), Paul Monroe, *The Founding of the American Public School System* (1940), and Frederic Eby and

Charles F. Arrowood, *The Development of American Education* (1941). So, although Cubberley's *Public Education in the United States* was a pioneer text in the field of American educational history and certainly enjoyed great influence, its influence should not be exaggerated. In fact, Cubberley's main interest was actually school administration; only about a dozen students finished their doctorate under his direction, and only one of them, Flaud Wooton, was a historian of education.

It was Paul Monroe's students who became the next generation of historians of education. And Monroe's perspective on history of education as a field of study was a liberal one. Monroe was brought to Teachers College in 1901 to develop history of education. His *Textbook in the History of Education* (1905) became a standard in the field of history of European education. With his editorship of *The Encyclopedia of Education* in 1912, he became the country's most influential historian of education. Among Monroe's students were Edgar Knight, Stuart Noble, Frederick Eby, Edward Reisner, Thomas Woody, Willystine Goodsell, and Harlan Updegraff. During the 1920s, besides the above, another group of historians of education, many trained in history departments of top American universities or colleges, were employed on education faculties, including James Mulhern at the University of Pennsylvania, Edgar B. Wesley at the University of Minnesota, Adolph Meyer at New York University, Allen O. Hansen at the City College of New York, Herman G. Richey and Newton Edwards at the University of Chicago, Frederick Eby and Charles F. Arrowood at the University of Texas, and Harry Good at Ohio State University, as well as Flaud Wooton at UCLA. There was the beginning of a modest monographic literature, and the appearance of Knight's *Education in the United States* (1929), which challenged the sovereignty of Cubberley's text.

So, by the late 1920s, history of education seemed favorably positioned for the future. Nevertheless, it was beset by the same old criticism from colleagues in education: its liberal orientation was not functional in the professional program. Edward Reisner, Monroe's protégé and successor at Teachers College, answered that any shortcomings of history of education courses resulted not from problems inherent in its liberal arts orientation but from a dearth of monographs and source materials.[23] Other historians of education, like Knight, Good, and Eby, argued that history was already functional—it shook up prejudices, enlarged horizons, provided perspective, and shed light on the origins of present problems in education or on the environment in which those problems would have to be resolved.[24] This liberal conception of the function of history of education would soon be more severely tested than ever before.

IV.

In the 1930s, the demand that history of education be more directly relevant to present-day problems received unexpected impetus from two sources: "social reconstructionists" on education faculties and progressive historians on liberal arts faculties.

The Depression lent great influence to educationists like George S. Counts, William H. Kilpatrick, and Harold Rugg of Teachers College, who had long wanted professional education to become more socially relevant and socially involved. In the early 1930s, Counts, Kilpatrick, Rugg, and others in their Teachers College Discussion Group moved quickly to bring professional education into the center of the political arena. The social reconstructionists assumed and sometimes explicitly stated that the new social order should be some form of cooperative or collectivistic economy, the exact form would be worked out later. They regarded the schools as general headquarters for the new social order, with teachers leading the way. In their attempt at turning the schools around to the social view, the reconstructionists in education found allies among progressive historians, like James Harvey Robinson, Carl Becker, and Charles Beard, who were calling for a new history that would contribute directly to the solution of contemporary social problems.[25]

The social reconstructionists placed great responsibility on the shoulders of professors of education, the "teachers of teachers." If teachers were to be politicized and play their assigned role in social reconstruction, teacher training would have to be reconstituted. The subject-centered specialists, the discipline-oriented faculty—those who believed that their subjects best served the professional program when they adhered to the ideal of liberal education—were put down firmly by social reconstructionists.[26] History of education was singled out for censure. As Rugg delicately put it, "there was a deep hiatus between what historians of education wrote in their books and the life going on around them." Historians of education would have to relinquish the "formal tradition" and adopt the "social point of view." The historians of education defended themselves forcefully. Stuart Noble rejected those who would obligate educators to visualize the requirements of a future state of society and set the schools to the task of creating a new social order. Reisner complained about the use of history in the service of "immediate utilitarian ends," pointing out that the values of history were long-term values. History, properly conceived, "aims not at direct action but at stimulating, sharpening, and regulating thinking."[27] But the question of the function of the history of education refused to go away. By the mid-1930s, Noble, Reisner, Eby, Knight, and historians of education who thought like them were placed increasingly on the defensive. The immediate cause was the emergence of "social foundations of education," the curricular embodiment of the social reconstructionist view that the teacher of teachers must play a strategic role in the reconstruction of society.

V.

The original inspiration for the social foundations of education came from the Teachers College group of social reconstructionists. The idea was that philosophy, psychology, sociology, economics, comparative education, and the history of education would be fused or integrated into a course on the foundations of education. These subjects would be mined for materials that would bear on the contemporary problems of school and society in America while indoctrinating prospective teachers and school administrators in the proper social and political beliefs. In 1934, Rugg and Kilpatrick at Teachers College spearheaded one of the most famous if not most influential innovations in American teacher education of the first half of the twentieth century: a two-semester course called "Social Foundations of Education."[28] In the 1940s, the concept of foundations spread to many other teachers colleges and schools of education, most significantly in the late 1940s to the College of Education at the University of Illinois.

The heart and soul of the new social reconstructionism was the foundations faculty at the College of Education: William O. Stanley, Kenneth D. Benne, and B. Othanel Smith, all philosophers of education, and Archibald Anderson, a historian of education, formed the nucleus of the group. Under their leadership in 1947, the College of Education began a thorough reorganization of its program.[29] The most important result of the reorganization, completed in 1950, was the establishment of a Division of Historical, Comparative, Philosophical, and Social Foundations of Education, and the subsequent publication of its justificatory manifesto, *The Theoretical Foundations of Education* (1951). In the grand scheme, history of American education was to be "a general foundation course in education rather than an academic course in history," and designed to be "functional" in the "development of professional competence to deal with important contemporary educational problems."[30] Historians of education, however, remained recalcitrant, and now more deeply divided than ever.

In the late 1940s and early 1950s, the foundations of education group at the University of Illinois reigned supreme, the philosopher-kings of American education. Their textbooks were basic works in the field. They had established themselves as the country's leading theoreticians and spokespersons for progressive education. They occupied the key positions in some of the most influential professional educational organizations in the country, including the Progressive Education Association, the Philosophy of Education Society, the John Dewey Society and, significantly for historians of education, the National Society of College Teachers of Education (NSCTE).

In 1948, a small group of historians of education—Anderson; R. Freeman Butts of Teachers College; John S. Brubacher of Yale University; and Claude Eggertsen of the School of Education at the University of Michigan—persuaded the NSCTE to let them organize a History of Education Section (HES), a first. They also persuaded the NSCTE to sponsor and finance a *History of Education Journal (HEJ)*, another first. An NSCTE/HES coordinating committee was appointed, composed of Butts, Eggertsen, the ubiquitous Anderson, Arthur H. Moehlman, William F. Drake, Harry Good, and Flaud Wooton, which subsequently became the NSCTE Committee on Historical Foundations. Butts became chairman of the committee and head of the editorial board of *HEJ*.[31] Eggertsen, a social reconstructionist and an advocate of "foundations," became editor of the *HEJ,* with Anderson as associate editor.

It seemed like the beginning of a new era for history of American education. But the alliance with the NSCTE was not to come cheap. HES meetings were coordinated with the annual NSCTE meetings, and *HEJ* was utterly dependent on NSCTE for financial support. There was a risk that HES would become simply a handmaiden of NSCTE and *HEJ* simply the latter's house organ. Indeed, the *HEJ* emphasized less what history of education might contribute to scholarly research than what it might contribute to the professional program. This is clear from the editorial in the first issue of *HEJ*, which set three purposes for the History of Education Section: to provide opportunities for interested members to communicate with one another; to study the role of history of education in preparing members of the educational profession to work with other committees and sections of the NSCTE in promoting the improvement of teacher education; and to apply the "discipline of the historical approach and methodology to the current controversies that beset the making of educational policy."[32]

In the meantime, the first assignment for the Committee on Historical Foundations was to launch a survey of attitudes toward history of education in the country as a preliminary step toward defining once and for all the function of history of education in the program of professional education. The committee hoped to demonstrate a general consensus that history of education should make itself functional in the professional program by adopting a contemporary problems-oriented approach. Events soon revealed that most historians of education disagreed sharply with the committee on how history of education could contribute to the professional program.[33]

The lack of consensus, indeed the incompatible views among historians of education, became strikingly apparent in three papers delivered before the Committee on Historical Foundations at the annual conference of the NSCTE in 1949, whose theme was the role of the history of education in educational policy-making. Anderson delivered one of the papers. Responses came from more senior historians of education, Newton Edwards and Stuart Noble. Anderson curtly disclaimed any concern for the history of education as a branch of social or intellectual history, as a research specialty, or as a field of specialization for doctoral study and focused on the functional role of the historian of education in the professional preparation of the teacher. He pointed out that although recent interest in philosophy of education had revived interest in history of education, it would not do for historians to sit back complacently. Whatever the impetus for revival of history of education, it was only temporary. The discipline had to break free from the shackles of "hidebound academics," and abandon subject matter used in "traditional academic courses" in favor of subject matter dealing with contemporary problems of educational and social policy. Anderson concluded with a warning—that if historians of education did not follow his prescription, education schools would eliminate their courses. In his response, Edwards opposed any effort to subordinate history of education to contemporary problems. History, he said, may give "insight" into the problems of one's own time, but only if regarded as a "seamless web."[34] It was "a mistaken view of history to regard it as a warehouse of antique furniture from which a few pieces may be selected to grace a living room fitted out . . . with the latest designs from Grand Rapids." Noble was equally emphatic in rejecting Anderson's position. The wording of the general theme of the conference, Noble remarked, seemed to imply that the history of education was a "functional" rather than a "liberal" study:

> If this be true, I wish to dissent at the outset, for I do not think it either necessary or desirable to teach the subject with the motive of relevancy to current problems. I am positive in the conviction that the history of education should be taught with the liberal rather than the functional values in mind.[35]

There were other indications of trouble ahead for Anderson, Brubacher, Butts, and the Committee on Historical Foundations. Not only did the older generation of historians of American education like Reisner, Good, Eby, Edwards, and Noble find the orientation of Anderson, Eggertsen, Brubacher and Butts repugnant, but evidently many junior faculty members did as well. In fact, most historians seemed to be preoccupied with the problems of the historiography of American education rather than with the problems of American society or of American education. Philip Perdew's survey of the writings of prominent historians of education in 1950 found a general consensus that history of education should be concerned with "education as a social process . . . intimately related to other social processes." He found some historians of education urging their colleagues to define education as "those activities . . . by which the culture of a society is transmitted from one generation to the next."[36] Shades of Bernard Bailyn.

Clearly, a new approach to history of education was being developed, but it was in the direction of history of education as a liberal study, not as a professional study. To Anderson and Brubacher, such a conception of history of education was nonfunctional, even professional suicide. Brubacher had a solution: "[If] we can dig out segments of educational history cut to size, then history's contribution would not only be welcome, but would be sought after." Of course, he continued, "there will be some who have an antiquarian interest in the past as the past, but they are not likely to be many among professional students of education. Such students will have an interest in history . . . if at all, because it illuminates the contemporary problems with which they have to deal."[37]

R. Freeman Butts, Reisner's junior colleague at Teachers College and the most sophisticated theoretician among the generation of historians of education of the 1940s and 1950s, tried to stake out a middle position between Anderson's and Brubacher's approach and Noble's and Edwards's approach: problems-be-damned; we study history for its intrinsic value. The history of education, Butts observed, has been taught in a chronological way that has failed to translate the past to the present, and failed to indicate the meaning of historical generalizations for the present. Much of this emphasis, he said, stemmed from an overly academic view of historical research that borrowed its methods from the physical sciences and was concerned only with facts for their own sake, to the exclusion of their meaning for present problems. But history must have meaning for the present. The problem was how to give past facts and past events present meaning while upholding the integrity of the past. Butts tried to find a balance. Historians would have to admit their biases—in Butts's case, a "frankly critical, experimental, and progressive" perspective. But the craft imposed certain restrictions on historians. They cannot alter or shape their material as they please. Their "frame of reference of things deemed necessary and desirable" must not interfere with the ideal of objectivity; pertinent and relevant evidence must not willfully be overlooked or mutilated in order to fit what the historian would like to find. History of education would then contribute both to the solution of the major problems confronting American education and to American social and intellectual history.

Butts expressed "great regard for intellectual achievement and scholarship" but held that "if academic scholarship is the only concern the teachers college loses touch with the realities of education and society." Historians of education must be concerned with the educational and social problems of the day. Butts asked:

> Shall universities be centres of purely intellectual concerns or shall they point the way to social responsibility? Shall they be devotees of the "life of the mind" or advocates of social and public service? Shall they be ivory towers or watch towers . . . ? What is the life of the mind without service, and what is service without the life of the mind?[38]

VI.

As the NSCTE Committee on Historical Foundations labored through the early 1950s, the roof caved in on progressivism in American education. Members of the arts and sciences faculty at the University of Illinois, no less—Harry J. Fuller, a biologist; Stewart S. Cairns, a mathematician; and Arthur E. Bestor, Jr., a historian—launched the attack;

the College of Education faculty, particularly the foundations of education faculty, provided the main target. The historian, Bestor, had the strongest impact. He anathematized schools of education in articles in national journals, in speeches at the annual conventions of the American Historical Association, and in two widely publicized books: *Educational Wastelands* (1953) and *The Restoration of Learning* (1955).[39] Of the two, *Educational Wastelands* was the more important and influential. Bestor charged that in setting up their own courses in history and philosophy, schools of education had shown "no real interest in interdisciplinary cooperation and no sense of academic partnership."[40] He condemned the "warping of the great intellectual disciplines" to serve the "narrow purposes of indoctrination and vocationalism." With specific reference to history of education, Bestor complained that, torn from its context of general historical change, the history of education "becomes a chronicle almost devoid of meaning. Worse than that, it may easily become the kind of distorted history which presents the past as a mournful catalogue of errors, redeemed by some few feeble gropings toward that perfection of wisdom which the present generation . . . alone possesses."[41] The integrity of the disciplines must be inviolate: philosophy of education must be taught philosophically and the history of education historically. Bestor called for a "process of devolution" through which subjects like history of education taught in colleges of education would be absorbed into existing university and college liberal arts departments and the rest eliminated.

The National Society of College Teachers of Education, the Progressive Education Association, and allied organizations responded defensively.[42] The History of Education Section and the *History of Education Journal* became embroiled in the conflict. Anderson, as the leading light in the College of Education at the University of Illinois and the editor of *Progressive Education,* was compelled to meet the "attacks on public education" and coordinate the counterattack. The *HEJ,* financially dependent upon NSCTE, was forced to give over its pages to an NSCTE newsletter. The Committee on Historical Foundations was polarized. William Brickman, for example, editor of *School and Society,* threw the journal open to Bestor and condemned *Progressive Education* for its "constant injection of ideological slant" in its pages.[43] Further divisions among historians of education became evident when Lawrence Cremin, Butts's junior colleague at Teachers

College, gave Bestor's *Restoration of Learning* a positive review after Butts had critically reviewed Bestor's *Educational Wastelands* a few years earlier.[44]

In 1955, the report that the Committee on Historical Foundations had called for in 1950 finally began to appear. The three parts making up the report came out one by one. First, in the fall, came Cremin's "The Recent Development of the History of Education as a Field of Study in the United States," an innocuous chronicle.[45] The second installment, Anderson's "Bases of Proposals Concerning the History of Education," appeared in the winter. Anderson once again returned to his familiar theme—the "precarious" position of history of education—warning that the subject might lose its place in the teacher-training curriculum, either by disappearing "into the anonymity of integrated courses in 'social foundations'" or by being eliminated altogether if it continued to be "academically-centered rather than professionally-centered."[46] In the spring of 1956 came the final part of the report, written by a junior historian of education, Michael Chiappetta, a former student of Eggertsen's and a partisan of "foundations" and contemporary problems as an approach to history of education. Chiapetta's report, a rehash of the thinking of the social reconstructionist group at the University of Illinois, was a pyrrhic victory for Anderson, Butts, Brubacher, and Eggertsen. Its recommendations were echoes of positions from the 1930s and 1940s, which, by the 1950s, had ceased to resonate. By the late 1950s, all the problems of the field had caught up with it. Bitterly divided internally, beset from the outside, this was the nadir of the history of education as a field of study in the United States.

VII.

By the late 1950s the Progressive Education Association was no longer in existence, the John Dewey Society and the National Society of College Teachers of Education were moribund, and the History of Education Section of the NSCTE was demoralized. Lawrence Cremin, joined by a few like-minded young historians of education—Merle Borrowman, Gordon C. Lee, Raymond Callahan, Edward Krug, and Theodore Sizer—picked up the pieces.

Cremin had been involved in the wars over history of education in the 1940s and 1950s, but more as a bystander than as a partisan.

Cremin abhorred partisanship and strong ideological commitment as antithetical to sound historical scholarship.[47] The function of the historian of education was to provide "insight" and "perspective," not solutions. Cremin's strategy for reviving the history of education was to repair the bridge between history of education and its parent discipline, history, maintaining contacts and mending fences with leaders in the field of professional education while overlooking, for fear of exacerbating, the recent deadly conflict among historians of education. Cremin became president of the NSCTE in 1960. Under his guidance, the History of Education Section was dissolved in 1960, and a new, independent History of Education Society was organized in its place, with headquarters at the School of Education at the University of Pittsburgh. At the same time, the *History of Education Journal* was terminated and replaced in 1961 by a new *History of Education Quarterly (HEQ)*, sponsored by the University of Pittsburgh and edited by Ryland Crary, formerly a colleague of Cremin's at Teachers College. In line with Cremin's liberal conception of history of education, Crary outlined the position of *HEQ* in his very first editorial: "The history of education should be related more closely to the historical profession; . . . it should develop particularly its roots in and relations with the areas of social, cultural, and intellectual history; [and] it should diminish its parochial and sometimes narrow emphasis."[48]

VIII.

Now, to return to the beginning of this chapter. I think I've supplied a fuller context in which to appraise the work of the Committee on the Role of History in American Education, Bailyn's *Education in the Forming of American Society*, and Cremin's *The Wonderful World of Ellwood Patterson Cubberley*. Now we perceive more clearly that Bailyn implicitly put down some contemporary historians of education hard and where it hurt. Recall some of his criticism. Uninterested in the past except as a "seedbed" of present issues, "they lost the understanding of origins and of growth which history alone can provide." To these historians "the past was simply the present writ small." Then the crowning insult. For all their efforts, "we have almost no historical leverage on the problems of American education." Cremin's *The Wonderful World of Ellwood Patterson Cubberley* documents not so much Cremin's and his generation's break with Cubberley as their break with their elders and mentors, and their deliberate decision to overlook or suppress the project of Anderson, Eggertsen, Butts, and Brubacher.

The efforts of Cremin and the new History of Education Society to revive history of American education as a liberal study in the professional program were aided by another crisis in education, this one specifically concerned with teacher training, which broke out in the late 1950s and peaked in the early 1960s with the publication of James B. Conant's polemic, *The Education of American Teachers* (1963). Conant saved his sharpest condemnation for courses in foundations of education. He asserted that those in charge of these courses, often inadequately trained in any of the parent disciplines, frequently attempt to patch together scraps of history, philosophy, political science, sociology, and ideology. Conant advised elimination of such courses—they were worthless and gave education departments a bad name. In 1966, the HES terminated its relationship with the University of Pittsburgh group, which had been closely identified with "social foundations" and the old history of education, and moved to New York University, where a new generation of historians began to take over leadership roles in the History of Education Society and the *History of Education Quarterly*. The HES severed all connections with the NSCTE. In 1968, a new Division F (History and Historiography of Education)—initiated by the HES—was accepted into the American Educational Research Association. At about the same time, the HES became an affiliated society of the American Historical Association.

The activities of Bailyn, Cremin, and the Committee on the Role of History in American Education had some influence among the historical profession in general; but they had more influence, I think, among historians of education on faculties at teachers colleges and schools of education. It was Cremin, in 1961, who exemplified one aspect of the "new" history of education with *The Transformation of the School: Progressivism in American Education, 1876–1956*. Cremin situated the history of education squarely in the mainstream of American social and intellectual history. Cremin located progressive education as part of broader turn-of-the-century progressive movements; the educational manifestation of the progressive era. When *The Transformation of the School* won the Bancroft Prize in American History in 1962, many junior historians of education on faculties of schools of education thought it marked the beginning of a new era. It was liberating to be encouraged to integrate the study of history of American education with all that seemed vital in contemporary American history. It meant, if historians of education so desired, the possibility of emancipation from foundations courses. And it became possible for historians of education, if they chose, to renounce the concept of the function of history of education that required it to be immediately germane to current problems, dilemmas, and crises of contemporary education. Within a decade or so, a new history of education—one liberally conceived and closely allied with the field of social and intellectual history—came into existence. However, a price was exacted: the deliberate forgetting or repression of those historians of American education who belonged to the generations between Cubberley and Bailyn and Cremin and whose general perspective on history of education, though not perhaps demonstrated in their published research, was similar to that of Bailyn and Cremin.

IX.

Historians of education hardly had a chance to assimilate the significance of Bailyn's and Cremin's new history of education when a new social reconstructionist, or "radical revisionist," school of educational historians made its appearance. The new social reconstructionists —a disparate group including Michael Katz, Clarence Karier, Joel Spring, and Paul Violas, among others—emerged on the scene in the late 1960s.[49] Here was a generation trained in a campus atmosphere of civil rights agitation, vigils protesting the Vietnam War, and New Left politics. The new reconstructionists broke with the consensus and romantic view of American educational development they associated with Bailyn and Cremin and which they perceived as a homogenizing and naïve history of education, a history willfully blind to education as an arena of conflict. Far from perceiving education as the great instrument in the triumphal advance of democracy, they saw education as "bureaucratic, racist, and class-based." Like Butts and an earlier generation of social reconstructionists, the radical revisionists were eager to engage in the political struggle and tried to balance a commitment to historical scholarship with a commitment to social and educational reconstruction. Katz declared in *The Irony of Early School Reform: Educational Innovation in Mid-Nineteenth Century Massachusetts (1968)*, that there was "no excuse for boredom with a subject that can contribute so significantly to both historical understanding and contemporary reform."[50] With these new reconstructionists—the radical revisionists, too—a vehement critical reaction was not long in coming;

historians of American education were once again polarized.[51] The controversy over radical revisionism petered out in the early 1980s, but it left bruised feelings all around. Anyone familiar with the history of the history of American education could be forgiven a feeling of déjà vu, a feeling that we had passed this way before.

If readers have come this far, the past of the history of education as a special field of study is no longer so foreign a country; they may even recognize some familiar landmarks.

What can we learn from this tour of our past? Is it that the history of the history of education is a "progress [resting] upon the opposition between successive generations"? Or is it that in the history of the history of American education a fairly small fund of essential attitudes toward the function of the history of education in the professional program is repeated, again and again, variations on the same theme, to the end of time? Or is it that we don't seem to learn from history? Are there any other lessons here? The answer to all of these questions is (provisionally) "yes."

Perhaps the most striking feature of the past of the history of education is the enduring nature of the controversy over the "function" of history of education; the terms, the rhetorical tone, the arguments seem scarcely to have changed from the turn of the century to the present. The great controversies about the function of history of education in the professional program are few and they remain curiously fixed. The question that has continuously agitated historians of education and caused the most contentiousness through the years has had to do with political engagement; whether and to what extent or how historians of education should direct their projects with the problems of the day—educational, social, or both—uppermost in mind.

Another landmark of our past is that the demand that history of education function in its technical and professional sense—to provide a "usable" past to contribute to the solutions of present-day problems of education or society—is not American educational historiography's founding myth, as many think. It seems that way only because the demand that history of education be usable in the cause of social or educational reconstruction has been so loud and insistent through the years. Still another important feature of our past highlighted by this journey is that the demand that history of education function in some immediately usable way has always been contested by the liberal conception of history, and that the latter has always been practiced under threat. Throughout the history of the history of education there have been alarums raised that if history of education was not usable to educational policy-makers or school or social reformers, the sky would fall; history of education would be pushed out of the professional program. Readers will experience a shock of recognition in Geraldine Joncich Clifford's admonition: "It takes courage for historians [of education] to point their work toward its 'lessons' for the present and future. But if it is not attempted, has the scholar who is positioned in a professional school *earned* his or her bread?"[58]

The crisis plot recurs insistently in the history of the history of American education. Coming, however, from so usually subtle and discreet a historian of education as Clifford, such implicit anxiety about the future of history of education, and the explicit warning, though familiar, must give historians of education pause. Clifford raises all over again, in the starkest of terms, the question of what degree of autonomy historians of education possess. My answer is different from hers. I think history of education has persevered because there have always been historians of education who have resisted having their function defined by colleagues or institutional pressures and have found different ways of being useful in the professional program. I would like to encourage those historians of education.

Much of the historiography of American education today *is* presentist: problems-centered, policy-oriented, and Whiggish. The quest for a usable past is the dominant position on the function of history of education. How short our memories are. We are submerged in the same presentist assumptions criticized by Bernard Bailyn and Lawrence Cremin: a history motivated by the quest for a past immediately usable in solving present problems of education is a history that leads to "wrenching of events from historical context," "persistent anachronism," and "isolation from the . . . shaping minds of twentieth-century historiography." Without disparaging the efforts of David Tyack, who has done more in the past fifteen or so years than anyone else to keep the history of education in the professional and public view, I think we have to face up to how meager the results of the presentist project have been. I think we have to confront our claims and the reality of our achievements with a little less innocence and a little more irony. An attitude of ironic skepticism, if I may describe it thus, may be the precept for a more modest but more fruitful and usable conception of the history of education today.[53]

The notion of history as constituted and provisional will hardly be news to anyone familiar with the new cultural history or current historiographical debates, but it needs to be stressed nonetheless. History cannot bear the weight of solving the problems of education or society. The historical enterprise is too problematic for that. In light of contemporary developments in historiography, I don't see how we can continue to act as if written history were something solid and stable or maintain with such certainty that its lessons for the present are so easy to read. This should not cause us to despair about our prospects, however. To give up certainties for what James Kloppenberg calls "pragmatic truth" or "pragmatic hermeneutics" and what Joyce Appleby, Lynn Hunt, and Margaret Jacob call "practical realism" allows us to live with contingency and ambiguity. Theirs is a perspective that takes into account the powers and limitations of the writing of history. Pragmatic realists accept the imperfections inherent in signification as part of the human condition and do not allow it to deflect us from our path of rational inquiry.[54]

I think it is ultimately non-functional for historians of education to claim to be directly relevant and useful to prospective teachers or educational policy makers, or to become silent (or vocal) partners in this or that cause of educational reform (but indispensable; presentist history provides a space for those historians of education who have different conceptions of their potential value to the professional program).[55] This is not to say that we do not provide knowledge that is useful for teachers, educational policy makers, or school reformers. History increases the range of choices. We offer insight. Ah, historical "insight" and "wisdom"; historical "perspective." But where have we heard this before?

I believe the issue goes even beyond how to define terms like "usable" and "useful," to what self-image the discipline of history of education wants to project, or what self-image historians of education want to project. I think we have some leeway about how to define "useful" and about how to describe or redescribe ourselves. If I say that it is time to change the conversation about history of education, I do not mean that this necessarily entails inventing an altogether new language or literally restoring an old one. One reason we reconstruct the past is so that we can, if we want to, converse with it. The history of the history of education offers many points of entrance to the conversation about the function of history of education in the professional program. Is it possible to articulate a new kind of liberal function for history of education in light of contemporary developments in historiography?

The new cultural historiography provides a recognition that there are other ways to be relevant and useful to the profession: useful in challenging orthodoxies in education, raising questions about "solutions" in education, providing historical contexts for critical thinking about the present moment in education, and helping to make our colleagues, our students, and the general public more sophisticated consumers of history.

Historians of education seem to need to constantly reassure themselves that their enterprise is useful. But useful to whom? We write for and speak to different audiences: historians of education, professors of education, students in the field of history of education, their fellow students in education schools, school administrators, policy makers, and the general public. These diverse audiences have different perspectives, interests, and horizons of expectations. They each see the role of history of education differently and evaluate the usefulness of the history of education as it relates to their own purposes, needs, and interests. But then who really knows what the present (or the future) will find useful in our work? As Dawn Powell remarks, there's no such thing as present sight. There is only hindsight and foresight. As Nietzsche observed: "We 'know' (or believe or imagine) just as much as may be *useful* in the interests of . . . the species, and even what is here called 'utility' is ultimately also a mere belief, something imaginary." Perhaps we can drop the language of "useful" and "usable" history altogether and replace it with the language of curiosity, enjoyment, pleasure, the excitement of the hunt. And—who knows— some of our colleagues, our students, and the general public might still find history of education useful if we were simply to attempt for such personal reasons to increase the store of historical knowledge of American education, as problematic as any knowledge of the past may be. And since, as Faulkner reminds us, the past is not dead—it is not even past, increasing our store of historical knowledge might deepen our understanding of the present as well.

X.

My intention has been not to prescribe but to stimulate discussion and keep a conversation going about the function of history of education. From the past we cannot determine what must be done. The history of the history of education as a field of study provides a salutary reminder that Clio has her own way of springing surprises. As Pieter Geyl observes: "History is an argument without end." Or as a postmodern historian observes: "History is a written discourse as liable to deconstruction as any other."[56] We should all be careful about making dogmatic claims about our histories and in our histories, and about the rhetoric we use in making claims at all. There is never a last word. Or rather, there is a last word, but some other historian will enjoy it.

Notes

1 David Lowenthal, *The Past Is a Foreign Country* (Cambridge, Mass., 1985), pp. xv–xvi.

2 I'd like to thank Russell Jacoby, who, recently coming over to a department of education from a history department to teach courses in the history of education, reminded me of the continued salience of the issue.

3 Paul H. Buck et al., *The Role of Education in American History* (New York, 1957), p. 2; Committee on the Role of Education in American History, *Education and American History* (New York, 1965), pp. 3–4.

4 Chapel Hill, 1960. See also Bernard Bailyn, "Education as a Discipline: Some Historical Notes," in John Walton and James L. Kuethe, eds., *The Discipline of Education* (Madison, 1963), ch. 6.

5 Boston, 1919.

6 Bailyn, *Education in the Forming of American Society*, pp. 3–14.

7 Ibid., p. 14.

8 Wilson Smith, "The New Historian of American Education," *Harvard Educational Review*, 31 (1961): 36, 38, 142–143.

9 *The Wonderful World of Ellwood Patterson Cubberley: An Essay on the Historiography of American Education* (New York, 1965), p. 39.

10 Ibid., p. 2. And almost a decade earlier, there had appeared R. Freeman Butts and Lawrence A. Cremin, *A History of Education in American Culture* (New York, 1953), with a second edition in 1955.

11 *The Wonderful of Ellwood Patterson Cubberley*, pp. 46–47.

12 Ibid., pp. 48, 51.

13 In his review of Bailyn, *Education in the Forming of American Society*, *Mississippi Valley Historical Review*, 47 (1961): 678.

14 Jesse B. Sears and Adin D. Henderson, *Cubberley of Stanford* (Palo Alto, Ca., 1957), p. 63.

15 E.g., Gabriel Compayré, *The History of Pedagogy,* trans. by W. H. Payne (Boston, 1886); Franklin V. N. Painter, *A History of Education* (New York, 1886); Robert H. Quick, *Essays on Educational Reformers* (New York, 1890); and Thomas Davidson, *History of Education* (New York, 1900).

16 New York, 1904. Dexter's concern with "facts" was deliberate: "The most crying need of the student of our educational history is a considerable mass of definite fact upon which to base his own generalizations . . . That the work is

perhaps more appropriately termed a chronicle than a history is a part of the plan, . . . for of the two evils, the lesser has seemed to me to be the omission of the philosophy rather than the fact," p. iv.

17   I borrow the terms "liberal" and "technical" from Merle L. Borrowman, *The Liberal and Technical in Teacher Education* (New York, 1956).

18   William H. Burnham and Henry Suzzallo, *The History of Education as a Professional Subject* (New York, 1908), p. 53.

19   Henry Johnson, *The Other Side of Main Street* (New York, 1943), pp. 203ff; Lawrence A. Cremin, David A. Shannon, and Elizabeth Townsend, *A History of Teachers College, Columbia University* (New York, 1954), p. 46.

20   Michael B. Katz, "From Theory to Survey in Graduate Schools of Education," *Journal of Higher Education,* 3 (1966): 325–331.

21   Where Cubberley can be criticized—his xenophobic depiction of southern and eastern European immigrants and his limited conception of "assimilation and amalgamation"—Bailyn and Cremin were silent.

22   Sears and Henderson, *Cubberley of Stanford,* ch. 7; Richard E. Thursfield, "Ellwood Patterson Cubberley," *Harvard Educational Review,* 9 (1939): 43–49; George E. Arnstein, "Cubberley: The Wizard of Stanford," *History of Education Journal,* 5 (1954): 73–81.

23   In 1931, McGraw-Hill launched under Reisner's editorship a series of source collections, the "McGraw-Hill Education Classics." Even earlier, in 1926, the Harvard Graduate School of Education had begun a series of source collections, "Harvard Documents in the History of Education."

24   Frederick Eby, "The Educational Historians Prepare to Strike Back," *Education,* 48 (1927): 92–101.

25   Charles Crowe, "The Emergence of Progressive History," *Journal of the History of Ideas,* 27 (1966): 109–124; Richard Hofstadter, *The Progressive Historians: Turner, Beard, Parrington* (New York, 1968); Peter Novick, *That Noble Dream: The "Objectivity Question" and the American Historical Profession* (Cambridge, Mass., 1988), ch. 6.

26   William H. Kilpatrick, *Education and the Social Crisis* (New York, 1932), p. 80; William H. Kilpatrick, Boyd H. Bode, John Dewey, John L. Childs, R. B. Raup, H. Gordon Hullfish, and V. T. Thayer, *The Educational Frontier* (New York, 1933), pp. 271, 290.

27   Edgar B. Wesley, "Lo, The Poor Historian of Education," *School and Society,* (13 May 1933): 619–621.

28   Harold Rugg, *The Teacher of Teachers* (New York, 1952), pp. 208ff, 224ff. See also Charles J. Brauner, *American Educational Theory* (Englewood Cliffs, N.J., 1964), pp. 202–204; Cremin, Shannon, and Townsend, *A History of Teachers College,* pp. 139ff; and Borrowman, *The Liberal and Technical in Teacher Education,* pp. 218–220.

29   The key book in the reconstructionism of the 1940s is Bruce Raup, George E. Axtelle, Kenneth D. Benne, and B. Othanel Smith, *The Discipline of Practical Judgment in a Democratic Society* (Chicago, 1943).

30   Archibald W. Anderson, William O. Stanley, B. Othanel Smith, Kenneth D. Benne, and Foster MacMurray, *The Theoretical Foundations of Education: Historical, Comparative, Philosophical, and Social* (Urbana, Ill., 1951).

31   Cremin, "The Recent Development of the History of Education as a Field of Study in the United States," *History of Education Journal*, 7 (1955): 34.

32   "Editorial Commentary," *History of Education Journal*, 1 (1949): 1–4.

33   By 1950, the Committee on Historical Foundations comprised the seven original members of the HES coordinating committee (Eggertsen, Anderson, Butts, Drake, Good, Wooton, and Moehlman), and also William Brickman, John S. Brubacher, Lawrence A. Cremin, and Andrew S. Clayton.

34   Newton Edwards, "Social Forces in American Education," *History of Education Journal*, 1 (1949): 72–73.

35   Stuart G. Noble, "The Relevance of the History of Education to Current Problems," *History of Education Journal*, 1 (1949): 78–79.

36   Philip W. Perdew, "Analysis of Research in Educational History," *Phi Delta Kappan*, 32 (1950): 134–135.

37   John S. Brubacher, *A History of the Problems of Education* (New York, 1947), p. vii.

38   R. Freeman Butts, *Assumptions Underlying Australian Education* (New York, 1957), pp. x–xii, and ch. 1, "Frame of Reference"; *A Cultural History of Western Education* (New York, 1947); and *The College Charts Its Course* (New York, 1939), ch. 18.

39   *Educational Wastelands* (Urbana, Ill., 1953); and *Restoration of Learning* (New York, 1955).

40   *Educational Wastelands*, p. 144.

41   Ibid., pp. 144ff; *Restoration of Learning*, pp. 251–252.

42   C. Winfield Scott and Clyde M. Hill, *Public Education Under Criticism* (Englewood Cliffs, N.J., 1954).

43   E.g., the series of articles by Brickman in *School and Society*, "Attack and Counterattack in American Education" (27 October 1951): 262–269; "Criticism and Defense of American Education" (20 June 1953): 390–395; and "Education, Pedagogy, and Dr. Bestor" (14 November 1953): 153–154.

44   Butts's review appeared in *Teachers College Record*, 55 (1954): 340–344; Cremin's, ironically, was published in *The Progressive*, 19 (1955): 38. See also Cremin's discussion of Bestor in *The Transformation of the School:*

Progressivism in American Education, 1876–1956 (New York, 1961), pp. 344–346.

45   Subsequently published in *The Role of the History of Education in the Professional Preparation of Teachers*, monograph 4, National Society for College Teachers of Education, 1957, pp. 1–35.

46   Archibald W. Anderson, "Bases of Proposals Concerning the History of Education," in *The Role of the History of Education in the Professional Preparation of Teachers*, p. 56.

47   Cremin observed of the decline of the progressive education movement: "Factions developed, and within the factions cults, cliques, and fanatics . . . dominated by the feuding of minorities . . . the result was intellectual bankruptcy." *The Transformation of the School*, pp. 348–349.

48   "Editorial Commentary," *History of Education Quarterly*, 1 (1961): 1–2.

49   Michael B. Katz: *The Irony of Early School Reform: Educational Innovation in Mid-Nineteenth Century Massachusetts* (Cambridge, Mass., 1968) is the seminal work. See also *Class, Bureaucracy, and Schools: The Illusion of Change in America* (New York, 1971); *School Reform: Past and Present* (Boston, 1971); and *Education in American History: Readings in the Social Issues* (New York, 1973). See also Clarence J. Karier, ed., *Shaping the American Educational State, 1900 to the Present* (New York, 1975); Clarence J. Karier, Paul Violas, and Joel Spring, *Roots of Crisis: American Education in the 20th Century* (Chicago, 1973); Joel Spring, *Education and the Rise of the Corporate State* (Boston, 1972).

50   Katz, *Education in American History*, p. ix.

51   Carl F. Kaestle, "Social Reform and the Urban School," *History of Education Quarterly*, 12 (1972): 211–228; Marvin Lazerson, "Revisionism and American Educational History," *Harvard Educational Review*, 43 (1973): 269–283; Patricia T. Rooke, "From Pollyanna to Jeremiah—Recent Interpretations of American Educational History," *Journal of Educational Thought*, 9 (1975): 15–18; Wayne J. Urban, "Some Historiographical Problems in Revisionist Educational History," *American Educational Research Journal*, 12 (1975): 337–350; Diane Ravitch, *The Revisionists Revised: Proceedings of the National Academy of Education*, 4 (1977); Joseph Kett, "On Revisionism," *History of Education Quarterly*, 19 (1979): 229–235.

52   At the conclusion of her review of Jurgen Herbst, *And Sadly Teach: Teacher Education and Professionalization in American Culture* (Madison, 1989), *History of Education Quarterly*, 30 (1990): 447.

53   I think a few other historians of education are at this point. Marc Depaepe, "History of Education Anno 1992," *History of Education*, 22 (1993): 8–10; and David N. Plank, most recently in the "Forum" discussion of David Tyack and Larry Cuban, *Tinkering Toward Utopia: A Century of Public School*

Reform (Cambridge, Mass., 1995), *History of Education Quarterly*, 36 (1996): 483–487.

54   *Telling the Truth About History* (New York, 1994), pp. 283–286, 306–309; James T. Kloppenberg, "Objectivity and Historicism: A Century of American Historical Writing," *American Historical Review*, 94 (1989): 1026–1030.

55   E.g., Maris A. Vinovskis, "An Analysis of the Concept and Uses of Systematic Educational Reform," *American Educational Research Journal*, 33 (1996): 73; Diane Ravitch and Maris A. Vinovskis, eds., *Learning from the Past: What History Teaches Us about School Reform* (Baltimore, 1995).

56   Keith Jenkins, *Re-Thinking History* (London, 1991), p. 66.

Chapter 2

Revisiting the History of Urban Education: Historiographical Reflections

> Men make their own history, but they do not make it just as they please, they do not make it under circumstances chosen by themselves, but under circumstances directly encountered, given and transmitted from the past.
>
> Karl Marx

> Every text refers back to previous texts.
>
> Umberto Eco

I.

Marx's observation may be read as a prescient commentary on the nature of writing history as well as the nature of historical events. To write history is to write within a tradition defined by earlier writings, which each new history partially recapitulates or transforms.

One tenet of contemporary intertextuality is that the practice of writing (or reading) history is already informed by a rich (or, as the case may be, impoverished) network of texts and traditions of discourse. Every history of education takes its place in an intertextual field that consists of a preexisting canon of texts, citable authorities, and inherited topics and debates; and the very meaning (and critical reception) of any new work in the history of education is in large part created by this intertextual network, even if it is not acknowledged as such within the work itself.

Among the perennial problems debated in the historiography of urban education in the United States in the twentieth century are these: (1) whether and how or to what degree historians of education should engage the educational or sociopolitical problems of the present;[1] and (2) which of the two main competing narrative formulas—romance or comedic, the public school movement triumphant and progressive; or satiric or tragic, the public school movement triumphant and reactionary—would gain ascendancy. The fierce controversy over "radical revisionism" in urban historiography, which roiled the history of education in the United States (and Canada) beginning in the late 1960s and lasting into the early 1980s, still haunts the present. But as the past recedes, so does memory. The following reflections are for historians of education who lived through this period and may be forgetting, and for their students or a younger generation of historians of education, who may have heard about the revisionist controversy only second-hand or may not have heard about it at all.

II.

It took a long time for historians of American education to develop an interest in the history of urban education.

The transition from a predominantly rural to a predominantly urban pattern of living was one of the most striking and significant of all the social changes that have occurred in the United States. The rise of the city left no basic institution untouched—not the home or family, not the church, and not the school. As early as 1889 John Dewey was urging that the congregation of people into cities was one of the most conspicuous features of modern America and that no theory of education could possibly disregard the phenomenon of urbanization. Indeed, *the* problem of education, as Dewey saw it in *The School and Society* (1900), was how to adjust the child to life in the city.

In 1890, the U.S. Bureau of the Census announced that the western frontier was no more. Nevertheless, Frederick Jackson Turner's frontier thesis cast such a long shadow over American historiography that for a long time afterward the role of the city remained little explored or understood. The city or urban development as a synthesizing principle around which to write a history of the United States was first put forward by Arthur Schlesinger in 1940, when he submitted a plan for a "reconsideration of American history from the urban point of view." Schlesinger's pioneering efforts found few followers for another two decades. Then, beginning in the early 1960s, there was a burgeoning interest in urban history, accompanied by an enormous and disparate literature in such genres as urban bibliography, surveys

of urban development, and urban or city biographies, along with what
Eric Lampard called the "orbis et urbis approach" to urban history,
treating of "virtually anything . . . and the City."

Urban history quickly won a place for itself as a specialty in the
broader field of history. Still, the response of historians of American
education to the rise of the city was for a long time largely neglect or
indifference. The historian of education Stanley K. Schultz started to
write a comparative history of Boston, Chicago, and St. Louis, but,
"struck with the paucity of respectable and useful historical writing on
the establishment and growth of even one urban school system," he
abandoned his comparative project and decided to concentrate on Boston.[2] In the late 1960s, after half a century of neglect, the history of
urban education in the United States finally emerged as an object of
intensive historical inquiry and established itself as the liveliest and
most significant subfield within the general field of history of education. Why did it take so long for historians of education in such a
heavily urbanized society as the United States to develop an interest in
the history of education in cities? There is always a close connection
between the historical scholarship of a period and the fundamental
concerns and characteristics of the society in which historians are living. But in the case of historians of education the nexus is institutional
as well as sociopolitical.

III.

History of education as a special field of study in the United States
dates back to the turn of the twentieth century, when it was one of the
most widely offered courses in American teachers colleges and schools
or departments of education. From the beginning, however, historians of education had to face the skepticism of academic colleagues
toward the profession of education in general, the reservations of colleagues in schools or colleges of education about the role or "function" of history of education in a professional program, and disagree-
ments among themselves as to whether history of education should be
taught as a "liberal," as a "technical" or professional, or as a "problems of school and society" subject while at the same time having to
cope with the general problems of a field seemingly infinitely broad
and indeterminate in scope.[3]

For a long time, problems of staffing and resources inhibited the
development of any special research interest in the history of educa-

tion, period. At the outset, few American teachers colleges or schools or departments of education had trained historians on their faculties, and faculty members who taught history of education could not devote themselves full–time to the subject. Until relatively recently, there was never a very large corps of trained historians of education in the United States; there was always a shortage of faculty for research in history of American education in general, let alone in history of urban education. The dominant content of courses in history of education in American teacher training institutions in the first two decades of the twentieth century was essentially the history of European education. Almost all of the textbooks in the field were histories of European educational thought, which emphasized developments from antiquity to the nineteenth century. And the content of history of education as a subject in the professional curriculum was construed as vast in scope. One of the doyens of the history of education, Thomas Woody, recalled, tongue-in-cheek, I think, the historiographical frontiers of a course in the history of education like this: Greek and Roman society; the Christian era; the Renaissance; the Reformation; Marxism; the Industrial Revolution; history of education in India, Africa, China, and the Soviet Union; and "major problems" of American education. The only extant works in the history of American education before World War I were Richard G. Boone's *Education in the United States* (1889) and Edwin Grant Dexter's *A History of Education in the United States* (1904), both essentially chronologies, compilations of facts dealing with formal educational institutions, educational legislation, and school administrative codes.

Elwood P. Cubberley's pioneer *Public Education in the United States: A Study and Interpretation of American Educational History (1919)*, was an attempt to create a viable history of American education tailored to the needs of the professional program. Cubberley hoped to overcome the reservations of colleagues about the function of history of education in the professional program by shifting the emphasis from a history of European educational ideas to a history of American educational policies and practices, from problems of education in Europe in the past to contemporary problems of education in America in historical perspective *and* in the context of late–nineteenth–century social and political developments. Cubberley also sought to secure the place of history of American education in the professional program by making it inspirational. Though *Public Education in the United States* did contain a section on the rise of cities, interest in the history of urban education, per se, was not part of Cubberley's interpretive frame. Cubberley's narrative line had to do with "battles" to establish free, tax-supported, publicly controlled schools—battles waged not at the level of the city but of the *state*: "Our school systems are all state school systems."[4]

The emphasis on state school systems in *Public Education in the United States,* an enormously popular text that dominated the field for more than a decade, helped retard the development of any particular research interest in the history of urban education. Meanwhile, the history of education suffered from the intellectual isolation of its practitioners; until the late 1940s the discipline did not have its own journal or professional society. Through the 1930s and the 1940s, the time and energy of most historians of education went into teaching, the collection and publication of source materials, and the publication of monographs or textbooks; or their intellectual energies were consumed in debating the "function" of history of education in the professional program—liberal, technical, present problems, or social reconstructionist. They had little time, energy, or incentive to explore the history of urban education.

In 1957, at the nadir of history of education as a special field of study in the United States, the Ford Foundation's Fund for the Advancement of Education appointed a blue-ribbon committee of some of the country's most prominent general historians to investigate the history of education. The Committee on the Role of Education in American History and the two junior members invited to join the committee in the early 1960s—Bernard Bailyn of Harvard University and Lawrence Cremin of Teachers College, Columbia University—were enormously influential in the subsequent renewal of history of American education, but the history of urban education was not an important part of their "new" history. The committee ignored the role of education in the urbanization of America and recommended, as a new point of departure, study of the role of education in the "building of new communities on the frontier."[5] Cremin's pathbreaking exemplar of the new history of education, *The Transformation of the School: Progressivism in American Education, 1876–1957* (1961) was not an interpretation of the history of urban progressive education, as might have been anticipated; in fact, Cremin was at pains to demonstrate that progressive education had its roots in rural as much as urban school reform movements.

Furthermore, any nascent interest historians of American education might have had in the 1950s or early 1960s in the history of urban education was short-circuited by Bailyn's and Cremin's unconstrained conception of the new history of education. Bailyn, in his seminal *Education in the Forming of American Society* (1960), urged historians to consider education "not only as formal pedagogy but as the entire process by which a culture transmits itself across the generations" and in its "elaborate, intricate involvements with the rest of society."[6] In *The Wonderful World of Ellwood Patterson Cubberley: An Essay on the Historiography of American Education* (1965), Cremin defined the scope of history of education only a little less (or more?) expansively, suggesting that historians consider "what agencies, formal and informal, have shaped American thought, character, and sensibility over the years, and what have been the significant relationships between these agencies and the society that has sustained them?"[7] These definitions are so abstract and encompassing that they raise the question: What is educational history and what isn't? Two points can be made. One, while seeming to suggest that historians of American education should be concerned with everything that educates, Bailyn and Cremin implied that historians of education were surrounded by historiographical frontiers of equal urgency. Two, Bailyn and Cremin, influential as they were among historians of American education, did not include history of urban education among their historiographical priorities. In the late 1960s, however, there was an eruption of interest in history of urban education that would leave the committee, Bailyn, and Cremin far behind, indeed. This would be a very curious phenomenon if we did not recall the context.

IV.

The remarkable upsurge of interest in urban educational history in the United States in the late 1960s and 1970s came at a particular moment of American political, social, and intellectual history: the urban crisis; the turbulent social and political atmosphere of the 1960s; and the emergence of urban history as an exciting and legitimate historiographical specialty. The catalyst for the redirection of historical scholarship in American education was the emergence of a "radical revisionist" school in the historiography of American education.[8] I include among the radical revisionists—by no means a homogeneous group in their methodology, their theoretical sophistication, or the quality of their published work—Joel Spring, Clarence Karier, Paul Violas, Edgar Gumbert, and the most important practitioner, Michael Katz.[9]

The radical revisionists came on to the scene at a turning point in American life, the tail end of the 1960s. The sources of their radicalism were those that produced alienation and rebelliousness throughout American society in the late 1960s and early 1970s—the war in Vietnam, poverty, racial discrimination, lawless politics (the siege of Chicago in 1968), and the appearance of a whole range of ominous and seemingly intractable urban problems. They were greatly influenced by the civil rights movement, the campus New Left and free speech movements, and the New Left movement in politics in general, as well as by critical social theorists like Paul Goodman, Ivan Illich, and Theodore Roszak; the philosopher Walter Feinberg; the historians Stephan Thernstrom, James Weinstein, and Gabriel Kolko; and the economists Herbert Bowles and Samuel Gintis.

In the winter of 1969 the historian of education James M. Wallace brazenly limned the project of the radical revisionists in the *Harvard Educational Review*. In its desire for academic respectability, Wallace claimed, history of education had bent over backward to be dispassionate and objective. Wallace called for the publication of "'anti-texts' in educational history" which would enable teachers in training to find "a usable, but historically sound past." Such an effort, Wallace conceded, "will doubtless result in some over-written, over-simplified, and over-stated history." But this, he said, is a risk that must be run "if history is to be relevant to a new generation of teachers." As the American teacher becomes politically more radical, Wallace concluded, hopefully, "it would seem both desirable and inevitable that there be an accompanying radicalization of the discipline's bearing on education."[10] Just a year earlier, Michael Katz had precisely fulfilled Wallace's hope. In *The Irony of Early School Reform: Educational Innovation in Mid-Nineteenth Century Massachusetts* (1968), Katz set the tone and the research agenda for much of the subsequent work in history of urban education in the United States. I think it can be said that after 1968 the historiography of American education changed for good.

In *The Irony of Early School Reform*, Katz focuses on three aspects of educational reform in antebellum Massachusetts: the controversy over the abolition of the public high school in the town of Beverly; the conflict between Cyrus Pierce and Horace Mann and the Boston schoolmasters over methods of teaching; and the arguments over the establishment of the state reform school at Westborough. Katz, however, was not really interested in these specific case studies as such.

He was interested in them for what they revealed about the "underlying dynamics" of urban school reform in America generally, not simply in mid–nineteenth-century Massachusetts.

Katz appealed to historians of education to cast off the myths that have pervaded their accounts of the origin of the common (public) school movement. Katz rejected the "noble story" that popular education in the United States emerged in response to the demands of an enlightened working class and the idealism and humanitarian zeal of far-sighted, benevolent philanthropists and social reformers. Promoters of urban schools were neither benevolent nor disinterested. School reform was advocated by an elite of wealth and position for its value in containing the social problems of urban-industrial society and protecting their own status. In alliance with this elite were aspiring middle-class people who saw the school as an agency of social mobility for their children. Educators joined the fight for school reform to enhance their precarious professional status.

The victory of school reformers was complete, but it was a victory for the forces of reaction. A common school system was established, but it was a system encrusted in a rigid bureaucracy and conceived as an instrument of social control, a powerful agency for imposing the values of the dominant economic class upon the working class who made up its chief clientele. The extension and reform of public education in the mid-nineteenth century, then, was not "a potpourri of democracy, rationalism, and humanitarianism." Rather, it represented "the attempt of a coalition of the social leaders, status-anxious parents, and status-hungry educators" to impose schooling "upon a reluctant, uncomprehending, skeptical, and sometimes . . . hostile citizenry."[11] Here was an "irony" of school reform. Promoters of urban public schools in the mid-nineteenth century "fostered an estrangement between the [public] school and the working-class community that has persisted to become one of the greatest challenges to reformers of our own time."[12]

Katz's use of social sciences and quantitative methodology was innovative and suggestive. The statistical computations that occupy sixty pages of appendices in the book are a novel attempt at recovering some of the variables which entered into the school debates of mid-nineteenth-century Massachusetts. Katz broke with Bailyn's and Cremin's culturalist definition of education and recalled the school to the center of educational historiography. Katz also broke with Cremin's liberal–progressive or consensus approach to the evolution of American society. Instead of a history of battles waged and victories won for the advancement of democracy and progress, Katz constructed a jeremiad lamenting decline and reaction. In the end, it was the rhetorical tone of *The Irony of Early School Reform*—Katz's moral passion, his polemical flair, and his apocalyptic language—that was to be decisive.

Katz conceived of *The Irony of Early School Reform* as at once a "scholarly historical study" and "a piece of social criticism." However, he sought to "emphasize connections between . . . past mistakes and the present disastrous state of formal education in our cities." *The Irony of Early School Reform* is permeated by a powerful action-oriented rhetoric. Katz offered no apologies for what he acknowledged as "the often partisan nature" of his argument: "The crisis in our cities must arouse a passionate response in all those who care about the quality of American life."[13] Katz interpolated from the public schools in Beverly, Massachusetts, in the mid-nineteenth century to the urban public schools of the entire country in the mid-twentieth century. Urban public schools had no redeeming features. They were elitist, anti-democratic, and irredeemably bureaucratic structures in the service of social control. Bureaucracy is anathema to Katz. He invariably uses the term as an epithet, heavy with odious connotations of rigidity, sterility, and class domination. "Social control," the counterpart of imposition, is his other *bête noire*. Urban public schools, he says, were deliberately conceived and promoted as agencies for social control. That is why their creators were determined to foist their innovations upon the community, "if necessary by force," that is, by making school attendance compulsory. School reform movements were another of Katz's targets—not simply their malevolent motives but their mystifying rhetoric of democracy, equality, and progress.

Katz dismissed school reform movements as a charade and school reform as an illusion. School reform, at least school reform based on some nostalgic vision of a "once vital and meaningful schooling" was the opiate of the liberals. "The diffusion of a utopian and essentially unrealistic ideology that stressed education as the key to social salvation," Katz asserts, "created a smoke screen that actually obscured the depth of the social problems . . . and prevented the realistic formulation of strategies for social reform."[14] Any serious school reform movement must start from scratch: "We must face the painful fact that this country has never, . . . known vital urban schools, . . . We must realize that we have no models; truly to reform we must conceive and build anew." Hence reform will not do: a fundamental reconstruction of American society was required. Accordingly, "at this point in history, any reform worthy of the name must begin with a redistribution of power and resources. That is the only way in which to change the patterns of control and inaccessible organizational structures that dominate American life. It is the only way in which to make education, and other social institutions as well, serve new purposes."[15] Katz's new social history of education and his critique of school reform movements were intended to link up with and contribute to the larger contemporary reappraisal of American life and institutions and of liberal or progressive consensus historiography then taking place in the historical profession at large.

Neither *The Irony of Early School Reform* nor the work of other radical revisionists would escape critical scrutiny.[16] But all attempts at any real dialogue about the methodological and epistemological issues raised by *The Irony of Early School Reform* or radical revisionism in general were undercut by the passions aroused by the radical revisionists. I think Diane Ravitch's famously controversial "The Revisionists Revised: Studies in the Historiography of American Education" (1977) is worth separating out for comment because it occupies a special place in the dispute.[17]

Ravitch takes several critical tacks toward *The Irony of Early School Reform* (and radical revisionism in general). She accuses it of anachronism, selective instancing, oversimplification of motives, factual inaccuracies, and lack of objectivity. She scored points on some of her accusations and missed on others. Reading the past into the present? All historians struggle against anachronism. Katz's lack of "objectivity" and "balance," and his inability to appreciate any positive qualities in the public school? Of course, Katz proclaimed his partisanship. Given Katz's view of the social crisis of the time and the illocutionary or performative intent of his work, he never wanted to achieve any judicious "balance." His reductionism and his simplification of motive, that is, his discovery of "functions (of schooling) as though they were clandestine purposes hidden by capitalist conspirators"? A point for Ravitch, and one to which I will return. In any event, methodologically and philosophically, Katz was too much the more sophisticated historian than Ravitch for accusations of anachronism or lack of objectivity to carry much weight. Factual inaccuracies? Conceded on all sides. But factual information was not the point. It did not matter whether the facts of the school affair in the town of Beverly, Massachusetts, were in error. This is not what made *The Irony of Early School Re-*

form compulsory reading among historians in the late 1960s and 1970s. The controversy generated by the radical revisionists did not, as I'll try to show below, have its locus here.

Ravitch's methodological perspective was largely innocent of epistemology, and she was naïve and unreflective about her own ideological presuppositions. For example, Ravitch distinguishes between the "politicization of history" and the "political analysis of history." She claims, against Katz and the radical revisionists, that their histories fall under the rubric of the "politicization of history." She argues that "politicized historians select the passages and the quotes that make their case against American schooling and the liberal tradition" while the "political analysis of educational history asks a series of open-ended, empirical questions." Here, she overreached herself. The contrast that Ravitch made between "politicized history" and "political analyses of history" implied that she was writing from a disinterested, "open–ended, empirical," and objective position. But "The Revisionists Revised" was not less unbiased or more "objective" than *The Irony of Early School Reform*; it came not from an absence of position but from a different position—liberal or progressive—a position which excluded any critical consideration of class, racial, or ethnic conflict. Ravitch was so committed to the "noble story" of the public school movement and the Whig model of educational historiography that she couldn't see the ideological mote in her own eye. Katz and the radical revisionists had challenged her unshakable faith in the public school ideal and the ideal of America: the classless society.[18]

But there is a certain naïveté in the writings of Katz and the radical revisionists as well. It has to do with the issue of motive and whether public school systems were deliberately designed as instruments of coercion, manipulation, and inequality. The radical revisionists' imputation of conscious self-interest or promotion of class interests to school reformers rests on a utopian and perfectionist view of what constitutes sincerity and altruism. There is a clarity, finality, and hyper-rationality in the work of the radical revisionists that oversimplifies the ambiguities, the unintentionality, and sometimes the irrationality of events. They oversimplify the ambiguities and complexity of both motive and the educational process. Katz, as an ironic historian, can be seen in part as trying to perform a therapeutic function, seeking to expose illusions about American school and society. But ironically, *The Irony of Early School Reform* is not "ironic" enough. I think an ironic view of history would assume that consequences are rarely

exact reflections of intentions, and that any action can be and frequently is as morally ambiguous as its consequences are frequently
contrary to the original intention of the actor.[19]

The bitter conflict that raged around radical revisionism was largely
a conflict between rival interpretations and rival traditions—a conflict
of values.[20] But there was more involved. In the rancorous debate not
two but actually three camps defined themselves. The third camp accepted the radical revisionists' social conflict approach to the history
of education as providing a much more convincing explanation of the
principal dynamics of school and society in the United States than the
reigning Whiggish version, but this camp found the revisionists' noi-
some rhetorical style offensive. More about this below. Granted all its
deficiencies, *The Irony of Early School Reform* remains a landmark
in the history of educational historiography. Its contributions to American educational historiography are two—one, I think, ephemeral, the
other of lasting value. Katz's social control approach became very
influential among historians of American education; for a time in the
1970s it was the prevailing model for interpreting the history of urban
school reform movements. The social control approach opened up to
critical examination the grandiloquent rhetoric of motives of progressive school reformers and progressive school reform movements; the
latter's idealism and progressive nature could never be taken for granted
again. By the mid-1970s, however, as its deficiencies became apparent, the social control approach had lost much of its appeal. It was
unable to explain how individuals, groups, or social classes could behave as at least partially autonomous actors, capable of resistance or
of acting in their own best interests. And the more it was scrutinized,
the more simplistic it appeared, giving "social control" an exclusively
pejorative connotation of conformity or coercion.[21] One does not
choose to live in a society without social order and some mechanisms
of ensuring social order.[22] The public school system is society's social
control structure *par excellence*. A different and more interesting
question for historical investigation might be: What other functions
does schooling perform?

Michael Katz's enduring contribution to American educational historiography is this: he provided an alternative to Lawrence Cremin's
then-reigning progressive or romance interpretive framework. Until
Katz emerged on the scene in the late 1960s with the publication of
The Irony of Early School Reform, the dominant tradition in American educational historiography, the *only* historiographical tradition in

the historiography of American education, was liberal or progressive in its ideological implications and romantic in its genre or narrative line; it was a story of the evolution and inevitable triumph of the public school idea, a story of the advance of educational progress on behalf of democracy, equality, and the realization of the American dream. This is a genre that Cremin reinforced in *The Transformation of the* School. There is neither irony nor social conflict in the romance tradition of historiography.

The Irony of Early School Reform unfroze the romance genre in which the history of American education was becoming set. Katz shifted the focus from harmony, consensus, and unequivocal progress to class conflict, inequality, and social-historical discrimination. Katz brought the involvement, passion, and righteous anger of the historian as moral critic to the writing of educational history.[23] Historians of education in the late 1960s were settling into their ivory tower when Katz and the radical revisionists rebuked their complacency and disturbed their contemplation with the noise of current events. Katz provided a strong new idiom, an alternative vocabulary, to describe American education. He made it difficult for historians of education to continue to ignore the language of power, prizes, and group interests, to ignore questions like "Who has the power?" "Where is the power located?" and "Whose interests are served?" If one of the tasks of the historian is to undo denials, myths, and idealizations, then Katz's place in the historiography of American education is secure. Finally, by its radical critique of the prevailing romance genre of educational historiography, *The Irony of Early School Reform* and the radical revisionists aroused fresh interest in the history of education not only among historians, but among students in schools and colleges of education as well as educational policymakers and the informed public.

What was all the shouting about?

In the late 1960s and through the 1970s the conflict raging among historians of education over radical revisionism was a firestorm that almost consumed history of education as a field of study. The radical revisionists polarized the history of education community in the United States (and in Canada).[24] So what was all the shouting about? I think it was about power and civility.

Michel Foucault has taught us that no text is innocent. Texts are facts of power produced within a world of power struggle as well as or more than a contribution to the dialogic exchange of views. Texts compete and struggle for voice, for territory, for an audience. Warren

Susman, a sensitive observer of and participant in the historiographical conflicts over revisionism that were beginning to split the entire historical community asunder in the 1960s, anticipated Foucault by a decade. In the United States, history is a key subject. We all like to have history on our side. And the way people view the past has some consequences for the way they act in the present. Since problems in the present are frequently situated or contextualized by reference to the way history dealt with similar problems, control over the interpretation of the past becomes a burning cultural issue.[25] The challenge posed by the radical revisionist historians came down to this: Who would have the power to determine the nature and boundaries of permissible historical discourse? Who would have control over the interpretation of America's educational past? But there was something else at stake.

Many historians of education, myself included, thought there was a certain etiquette or set of manners of writing and of speech shared by all historians. That was another shock effect of the radical revisionists. Few historians of education were equipped to handle the radical revisionists' aggressive, in-your-face rhetorical style, their arrogance in argument, and their imputations of ignorance, bad faith, or self-seeking aimed at anyone who disagreed with them. (But then, almost everyone's judgment was affected. As Peter Novick notes in *That Noble Dream: The "Objectivity Question" and the American Historical Profession*, for all their interest in delving into the motives of past historical figures, historians are hard put to understand that their own activities are driven by any motive other than logic or rationality.) Diane Ravitch was targeted for vilification.

Reading it today, "The Revisionists Revised" is, I think, a fairly cool, contextualized, and balanced critique. Here and there, Ravitch gives *The Irony of Early School Reform* due respect—for example, acknowledging its "sophisticated effort to apply social science concepts to historical problems." Sharper critiques had appeared in print, but Ravitch—to repeat—was singled out. Why? I speculate as follows. Other critics published in innocuous journals, or journals with a limited audience. "The Revisionists Revised" was commissioned and published by the prestigious National Academy of Education (copies were apparently sent to publishing houses, deans of education, and prominent historians and other scholars). Lawrence Cremin, one of the founding members of the Academy, who abhorred controversy, chose Ravitch, his former student, for the assignment; everyone knew she was his spokesperson in the revisionist affair.[26] "The Revisionists Revised" helped to alter the intellectual climate. Ravitch provided an alternative and contrasting perspective for all those historians and other scholars who in the 1970s knew only the radical revisionist version of the history of American education. Thanks to Ravitch, everyone finally had a chance to hear Cremin's side of the debate.[27]

"The Revisionists Revised" stopped the momentum of radical revisionism cold and created a space to think. In the end, the radical revisionists were not able to dictate the terms of historiographical debate, or to establish the norms by which histories or historians of education would be measured. Lawrence Cremin's romantic metanarrative of the course of American education in the twentieth century was decentered, but so was the satiric metanarrative of Michael Katz and the radical revisionists. Historians of American education would not be held to any single mode of interpreting America's educational past.

V.

The controversy that swirled around radical revisionism was a bruising experience for everyone. It did not really come to a resolution but sputtered along into the early 1980s.[28] While the controversy dragged on, it stimulated a handful of historians of education to produce subtler and more complex versions of the history of American urban education.

In the early 1970s, perhaps a dozen articles in the "orbis et urbis" genre of urban educational historiography made their appearance.[29] Still, they didn't add up to much. As we noted above, Stanley Schultz started to write a comparative educational history of Boston, Chicago, and St. Louis. But struck by "the paucity of respectable and useful historical writing on the establishment and growth of even *one* urban school system" (italics mine), Schultz abandoned the comparative history project to concentrate on Boston. Because of the recency of interest, and the fragmentary nature of the published research (there was, remarkably, still no history of education of any city in the far west or in the southern part of the country), such studies provided little cumulative knowledge of the history of urban education. Nevertheless, in 1974, David Tyack's *The One Best System: A History of American Urban Education* made its appearance.[30] Here was an ambitious interpretation of the history of American urban education in terms of the "organizational factor" or the "organizational revolution" by one of the country's most productive historians of education.

To briefly summarize Tyack's argument: in the latter part of the nineteenth century the local ward system—community control of schools with a vengeance—was prevalent in American cities, a legacy of earlier village or small town patterns. School leaders, an interlocking directorate of university presidents, professors of educational administration, leading businessmen and lawyers, and publishers of leading newspapers and journals of opinions, condemned the ward system as corrupt and inefficient. The ward system would be replaced by a system based on the model of large-scale industrial bureaucracies emerging at the turn of the century. The "administrative progressives" (as distinct from "pedagogical progressives" and "social progressives")— Tyack's useful label for the men, and they were almost all men, who conceived and led the drive to implement the "one best system"—were convinced that what worked in business and industry was eminently applicable to the schools. Their watchwords were centralization, efficiency, economy, and nonpolitical control. School boards were to be small, nonpartisan, preferably composed of successful businessmen, and purged of all connection with political parties and elected officials; school reformers preferred a "relatively closed system of politics" to "pluralistic politics."

The desire to bring order to increasingly disorderly cities prompted the drive to expand urban school systems. The need to bring efficiency to increasingly large and complex urban school systems prompted the move to centralization, standardization, and bureaucratization. In order to make the "one best system" work, school leaders also had to classify children and develop differentiated courses of study and standardized examinations. With classification and differentiated curricula came new job categories, new programs of professional preparation, more administrators, more bureaus, bureaucracy, and scientific management; the "one best system." Here is an irony of school reform. Progressives sought in part to counteract the inhumanity of the industrial revolution through the school, and the school was modeled on the very essence of the industrial revolution—the factory. The trend toward centralization, bureaucracy, and scientific management emerged first in school systems in cities in the American northeast, then spread south and west and in a short time into rural and smalltown school systems. Tyack maintains that administrative progressives were able to develop a consensus in their search for the "one best system," and by 1920 or thereabouts largely succeeded in implementing it. Their success, Tyack concludes, "so framed the structure of urban education that the subsequent history of [American urban schools] has been in large part an unfolding of the organizational consequences of centralization."[31]

The One Best System had many of the strengths of the new urban history: strong application of the social sciences; bold speculation; an effort to reinterpret well-known events from the perspective of those on the bottom, those "victimized by their poverty, their color, their cultural differences." Tyack's insights are frequently penetrating; for example, his analogy between "black power" in urban education in the 1960s and "Catholic power" in urban education in the 1830s and 1840s, and his observation that in the politics of urban education, what is frequently at stake is cultural rather than pedagogical issues, and there are interesting comparisons of school systems with police departments and other municipal organizations. *The One Best System* is also the most ambivalent and interesting—interesting because it is ambivalent—example of the presentist, advocacy historiography of the 1970s. It is definitely socially engaged and presentist, like the historiography of Katz and the radical revisionists. In contrast to the latter, however, Tyack approached his project in a more formal, polite historiographical tradition. Tyack introduces his book as "exploratory and tentative," a "dovetailing of old and new scholarship," and he states that he is open to modifications, critiques, and suggestions. On the other hand, in contrast to Cremin and Ravitch, Tyack's was a much more critical approach to the history of American education.

The One Best System aimed to provide a new interpretive framework for history of American education and also a usable past for the present by explaining how we arrived at the "present crisis in urban education" and how we can "serve the quest for social justice." Tyack asserts that he "does not share the view that urban schools have abysmally declined; this is an exaggeration as misleading as the mindless optimism of those who recently saw only progress." He also states, "I endorse neither the euphoric glorification of public education as represented in the traditional historiography nor the current fashion of berating school people and regarding the common school as a failure." But, he declared, "in this book I shall stress persistent problems."[32] And he does. For example: "Despite frequent good intentions and abundant rhetoric about 'equal educational opportunity,' schools have rarely taught the children of the poor effectively—and this failure has been systematic, not idiosyncratic," and "urban schools did not create the injustices of American urban life, although they had a systematic part in perpetuating them." Tyack does not overlook the positive qualities of urban public education for racial and ethnic minority groups, women, and the "dispossessed." He acknowledges that many reformers acted "with the best of conscious motives" and that urban schools "opened up opportunities that many of the students might otherwise never have had." And he acknowledges that there was always the possibility of resistance. Dissent generally came on the local level and in the rhetoric of the preservation of diversity. For example, opposition to the common school arose in many Catholic urban communities. Angered by discrimination and what they perceived as Protestant bias, Catholic parents withdrew their children from urban public schools and placed them in their own parochial school system. German Americans in a number of cities mobilized for bilingual education. African Americans in some northern cities sought their own schools and fought discrimination and separation in the courts. These actions demonstrated that a diverse American population could not be encompassed by a single-minded, centralized bureaucratic order. Thus the "one best system" was neither omnipotent nor omniscient. And the clientele of the urban public school was not passive: various groups could and did stand up for their own interests.

The narrative line of *The One Best System*, however, is so structured that the school's positive features are discounted, its virtues downplayed. It is as if to credit the school would be to legitimatize the apologists for urban schools and thus to disarm the school's critics. In terms of the poetics of history, it is interesting to speculate how much Tyack was trapped by his commitment to advocacy history. Tyack was "literally" committed to a narrative line which he himself had warned against and to which he was apparently opposed. (Recall his assertion that he "does not share the view that urban schools have abysmally declined.") But with *The One Best System*, as with *The Irony of Early School Reform*, neither its documentary content, or in Hayden White's terminology, its mode of emplotment, is as significant as its overarching argument, the explanatory power of its interpretive framework.[33]

In the early 1970s, historians were beginning to devote increasing attention to the organizational factor in American history, to the development of those sprawling networks of large-scale organizations that had begun to dominate the United States and other industrial societies.[34] In 1967, Robert H. Wiebe published an interpretation of modern American history along organizational lines: *The Search for*

Order, 1877–1920. With *The One Best System*, Tyack cut loose from both the satiric emplotment of Katz and radical revisionists and the romance emplotment of Cremin and progressive historians of education, and turned to the organizational school of historiography for an alternative conceptual framework. Tyack's discussion of structural constraints on school reform has provided a point of reference for the historical examination of the formation of educational policy and the implementation of educational reform. I think Tyack's lasting contribution to the historiography of American education, however, is that he brought the organizational revolution that took place in American schooling in the twentieth century to the forefront of the attention of historians of American urban education. Thanks to Tyack, no subsequent history of twentieth-century progressive school reform movements nor of the "transformation" of the school would be able to ignore the organizational factor.

VI.

"In a sense," Tyack avers about *The One Best System*, "this synthesis is premature since a new generation of talented scholars is directing its attention to monographic studies of urban schooling."[35] Beginning in the early 1970s, the works of four members of that new generation of scholars—Stanley Schultz, Carl Kaestle, Selwyn Troen, and Julia Wrigley—made their appearance and proved that Tyack was wise to provide so generous a preamble to his own work.[36] The subjects of Schultz, Kaestle, Troen, and Wrigley, respectively, are the public school systems of Boston, New York City, St. Louis, and Chicago. Their histories indicate that the historiographical project is not just one version replacing another—that, at least in the historiography of urban education, progress can be cumulative as well as corrective. All demonstrated that there was still much life in studying the history of public school systems.

The point which clearly emerged from these studies is that urban public school systems in the United States developed as a response to the first shocks of modernization—felt earliest and most intensely in America's eastern coastal cities, especially Boston and New York City. None of the studies condemns or celebrates. The schools have been asked to perform many and varied services and to satisfy many constituencies. Schooling has unintended and even unpredictable consequences. The schools have been an instrument of both social control and social advancement, of both democracy and social inequality. All abjure the premise that American public schools have been an un-equivocal failure; all portray the schools as a focal point of idealism as well as self-interest. Urban school systems emerged as a response to the influx of immigrants and to the social friction and disorganization pursuant to rapid and disorderly urban growth. The public schools— tax-supported, publicly controlled, and free—were to be a major in-strument in Americanizing the immigrants and forging a new national cohesion.

The advocates of public schooling set out to shore up society. They were aided by schoolmen who found in the development of public schools a device by which they could enhance their own professional status and dominance. All believed, however, that education would improve the conditions of the poor. The rapid expansion of the school population, the swelling economic investment in schools, and the pro-liferation of schools and schoolteachers led to a demand for efficiency, economy, systematization, and bureaucracy. It was inevitable that the nascent urban school systems would be organized along the lines of the New England factory system. Centralization, bureaucracy, and ef-ficiency and economy of operation were essential if the systems were to be universal. Finally, those who established school systems were not following some predetermined path. The process of building ur-ban public school systems went something like this: there was an ur-gent social problem or "crisis" followed by pressure on the schools and then hasty and makeshift solutions. The ramshackle creations of the people who built the urban school systems illustrated neither an inevitable working out of the spirit of progress nor a conspiracy of one class against another.

To reacquaint readers, Kaestle's *The Evolution of an Urban School System* attempts to explain why and how the public schools of New York City became organized into "a single, articulated, hierarchical system that was amenable to uniform policy decisions."[37] In response to increasing vagrancy, intemperance, and crime, the city's leaders turned to public schooling as an instrument for the socialization of the children of the poor. The public school system was expected to trans-mit not only literacy but the cultural traditions and moral attitudes appropriate to a safe transition to the new urban, industrial America. Kaestle concludes that it was not so much class and cultural bias on the part of school leaders as common sense which mandated the bu-reaucratization of the schools. The sheer numbers of children and schools dictated centralization and bureaucracy. School leaders in New York City were concerned with efficiency, economy, and standardization, but there was more involved: "the desire to be fair to all those who would accept the rules of the system, and [the] desire to raise the quality of teaching."[38] Kaestle concludes that New York's public school system was a reflection of the city's consistent institutional approach to urban problems, "one which has aimed ideally to uplift, hopefully to reconcile, and minimally to control, its turbulent population."[39] Schultz's argument was in many ways similar to Kaestle's. The public school movement in Boston evolved in response to mounting concern over immigration, pauperism, and rising crime rates. The public school system was promoted "to secure order in a disorderly age." Still, Schultz concludes, to the extent that schools succeeded in reaching the children of the poor, the working class, and the foreign-born, they opened opportunities for social advancement.[40] In their attempt to create a *system*, school leaders in Boston turned to the factories of New England, "the perfect model for retooling the schools."[41] Both Schultz and Kaestle made extensive use of quantitative evidence to demonstrate that in fact children from a wide variety of socioeconomic classes attended the public schools.

Troen's study of the public school system in St. Louis and Wrigley's of public schools in Chicago provide invaluable midwest counterparts to the more widely studied school systems of New York City and Boston. Troen rejects what he calls hostile historical analyses of urban school reform and refers to the development of systems of public education as one of the great accomplishments of nineteenth-century urban society.[42] Troen dissents from the social control model of urban educational historiography as well as from the view that bureaucratic reforms were an upper-class attempt to dominate the public schools. Like David Tyack, Troen emphasized the "importance of the rationalizing processes that characterized modernizing institutions."[43] Changes in city schools were not preordained; they "flowed from the system's responses to changes in urban life, political pressures, educational theory, and the decisions of students and parents."[44] Administrative and curricular reforms were widely supported. School administrators were careful to educate the public about the school system's work and to seek public support, and this made the transition to centralization and bureaucracy relatively free from conflict.

Wrigley's *Class Politics and Public Schools: Chicago, 1900–1950,* which appeared in 1982, put a period to an era in the historiography of American urban education. Wrigley challenged the radical revisionist position that public schools were fostered by an economic elite as a means of social control and that schools were imposed on the working class.[45] She concluded that in Chicago, business and professional groups, rather than conceiving of the public school system as a powerful agency of social control, which consequently should be generously supported, often viewed the public school system as a drain on the finances of the city and opposed its expansion. She found, on the other hand, that the labor movement in Chicago provided consistent support for the public school system and fought for its expansion. And far from being docile, the labor movement resisted school reforms deemed not in its interests and fought for its own educational ideals and school reform programs: "The history of educational development in Chicago is the history of struggle, compromise, and resistance, not of simple elite domination."[46] And Chicago, like Boston, St. Louis, and New York City, as we now know, was not exceptional in this regard.

VII.

Historians of education in teachers colleges or on the faculties of schools or departments of education practice their craft under particularly acute tension. They carry commitments both to the discipline of history and to the professional education program. Their loyalties are claimed by the demands of both past and present. Richard Hofstadter remarked in 1970, at the beginning of a bitter conflict over radical revisionism among general historians, that historians are caught between their desire to count in the world and their desire to understand it, between their desire to do good and to do good historical scholarship, between their desire to create a historically sound past and to create a usable past for the present. The problem is that such desires are at odds with each other, or that they are compatible only within narrow limits. On the one hand, the desire to understand the past points back to a commitment to detachment, neutrality, and the scientific ideal. On the other hand, the urgency of present problems exacerbates the desire to derive some lessons from history that will serve the needs of the time, and this frequently overrides the importance of comity, so essential for the survival of the community of historians.[47] The passage of time hasn't diminished the relevance of the dilemma Hofstadter so eloquently pinpointed in 1970. The conflict between their desire to create a historically sound past and their desire to create a past that is usable for the present remains unresolved for historians of American education.

Now that we have revisited the history of urban education, I promised some historiographical reflections.

About the importance of comity for the survival of the community of historians of education: I think this is just common sense and not debatable. As for revision in the historiography of education: of course, revisionism is the lifeblood of the discipline. History is continually rewritten according to the needs and interests of each generation. What about "radical revisionism"? The radical revisionists left this legacy, among others: a conviction that historians of education cannot distance themselves from the problems of their times. They should join the struggle and use history as a weapon in the cause of social or educational reconstruction.

So did the radical revisionists of the 1970s implicitly believe, and do many historians of education implicitly believe today, that the problems of school and society are not so intransigent that they cannot be solved by historians of education? Or did radical revisionists in the 1970s implicitly believe, and do many historians of education and others implicitly believe today—as Hayden White and Richard Rorty seem to believe—that the provisional nature of history and its infinite redescribability offer a "lever by means of which we may move the weight of the past," liberate the present from the "burden of history," and begin anew?[48] But if the past can be infinitely redescribed, it can support countless plausible and (by a historian's own methodological lights) equally legitimate histories; it can provide whatever historians think useful to different groups: various "origins, legitimating antecedents, explanations, and lines of descent . . . useful for them as they try to be in control, so that they can make the past their past."[49] Is this not to reduce histories to arbitrary political or ideological preference? And then what are we left with? History as one likes it?[50]

As Umberto Eco argues, the past exists. Since it cannot really be destroyed, it must be revisited—but with irony, not innocently. The new developments in historiography associated with the idea of written history as constituted and provisional need to be stressed. As I noted in the previous chapter, history cannot bear the weight of the appeal to help solve the urgent problems of present-day schools or society. The historical project is too tentative, contingent, and unstable, too liable to deconstruction. This leads not to the "end of history" but to a conception of history of education as one voice in the conversation about education (which, in reality, it is anyway), without claiming to be a privileged voice.[51] If this is not enough for historians of education nostalgic for the engagement and excitement of the 1970s, well, *that* radical revisionism is gone. The cultural space it once occupied is now taken.[52] But I have a modest proposal for a new radical revisionism for historians of education.

In "The Discourse of History," Roland Barthes argues that the past can be represented in many historians' modes and tropes, some of which are less mythological and mystifying than others, inasmuch as they deliberately call overt attention to their own processes of production and explicitly indicate the constructed rather than the found nature of their referents. To engage history of education in the way suggested by Barthes is to do history in a way that concerns itself with the past but allows for its continual reinterpretation and which keeps in mind the importance of unintended consequences in history and in historical writing as well.

How might such an approach to history of education—an approach to the past laced with more irony and less innocence—be realized? Two things are needed. First, following the work of Hayden White, Dominick LaCapra, and Hans Kellner, among other historians who can be cited, is a self-reflective and critical methodology about the role of rhetoric, language, and mode of emplotment in our representations of the past—that is, a willingness to be more introspective about the rhetorical and linguistic processes by which we construct meaning from past reality and represent ourselves and the past to our readers. And second, a willingness to challenge orthodoxies, mystification, and obfuscation not just in histories of education but in educational discourse generally wherever we find them. Here is a new radical revisionism: history of education as counternarrative, a kind of history of which film—what Robert Rosenstone calls the other "chief carrier of historical messages in our culture"—provides the foremost example.[53] I refer particularly to films set in or around high schools that contest official "ways of seeing," the "common script," the "regimes of truth," the "orthodoxies" of present-day educational discourse so provocatively that they force us to revisit the past of education, now no longer with innocence, but with irony. I am not unaware of the marginal position of history of education in the professional program today. I don't know if it will make our discipline more central, but as we approach the millennium and if history of education has to be practiced under new historical conditions, what have we got to lose? In this new radical revisionism—self-reflective, provisional, and unafraid of philosophical introspection or of becoming literary—our colleagues, our students, educational policy makers, and the public may find a more interesting, more complex, and even a more usable history of education.

Notes

1   "Whether" is not quite the word I want. All written history bears marks of its present.

2   *The Culture Factory: Boston Public Schools, 1789–1860* (New York, 1973), pp. x–xi.

3   See Chapter 1 in this volume.

4   Cubberley, *Public Education in the United States*, pp. 487–495.

5   Paul H. Buck et al., *The Role of Education in American History* (New York, 1957), p. 10; Committee on the Role of Education in American History, *Education and American History* (New York, 1965).

6   *Education in the Forming of American Society: Needs and Opportunities for Study* (Chapel Hill, 1960), p. 14.

7   *The Wonderful World of Ellwood Patterson Cubberley: An Essay on the Historiography of American Education* (New York, 1965), p. 48.

8   The label "radical revisionists" is not very satisfactory. Michael Kammen has sagely warned of the risk of categorizing historians into schools: "Some of us fall into schools unknowingly; others are too hastily pigeonholed . . . and some of us simply change our minds." *Selvages and Biases: The Fabric of History in American Culture* (Ithaca, N.Y., 1987), p. 31. Nevertheless, I use the term here because of its familiarity. In another place, I use the term "new reconstructionists."

9   Michael B. Katz, *The Irony of Early School Reform: Educational Innovation in Mid-Nineteenth Century Massachusetts* (Cambridge, Mass., 1968). See also his *Class, Bureaucracy, and Schools: The Illusion of Educational Change in America* (New York, 1971); *School Reform: Past and Present, Boston* (New York, 1971); and *Education in American History: Readings in the Social Issues* (New York, 1973). See also Clarence J. Karier, ed., *Shaping the American Educational State, 1900 to the Present* (New York, 1975); Clarence J. Karier, Paul C. Violas, and Joel H. Spring, *Roots of Crisis: American Education in the 20th Century* (Chicago, 1973); Joel H. Spring, *Education and the Rise of the Corporate State* (Boston, 1972); Edgar B. Gumbert and Joel H. Spring, *The Superschool and the Superstate: American Education in the 20th Century, 1918–1970* (New York, 1974); Paul C. Violas, *The Training of the Urban Working Class: A History of Twentieth-Century American Education* (Chicago, 1978).

10   Review of Patricia A. Graham, *Progressive Education: From Arcady to Academe, Harvard Educational Review*, 39 (1969): 190–197.

11   Katz, *The Irony of Early School Reform*, pp. 112, 218.

12   Ibid., p. 112.

13   Ibid., p. viii.

14   Ibid., pp. 211, 218.

15   *Education in American History: Readings in the Social Issues,* p. 348.

16   E.g., Carl F. Kaestle, "Social Reform and the Urban School," *History of Education Quarterly,* 12 (1972): 211–228; Marvin Lazerson, "Revisionism and American Educational History," *Harvard Educational Review,* 43 (1973): 269–283; Wayne J. Urban, "Some Historiographical Problems in Revisionist Educational History," *American Educational Research Journal,* 12 (1975): 337–350; Patricia T. Rooke, "From Pollyanna to Jeremiah—Recent Interpretations of American Educational History," *Journal of Educational Thought,* 9 (1975): 15–18.

17   "The Revisionists Revised: Studies in the Historiography of American Education," *Proceedings of the National Academy of Education,* 4 (1977).

18   More attentive to conflict is Ravitch's *The Troubled Crusade: American Education, 1945–1980* (New York, 1983).

19   These comments are based on Katz's use of irony and on my own preference for an ironic mode of doing history. Katz was more adroit in "Education and Social Development in the Nineteenth Century: New Directions for Inquiry," in Paul Nash, ed., *History and Education: The Educational Uses of the Past* (New York, 1970), ch. 4.

20   Most perceptive is Joseph F. Kett, "On Revisionism," *History of Education Quarterly,* 19 (1979): 229–235.

21   William Muraskin, "The Social-Control Theory in American History: A Critique," *Journal of Social History,* 9 (1976): 550–559; Peter N. Stearns, "Toward a Wider Vision: Trends in Social History," in Michael Kammen, ed., *The Past Before Us: Contemporary Historical Writing in the United States* (Ithaca, N.Y., 1980), pp. 216–217.

22   By definition, Brian Davis observes, "the social is control. Social control is the ubiquitous condition of society." *Social Control and Education* (London, 1976).

23   Cf. John Higham, "Beyond Consensus: The Historian as Moral Critic," *American Historical Review,* 57 (1962): 609–625.

24   Some historians of education who lived through this decade must have had mixed feelings as they read Harvey Graff's recent memoir: "By 1970 . . . the rejuvenated *History of Education Quarterly,* newly under the editorial direction of Paul Mattingly, became for a decade the journal of record for the field in North America and a major site for revisionist scholarship *and* its best criticism." "Towards 2000: Poverty and Progress in the History of Education," *Historical Studies in Education/Revue d'histoire de l'éducation,* 3 (1991): 191–210.

25   Warren I. Susman, "History and the American Intellectual: Uses of a Usable Past," *American Quarterly*, 16 (1964): 243–263.

26   In Barthes's formulation, Ravitch was the "guest" of the text, not its creator. That Ravitch's innocuously titled article, "The Revisionists Revised: Studies in the Historiography of American Education" was subsequently published as *The Revisionists Revised: A Critique of the Radical Attack on Schools* (1978) further infuriated the radical revisionists. See Katz's "An Apology for American Educational History," *Harvard Educational Review*, 49 (1979): 256–266. See also Katz, "The Politics of Educational History," in *Reconstructing American Education* (Cambridge, Mass., 1987), ch. 5.

27   In a comment in the 1970s on the revisionist controversy— and it is only implicit—Cremin observed: "On balance the American educational system has contributed significantly to the advancement of liberty, equality, and fraternity. . . . The aspirations of American education have been more noble than base." *Traditions of American Education* (New York, 1977), p. 127. Cremin makes another brief comment on the controversy in the course of a lengthy footnote in *American Education: The National Experience, 1783–1876* (New York, 1980), pp. 549–550. "My own interpretation," Cremin remarks, "suggests that Katz overgeneralizes from specific findings."

28   Jurgen Herbst, "Beyond the Debate over Revisionism," *History of Education Quarterly*, 20 (1980): 133; Laurence Veysey, "The History of Education," *Reviews in American History*, 10 (1982): 285; J. Donald Wilson, "Historiographical Perspectives in Canadian Education History," *Journal of Educational Thought*, 11 (1977): 51–53; Konrad H. Jarausch, "The Old 'New History of Education': A German Reconsideration," *History of Education Quarterly*, 26 (1986): 239.

29   E.g., Ronald D. Cohen, "Urban Schooling in Twentieth-Century America: A Frame of Reference," *Urban Education,* 8 (1974): 423–437; Edwin B. Gumpert, "The City as Educator," *Education and Urban Society,* 4 (1971): 7–24; Carl F. Kaestle, "School Reform and the Urban School," *History of Education Quarterly*, 12 (1972): 211–228.

30   Cambridge, Mass., 1974.

31   Ibid., p. 127.

32   Ibid., pp. 11–12.

33   White defines emplotment as the "encodation of the facts contained in a chronicle as components of specific kinds of plot structures." See in general "The Historical Text as Literary Artifact," in *Tropics of Discourse: Essays in Cultural Criticism* (Baltimore, 1978).

34   Robert H. Wiebe, *The Search for Order, 1877–1920* (New York, 1967); Louis Galambos, "The Emerging Organizational Synthesis in Modern American History," *Business History Review*, 44 (1970): 279–290.

35 *The One Best System*, p. 3.

36 Schultz, *The Culture Factory*; Carl F. Kaestle, *The Evolution of an Urban School System: New York City, 1750–1850* (Cambridge, Mass., 1973); Selwyn K. Troen, *The Public and the Schools: Shaping the St. Louis School System, 1838–1920* (Columbia, S.C., 1975); Julia Wrigley, *Class Politics and Public Schools: Chicago, 1900–1950* (New Brunswick, N.J.,1982).

37 Kaestle, *The Evolution of an Urban School System*, p. viii.

38 Ibid., pp. 177–179, 190.

39 Ibid., p. 191.

40 Schultz, *The Culture Factory*, p. x.

42 Ibid., pp. xi–xiii.

42 Troen,*The Public and the Schools*, p. 224.

43 Ibid., p. 1.

44 Ibid., p. 4.

45 Wrigley, *Class Politics and Public Schools*, p. 15.

46 Ibid., pp. 261–269.

47 Richard Hofstadter, "The Importance of Comity in American History," *Columbia University Forum*, 13 (1970): 12–16.

48 The task of the historian is "less to remind men of their obligation to the past than to force upon them an awareness of how the past could be used to effect an ethically responsible transition from present to future." Hayden White, "The Burden of History," *Tropics of Discourse: Essays in Cultural Criticism*, pp. 40–41, 49. And quoted in Michael B. Katz, "The Origins of Public Education: A Re-Assessment," *History of Education Quarterly*, 16 (1976): 382.

49 Keith Jenkins, *Re-Thinking History* (London, 1991), p. 65.

50 Peter Novick's last three chapters in *That Noble Dream: The "Objectivity Question" and the American Historical Profession* (Cambridge, England, 1988) are relevant here: "Every Group Its Own Historian," "The Center Does Not Hold," and "There Was No King in Israel."

51 I take it that this is also Marc Depaepe's position in "History of Education Anno 1992," *History of Education*, 22 (1993): 8–10. He refers to education as "a sobering and relativizing discipline that leads to the demystification of the traditional educational discourse rather than to the advancement of one or another educational theory." See also David N. Plank's contribution to the "Forum" discussion of David B. Tyack and Larry Cuban, *Tinkering Toward Utopia: A Century of Public School Reform* (Cambridge, Mass., 1995), *History of Education Quarterly*, 36 (1996): 483–487.

52   E.g., Peter McLaren, *Revolutionary Multiculturalism: Pedagogies of Dissent for the New Millennium* (Boulder, Col., 1997).

53   Robert A. Rosenstone, ed., *Revisioning History: Film and the Construction of a New Past* (Princeton, 1995), p. 3.

Chapter 3

Representations of History in the Linguistic Turn

What is omnipresent is imperceptible. Nothing is more commonplace than the reading experience, and yet nothing is more unknown. Reading is such a matter of course that, at first glance, it seems there is nothing to say about it.

Tzvetan Todorov

I.

"What do you read, my lord?"
"Words, words, words."

Hamlet is having fun at Polonius's expense. But if taken straight, the exchange between Hamlet and Polonius might be echoed by historians of education who are asked to state the basic material of their practice. Yet we don't pay much attention to language, rhetoric, words, the words we use in our histories or the words other historians use in their histories, and how we read them.

Historians have always had to deal with textual sources. We have always been concerned with the reading of texts. But our concern with reading has been largely unreflective. "In a sense," LaCapra maintains, "historians are professionally trained not to read." Historians are trained to give texts a "documentary" reading, to read texts in narrow, utilitarian ways. We speed through texts, mining them for factual information about given times and places. There is no grappling with language; we do not engage texts as "texts." I think historians need to think more deeply about the nature of historical explanation and need to acknowledge more fully the theoretical dimension of reading (and writing). Although we are all readers first and foremost, how little we reflect about this ubiquitous activity: the semiotics of text production, how meaning is made in text, how readers take meaning from text, the status of authorial intention versus the reader's interpretation, the role of the community of discourse in the reception of text, and so forth. I think we are overlooking something very important about the problematics of our craft.

By reminding historians of the irreducible rhetorical or poetic nature of historical discourse, Hayden White, Hans Kellner, and Dominick LaCapra, among others we could cite, challenge us to domesticate ourselves in the world of rhetoric and literary theory (and epistemology) and to become more reflective about the nature and problematics of our craft as readers (and writers).[1] This challenge, so far as historians of American education are concerned, has for the most part fallen upon deaf ears. For example, whether one agrees with White or not, his work cannot be ignored. It is quite astonishing that in the quarter-century since the publication of *Metahistory: The Historical Imagination in Nineteenth-Century Europe*, White has had so little visible impact on historians of American education. A positivist tradition of mimesis dominates the historiography of American education while, with the notable exception of Richard Angelo, the conventions of romance, comedy, satire, and tragedy flourish unrecognized in our histories of education.[2]

In this chapter I want to introduce some of the core ideas and leading theorists of the "linguistic turn" in general historiography and draw out their implications for the writing, reading, and critical reception of histories of education.

II.

During the past two decades, the nature of reflection about history has changed significantly. The linguistic turn has forced historians to rethink traditional ideas about the nature and function of language, and the relationships between language and historical knowledge, between language and historical representation, between author and text, and between text and reader. The turn toward language has induced one group, led by the English historian of political thought John G. A. Pocock, to develop a new framework for practicing history in which language is considered an event or action, as real or material as any nonlinguistic event or action, in which language systems become the basic unit of historical investigation and in which language generally—its use, production, diffusion, and appropriation over time—is moved to the center of the historian's concern. This approach is currently being pursued by a handful of historians of the French Revolution, including Keith Baker, William Sewall, Lynn Hunt, and Linda Orr.[3] Another group of historians, including Frank Ankersmit, Allan Megill, and Stephen Bann have been inspired to probe more deeply into the relationship between language, linguistic structures, and historical epistemology.[4] And another group of historians, rallying around Hayden White, are exploring the relevance of literary theory for the writing and reading of historical narratives. It is the work of this last group that is the primary focus of this chapter.

One of the founding myths of modern historiography is the strict separation of history and literature. It is generally assumed that as a species of realistic or nonfictional prose discourse, history is independent of literary or rhetorical constraints and the entanglements posed by the nature of language—more science than art. During recent years, however, the linguistic turn has forced a reconsideration of the role of language, rhetoric, and narrative structures in the writing of history. It is now possible to discuss the relationship between history and language and between history and literature, and how literary theory and linguistic studies can illuminate our historical projects in ways that would have been thought eccentric even a decade ago. White's is the most fully and carefully articulated theory of a poetics of historiography; it constitutes the basic framework of my approach in this essay and warrants extended discussion.[5]

White insists on what most historians choose to deny or ignore, what Roland Barthes has called, in a different but related context, the "sovereignty of language." History is always bound up with linguistic structures, which crucially influence and complicate its logical workings. White's starting point is that historical writing is writing first of all, a form of narrative prose discourse. Historical narratives are constructions governed by the same rules and constraints of language and rhetoric as any other kind of literature. Consequently, modes of rhetorical analysis hitherto applied mainly to literary texts are indispensable for the analysis of historical texts. Histories can and should be studied for the art of their composition, the rhetorical demands required by their plot structure and argument, and the rhetorical means by which they claim to represent historical truth or historical reality.

White thus challenges the conventional boundary between history and literature and argues that historical narratives have much more in common with literary narratives than historians are usually willing to allow. White's project is to emend the epistemological innocence of historians: their reluctance to consider the constructed quality of historical narratives, "the contents of which are as much *invented* as *found* and the forms of which have more in common with their counterparts in literature than they have with those in the sciences."[6] White does not deny the reality of the past; he is saying only that as representations of the past, histories possess an irreducible literary or textual dimension. Before historians can represent, explain, or evaluate the data of a historical field, they must prefigure the field as an object of mental perception. This a priori constitutive act is "generally poetic, and specifically linguistic in nature."[7] In short, the historian is, at the least, a storyteller.

One of the most significant contributions that White makes to the poetics of history relates to the idea of "emplotment," which he defines as the "encodation of the facts contained in a chronicle as components of specific kinds of plot structures." Historians grasp the meaning of historical events by choosing what is a fact, an event, and then arranging selected events into a particular narrative plot structure—that is, a story. Indeed, first comes the plot structure or the emplotment, the historian's prefiguration of a sequence of events as a story of a particular kind. To give meaning to the inchoate mass of data constituting the past, historians tell now one and now another kind of story about it. The number of possible story forms or emplotments available for endowing the past with meaning is not infinite, however, but is "coterminous with the number of generic story types available in a historian's own culture."

Following the literary critic Northrop Frye, White identifies a stock of four generic story forms or archetypal plot structures which constitute the historian's initial literary resources: romance, comedy, satire, and tragedy (which may, within limits, be mixed or combined).[8] Furthermore, these four prefigurative modes or emplotments correlate in a general way with four principal modes of ideological implication: anarchist, conservative, radical, and liberal. That is, how one emplots history engages larger social and cultural questions. White emphasizes that there is no neutral or value-free mode of narrative emplotment. The historian's choice of a story form or plot structure carries a certain ideological freight; it is an index of a particular moral and political sensibility. Moreover, historical narratives are social transactions. They are produced by someone for someone in a special situation—a pre-existing or ongoing debate, argument, discourse. There is always an audience. The intention of all histories is to persuade as well as to inform. That is, histories have a performative dimension: they are acts in some particular discourse of their time; they are written with some sociopolitical or ideological aim in view. The rhetorical conventions employed by historians are intended to persuade readers that his or her version of the past is truer or worthier than another version and to persuade readers to assume a particular attitude toward the past and thus toward the present.

Now that White has called our attention to it, we seem to have always known that the past with which historians are professionally concerned is mediated by written discourse—which is to say language. Of course, before it can be read, historians have to convert knowing all that research into telling—writing it up into "a story of a particular kind."[9] Disputes among historians are frequently not so much about what really happened, or about whether historians should emphasize class struggle or consensus so much as they are disputes about different rhetorical strategies for constituting the past, each of which possesses its own ideological implications: "What one historian may emplot as tragedy another may emplot as comedy or romance."[10] And of course, our choice of rhetorical devices has a performative dimension in the sense that we write history for someone as well as for something: for someone, in the sense of a specific audience or social group or community of discourse; and for something, in the sense that histories take part, that is, take sides, in some particular discourse of their time. Our (most often unreflective) language and rhetorical strategies are chosen for the purpose of persuading readers that one version of the past is truer or more objective than another, and to lead them toward a particular course of action or emotional response in the present.

Serious theoretical issues are raised by Roger Chartier, Lionel Gossman, Russell Jacoby, and the authors of *Telling the Truth About History*, about White's approach. For example, what is the status of reference in history? How does genre or emplotment hook on to past reality? What is the relation between language and reality? Between history and fiction? Between facts and interpretation, between story and truth, between history's fictions and its truths? How can we acknowledge the constructedness of historical knowledge and yet maintain that it is possible to give true or truer accounts of a "real" past?[11] What about White's tropes? Are they essential or are they constructions of which there may be four or five or more and which we are free to use if and as we see fit? Nonetheless, for historians of education, White's central insights cannot be ignored. The essential implications of White's theorizing on the nature of historical discourse are at least two: (1) It reminds us that truth in our histories is a more complex and subtle matter than we usually think—an insight that might, if not temper, at least help us make better sense of some of our more intense historiographical disputes. (2) It opens up the possibility of applying to our histories some strategies or technologies of interpretation originally worked out in literary texts. That is, White enables us to read meaning into histories of education by reference to their predominant form, mode of emplotment, and rhetorical strategies, in addition to or as an alternative to our usual way of reading, which focuses on a content, existing outside or prior to its form, the supposed neutral or transparent container that transmits the content. This approach enables us to read new meaning in old histories of education and to find more layers of meaning in any history of education than it would seem to contain or than the author may have intended to convey.

What follows is an exercise in the application of historiographical poetics and narrative theory to a reading of two histories of American education: Bryce E. Nelson, *Good Schools: The Seattle Public School System, 1901–1930;* and David F. Labaree, *The Making of an American High School: The Credentials Market and the Central High School of Philadelphia, 1838–1939*, winner of the American Educational Research Association's and the (American) History of Education Society's Outstanding Book Awards for 1989.[12]

This exercise is intended as illustrative and suggestive. There is no one right way of reading these histories; there are only ways of reading.[13] What I hope to demonstrate is that rhetoric, as J. H. Hexter nicely put it, is not mere "icing on the cake of history, it is mixed right into the batter,"[14]—and that form itself, or the genre of emplotment of a history, is determining; it shapes content. As White argues, even form has a content. I hope to demonstrate that a reading which engages the poetics of historical representation in a fully attentive and responsive way can yield new insights, help us to discover meaning in unexpected places, and increase the pleasures of reading histories.

III.

The mythopoetic titles of many histories of education—for example, *The Transformation of the School, The Irony of Early School Reform, The Troubled Crusade, The Imperfect Panacea, Land of Fair Promise,* and *The Myth of the Common School*—are revelatory of their mode of emplotment. The mode of emplotment of *Good Schools* is that of romance; its mode of ideological implication is progressive. Nelson is an advocate of progressive education; Seattle's "good schools" are progressive schools and its schools are the key to Seattle's progressive self-image. *Good Schools*, at least in a first, conventional reading, is squarely situated in the romantic historiographical tradition set by Lawrence Cremin's *The Transformation of the School: Progressivism in American Education, 1876–1957* (1961). A second, rhetorical reading, however, discloses a surprising variation on this familiar formula.

Nelson begins his history of the Seattle public schools with one of the most artless and transparent of literary conventions, a formula of the romance genre: "once upon a time" or a wish-fulfillment dream. The book's first sentence actually reads: "Imagine yourself attending grade school in 1915."[15] But the beginning of *Good Schools* must be quoted at length:

> You walk a few blocks from home to a new, landscaped brick building. . . .
> There are only about 400 pupils in your school, and you know most of
> them. . . . Teachers, neighbors, and students know you. . . . In your grade
> school you try out new skills, using both your mind and hands. You learn to
> read and write, but you also learn to sing, play sports, garden, cook, use hand
> tools, and draw. . . . Informal and extracurricular lessons are as important
> as those from the books: learn right from wrong, and act accordingly; take
> responsibility; cooperate; and be a healthy, productive citizen. In these grade
> schools, children . . . grow slowly into early adolescence.[16]

This, however, is no utopian dream but historical reality: "Such grade schools were in fact built in Seattle from 1901 through 1917."[17] The romantic beginning not only reveals the attitude with which Nelson approaches his project but prefigures the trajectory his subsequent narrative will take.

The romance genre calls for an element of contrast: good versus bad, virtue versus vice. Nelson contrasts the bad eastern and midwestern urban public school systems "imposed by an elite . . . a tool for social control" with the good Seattle public school system, where labor unions, socialists, and political progressives all "shared a progressive vision of schooling" in which selfish class or group interests were reconciled. The romance genre requires a hero. The hero (depicted in what Frye would call the "high mimetic mode") of *Good Schools*, the man of vision, the leader who developed Seattle's "good schools," is Frank B. Cooper, superintendent of schools from 1901 to 1922.

If we attend to the way Nelson emplots his narrative, its deep structural content exemplifies the romance genre. *Good Schools* starts at the turn of the century with small beginnings, followed by (at the center of the narrative) an "adventure quest" for good schools, then victory; the quest is a success around the time of World War I. Individual chapters in *Good Schools* deal with major components of progressive education before 1920—the education of the whole child, learning by doing, the expanded curriculum, the school as social agency. The chapters are composed on an evolutionist frame, as if each successive development in Seattle public education is an advance, a triumph for progressive education, at least until we get to the post–World War I period. The romantic trajectory of Nelson's narrative takes a downward turn in about 1919. Disaster strikes in the guise of educational "conservatives," and "tax-cutting groups" who raise questions about the cost, scope, and purpose of Seattle's school system and challenge the leadership of Cooper and his progressive allies. In the wake of the postwar "red scare" and the Seattle general strike of 1919, the informal coalition of progressives, socialists, and labor unions breaks up, and is replaced by interest–group politics, the emergence of a conservative, counterprogressive education movement, and the subsequent "triumph of efficiency," the nadir.

Cooper's resignation in 1922 marks the end of an era, the end of Seattle's progressive vision of schooling and its good schools. But this story cannot end on a note of defeat. Nelson concludes *Good Schools* with an epiphany; after the Fall comes the happy ending and the uplifting moral required of all historical narratives rendered in the romantic mode. Seattle's pre–World War I public schools can provide a model for American public education today. America needs no new wave of school reform. All America needs to do is adopt Cooper's vision of education and Seattle's model of good schools, circa 1901–1919, when, as depicted in Nelson's final paragraph:

> Urban grade schools [were] small, humane places where staff really knew the children and their families; and grade and high schools . . . included a traditional liberal arts curriculum, enriched with lessons from real life, and taught with a variety of methods [with] high schools and night schools with open doors . . . and a social welfare aspect to schooling . . . with a fundamental emphasis on the conditions under which good teaching could occur.[18]

"All of these characteristics of Seattle's pre-World War I public schools," Nelson concludes, in his last sentence, "were—and still are—the basic and enduring ingredients of 'good schools.'"

Thus, in a terminating maneuver worthy of the romance genre, time has been made to stand still. We can go back to the future. Nelson's ending is intended to reveal a great lesson, not just about a tiny patch of the world of American public education in the pre-World War II period, but about American public education in the present. Seattle's progressive "good schools" live on. Time is not the enemy; our faulty memory is. Nelson's project has been to restore and recall for our remembrance a model of good schools which, presumably, Americans have forgotten (amnesia and the subsequent restoration of memory are another staple of the romance genre), but which endures for all time, and holds the solution to the crisis of American education today.

IV.

On a first encounter, *Good Schools* is predictable to any reader familiar with the romance idiom. On a closer, rhetorical reading, however, it comes through as a tense, ambivalent, and conflicted work. It thus ultimately fails of its intended effect but becomes a more interesting and more significant work.

Beginnings and endings of all literary constructions, not excluding written histories, are the most important and the most difficult to get right.[19] Nelson's ending poses an interesting rhetorical problem. Can Nelson really believe that his utterly mundane list of characteristics of Seattle's public schools "were—and still are—the basic ingredients of 'good schools'"? His ending seems absurdly inadequate and implausible. The final paragraph of *Good Schools* is a literary convention prefigured or determined by the beginning of the work. Nelson was "literally" forced to compose an ending with some symmetrical relationship to the romantic "once upon a time" formula with which he began *Good Schools*. But it is an ending that evokes not so much affirmation or hope for the future as nostalgia and rue for a vanished past, for the good old days. In this context, Nelson's use of photographs is of particular interest.

Recall that histories have a performative dimension—to persuade the reader to act, feel, or value in a particular way. They not only have this performative dimension but they are (again, usually unreflectively) structured to have that particular effect: the paratext, *all* their constituent parts—title, preface, acknowledgments, footnotes, bibliography, appendixes, and so forth—may be thought of as rhetorical devices or rhetorical strategies. The most conspicuous rhetorical device Nelson employs in *Good Schools* is the photograph. There are forty photographs. What do they do? What is their function? What is their meaning? Nelson takes us into the realm of the "seen" or scene and leaves it at that. It is as if these pictures were not to be read; their mere presence is what is counts. However, suppose we do read these pictures.[21] From our textualist perspective, Nelson's use of photographs is a rhetorical device in the service of authenticity, intended to enhance the "reality effect"(Roland Barthes's useful term) of *Good Schools.* Their function is to bear witness to the reality, verisimilitude, and accuracy of its documentary content. Here, they say, is objective evidence, concrete proof that these schools once really existed, that they were "good," and that they can serve as a model for us today.

Upon closer examination, we see idealized images of teachers, students, and classrooms frozen in time and place; the prewar decade in Seattle. Here are the teachers, all of them white. The women are covered from neck to foot in Gibson Girl dresses or white shirtwaists and long black skirts, some wearing bonnets, looking maternal yet in control in the classroom or relaxing at lunchtime and drinking tea at a table set with china. The men are dressed in suits, white shirts, and ties, some wearing boaters or straw hats, fingers crooked in vests, looking friendly but masterful. Here are the students, all of them white except for a handful of Japanese girls dressed ceremonially for the photographic occasion; girls in their best dresses, boys wearing white shirts, ties, dark suits, and black or brown shoes. Here is the garden. Here are the classrooms, laboratories, and workshops—spacious, well-lit, well-furnished. The students all look interested, busy, orderly, quietly active whether at play, at morning calisthenics on the lawn, or learning by doing: building birdhouses or sailboats or working on Model T's. And here is Superintendent Frank B. Cooper himself, captured in an expensive suit with a pearl stickpin in his carefully knotted cravat, gazing presciently at us through rimless spectacles, obviously a man of affluence, stature, and wisdom.

Who can doubt that Cooper is a leader of vision and that these are good schools? Yet the rhetorical force of the photographs remains ambiguous. As a rhetorical device whose purpose is to glorify Seattle's good schools and to provide inspiration and hope in the present, the photographs don't work; they only elicit nostalgia for the good old days. Nelson is still working in the genre of romance: the illusion that what is gone, what is irretrievably past, can be brought back as it really was. But these photographs constitute a memorial to a vanished era in the history of American education, an era which cannot be resurrected and to which we cannot return. There will be no happy ending to this story. The photographs, finally, evoke an elegiac mood. Now Nelson's once upon a time rendering takes on a different meaning. This is the romantic pathos of "remembrance of things past."[22] Time *is* the enemy. Seattle's pre-World War II good schools cannot be a viable model for present-day American education. Now, thanks to these pictures, regardless of Nelson's intentions, we finally come to understand *Good Schools* as a melancholy depiction of a vanished world, paradise lost. The schools it depicts have passed away. America will have to look elsewhere for its educational salvation. At some level, Nelson may have known this, but he was trapped by the form in which he prefigured his narrative. Thus, the meaning and significance of *Good Schools* goes far beyond Nelson's intention or control.

V.

The Making of an American High School: The Credentials Market and the Central High School of Philadelphia, 1838–1939 is emplotted in the mode of satire, a reverse or a parody of the idealization of American public education that characterizes *Good Schools* and the romance genre in American educational historiography. *The Making of an American High School* belongs to the satiric genre of Michael Katz's *The Irony of Early School Reform: Educational Innovation in Mid-Nineteenth Century Massachusetts.* But in the end the political and educational ideology implicated in *The Making of an American High School* is still progressive, like that encoded in *Good Schools*—further to the left perhaps, but not radical. The main narrative trajectory of *The Making of an American High School* is a downward spiral. Its predominant mood is anger and disillusionment with the deterioration or subversion and fall from grace of American public secondary education. This trajectory, though the reverse of Nelson's, is equally formulaic; from promising democratic origins to conflict, to decline and fall, and finally to the hope of resurrection.

Labaree's work is modestly titled *The Making of an American High School—an*, not *the*—but Labaree, like Nelson, has much grander aspirations than simply to portray a local educational phenomenon during a particular time in the past. The American high school Labaree is concerned with is Central High School (CHS) in Philadelphia. Labaree's aim was not to pick a typical high school but "to choose one that is exemplary."²³ The history of CHS is explicitly intended to represent the development of the whole of American secondary education not just from 1838 to 1939 but from 1838 to the present, and to speak to present educational issues in American secondary education.

The story line of *The Making of an American High School*, as noted above, is primarily from democratic origins to conflict and decline and fall. The conflict is between egalitarianism and "market values"; between the early democratic aspirations of Central High School—to educate a virtuous and informed citizenry for the new republic—and its latter–day function as an "elitist vehicle for individual status attainment," controlled by a middle class whose goal was to ensure that its children received the educational credentials which would entitle them to become the entrepreneurs and managers of America's capitalist society. The decline and fall of secondary education at CHS occurred in the 1890s (not only at CHS, but throughout the United States). At that time, CHS had to somehow reconcile its democratic commitment to access to secondary education for all young people with its commitment to "market values." In 1899 Philadelphia's school officials devised what "has become the main solution to this perennial American educational dilemma: tracking or 'stratification.'"²⁴ Labaree stresses the relationship between "market values" and the growing dominance of bureaucratization and meritocratic values, with their oppressive effect on every aspect of CHS (and, again, on American secondary education, generally): governance, pedagogy, the curriculum, the students. As befits the satiric mode of emplotment, Labaree condemns the "market" conception of secondary education from, to use Frye's term, a "high moral line," that of democracy and egalitarianism.

To repeat, the narrative trajectory of Labaree's book is a downward spiral. Its predominant mood is anger over the deterioration and fall of American public secondary education. But the lugubrious narrative unexpectedly takes a comedic or romantic upward turn at the very end, in fact, in the last paragraph, when Labaree foresees a transformation of the American high school. Labaree's ending looks optimistically toward the future, in stark contrast with the previous chapters. The American high school may be a servant of the marketplace now, and a failure even at that, but the high school can be transformed, as in a wish-fulfillment dream or a fairy tale, into the kind of high school its democratic advocates had always envisioned. In Labaree's own words: "As a market institution, the contemporary high school is an utter failure; yet, when rechartered as a common school, it has great potential." The common high school "would be able to focus on equality rather than stratification and on learning rather than the futile pursuit of educational credentials." Stripped of its "disabling market concerns, the common high school could seek to provide what had always eluded the early selective high school: a quality education for the whole community."[25] The End. As to how this magical transformation is to occur, Labaree is silent.

Labaree's ending, like Nelson's, is underdeveloped and implausibly optimistic, even utopian. It is an ending that, like Nelson's, poses an interesting rhetorical problem.

As I noted in connection with *Good Schools*, the problem of beginnings and endings of histories is fascinating because the latter demonstrate in an obvious and fundamental way, once we are made aware of it, how our decision to start and stop writing at a certain point is literary or rhetorical, and how this decision affects the stories we tell, the histories we write. If we take a closer look at Labaree's ending, the last line of his book suggests that we may be at the dawn of a new age. This ending, like Nelson's, is a familiar literary convention. The problem is that it doesn't fit the satiric mode of emplotment which characterizes the main narrative line of *The Making of an American High School*.

The underlying thrust of *The Making of an American High School* is that nothing has changed in American secondary education between the 1890s and 1939 or the 1890s and the present; yet Labaree would have us believe that things will be different in the future. The satiric trajectory of Labaree's narrative should lead inexorably to the conclusion that we must resign ourselves to the world of secondary education as it is—alas, we live unhappily ever after, or rather, we go to school unhappily ever after—or to the conclusion that unless radical action is taken nothing will change. Instead, *The Making of an American High School* ends with another staple of the romance genre, a reference to the world of desires and dreams; we can escape the burden of the past. The "market forces" will be overcome. The high school may now be a servant of the marketplace, but it can be transformed. How might this come about? How will the dark forces of the market be overcome? One can make happen only what one dreams about first; the dreamer says, "Let there be common high schools."

Labaree's ending is no more plausible or convincing than Nelson's. The concluding statement of hope and promise does not follow from what precedes. What happened? Something like the following, I think. The public high school is very much at the center of debate in American education. Labaree is committed to the ideal of public, "common" secondary education. *The Making of an American High School* could not end in a call for revolution; Labaree presents himself as a liberal-progressive, not as a radical or an anarchist. Nor could *The Making of an American High School* end on a note of resignation. (Readers must be left with a hope that somehow, sometime, change for the better can be effected in the public high school, or else they might flee to the private school sector, the *bête noire* of American liberals.) Labaree's attempt at a happy ending may be inconsistent with his satiric plot structure, but it is required by his liberal sensibilities. Since Labaree is committed to the public high school, *The Making of an American High School* cannot end on a note of despair. The moralist in Labaree will not permit it, although nothing in his narrative justifies anything else.

VI.

Labaree employs two major rhetorical devices in *The Making of an American High School*: the "market" metaphor and the technical and linguistic apparatus of quantitative research. Labaree constantly refers to "market values," "market pressures," "market forces," and the "intrusion of the market." Readers are supposed to understand what Labaree intends to signify by the metaphor—a crass and malignant quality or essence of American secondary education—and to agree with him that the high school's concern for "market values" is undemocratic and inegalitarian. Labaree takes this for granted. Labaree does not entertain the idea that the "market" might also stand for deregulation, freedom of choice, empowering parents, or accountability, for example—none of which would seem to infringe adversely on democratic ideals, and all of which might possibly advance the goal of democracy and egalitarianism in education. Nevertheless, the "market" is a heuristically useful metaphor which enables Labaree to discuss an aspect of American education that is omitted in romance emplotments of histories like Nelson's.

Something else of interest and significance is also going on in *The Making of an American High School*: Labaree's use of quantitative research methodology.

The Making of an American High School contains fifteen statistical tables as well as four appendixes in what is a brief work (only about

180 pages of text). Two samples will give the flavor of the whole. The first is from "Appendix B: Social Class Categories":

> Table B.1 Wealth of Central Parents by Class, 1860 and 1870 Combined [with columns for] "Class," "Mean," "N," and "S. D."
>
> Table B.2 Occupational Distribution of Household Heads, CHS versus Philadelphia, 1880. [With columns for] Central High (%), Philadelphia (%), Index of Representativeness.

The second example is from "Appendix C: Multiple Classification Analysis":

> The primary technique used in analyzing student achievement was multiple classification analysis (MCA), a form of multiple regression using categorical predictor variables (called factors). MCA constructs a beta for each factor as a whole rather than for each level of this variable as is done in regression with dummy variables.
>
> There is one assumption of both regression and MCA which was violated routinely during my analysis, the assumption of homoscedasticity. My primary dependent variable, graduation, is not interval-level, but dichotomous. . . . The consequences of this are twofold: (1) the regression equation no longer provides the best linear estimate (its variance is not minimized), and (2) tests of significance are no longer unbiased.[26]

Labaree has been diligent in finding and mining a trove of empirical data ("based on a sample of two thousand students drawn from the first hundred years" of CHS). But suppose we ask the same questions of Labaree's tables and appendixes that we asked of Nelson's photographs. What do they mean? What is their function? What do they do? How do they work? How should we read them? The point I'm trying to make is not about quantitative history; it's not about numbers or counting or "60%" or "8%" versus "many" or a "handful." The point is that numbers are not needed here—their presence is a kind of rhetorical overkill. For all the numbers and statistics, we are not much wiser than before. So what is their function in the text? As noted above, histories have a performative dimension: to persuade an audience to act, feel, or value in a particular way. They are structured to have that particular effect; all their constituent parts may be thought of as rhetorical strategies.

The Making of an American High School possesses some complexity and depth, if not breadth; it is a competent enough story. But it is as if Labaree were at some level dissatisfied with narrating a mere story or with that story's formal, rhetorical properties—its satiric mode of emplotment, its metaphoric mode of argument, its storybook ending—so he puts on positivist airs. But Labaree's piling on of beta factors, chi squares, dummy variables, multiple regressions, and MCAs does not help us understand the drift of his argument any better. That is to say, all this statistical detail—like the photographs in *Good Schools*—is to be understood as a rhetorical strategy in the service of the "reality effect." From a textualist perspective, the statistical tables and appendixes in *The Making of an American High School* are not actually there to be read; they are simply there to be seen. Their sheer presence in the text is what "counts."[27]

VII.

I do not want to be misunderstood. The point of this chapter was not to reprove Nelson or Labaree but to demonstrate how a rhetorical or "crooked" reading may yield new insights into our histories.

By way of summary. One direction the linguistic turn has taken among cultural historians in recent years is toward greater self-reflectiveness about the nature of history as narrative or history as story. As we learn from Hayden White and Hans Kellner, among others, historians are tellers (and readers) of "stories." To claim that history is a story does not imply that the past is nonexistent or unrecoverable; it is simply to assert that histories, whatever else they are, are constructions of language and rhetoric. It is to underscore Kellner's point that a written history is "everywhere (not just in the final stages) linguistic, shaped and constrained from the start by rhetorical considerations that are the 'other' sources of history."[28] Neither White nor Kellner views these revelations as a devaluation of history. On the contrary, they view the acknowledgment of the decisive role of language, rhetoric, and the literary conventions in histories, as an antidote to our tendency to become captives of ideological preconceptions that we do not recognize as such but honor as the only correct representation of reality.

Within this frame of reference, to ask of Nelson's and Labaree's histories whether they have gotten it right—or which one has it more right—is not the question I've chosen to address. There are other, equally interesting questions. For example, how do historians try to persuade readers that their version of what happened in the past is true? How do historians try to convince an audience that one of the competing accounts of what happened in the past is truer than another? How do we (or how should we), as historians or readers of histories, decide among historical interpretations? In this light, to read *Good Schools* and *The Making of an American High School* side by side becomes a fascinating exercise. With their differing narrative formulas—romance and satire or tragedy—they represent the two main competing and alternative genres or forms of emplotment in American educational historiography today. Which or whose version is truer? How can we decide between them? There is no easy answer to these questions. We usually don't reflect much (and we need to reflect more) about what makes us prefer one interpretation of the past to another. Neither Labaree's nor Nelson's history can be compared with its subject as it really was, since there is no basic, canonical version to compare them with; there are only versions.

Where does this leave us? We could say, following White, that historians of education and their readers are indentured to a choice among competing narrative strategies, and that the grounds for choosing one interpretation of history of education over another are ultimately aesthetic and moral rather than epistemological. But, here, White is vulnerable; at least, this is too relativist a position for me. Not all historical narratives are equal. I think it is possible to distinguish history's truths from its fictions, to evaluate the verisimilitude or veracity of different versions of past reality. But this would require a different, more traditional reading than I've done here—one which puts into play what Michel de Certeau calls the "historiographical operation," an analysis of the historian's retrieval and treatment of evidence, and the relation between evidence and interpretation. Where does that leave us? At this point, I think we have to acknowledge, first, the multidimensionality of historical reality and, second, we have to say that those who have no knowledge of histories of education can believe any history of education. Which is to say that not only writers of histories have to make choices; readers have responsibilities as well.

My intention in this chapter has been to call the attention of historians of education to some alternative approaches to the reading (and writing) of histories. If the linguistic turn teaches us anything, it teaches us to read differently. And, to paraphrase Jacques Derrida, if we begin to read differently, we must begin to write differently. There is no single correct approach to reading a historical text; there are only ways of reading. Different reading strategies will constitute a historical text in different ways. The linguistic turn forces us to reconsider what kind of act the writing of history is, what our form of emplotment permits or constrains, what kind of story we want to tell, and what kind of story we actually do tell. Historians of education are storytellers and story readers. As tellers and readers of stories, we possess an initial stock of rhetorical devices that can be expanded as we learn more about stories. We have much to learn from literary theory (and philosophy), where theorizing about language, reader reception, and the nature of the text has been going on for some time.[29]

Notes

1   The conception of history writing as preeminently a rhetorical activity has led Kellner to elaborate a "crooked" way of reading. We have to quote Kellner: "Getting the story crooked means looking at the historical text in such a way as to make more apparent the problems and decisions that shape its [rhetorical] strategies. . . . It is a way of looking . . . at the *other* sources of history, found not in archives or computer databases but in discourse and rhetoric." *Language and Historical Representation: Getting the Story Crooked* (Madison, 1989), p. vii.

2   Richard Angelo, "Ironies of the Romance: The Romance with Irony," *Educational Theory* (1990): 443–452; "Myth, Educational Theory, and the Figurative Imagination," *Philosophy of Education, Proceedings*, 1978, pp. 227–238; and "The Freedom We Have in Mind," *Educational Theory*, 28 (1978): 77–83. See John Calam's review of David Tyack and Elisabeth Hansot, *Managers of Virtue: Public School Leadership in America, 1820–1980* (New York, 1982), *Journal of Educational Thought*, 18 (1984): 115–116.

3   Keith M. Baker, "On the Problem of the Ideological Origins of the French Revolution," in Dominick LaCapra and Steven L. Kaplan, eds., *Modern European Intellectual History: Reappraisals and New Perspectives* (Ithaca, N.Y., 1982); and *Inventing the French Revolution: Essays in French Political Culture in the Eighteenth Century* (Cambridge, England, 1990). See also Lynn Hunt, *Politics, Culture, and Class in the French Revolution* (Berkeley, 1984), Part I, "The Poetics of Power"; and William H. Sewall, Jr., *Work and Revolution in France: The Language of Labor from the Old Regime to 1848* (Cambridge, England, 1980). And see Janis Langins, "Words and Institutions During the French Revolution," and Dorinda Outram, "*La langue male de la vertu*: Women and the Discourse of the French Revolution," both in Peter Burke and Roy Porter, eds., *The Social History of Language* (Cambridge, England, 1987).

4   Frank Ankersmit and Hans Kellner eds., *A New Philosophy of History* (Chicago, 1995).

5   The essential texts are White, *Metahistory: The Historical Imagination in Nineteenth–Century Europe* (Baltimore, 1973); *Tropics of Discourse: Essays in Cultural Criticism* (Baltimore, 1978); and *The Content of the Form: Narrative Discourse and Historical Representation* (Baltimore, 1987). See also Kellner, *Language and Historical Representation*; Dominick LaCapra, *History and Criticism* (Ithaca, N.Y., 1985), ch. 1, "Rhetoric and History"; Philippe Carrard, *Poetics of the New History* (Baltimore, 1992); and H. Aram Veeser, ed., *The New Historicism* (New York, 1989).

6   White, *Metahistory*, p. ix. "The processes of the historical imagination," Kellner argues, "are everywhere (not just in the final stages) linguistic, shaped,

and constrained from the start by rhetorical considerations that are the 'other' sources of history." *Language and Historical Representation*, pp. 325–326.

7   White, *Tropics of Discourse*, p. 82.

8   Northrop Frye, *Anatomy of Criticism: Four Essays* (Princeton, 1957), sec. 3, "Archetypal Criticism: Theory of Myths"; and *Fables of Identity: Studies in Poetic Mythology* (New York, 1963), ch. 1, "The Archetypes of Literature."

9   White, *Metahistory*, p. xii.

10 White, *Tropics of Discourse*, pp. 22, 58.

11 Joyce Appleby, Lynn Hunt, and Margaret Jacob, *Telling the Truth About History* (New York, 1994); and Lionel Gossman, *Between History and Literature* (Cambridge, Mass.,1990). More critical is Roger Chartier, *On the Edge of the Cliff: History, Language, and Practices* (Baltimore, 1997), ch. 2, "Four Questions for Hayden White." See also Russell Jacoby, "A New Intellectual History?"*American Historical Review*, 97 (1992): 407–413.

12 Respectively, Seattle, 1988; and New Haven, 1988.

13 Compare three reviews which take a different approach than I do and which are informative in their own way: David E. Hanson's review of *Good Schools*, *History of Education Quarterly*, 30 (1990): 112–114; William Cutler's review of *The Making of an American High School*, *History of Education Quarterly*, 29 (1989): 327–329; and Marvin Lazerson's review of the same book in *Historical Studies in Education/Revue d'histoire de l'éducation*, 2 (1990): 375–377.

14 "The Rhetoric of History," *Doing History* (Bloomington, Ind., 1975), p. 68.

15 *Good Schools*, p. 3.

16 Ibid., pp. 3–4.

17 Ibid., p. 4.

18 Ibid., p. 173.

19 There is an elegant discussion of the rhetorical problems posed by beginnings and endings of historical narratives in Kellner, *Language and Historical Representation,* pp. 2, 7–8, and ch. 3, "Boundaries of the Text."

20 Carrard, *Poetics of the New History.*

21 "The Photographic Message," in Roland Barthes, *Image-Music-Text,* trans. by Stephen Heath (New York, 1977), pp. 15–31. A helpful discussion is David Tyack and Elisabeth Hansot, "Using Photographs as Evidence of Gender Practice in Schools," in *Learning Together: A History of Coeducation in American Schools* (New Haven, 1990), pp. 293–296.

22   Frye observes that the wish-fulfillment formula of the romance genre is characterized "by its extraordinarily persistent nostalgia, its search for some kind of imaginative golden age in time or space." *Anatomy of Criticism*, p. 186. And, a story "becomes more romantic in its appeal when the life it reflects has passed away." Ibid., p. 307.

23   *The Making of an American High School*, p. 2.

24   Ibid., p. 7.

25   Ibid., p. 182.

26   Ibid., p. 187. Appendix A deals with "Student Data Methods." Appendix D is "A Close Look at the Multiple Classification Analyses of Graduation."

27   Cf. Donald Warren's observation: "Valuable and tough-minded, quantitative history risks being unreadable and enigmatic." "A Past for the Present," in Warren, ed., *History, Education, and Public Policy: Recovering the American Educational Past* (Berkeley, 1978), p. 2. A critical discussion is Carl F. Kaestle, "Recent Methodological Developments in the History of American Education," in Richard M. Jaeger, ed., *Complementary Methods for Research in Education* (Washington, D.C. 1986), pp. 64–67. A recent critique in the ironic mode is Theodore M. Porter, *Trust in Numbers: The Pursuit of Objectivity in Science and Public Life* (Princeton, 1995), ch. 1.

28   White, "Historical Pluralism," *Critical Inquiry,* 12 (1986): 483. Kellner, *Language and Historical Representation,* pp. 325–326.

29   I have found the following collections still the most helpful: Josué V. Harari, ed., *Textual Strategies: Perspectives in Post-Structuralist Criticism* (Ithaca, N.Y., 1979); Jane P. Tompkins, ed., *Reader-Response Criticism: From Formalism to Post-Structuralism* (Baltimore, 1980); Susan R. Suleiman and Inge Crosman, eds., *The Reader in the Text: Essays on Audience and Interpretation* (Princeton, 1980). And also Robert Scholes, *Semiotics and Interpretation* (New Haven, 1982).

Chapter 4

Language and History: A Perspective on School Reform Movements and Change in Education

To change the way we talk [is to change] what we want to do and is to change
. . . what we are. . . . What matters in the end are changes in the vocabulary.

Richard Rorty

I.

The potential histories of school reform movements are numberless.
We need an enabling postulate, a prefigurative move in thought, before we can proceed. Assuming, with Hayden White, that the historian does not find patterns of meaning in the past but constructs meaning from or imposes meaning on the inchoate sources which make up
the past, I call attention here to a way of viewing school reform movements and change in education which does not yet figure in historical
accounts.

In this chapter I radically foreground language, or place a magnify-
ing glass on language and the discursive landscape of American education. My basic unit of study is not individuals, economic or political
factors, or social forces, but the language or languages of education
or educational discourse. My controlling assumption is that language
has meaning only in the context of a particular language system and
that fundamental change in education will take the form of a revolution in which one language system displaces another.

II.

Change in education is one of the most significant yet troublesome problems confronting the historian. In spite of preoccupation with school reform movements and change in education, our histories of education are marked by a dearth of theoretical thinking on the subject of change. Four questions about change in education insistently present themselves and just as persistently have defied solution. One, under what conditions can we speak of fundamental change in education? Two, how can we document the influence of school reform movements on fundamental change in education? Three, how and in what form do ideas become influential, and how can we estimate their influence? Four, how can we document the influence of ideas on fundamental change in education?

Histories of school reform movements always include the further question of influence. But historians of education rarely make explicit the mechanics of change or the theoretical or methodological assumptions underlying their discussions of reform movements and educational change. Still, there is always some model or theory of change in place. Our explanatory model implicitly runs to three archetypal approaches: (1) Romance; there is conflict, but democratic forces overcome and change is cumulative and progressive. (2) Tragedy; there is conflict, but in the end the forces of reaction are victorious and change is a fall or a decline—things go from good to bad or bad to worse. (3) Satire or irony; there may or may not be conflict, but change is an "illusion," a "myth." As to how ideas influence change in education, our explanatory model rests on change as imposition by the dominant social classes or powerful vested interests, or on a "great man or woman" theory, or on the assumed influence of legislation, court decisions, or social forces—dramatic events or crises like war or economic depression. As regards gauging the extent or the success of efforts at change, historians of education rely on either a vaguely intuited progress or decline based on some a priori ideological position; or they rely on quantification, that is, a positivist renumeration of more or less of something—enrollments, curricula, special services, financial support, and so forth. Sometimes, counting can be useful, but quantification can hardly pick up the deeper or more subtle processes of influence or change in education. Thus, influence and change remain problems. (I still remember the historian of education, who, with admirable candor or naïveté, threw up his hands: "No attempt will be made to determine the degree to which [ideas] actually influenced practice in schools.")[1] The "absence of 'maps' that trace influence in specific and convincing ways," as Geraldine Joncich Clifford pointed out some years ago, continues to frustrate historians of education.[2] Before we can get a handle on the subject, we need some appropriate conceptual tools, an appropriate theoretical framework.

I have gone to the linguistic turn to find the approach most satisfactory to me, one which opens up a whole new way to map influence and document change in education. In this approach the critical datum is language and the basic unit of study is the language or languages of educational discourse. My controlling assumptions are these: that language or language systems are a class of phenomena or historical source that can be studied as acts, events, or practices, as real and meaningful as any phenomena in the social world; that the field of education is a single discursive field; that we can track the influence of school reform movements through the diffusion and appropriation of language; and that fundamental change in education can be marked through change in the language system. Which is to say that fundamental change occurs when one language system, formerly marginal, displaces another, formerly dominant, in the total discursive field of education. By way of concrete illustration I explore the contribution the linguistic turn suggests to our understanding of the stubborn historiographical problem of progressive education and change in American education in the twentieth century. Before proceeding, I should briefly describe the theoretical basis of my approach to change, which rests on contemporary developments in linguistic theory and general historiography.

III.

Over the past twenty years, scholars in various disciplines have been questioning long-held ideas about the nature and function of language and rethinking the relation between language and thought, language and action, and language and the practice of history. The new methodologies and insights that have arisen in connection with the linguistic turn have not gone unnoticed by intellectual historians here and abroad.[3] They have led one group of historians—Hayden White is the seminal figure here—to apply the insights of literary theory to the writing, reading, and interpretation of historical texts.[4] The linguistic turn has led another group of historians, the English historians of political thought John G. A. Pocock, Quentin Skinner, and John Dunn, to language itself as the subject and basic unit of historical investigation, in which questions of language generally—its use, production, diffusion, and appropriation over time—become the center of the historian's concern. The focus on language not only opens up for study a whole new category of historical events, facts, or sources, a whole new family of historical acts, but calls attention to language as basic for understanding the problem of change and for gauging the extent of change. This is the approach I intend to follow here.

The case for language as a basic unit of historical study was put forward most persuasively by Pocock in 1971 in his pathbreaking essay, "Languages and Their Implications: The Transformation of the Study of Political Thought," in which he urges that the history of political thought should become the history of the emergence and transformation of the languages of political discourse.[5] Pocock's attempt at theorizing a new history of political thought rests on the structural linguistics of Ferdinand de Saussure, the speech–act theory of J. L. Austin, the historicism of Thomas Kuhn, and the discourse/power theory of Michel Foucault.

Pocock isolated language or language systems as the defining subject matter of intellectual history.[6] Pocock repudiated the historian's practice of referring to the extralinguistic as "reality" and the linguistic as somehow less real. Against those historians who consider language, at least by implication, as nonreality, mere epiphenomena of some superior order of reality, Pocock emphasized that language is a part of reality, that it is even a historical act or event, and that it is not subordinate to the extralinguistic: "The real world does not operate independently of language. When we study language, we are studying an aspect of reality."[7]

Rehabilitating Austin's long-overlooked speech-act theory (from *How to Do Things with Words*, 1955), Pocock stressed the performative dimension of language: language as act or agency. Pocock assumes that the use of language is an *act*, a speech act, a form of social action by which a speaker or writer defines his or her position in the world and attempts to persuade listeners or readers to adopt that language and thus to accept or occupy that position. With Kuhn, Pocock also assumes that language implies a specific ideological posture and worldview. Once individuals adopt a vocabulary, its users are drawn not only into a language system but into a common value system, a particular community of discourse. The world is experienced and perceived differently in different language communities. The adherents of rival languages not only hold different beliefs but, as Kuhn puts it, they "practice their trades in different worlds." Language creates a "reality" without its users' needing to be aware of it in a self-conscious way. "By the mere act of using a particular language," Pocock argues, "we commit ourselves to a tissue of political implications, to a variety of political functionings, and to the recommendations of a variety of authority structures." Language, as Clifford Geertz explains, is "symbolic action," and is always more revelatory than its users think or even intend.[8] The question is always: to what system does the language or its pivotal or key words belong? Pocock adds this cautionary note: we need to avoid conflating "words" and "language." By language is meant not merely individual words, but words as elements in a language *system* that provides words with their full range of nuances, overtones, and moral resonance; it is this *system* which endows words with meaning.[9] Equally apposite to our concerns, Pocock emphasizes language use as an *event* or *act* in history and isolates language as the key to identifying fundamental change or even a revolution in a polity.

Any particular phenomena in language can be studied synchronically or diachronically. A language may be seen as part of a total discursive system simultaneous with itself, or it may be seen as part of a historical sequence of related phenomena. Saussurian linguistics emphasizes the former; it is primarily synchronically oriented and has relatively little interest in historical change. Pocock added the essential diachronic aspect which makes linguistics so useful to historians. Pocock borrowed from Kuhn's model of scientific revolutions, as well as Foucault's notion of discourse/power, for his model of change in the realm of political thought. Pocock views fundamental change along the lines of Kuhn's model of scientific revolutions: not cumulative and linear but discontinuous; not evolutionary but revolutionary.

Where the history of ideas is concerned, Pocock rejects the Whiggish concept of a progression or continuity between past and present as possessing little heuristic value and with Kuhn, urges historians to think in terms of ruptures, breaks, and discontinuities. Pocock's conceptual framing goes something like this. In any given society at any particular historical moment, a variety of languages of political discourse are available, with one language or one discourse dominant. There comes a time when the discourse loses its ability to solve the problems of import to this community. There may be innovations within the discourse, or a time comes when the discourse loses its constituency and slips into a state of crisis. New, alternative, and competing languages of political discourse vie for hegemony. That language is a site of struggle among conflicting interests is another key to Pocock's theory of change. With Foucault, Pocock locates power strategically in language: "Language is power . . . a mode of exerting power." Since relations of power are realized in language, the terrain of language becomes the object of a struggle for power and one of the decisive stakes of power. If in any particular society, a formerly marginal language or a new language achieves dominance, the result is so fundamental a change in the political culture of that society it can be called a paradigm shift, a revolution.

Pocock challenged intellectual historians to treat language as their basic unit of investigation, to identify and reconstruct the main systems of discourse available in a given society at any particular time, analyze their hierarchical relations, and then uncover the critical shifts in linguistic hegemony or the reversals in discursive practice that occur over time. In the past decade a number of historians have taken up Pocock's challenge and developed linguistic reinterpretations of the French Revolution.[10] Keith Baker's approach is highly relevant to the approach to the problem of change in education that I intend to follow; thus it also requires some elaboration.

Baker is exploring the French Revolution in terms of competing discourses or language systems in a struggle for dominance. These competing discourses are arranged hierarchically but are in a state of constant tension: the dominant language struggles to retain its dominance; the subordinate language seeks to gain dominance. Baker interprets the revolution as a struggle for dominance between the hegemonic language of the *ancien régime*, with its key words like royalism, aristocracy, and privilege; and the new revolutionary discourse, with its key words like equality, liberty, republic, and the social contract—a marginal discourse in the decades preceding the revolution. Words or concepts that in the 1750s and 1760s were subordinate in the discourse of the politics in France became dominant by the late 1780s; words or concepts that used to be dominant became marginal or even taboo. The result, according to Baker, was a "transformation of the discursive practice of the community."[11] This is what occurred in France in the late 1780s. The revolution succeeded in imposing not only its laws but its language.

What if we were to borrow Pocock and Baker's approach and apply it to school reform movements and change in education? What if we redescribed the history of school reform movements and change in education in terms of the history of change in the languages of educational discourse over time? What if we prefigured education as a discursive field comprising opposed and competing language systems vying for hegemony, and studied educational transformations in terms of change in the languages of educational discourse? And what if we assumed that fundamental change in education is, above all, a fundamental change in language, the displacement of one language system by another? I think the consequences would be far-reaching. We would now be able to perceive the course of development of American education in the twentieth century as we have not perceived it before. Consider the troublesome historiographical problem of the progressive school reform movement and its influence on American education.

IV.

Lawrence Cremin's Bancroft Prize-winning, *The Transformation of the School: Progressivism in American Education, 1876–1956* (1961), is among other things a history of change in education. It is evidently a history of the influence of "progressive education" on the "transformation" of the school, and it illustrates in an exemplary way many of the difficulties historians of education have with change in education.

In the first place, Cremin runs into trouble defining progressive education. Cremin's narrative line lies in the literary genre which Northrop Frye has designated romance, and that may be part of the problem. The romance genre tends to "conventionalize content in an idealized direction."[12] Cremin attempts several definitions. For example, he claims, "the word *progressive* provides the clue to what it really was: the educational phase of American progressivism writ large." And progressive education was "part of a vast humanitarian effort to apply the promise of American life . . . to the puzzling new urban-industrial civilization [and] a many-sided effort to use the schools to improve the lives of individuals."[13] All this is so exceedingly general that it is not clear what is *not* "progressive education." As regards the "transformation" of the school, the very naming of great men and women, books, and commissions and committees almost seems reason enough for Cremin to infer change. When Cremin does attempt to offer evidence of the "unmistakable imprint" of progressive education, he provides a list: a steady extension of educational opportunities, a broadening of the curriculum at all levels, a reorganization of the school ladder, an expansion of the extracurricular, improvement in the materials of instruction, changes in school architecture. But the word "transformation" in the main title of Cremin's work, if it signifies anything, implies some sort of fundamental or radical change in American education. Here we encounter a problem. In the first place, without some sense of the "before"—of what preceded the changes presumably caused by "progressive education"—these changes have little meaning. In the second place, even if the changes listed by Cremin may all be worth mentioning, they do not add up to a "transformation." Where does that leave us?

I think, with Cremin, that, beginning in about the last decade of the nineteenth century, there was a school reform movement that can usefully be labeled "progressive education." I think, with Cremin, that between about 1890 and 1950 there occurred so basic and irrevocable a change in American education that it can be called a "transformation." And, I think, again with Cremin, that this transformation was wrought by progressive education. But now, departing from Cremin, or supplementing Cremin, I take the linguistic turn and offer a redescription of both progressive education and the transformation of the school in terms of language. The linguistic turn (Daniel Rodgers some years ago attempted something like this with the Progressive Movement) preserves both categories as meaningful, but in radically altered form.[14] I will define progressive education as a system of language occupying a total discursive field with what I will call the moral-intellectual system of language. I then define the transformation of the school as first of all a revolution in the language of American educational discourse: the displacement of a traditional and formerly hegemonic system of verbal culture, the moral–intellectual, by a once marginal, alternative, and incommensurate system of language, the progressive. The transformation of American education in the twentieth century took the form of an upheaval in the discursive landscape of American education, which can be tracked through vocabulary, through the language of educational discourse; the transformation of the school can be measured in words.

V.

The history of the discursive landscape of American education is uncharted territory. Given the constraints of space I can set down only a few moments in the history of the languages of education taken from different periods of American history, beginning in the colonial period and ending in the 1950s. The succession, in terms of the language of educational discourse, from the founding generation to Horace Mann in the 1840s to William Torrey Harris in the 1890s, is linear, a continuity. But beginning with Francis Parker and G. Stanley Hall—or better, with John Dewey—we come across something different: a displacement, a rupture, a revolution in the language of educational discourse. The subsequent triumph by about 1950 of the discourse of progressive education marks a radical discontinuity, a Foucauldian epistemic break in the history of American education. The full extent of the break can be gauged only by comparing the discourse of progressive education with the language of educational discourse that progressives in education contested, repudiated, and by 1950 displaced from its position of dominance—the discourse of the moral-intellectual tradition of education.[15]

What did the discursive landscape of American education look like in the colonial period? What were its key words? Among the founders there was widespread agreement on the goal of "creating a republican form of government that would be free but also virtuous," and that "to ensure both freedom and virtue, the citizenry would require education."[16] Or consider the language of Horace Mann, the architect of the American common school system in the mid-nineteenth century. The key words or key terms used by Mann to describe the ends of American education are "morality," "self–government," "self–control," and the "laws of reason and duty." Here is how Cremin summarizes the "republican style" in American education as it emerged in the mid-nineteenth century. Its aim was the creation of a "new republican individual, of virtuous character, abiding patriotism and prudent wisdom, fashioned into an independent yet loyal citizen."[17] A proper republican education "consisted of the diffusion of knowledge, the nurturance of virtue, and the cultivation of learning."[18]

We move next to William Torrey Harris, the leading educator of his time, the educator who best articulated the consensus of the public school movement in America in the late nineteenth century. Here is a sample of Harris's rhetoric:

> Educate the heart? Educate the character? Yes, these are the chief objects, but there is no immediate way of educating these. They must be educated by two disciplines: that of the will in correct habits, and by that of the intellect in a correct view of the world.[19]

Here is a sample of the language of two influential reports that bear Harris's fingerprint. From the National Education Association (NEA) *Report of the Committee of Fifteen on Elementary Education* (1895):

> The child is trained to be regular and punctual and to restrain his desire to talk and whisper—in these things gaining self-control day by day. The essence of moral behavior is self-control.[20]

And from the National Education Association, *Report of the Committee of Ten on Secondary School Studies* (1893):

> [All the main subjects] would . . . be used for training the powers of observation, memory, expression and reasoning. . . . It would make no difference which subjects [the pupil] had chosen for his programme—he would have had four years of strong and effective mental training.[21]

The key words in Harris's discourse are character, will, virtue, discipline, morality, mental training, the faculties of the mind, the tools of thought.[22] This was the vocabulary of American education from the founders to Harris. But Harris, the Committee of Ten, and the Committee of Fifteen represent the culmination of an epoch in the history of the language of American educational discourse and of American education. What follows after Harris is not a succession or a progression, but so fundamental a discursive change in education that it can be called a revolution, a transformation of the school.

VI.

"Whatever else they may be," as Dominick LaCapra says, "texts are events in the history of language."[23] Some texts are revolutionary or express a revolutionary situation. These are texts which introduce a new language to the discourse of their time.

Some texts are significant as events or moments in the shift from the moral-intellectual discourse of education to the progressive discourse of education. Which are the revolutionary texts of American education in the twentieth century? Which texts introduced a new language to the educational discourse of our time? Which texts are significant as events in the history of progressive education as a language of discourse? A short list would begin with John Dewey, *The Child and the Curriculum* (1900), *Schools of Tomorrow* (1915), and *Democracy and Education* (1916). The list would then go on to U.S. Bureau of Education, *Cardinal Principles of Secondary Education* (1918); Harold Rugg and Ann Shumaker, *The Child-Centered School* (1928); Vivian T. Thayer et al., *Reorganizing Secondary Education* (1939); Educational Policies Commission, *Education for All American Youth* (1944); and U.S. Bureau of Education, *Life Adjustment Education for All American Youth* (1951).

Tracing chronology in the history of discourse is a difficult matter. The discourse of progressive education was not created all at once; but, beginning in the late 1890s, various linguistic components were added in the pre–World War I era and the 1920s, 1930s, and 1940s, until that discourse reached its mature form by about 1950. The new era may be said to have begun in the late 1890s with Dewey, the most commanding figure in the history of American education in the twentieth century. Take this utterance from *Democracy and Education* (1916):

> When it is said that education is development, everything depends upon how development is conceived. Our conclusion is that life is development, and that developing, growing, is life. Translated into its educational equivalents, this means (i) that the educational process has no end beyond itself; it is its own end, and that (ii) the educational process is one of continual reorganizing, reconstructing, transforming.[24]

Next, we turn to the language of another NEA report, this one from 1918, "The Cardinal Principles of Secondary Education":

> It is the firm belief of this commission [the NEA's Commission on the Reorganization of Secondary Education] that secondary education in the United States should aim at nothing less than complete and worthy living for all youth.

Or:

> There are various processes, such as reading, writing, arithmetical computations, and oral and written expression, that are needed as tools in the affairs of life. Consequently, command of these fundamental processes, while not an end in itself, is nevertheless an indispensable objective.[25]

How far removed we are from the world of William Torrey Harris. Contrast the discursive landscape in American education as revealed in the writings of Harris and Dewey or contrast the language of the "Report of the Committee of Ten on Secondary School Studies" with that of "The Cardinal Principles of Secondary Education." With Dewey and "The Cardinal Principles," we have entered the new world of progressive education.

If we conceive of progressive education as a language system evolving and achieving its mature form by about 1950, some other essential linguistic components of progressive education follow. Here are a few key phrases from a classic work of the 1920s, *The Child-Centered School*:

> The vocabulary of the new school has coursing through it a unitary integrating theme: individuality, personality, experience.

> I would have a child say not "I know" but "I have experienced."

> Tolerant understanding and creative self-expression, the two foci of the new education.[26]

Or listen to the language from another classic progressive text, from the late 1930s—the Progressive Education Association's *Reorganizing Secondary Education*:

> In conclusion, it may be said that using [adolescents'] needs as a basis for revising educational goals and processes does not mean . . . specifying particular knowledges, skills, and attitudes. . . . Instead it means seeking clues to the desirable reconstruction of the whole self in the adolescent's personality.[27]

We have come a long way from Horace Mann and William Torrey Harris. The distance can be measured in words, in the language of educational discourse.

Radical change does not have to occur radically, as it were. Some revolutions occur quietly. No marching, no picketing, simply a change in language. "Every revolution creates new words," as David Hare remarks in *Fanshen*, a play about the cultural revolution in China. New words and concepts enter our vocabulary; old words and concepts disappear or become marginalized. So it was with the progressive movement in American education.

As I observe above, the struggle of competing languages over time is difficult to document. We can date approximately the moment of victory of one language over another, but the stages of conquest are less clearly visible. In the 1920s the discourse of progressive education was the possession of an influential, but still only a small, community of discourse. Gradually, in the 1930s and 1940s, the language of progressive education began to saturate textbooks in education. The critical evidence is language. It would be possible, if there were space, to identify a distinctive progressive discursive mode shared by all the important education texts of this period. The point is that it is here, in the cumulative process of the sedimentation of language, that we can trace the influence of progressive education. Gradually, through the provision of a vocabulary, of a nomenclature and language of discourse, the progressive language of discourse filtered into the vocabulary and consciousness of policy makers and influential publics; their way of comprehending education had changed. By the early 1950s, long-existing conventions of educational thought and language crumbled; progressive education had preempted the discourse of education. Cremin unwittingly lends support to this point of view. By mid-century, he asserts, progressive education had become the "conventional wisdom" of American education. Its language had become slogans and clichés; "a cant, . . . the peculiar jargon of the pedagogues."[28] For Cremin, that its language had become a "cant" marks the nadir of progressive education. From the perspective of the linguistic turn, however, the fact that the language of progressive education had become a ritualized invocation marks the triumph of progressive education; its key words had become ubiquitous in American educational discourse. The reversal of hierarchy in the discursive field of American education is a change so basic that it can be called a "transformation" of the school.

VII.

What I have attempted to do in this chapter is (1) to sketch a new approach to the problem of school reform movements and change in education in terms of language, and (2) by way of a case study, to sketch the influence of the progressive movement on American education in the twentieth century in terms of language. To restate my thesis: change in education also passes through language. My hope has been to persuade historians of education that language is so intimately involved with the processes of educational change that we have to give language much more attention than we have given it in the past. Language, discourse, and discursive contexts are crucial to our understanding of school reform movements and the problem of influence and change in education. The turn toward language provides a rich and untapped source of empirical evidence for documenting educational change and the influence of ideas on educational change. I have argued that if we foreground language, move the language of educational discourse into the forefront of historical inquiry in education, it transforms our understanding of the problem of school reform movements and educational change and enables us to break new ground in the investigation of how and in what form ideas about education are transmitted, how they become influential, and how to gauge their influence. In this regard, it is difficult to say which has been the more striking experience for me—the excitement of "discovering" language or astonishment that language ; with Jeffrey Mirel, David Tyack and William Tobin as recent exceptions, has been so long neglected or overlooked by historians of education.[29]

I have argued that there was a fundamental change—a "transformation"—in American education in the first half of the twentieth century, and that "progressive education" as a *language system* played the central role in this transformation. The means the progressive movement in education used, the field on which it fought, was language; the stakes were control of the language of educational discourse. If, with Pocock and Baker (and Foucault), we consider discourse as the object of a struggle for power and one of the decisive stakes of power, then by about 1950 there had occurred a shift in the power relationships in American educational thought, the displacement of the moral-intellectual discourse from its long-established position of dominance in American educational discourse by the progressive discourse of education. Now we can better grasp the transformation of the school. The transformation of the school occurred in the language of educational discourse—the displacement of one system of verbal culture, the moral-intellectual, by another, the progressive.

I do not claim that the approach to change expounded here is canonical or *the* correct one. There are many ways of approaching the problem of school reform movements and change in education. Neither the whole of the linguistic universe of the moral-intellectual discourse nor that of progressive education has been depicted here. That was far beyond the scope of this chapter. And my portrayal of both language systems no doubt gives an impression of more cohesion or unity than they actually possessed. Other students of change in education might map the discursive landscape of American education quite differently.[30] I am also aware that moving language into the forefront of the historical study of change in education radically displaces individuals, interest groups, and "social forces" (though language is itself a "social force") traditionally emphasized in historical accounts of change in education.[31] In this sense, the approach through language is an attempt to rectify an imbalance.

I do claim that, as a heuristic device, if we foreground language and discourse, it would not only enable us to break new ground in the historical investigation of school reform movements and change in education, but provide us with a way to map the influence of ideas "in specific and convincing ways" on change in any educational system— a method which historians of education have not possessed before, and which can be used whenever other approaches to educational reform movements and change prove unsatisfactory, as no doubt from time to time they will.

Notes

1 Joseph A. Diorio, "The Decline of History as a Tool of Moral Training," *History of Education Quarterly*, 25 (1985): 74.

2 *American Educational Research Journal*, 7 (1970): 468.

3 E.g., John E. Toews, "Intellectual History After the Linguistic Turn," *American Historical Review*, 92 (1987): 879–907; and in general, Peter Novick, *That Noble Dream: The "Objectivity Question" and the American Historical Profession* (Cambridge, England, 1988), ch. 15; and Dominick LaCapra and Steven L. Kaplan, eds., *Modern European Intellectual History: Reappraisals and New Perspectives* (Ithaca, N.Y., 1982).

4 Hayden White, *Metahistory: The Historical Imagination in Nineteenth-Century Europe* (Baltimore, 1973); *Tropics of Discourse: Essays in Cultural Criticism* (Baltimore, 1978); *The Content of the Form: Narrative Discourse and Historical Representation* (Baltimore, 1987). See also Hans Kellner, *Language and Historical Representation: Getting the Story Crooked* (Madison, 1989); Lloyd S. Kramer, "Literature, Criticism, and Historical Imagination: The Literary Challenge of Hayden White and Dominick LaCapra," in Lynn Hunt, ed., *The New Cultural History* (Berkeley, 1989), ch. 4.

5 J. G. A. Pocock, *Politics, Language and Time: Essays on Political Thought and History* (New York, 1971), pp. 3–41. See also Pocock, "Intellectual History," in Juliet Gardiner, ed., *What Is History Today?* (London, 1988), pp. 114–116.

6 "The appropriate focus of the history of ideas is . . . linguistic. . . . It is essentially a linguistic enterprise." Quentin Skinner, "Meaning and Understanding in the History of Ideas," *History and Theory*, 8 (1969): 49.

7 *Politics, Language and Time*, p. 38.

8 Clifford Geertz, "Thick Description: Toward an Interpretive Theory of Culture," in *The Interpretation of Cultures: Selected Essays* (New York, 1973), ch. 1. And in general, see William J. Bouwsma, "Intellectual History in the 1980s: From History of Ideas to History of Meaning," *Journal of Interdisciplinary History*, 12 (1981): 279–291.

9 And see Raymond Williams, *Keywords: A Vocabulary of Culture and Society* (London, 1983), pp. 21–23.

10 Keith M. Baker, "On the Problem of the Ideological Origins of the French Revolution," in Dominick LaCapra and Steven L. Kaplan, eds., *Modern European Intellectual History: Reappraisals and New Perspectives* (Ithaca, N.Y., 1982), pp. 197–219, and Baker, *Inventing the French Revolution: Essays in French Political Culture in the Eighteenth Century* (Cambridge,

Mass., 1990); and Lynn Hunt, *Politics, Culture and Class in the French Revolution* (Berkeley, 1984), Part I, "The Poetics of Power." See also Janis Langins, "Words and Institutions during the French Revolution"; and Dorinda Outram, "*La langue male de la vertu*: Women and the Discourse of the French Revolution," both in Peter Burke and Roy Porter, eds., *The Social History of Language* (Cambridge, England, 1987); and Ann Rigney, *The Rhetoric of Historical Representation* (Cambridge, England, 1990).

11   Ibid., p. 217.

12   Northrop Frye, *Anatomy of Criticism: Four Essays* (Princeton, 1957), pp. 136–137.

13   Lawrence A. Cremin, *The Transformation of the School: Progressivism in American Education, 1876–1957* (New York, 1960), p. viii.

14   "In Search of Progressivism," *Reviews in American History* (1982): 113–132. Rodgers influenced Jeffrey E. Mirel's thoughtful venture into language theory, "Progressive School Reform in Comparative Perspective," in David N. Plank and Rick Ginsberg, eds., *Southern Cities, Southern Schools: Public Education in the Urban South* (New York, 1996), especially pp. 158–161.

15   I take up another aspect of this project in Chapter 5.

16   Lawrence A. Cremin, *American Education: The Colonial Experience, 1607–1783* (New York, 1970), p. 569.

17   *American Education: The National Experience, 1783–1876* (New York, 1980), p. 137.

18   Ibid., p. 124.

19   William Torrey Harris, "Psychological Inquiry," *Addresses and Proceedings of the National Education Association* (1885), p. 47.

20   Sol Cohen, *Education in the United States: A Documentary History* (New York, 1974), vol. 3, pp. 1962–1963.

21   Ibid., pp. 1942–1943.

22   Lawrence A Cremin, *American Education: The Metropolitan Experience, 1876–1980* (New York, 1989), pp. 160–164. For other examples of the key words of the moral-intellectual language of discourse, though not interpreted as such, see Carl F. Kaestle, *Pillars of the Republic: Common Schools and American Society 1780–1860* (New York, 1983), ch. 5, "The Ideology of Common School Reform." See also David Tyack and Elisabeth Hansot, *Managers of Virtue: Public School Leadership in America, 1820–1980* (New York, 1982), Part I, "An Aristocracy of Character, 1820–1890"; and Robert L. Hampel, *The Last Little Citadel: American High Schools Since 1940* (Boston, 1986), ch. 3, "The Persistence of the Old Order."

23   *Rethinking Intellectual History: Texts, Contexts, Language* (Ithaca, N.Y., 1982), p. 65.

24   John Dewey, *Democracy and Education* (New York, 1916), p. 59.

25   U.S. Bureau of the Interior (Washington, D.C., 1918), p. 9.

26   Harold Rugg and Ann Shumaker, *The Child-Centered School* (New York, 1928), passim.

27   Vivian T. Thayer et al., *Reorganizing Secondary Education* (New York, 1939), pp. 365–367.

28   Cremin, *The Transformation of the School*, p. 328.

29   Mirel, "Progressive School Reform in Comparative Perspective." And David Tyack and William Tobin, "The 'Grammar' of Schooling: Why Has It Been So Hard to Change?" *American Educational Research Journal*, 31 (1994): 453–480.

30   E.g., Herbert M. Kliebard, *The Struggle for the American Curriculum, 1895–1958* (New York, 1987).

31   See Thomas S. Popkewitz, *A Political Sociology of Educational Reform* (New York, 1991); Diane Ravitch, *The Troubled Crusade: American Education, 1945–1980* (New York, 1983); and in general, the special issue on "Educational Reform in International Perspective," *International Perspectives on Education and Society*, 4 (1994).

Chapter 5

The Influence of Progressive Education on School Reform in the United States: Redescriptions

We can know only what we succeed in giving form to. . . . There is no reality outside of this, the form we manage to give to ourselves, to others, to things.

Luigi Pirandello

There are distances which are measured only in words.

Victor Lily

I.

The genesis of this essay was a request from Hermann Röhrs and Volker Lenhart to contribute a chapter on "The Influence of Progressive Education on School Reform in the U.S.A." for their handbook, *Progressive Education Across the Continents* (Frankfurt am Main, 1995)—as if the assignment were transparent or utterly unproblematic.

The influence of progressive education on school reform in the United States is a more difficult and complex matter than it would seem at first glance. It involves at least the prior question of whether the term "progressive education" is meaningful at all. If the answer is yes or perhaps, then there is the question of how one is to understand "progressive education." Or should the term be abandoned as mystifying? If there is something that can usefully be labeled "progressive education," there is the question of its influence, if any, on American education. And finally, there is the question of how to apprehend that influence.

If themes of progressive education and its influence on school reform in the United States preoccupy this essay, so does a concern with the concepts and methodologies which go under the synoptic name "linguistic turn." These preoccupations are not unrelated. Two aspects of the many-faceted linguistic turn concern me here: one has to do with the relevance of linguistics and literary theory for the writing and reading of historical narratives; the other has to do with making language itself a basic object and a methodological starting point for the historical study of change in education. In this chapter, I explore from another angle the implications of bringing the linguistic turn to bear on the historiography of progressive education.

New theories and methodologies usually spark free and lively historiographical debate. This has certainly been true of the reception accorded the linguistic turn by general historians. The linguistic turn occupies a central place in the process of recasting the subject matter boundaries of general social and intellectual history that is under way in the United States and on the European continent.[1] The turn to language has aroused some interest among historians of education outside of the United States.[2] So far, however, this has not been true of its reception by historians of American education. At the moment a discussion hardly exists. With few exceptions, historians of American education have remained indifferent to the way literary theory and linguistic studies can illuminate their projects.[3] This is curious, since the turn to language opens up a whole new world of social acts or social events. The linguistic turn not only offers exciting possibilities for intellectual history but greatly enlarges the terrain of the social history of education.

II.

Few topics in the historiography of American education are as troublesome as progressive education. Lawrence Cremin's history of progressive education, *The Transformation of the School: Progressivism in American Education, 1876–1957*, has had almost canonical influence over a generation of historians of education, in America and elsewhere. Cremin defined progressive education variously as "the educational phase of American Progressivism writ large," "a many-sided effort to use the schools to improve the lives of individuals," and "part of a vast humanitarian effort to apply the promise of American life" to the new urban-industrial society that came into being during the latter half of the nineteenth century.[4] Cremin left no doubt of the influence of "progressive education" on the "transformation" of the school. By way of documentation, Cremin listed items such as continuous expansion and reorganization of the curriculum at all levels, a reorganization of the school ladder, expansion of the extracurricular, improvements in textbooks, enrichment of other materials of instruction, modifications in school architecture, and so forth.

Though a winner of the 1962 Bancroft Prize in American History, *The Transformation of the School* has always had its critics. They say that Cremin first refused to define progressive education clearly and then went about defining it in ways that were excessively general and inclusive. Cremin's documentation of progressive education's transforming influence on school reform in the United States has also been criticized as unpersuasive. But even revisionist works by historians of education like Raymond Callahan, Michael Katz, and David Tyack, though seriously challenging the positive trajectory of Cremin's metanarrative, did not contest the category "progressive education," and they provided grist for keeping the historiographical debate over progressive education alive.

In 1986, the respected historian of curriculum Herbert M. Kliebard issued the most formidable challenge to date to Cremin's interpretation of progressive education. In *The Struggle for the American Curriculum, 1893–1958*,[5] in effect a history of American education in roughly the same period as Cremin's history, Kliebard questioned whether the term "progressive education" is meaningful at all and called for its complete abandonment. Despite a copious preexisting discourse on Cremin's work, Kliebard makes no effort to come to grips with scholarship on or interpretation of Cremin; he systematically excludes any mention of Cremin or of *The Transformation of the School* and Cremin's name does not appear in his index. A general tenet of poststructuralist literary theory is that what is said in a given text takes on significance as a referent to what is not said and as a referent to the absent text to which the given text is opposed. *The Transformation of the School* is the absent text to which *The Struggle for the American Curriculum* is opposed and which constitutes its essential context.

Kliebard's polemical intent is clear: to settle the historiographical problem of progressive education once and for all by discarding the category altogether. Kliebard's dismissal of progressive education must be quoted at some length:

> I was frankly puzzled by what was meant by the innumerable references I had seen to progressive education. The more I studied this the more it seemed . . . that the term encompassed such a broad range, not just of different, but of contradictory, ideas on education as to be meaningless. . . . I came to believe that the term was not only vacuous but mischievous. It was not just the word "progressive" that I thought was inappropriate but the implication that something deserving a single name existed and that something could be identified and defined if we only tried.[6]

Needless to say, Kliebard rejects any notion that progressive education had a transforming influence on school reform in the United States.

If Cremin interprets all school reform in the United States from the 1870s through the 1930s as but phases of "progressive education," culminating by about 1950 in a "transformation" in American education, Kliebard interprets the history of the American school curriculum in this period in terms of a struggle between four competing interest groups—humanists, developmentalists, advocates of social efficiency, and social meliorists—each with its own distinct agenda for school reform, none of which ever achieved dominance. Kliebard rejects the notion that any interest group had a transforming influence on school reform in the United States. The school curriculum did change over the decades, but the outcome "was not the result of a decisive victory of any of the contending groups, but a loose, largely unarticulated, and not very tidy compromise."[7]

In *The Transformation of the School* Cremin asked readers to view *his* history of progressive education as real "history," as opposed to a "morality play" or a "simple story [which] should never be confused with history." Kliebard apparently thinks that Cremin's history of progressive education is a "simple story," not worth mentioning, and that *his* is the truer and superior history. Now we have another question— what to make of the conflicting interpretations of progressive education—to put alongside the questions we initially posed above.

If the historiographical debate over progressive education is to continue, as I believe it should, then I think the challenge posed by Kliebard should be addressed first. The linguistic turn offers insights into how rhetorical structures operate in the construction of historical narratives; this helps make sense of the disputes over *The Transformation of the School* and the conflicting interpretations of progressive education. The linguistic turn also suggests a new evidentiary source and a new set of topics for historical investigation—language or language systems—which provide an approach to "progressive education" and the "transformation" of the school, while preserving both terms as meaningful entities, although with radically altered meanings, and re-invigorating historiographical debate on the subject.[8]

III.

First, the matter of conflicting historical interpretations of progressive education. I have been greatly influenced by Hayden White on the significance of literary theory for our understanding of the nature of historical narratives.[9] Here I wish to take readers briefly through some of the most relevant, for my purpose, of White's ideas.

White argues that histories, that is, our written descriptions of historical reality, are literary constructions first of all, which cannot be separated from the entanglements of language, rhetoric, and narrative structure. Historical narratives are "makings" rather than "findings." Historians do not find and then merely report the past "as it really was," but construct meaning from, or rather impose meaning upon, the profusion of sources which the past comprises. In converting knowing (all that research) into telling, the historian must prefigure a sequence of facts or events as a story of a certain kind. Where do historians get their model of a story? Following the literary critic Northrop Frye, White identifies a stock of generic story forms or archetypal plot structures (at least in the western world) that constitute the historian's initial rhetorical or dramatic resources: romance, comedy, tragedy, and satire or irony, which within limits can be mixed or combined. White's insights into the irreducible rhetorical nature of historical narratives adds an important new dimension to the reading and writing of histories. Historians cannot claim to be telling a particular story as if it were a definitive, universal, and objectively determined depiction of the past "as it really was." Instead, if one accepts White's view that histories are constructions, then we must acknowledge that disputes among historians of education are not so much about what "really" happened in the past as much as they are about different strategies of emplotment: what one historian of education may emplot as tragedy or satire another may emplot as romance or comedy.

White's retheorization of historical representation has significant implications for our understanding of the conflicting interpretations of progressive education. The histories of Cremin and Kliebard are different ways of making meaning of the history of American education. In constructing their differing versions, Cremin and Kliebard employ different narrative conventions and organize their evidence into different kinds of narrative plot structures. The narrative form in which Cremin has cast *The Transformation of the School* is romance. Kliebard has emplotted his history in the mode of satire. Certainly, there is no one right or definitive version of progressive education; but Kliebard is too much the scoffer. I suppose Kliebard can dismiss out of hand Cremin's version of progressive education. Any clever historian can solve the troublesome problem of progressive education by simply proclaiming that it never existed. But this is really too naïve.[10] We do not dismiss out of hand categories like "the Renaissance" or "the Reformation" or "the Progressive Era," problematic as these categories may be. Such categories are set up by us; they are not found ready-made. They are mental constructions, ways of imposing order on the past. We have to impose some form on the past to give it meaning. So we invent "eras" and "ages" and "periods." Of course, in a sense, they both do and don't "exist." The test is pragmatic. My problem with Kliebard is not about claims of truth: that there *really* was a "progressive education" or that there *really* wasn't. A category or concept like progressive education is just an instrument. The questions are: Does it still illuminate? Is it still useful? My answer to both questions is in the affirmative.[11]

It goes against the grain of the new cultural approach to historiography to make a monument of *The Transformation of the School* or any text. But progressive education is an object of persistent interest and ongoing historiographical study. Certainly, there is no end of books or articles on progressive education.[12] The term "progressive education" is fixed in the lexicon of historians of education and other scholars, who continue to assume its reality and importance. Arthur Zilversmit may be dubious that there was any transformation of the school, but he does not contest the category "progressive education." John L. Rury agrees that there was a progressive education but says that its history is yet to be written.[13] Paula Fass argues that the history of American education in the twentieth century is largely the history of progressive education, but that in spite of the existence of a rich and contentious legacy of scholarship, the picture of progressive education is still unfocused.[14] To accept Kliebard's position would mean the end of an important historiographical discussion. I agree with Cremin's perception that something special was going on in American education early in the twentieth century which can be called progressive education, and with his perception that something special—a critical transition—had taken place in American education by about 1950, a change so basic that it can be called a transformation. Nevertheless, *The Transformation of the School* has its problems.

One problem is that Cremin's latitudinarian definition of progressive education is too vague, even protean. Cremin calls virtually every educational reform in the Progressive Era "progressive education." This is not very helpful at all. So little is left out of Cremin's definition of progressive education that it loses all specificity. Another problem is with Cremin's documentation of the transformation of the American school.[15] The word "transformation" in the main title of *The Transformation of the School: Progressivism in American Education* implies some sort of fundamental or radical change in education. Cremin claims of the Progressive Education Association and progressive education that "the transformation they had wrought in the schools was in many ways as irreversible as the larger industrial transformation of which it had been part."[16] Cremin's catalogue of changes in American education may all be worth listing (it is strangely reminiscent of Elwood P. Cubberley's celebration of "educational services extended and perfected"), but I do not think it adds up to a transformation of the school.

The Transformation of the School fails to engage any theory of change.[17] Cremin does not give the reader a sense of any "before." Thus Cremin stumbles on his passage to the transformation of the school. There is no sense of competition between earlier and later theories of education or of any alternatives to progressive education. Without the depiction of some "before" to contrast with a progressive "after," we have very little sense of what fundamental change has taken place. Then, there is a lack of detail about the actual processes of transformation, or how progressive education, per se, is related to the transformation of the school. Cremin never found the theoretical approach to enable him to do this. To Cremin, as I observe previously, it is as if the very naming of educational theoreticians and policymakers, their ideas, and their books—of powerful interest groups and important associations and committees—seems justification enough to assume influence and subsequent change. In short, neither the term, "progressive education" nor the term, "transformation" is a fully comprehensible category within Cremin's conceptual framework. If these categories are to be preserved, that will have to be accomplished with an entirely different approach.

IV.

My intent is not to settle once and for all the historiographical problem of progressive education, nor to criticize Kliebard or Cremin. To
paraphrase Richard Rorty, criticism is not essential. What is essential
is telling a new story or, as Rorty might say, changing the conversation. I think it is possible to preserve the category "progressive education," and open up different and perhaps more fruitful lines of historical study and historiographical debate if progressive education is
redescribed solely as a language and its influence on school reform in
the United States is tracked solely in terms of language. That is what
I intend to do here: I intend to redescribe progressive education and
the transformation of the school solely in terms of language; more
precisely, in terms of change in the language of educational discourse.
My approach has been influenced mainly by the linguistic turn and
the approach to intellectual history suggested by the historian
J. G. A. Pocock.

The following aspects of the linguistic turn need emphasizing: (1) Perhaps the hallmark of the linguistic turn is the radical priority given to
language and the role of language in the social construction of reality.
(2) Language is a historical phenomenon, an event, a practice, or an
act, part of the social structure and not an epiphenomenon. (3) Every
language inscribes a system of meaning. Different language systems
represent differing conceptions of the world, which ultimately lead to
certain kinds of behavior and not others. (4) Language *systems*, not
words, per se, are the primary unit of meaning. Every language system, however, possesses an indicative vocabulary or key words. These
are the revelatory words, the words that stand as a proxy for a whole
language *system*. (5) Conversely, any language or language system is
itself situated in a discursive field containing other languages to which
it stands in a relation of difference and opposition. (6) Language has
extralinguistic effects. That is, the study of language cannot be divorced from questions of power—the power of language—as well as
the involvement of language with other forms of power.
(7) Because of its capacity to influence thought and behavior, language is a site of historical struggle, the object of a struggle for power
and one of the decisive stakes of power.[18] (8) Finally, this brings us to
language as a means of tracking the influence of ideas on fundamental
change in any aspect of a polity—the approach to intellectual history,
as noted above, suggested by Pocock.[19]

Here is the way Pocock approaches fundamental change in the history of political thought. In any given historical period, alternative and competing language systems occupy a single discursive field in a hierarchical relation. These languages or language systems struggle for hegemony. The dominant language struggles to retain its dominance; the marginal or subordinate language seeks to gain dominance. Change is marked by shifts within the total discursive system; for example, a previously dominant language becomes marginal or subordinate or, vice versa, a previously marginal or subordinate language achieves dominance. If a reversal of hierarchical relations within the total discursive field occurs, the result can be called a revolution.[20]

V.

The implications of the linguistic turn for the problem of influence and change in education in general should be coming into focus. Suppose historians of education were to assume the following. In any given historical period, as previously stated, education is a discursive terrain marked by struggle between competing and hierarchically situated languages. By investigating one language, say, the dominant one, synchronically at a particular moment in time and then comparing its place in the total discursive system of education at a later period in time, we can specify whatever diachronic changes in that system have taken place and how radical those changes are. From this perspective, fundamental change in education can now be defined as a reordering of linguistic hierarchies, a reversal of dominant and subordinate languages within a total discursive system over time. From the perspective of language, we can now approach "progressive education" and the "transformation" of the school in an entirely new way.

Note: Kliebard and Cremin do pay attention to language. Their histories are both basically histories of what "great men and women" have thought, written, or said about education. Kliebard considers the educational statements of spokespersons for his various interest groups as mere rhetoric, mere epiphenomena, "not as influencing the course of events," in schools.[21] Cremin also neutralizes or nullifies the full potential of language. He dismisses the language of progressive education as "shibboleths," "jargon," and "slogans": a "cant."[22] From the point of view of the linguistic turn, such characterizations of the language of progressive education obscure its real significance—the creation of new forms of educational discourse constituting radically new modes of educational theory, policy, and practice.

Now to return to the problem of the influence of progressive education on school reform in the United States.[23] In contrast to Kliebard's rival interest groups—humanists, developmentalists, social meliorists, and advocates of efficiency, each with a distinct "rhetoric" and no single, whole entity, "progressive education"—I intend to treat the diverse languages of these interest groups as strands of discourse constituting one language system, "progressive education," with the rhetoric of "developmentalism" as its core or final language. In contrast to Cremin, I define progressive education solely as a language system; what Cremin depicts as mere slogans and jargon constitutes its core terminology. I then prefigure the field of education as constituting but a single discursive formation comprising two alternative and competing languages of discourse: progressive education and what, for expository convenience, I call the moral-intellectual discourse of education. I assume that these two discourses not only inhabit the same linguistic universe but are situated hierarchically and in a state of tension, constantly vying for hegemony.

Through the late nineteenth century and up to about World War I, the moral-intellectual discourse of education was dominant and the discourse of progressive education was marginal. By the 1950s, we find their positions reversed. It is this shift which in my view delineates the influence of progressive education on the transformation of the school in the United States. The transformation of the school was a shift in the discursive landscape of American education in which one language of educational discourse, the progressive, displaced another, the moral-intellectual. The influence of progressive education lies here; its influence can be measured in words.

VI.

To discuss influence and change over time meaningfully, we need a description of some earlier or baseline state of affairs. Before we can depict the discourse of progressive education and trace its influence on school reform in the United States, we need to recover and identify the key words and terms of the moral-intellectual discourse of education—the "before" to progressivism's "after." Then, by comparing the dominant language system at the earlier date, the moral-intellectual, with the dominant language system at the later date, the progressive, we will be in a position to specify whatever changes took place and how radical these changes were.

What did the discursive landscape of American education look like at the turn of the twentieth century, when the moral-intellectual discourse of education was dominant? Given the constraints of space, a few of its key words will have to do.[24] Character and its handmaidens, will and intellect, were the key words in the discourse of American education from the founding generation to Horace Mann to William Torrey Harris, arguably the leading educationist of his time until his death in 1909. Character, or will, was to be educated, that is, strengthened, through myriad school rules and regulations: injunctions about order, work, effort, silence, obedience, neatness, accuracy, industry, and punctuality. Reason, intellect, and the correct view of the world were to be developed with the "tools of learning," and through the "accumulated wisdom of the past."

The discourse of secondary education emphasized "mental training," the development of the reasoning powers and the "faculties of the mind." Again, take this selection from the classic text in the moral-intellectual tradition which bears Harris's signature, the National Education Association *Report of the Committee of Ten on Secondary School Studies*:

> [All the main subjects] would be taught consecutively and thoroughly, and would all be carried on in the same spirit; they would all be used for training the powers of observation, memory, expression, and reasoning. . . . It would make no difference which subjects [the pupil] had chosen for his programme— he would have had four years of strong and effective mental training.[25]

This is the language of the moral-intellectual discourse of education. This language was the hegemonic, common, everyday language of most American educationists of the late nineteenth and early twentieth centuries.

At the same time, between the turn of the century and the period before World War I, important linguistic elements of the discourse of progressive education were already in place, a constituent language but still only a marginal language in the total discursive landscape of American education. The key words and phrases of this discourse had already made their appearance in the works of Francis Parker, G. Stanley Hall, and especially John Dewey. Again, the language of progressive education was not invented all at once; essential linguistic components were added at the time of World War I, and in the 1920s, 1930s, and 1940s. At the center of the mature language of progressive education is a core terminology that can be expressed in a number of key words, terms, or phrases: the school as miniature community, learning by doing, project method, development of personality, creativity, growth, activity, self-expression, experience, play, interest, freedom, the whole child, meeting the needs and interests of students, and social and emotional adjustment.

Certainly the key words and phrases of progressive education possess a dictionary or literal meaning. But recall Ferdinand de Saussure's tenet that meaning in language is relational and that the key words of a language are most fully understood not in terms of their literal content but oppositionally, in contrast with the key words and terms of other languages or language systems in the relevant discursive field. The defining quality of progressive education as a language is dependent on relations of contrast or opposition to the language of the moral-intellectual discourse of education. Compare Harris's language with the language of John Dewey in *The Child and the Curriculum* (1902):

> Not knowledge or information, but self-realization, is the goal. . . . Learning is active. . . . Literally, we must take our stand with the child and our departure from him. It is he and not the subject-matter which determines the quality and quantity of learning.[26]

Or, once more, compare Harris's language with Dewey's language in *Democracy and Education* (1916):

> When it is said that education is development, everything depends upon how development is conceived. Our conclusion is that life is development, and that developing, growing, is life. Translated into its educational equivalents, this means (i) that the educational process has no end beyond itself; it is its own end; and that (ii) the educational process is one of the continual reorganizing, reconstructing, transforming.[27]

With Dewey, we have entered the discursive world of progressive education.

Other essential linguistic components of progressive education were added in the 1920s, 1930s, and 1940s. For example, Harold Rugg's and Ann Shumaker's *The Child-Centered School* (1928) is a veritable encyclopedia of key words and terms of progressive educational discourse: "creative self-expression," the "active school," "child initiative," the "whole child," "personality and social adjustment," "centers of interest."[28] Or take a third-grade "Study of Boats," circa mid-1920s, from the Lincoln School in New York City, described in *The Transformation of the School*. Cremin calls this unit or lesson plan "the most celebrated of the Lincoln School units" and displays it over two pages as a concrete manifestation of the "changing pedagogical mainstream." Cremin says that "even a hasty glance" at the lesson plan reveals "how one imaginative teacher used the normal interests of children in the life around them" in designing a lesson, and leaves it at that. Let's take a closer look at this lesson plan. There is much that can be discovered here. Its headings are "'Stimulation," "Problems," "Subject Matter Content Which Helped Solve the Problems," and "Probable Outcomes," under which are listed "Desirable Habits and Skills," "Attitudes and Appreciations" (economic, social, recreational, aesthetic), as well as "Information" and "New Interests Leading Toward Further Activities." The hoped-for outcome of the unit is the "Total Personality as Modified by the Foregoing Experiences."[29]

I cite the lesson plan because from the perspective of the turn toward language it marks a moment in the history of American educational discourse. The language of this lesson plan exquisitely elucidates the discourse of progressive education (and Cremin's position in relation to that discourse).[30] Certainly, words like "stimulation," "interests," "attitudes," "appreciations," "activities," "experiences," and "personality" can be considered the jargon and shibboleths of progressive education. But these are key words in progressive discourse. If taken seriously as an event in the history of American educational discourse, the language of this third–grade lesson plan demonstrates graphically the authority beginning to be wielded by the discourse of progressive education in the mid-1920s, as well as the increasing marginality of the moral-intellectual discourse of education. That is, a further analysis of this lesson plan would also reveal an absent discourse, the moral-intellectual discourse, whose key words are character, will, virtue, discipline, morality, achievement, order, work, effort. Now, considered in juxtaposition with and opposition to the moral-intellectual discourse of education (but as part of the same discursive system), the key words of progressive education—even the commonplaces of progressive educational discourse spring to life—words or terms like "activities," "self-expression," "learning by doing," "creativity," "project method," and "personality development" become surprisingly nuanced, valued, and resonant.

VII.

The struggle for dominance of educational discourse in the United States began in the 1890s. As late as World War I, the moral-intellectual language of discourse was dominant; the language of progressive education was marginal—the possession of an influential but still only a minority community of discourse. By the late 1940s the discourse of progressive education had achieved hegemony across the discursive landscape of American education.

The struggle of competing languages over time is a bit more difficult to document than I have made out above. But we can date approximately the moment of triumph of progressive education over the moral-intellectual discourse of education. Cremin inadvertently makes the point for us. By 1950, progressive education had become the "conventional wisdom in the United States, espoused by lay people as well as professionals and embodied in the very language used to debate educational policy and practice."[31] Discussions of educational policy "were liberally spiced with phrases like 'recognizing individual differences,' 'the needs of learners,' 'persistent life situations,' 'personality development,' the 'whole child,' 'social and emotional growth,' 'creative self-expression,' 'intrinsic motivation,' 'teaching children, not subjects,' 'adjusting the school to the child,' and 'real life experiences.'"[32] Cremin calls these phrases the "cant" and "jargon of the pedagogues." After World War II, all that remained was a "collection of ready-made clichés."[33] From Cremin's perspective this represents the defeat and the ultimate demise of progressive education. But from my perspective and the perspective of the linguistic turn, the fact that the language of progressive education had become the "conventional wisdom," the "clichés," the "slogans," and the "jargon of the pedagogues" marks not the failure but the triumph of progressive education. As Roland Barthes puts it, when a language achieves hegemony, it spreads everywhere; it becomes the ordinary, everyday language of its time. This is what occurred in the United States. Which is to say, in the 1950s, when the key words and phrases of progressive education became the conventional wisdom, the "jargon of the pedagogues," it had achieved hegemony over the discursive field of American education. Now we can gauge the influence of progressive education on school reform in the United States.

To paraphrase Richard Rorty (and Thomas Kuhn), a revolution can succeed only when it employs a new vocabulary incommensurable with the old. The progressive and the moral-intellectual vocabularies are incommensurable. From my broad view, the point is not so much that progressives in education succeeded in imposing their policies but that they succeeded in imposing their language. Progressive education radically altered the way in which Americans talk about education. Progressive education marginalized the moral-intellectual discourse—the discourse of character, will, virtue, discipline, the tools of thought, and the faculties of the mind—and rendered that discourse for many years virtually inexpressible. The displacement of the moral-intellectual discourse of education from its long-established position of dominance in American educational discourse by the progressive discourse of education, marks so fundamental a shift in the discursive landscape of American education that it can be called a paradigm shift, ultimately constituting an act of redefining the character of American education. This is the "transformation" of the school. To repeat, the influence of "progressive education" on school reform lies here. Its influence can be measured in words.

VIII.

I have argued that the insights of Hayden White are indispensable for making sense of the conflicting historical interpretations of progressive education. I have also argued that the entities "progressive education" and "transformation" were worth preserving and worth continued historiographical debate but that both terms needed to be redescribed, and that the arena for debate needed to be reconstituted. With the aid of the linguistic turn, I sought to redescribe both progressive education and the transformation of the school in terms of language. My basis for this approach was its potential utility for historical analysis and explanation. I believe that if historians of education foreground or privilege language and systems within language, this will enable us to perceive with special clarity the meaning of progressive education as well as the full dimensions of the transformation of the school wrought by progressive education in the United States in the twentieth century.

Neither the whole of the linguistic universe of the moral-intellectual discourse nor that of progressive education was depicted here. That was beyond the scope of this essay. The discursive world of progressive education as well as the transformation of the school might be mapped quite differently, as I have done in my chapters on the mental hygiene movement and the medicalization of American education.[34] Other historians might define the transformation of the school differently, as David Tyack in effect has done with his organizational thesis in *The One Best System: A History of American Urban Education* (1974). Nor have I discussed the question of the distribution of the progressive discourse of education across social classes. (I think it is pretty obvious that this was widely diffused among the progressive-liberal, educated middle class.) Nor have I made any attempt to explore the ramifications of my redescription of progressive education for the present moment in American education. Suffice to say here that I understand the wave of school reform movements that fit under the umbrella name "excellence movement" as a counter-progressive movement whose implicit goal is to restore the moral-intellectual discourse of education to the educational discourse of our time and whose success will in part be gauged by its success in doing just that. Which leads me to reflect that the turn toward language raises an important issue which I have not addressed: if we consider the field of education as a site of cultural struggle, a struggle which has a vital linguistic dimension, as I do, and language as the object of a struggle for power, as I also do, what makes one discourse or language system gain hegemony over another or over the whole discursive field of education?[35]

Finally, I have by no means portrayed all the facets of the linguistic turn in this essay. Though I have found my involvement in the world of the linguistic turn exhilarating, its theoretical concepts and terminology remain a challenge with which I am still wrestling. Above all, whether they agree with my application of the linguistic turn to the debate about progressive education or not, this essay seeks to move the historiographical conversation about progressive education along and to further stimulate discussion of the linguistic turn among historians of American education.

Notes

1. Dominick LaCapra and Steven L. Kaplan, eds., *Modern European Intellectual History: Reappraisals and New Perspectives* (Ithaca, N.Y., 1982); Juliet Gardiner, ed., *What Is History Today?* (London, 1988), ch. 9, "What Is Intellectual History"; and Allan Megill, "Recounting the Past: Description, Explanation and Narrative in Historiography," *American Historical Review*, 94 (1989).

2. Peter Cunningham, "Educational History and Educational Change: The Past Decade of English Historiography," *History of Education Quarterly*, 29 (1989): 85–86; J. Donald Wilson, "The New Diversity in Canadian Educational History," *Acadiensis*, 10 (1990): 148–169; Marc Depaepe, "History of Education Anno 1992," *History of Education*, 22 (1993): 1–10.

3. But see Richard Angelo, "Ironies of Romance and the Romance with Irony: Some Notes on Stylization in the Historiography of American Education Since 1960," *Educational Theory*, 4 (1990): 443–452.

4. Lawrence A. Cremin, *The Transformation of the School: Progressivism in American Education, 1876–1957* (New York, 1961), p. viii.

5. London, 1986.

6. Ibid., p. xi.

7. Ibid., pp. xiii, 270; "Education at the Turn of the Century: A Crucible for Curriculum Change," *Educational Researcher*, 9 (1989): 23.

8. See also Jeffrey E. Mirel's turn to language in "Progressive School Reform in Comparative Perspective," in David N. Plank and Rick Ginsberg, eds., *Southern Cities, Southern Schools* (New York, 1990), pp. 158–161.

9. The essential texts are Hayden White, *Tropics of Discourse: Essays in Cultural Criticism* (Baltimore, 1978), and *The Content of the Form: Narrative Discourse and Historical Representation* (Baltimore, 1987). In general, see Lloyd S. Kramer, "Literature, Criticism, and Historical Imagination: The Literary Challenge of Hayden White and Dominick LaCapra," in Lynn Hunt, ed., *The New Cultural History* (Berkeley, 1989), ch. 4; and Hans Kellner, *Language and Historical Representation: Getting the Story Crooked* (Madison, 1989).

10. More discerning are Kliebard's "Vocational Education as Symbolic Action" and "Curriculum Theory as Metaphor," chs. 11 and 12, in *Forging the American Curriculum: Essays in Curriculum History and Theory* (New York, 1992).

11. Cf. Peter Filene, "An Obituary for the 'Progressive Movement,'" *American Quarterly*, 22 (1970): 20–34; David M. Kennedy, "Overview: The Progres-

sive Era," *Historian*, 37 (1975): 453–468; and John D. Buenker, John C. Burnham, and Robert M. Crunden, *Progressivism* (Cambridge, Mass., 1977).

12   Diane Ravitch, *The Troubled Crusade: American Education, 1945–1980* (New York, 1983); William J. Reese, *Power and Promise of School Reform: Grassroots Movements During the Progressive Era* (London, 1985); Kathe Jervis and Carol Montag, eds., *Progressive Education for the 1990s* (New York, 1991); Judith Rosenberg Raftery, *Land of Fair Promise: Politics and Reform in Los Angeles Schools, 1885–1941* (Stanford, Ca., 1992); Maurice R. Berube, *American School Reform: Progressive, Equity, and Excellence Movements, 1883–1993* (Westport, Conn., 1994). See also, in general, Hermann Röhrs and Volker Lenhart, eds., *Progressive Education Across the Continents* (Frankfurt am Main, 1995).

13   Zilversmit, *Changing Schools: Progressive Education Theory and Practice, 1930–1960* (Chicago, 1993); Rury, "*Transformation* in Perspective: Lawrence Cremin's *Transformation of the School*," *History of Education Quarterly*, 31 (1991): 67–76.

14   Paula S. Fass, *Outside In: Minorities and the Transformation of American Education* (New York, 1989), pp. 5, 34–35.

15   *The Transformation of the School*, ch. 8, "The Changing Educational Mainstream," passim.

16   Ibid., p. 353.

17   I discuss this point in a different context in Chapter 4 of this volume.

18   Peter Caws, *Structuralism: The Art of the Intelligible* (London, 1990); Richard Harland, *Superstructuralism: The Philosophy of Structuralism and Post-Structuralism* (London, 1987); and, in general, Pauline M. Rosenau, *Post-Modernism and the Social Sciences* (Princeton, 1992).

19   "Languages and Their Implications: The Transformation of the Study of Political Thought," in *Politics, Language and Time: Essays on Political Thought and History* (New York, 1971), pp. 3–41, and "Intellectual History," in Juliet Gardiner, ed., *What Is History Today?*, pp. 114–116.

20   The new methodologies and insights that have arisen in connection with the linguistic turn have not gone unnoticed. At one time, histories of the French Revolution were dominated by themes of class struggle. Now it is increasingly acknowledged by historians—like Keith Baker, Lynn Hunt, Janet Langins, Ann Rigney, and Lorinda Outram—that it is impossible to understand the revolution without examining the special discourse which the revolution generated.

21   *The Struggle for the American Curriculum*, p. x.

22   *The Transformation of the School*, p. 328.

23   What follows is a continuation of a project I began with my review of Cremin's *American Education: The Metropolitan Experience, 1876–1980* (New York,

1988), *Historical Studies in Education/Revue d'histoire de l'éducation*, 1 (1989): 307–326; and "Language and History: A Perspective on School Reform Movements and Change in Education," Chapter 4 of this book.

24   Readers might keep in mind Pocock's caution that to trace the history of a revolution, it is almost a necessity to start with a straw man. "Languages and Their Implications," p. 4.

25   Quoted in Sol Cohen, ed., *Education in the United States* (New York, 1974), vol. 3, pp. 1942–1943.

26   Chicago, 1902, p. 9.

27   John Dewey, *Democracy and Education* (New York, 1916), p. 59.

28   Harold Rugg and Ann Shumaker, *The Child-Centered School* (New York, 1928).

29   *The Transformation of the School*, pp. 283–286. Of Lincoln School, Cremin observed, "No single progressive school exerted greater or more lasting influence on the subsequent history of American education." *American Education: The Metropolitan Experience,* p. 244.

30   Cremin's vocabulary—"imaginative teacher," "normal interests of children in the life around them"—reveals his own position as one of the few mourners at the supposed demise of progressive education. And see also Cremin's description of "Farmville," the Educational Policies Commission's imaginary progressive education utopia. *The Transformation of the School*, pp. 330–331.

31   Ibid., p. 328; Cremin, *American Education: The Metropolitan Experience*, p. 241.

32   Cremin, *The Transformation of the School*, p. 328.

33   Ibid., pp. 332–333, 348.

34   Or some may attempt to refocus the discussion of Progressive school reform altogether, as James L. Leloudis claims to do in "Schooling the New South: Pedagogy, Self, and Society in North Carolina, 1880–1920," *Historical Studies in Education/Revue d'histoire de l'éducation*, 5 (1993): 204.

35   This is a point which Jurgen Herbst raises in an essay reviewing Röhrs and Lenhart, eds., *Progressive Education Across the Continents*. "Toward a Theory of Progressive Education?" *History of Education Quarterly*, 37 (1997): 58–59.

Chapter 6

Postmodernism, the New Cultural History, Film: Resisting Images of Education

The visual media are a legitimate way of doing history—of representing, interpreting, thinking about, and making meaning from the traces of the past. . . . that seriously deals with the relationship of past to present.

Robert A. Rosenstone

One could perhaps say that certain ideological conflicts animating present-day polemics oppose the pious descendants of time and the determined inhabitants of space.

Michel Foucault

My point can be stated simply. One of the major themes of the new cultural history is to collapse the boundaries and heirarchical distinctions between elite culture and academic culture, giving us new opportunities to cross the boundaries separating history from literature and the arts, the archival from the imaginative, and the book from the film.

There is a strong tradition among historians of education to privilege written sources in their research, and the book, article, or report in their teaching. But historical discourse cannot be confined to the "text" in the narrow sense of the term. The range of our sources can and should go beyond the archive and monographs, textbooks, and periodicals to encompass all cultural artifacts, including the symbolic and the imaginary. Despite a growing scholarly interest in film studies, movies have not yet secured a foothold among us. The issue is not whether film or written history is the better method "by which we make meaning from the remains of the past."[1] Rather, what I propose here is that we extend the range of what counts as historical source to include film, and that film be accepted as a legitimate form of historical representation and as important evidence for the historical exploration and interpretation of culture and of education.

What follows is offered in the spirit of an exploratory exercise, an attempt to open a dialogue between history and alternative representations of the world of education, particularly film. I offer it in the spirit of a postmodernist try at integrating film into the historiography of education. The limitations of a short essay make it necessary to concentrate on just one film for illustrative study. After a close viewing of about a score of Hollywood high school movies which appeared in the decade 1980–1990, and shortlisting *American Graffiti, Fast Times at Ridgemont High, Pretty in Pink, The Breakfast Club, Heathers, Teachers, Stand and Deliver, Ferris Bueller's Day Off*, and *Dead Poets Society*, I chose for my case study *Dead Poets Society* (DPS), 1989, directed by Peter Weir from a screenplay by Tom Schulman. DPS powerfully represents some of the enduring conflicts facing America: the tensions between self-expression and society, and between self-absorption and service; the restraints of tradition and the claims of the unbounded self. Though DPS is limited to the American scene, I hope my reading of it will provoke reflection on film and the history of education in a variety of national contexts.

In sections I and II, I sketch some of the more relevant theoretical considerations underpinning this essay. Then, using *Dead Poets Society* as an exemplar, I try to demonstrate that incorporating film into the historiography of education is both feasible and productive. In selecting my references, I emphasize works that I have found to be the most useful or relevant and that may also provide colleagues with some idea of the diversity of resources available to aid our critical understanding and use of film.

I.

This essay has significant points of contact with some of the more interesting theoretical developments in postmodernism, popular culture studies, and the new cultural history.

Postmodernism is a vast and extremely complex subject.[2] Of the many aspects of the discussion of postmodernism, I will emphasize here only a few "postmodernisms." One of the founding insights of postmodernism is Jean-François Lyotard's: "postmodernism cannot exist . . . without discovery of the 'lack of reality' of reality, together with the invention of other realities."[3] Perhaps the strongest commonality between the wide variety of discourses falling into the category of the postmodern is this: there is neither a primary real world nor one true representation of the world that then becomes the touchstone for the "real" or for the veracity of diverse kinds of representation of reality. What is called the "real" is merely conventional; "reality" is a constructed reality. A related core postmodernism is the radical textualization of reality: the dispersion of reality into text. If the Marxist (and modern) project is to privilege the extralinguistic level of experience, which by definition is primary and to which language is subordinate, there is a strong tendency in postmodernism to see "text" as constituting the primary realm of human experience. To get a handle on this matter, it is necessary that we come to an understanding of "text" different from our ordinary understanding. To postmodernists, the meaning of text expands far beyond the meaning of a piece of writing to include all cultural phenomena: "all events, all practices. Postmodernists consider everything a text."[4] All texts contribute to the construction of and provide access to reality.

My next postmodernism comprises two closely intertwined strands. One strand is the apotheosis of culture, in part because its definition has become so broad and unbounded. There is just "culture," defined by Clifford Geertz as a "network of meanings" that emerges from the apparently least cultural discourses and events.[5] The other strand is the erosion of the boundaries and hierarchical distinctions between high culture and popular culture. Postmodernism's effacement of the distinction between high and popular culture has led to a reevaluation of popular cultural practices as texts which carry significant cultural meaning, and thus to a shift from suspicion and distancing to a positive embrace. This is not to say that all texts are equal or that any text is as significant as any other. It is to say there is no a priori privileged text or set of texts. Cartoons, comics, advertisements, tourism, sport, religious festivals, TV soaps, pop music, and film have, along with the more traditional textual sources, all become part of the expanded text.[6] This leads to the last of my postmodernisms, one of the key concepts of postmodern discourse and of the new cultural history: intertextuality.

Mikhail Bakhtin is one of the seminal theorists of contemporary discussion of intertextuality. Simply put, no text is autonomous and self-contained; one text always alludes to another. To read a text is always to read it in relationship to other texts; all texts belong to a single cultural or discursive formation. In the broadest sense, intertextuality refers to the open-ended possibilities generated by all the discursive practices of a culture, what Bakhtin calls the "ensemble of discourses," the entire matrix within which a text is situated. High and popular culture inform each other. The relation between the two becomes intertextual, in the sense that no text has meaning in itself; meaning emerges from juxtaposition between texts. To put it otherwise, intertextualism operates within all cultural production. The popular converses with the highbrow and vice versa; the "most consecrated figures of the 'high' cultural tradition dialogue with 'low' culture and popular language."[7]

For the new cultural history, the concepts of constructivism, textuality, the expanded text, and intertextuality may be the most important interpretive concepts to be drawn from postmodernist theories. Suffice it to say that these postmodernisms have opened a whole new world of possibilities for reading history of education in any cultural phenomena—and for the opposite, interpreting any cultural phenomena as text in history of education. The new cultural history has the same project Raymond Williams urged upon historians in *The Long Revolution* (1975), but now its emphasis is on the textual dimension of reality, on the inescapable textuality of all sources, and on the fundamental task of interpretation. In Lynn Hunt's important collection of essays, *The New Cultural History* (1989), phenomena like frescoes, autopsies, and parades are interpreted as text in history.[8] In *The Clothing of Clio,* Stephen Bann has argued for the reintegration of all forms of representation—from chronicle to the novel, from taxidermy to painting, photography and film—into the practice of history.[9]

The past decade or so has witnessed an explosion of interest in film as a legitimate field for historical activity.[10] The historians Robert Rosenstone, Robert Sklar, John E. O'Connor, Robert Brent Toplin, and Natalie Zemon Davis, among others, have turned their attention to film as essential source material for social and cultural history. The American Historical Association and the Organization of American Historians have put their imprimatur on film.[11] Since 1989 there have been film review sections in the *American Historical Review* as well as the *Journal of American History.* A conference on history and film organized by the New England Foundation for the Humanities in 1993 brought together more than 800 people—historians, filmmakers, and the general public. I cannot quarrel with Rosenstone's contention that this was "a celebration of an idea whose time [had] come."[12]

But, granted its legitimacy in historiography, how shall we read film? Some historians are traditional and positivist in their approach and hold film to a standard of verisimilitude: "the past as it really was." Other historians choose to elide what Peter Novick has called the "objectivity question." Few have argued as persuasively as Robert Rosenstone on the merits of film for historians. Rosenstone approaches film at the level of discourse. What makes a film "historical" is its willingness to engage the ongoing discourse of history—the issues, ideas, and arguments raised in written histories.[13] For Robert Toplin, films point to contemporary historiographical questions and comment on the discourses that animate historical writing. Film, like written history, "bears markings of the present."[14] I follow Rosenstone and Toplin in this essay.

My thinking about film is to proceed without regard for any strong distinction among texts; it depends upon an understanding of "the complex interactions of meanings" in culture—there are only cultural artifacts in one vast interlocking web of human production. I assume that the school film is a report on the world of education, that all texts on education make up a single discursive field, and that the school film is one element in a broader discursive formation in which all texts have value in the representation of reality, and none are privileged a priori. Like any written academic text about education, the school film is a construction, a way of educational world making that is on the same level of the "real" and occupies the same discursive universe or cultural space with written texts about education. Neither film texts or other texts on education can be studied in isolation; they must be put alongside each other, all taking their place in a single discursive system or semiotic field.

Although I want to call serious attention to the importance of film for educational historiography, I don't want to privilege film. I approach film as one element in an intertextual network, part of an "ensemble of discourses" that includes diverse artifacts of popular culture, literary and artistic texts, historical, psychological, and sociological treatises, and so forth. A new cultural history of education would concern itself with the lateral relations between these diverse discourses.

II.

Dead Poets Society is a joy to look at, a visual feast. The cinematography is marvelous; it has a lush, painterly style of composition. The parade of images—of the New England countryside in two seasons, autumn and winter; of the charismatic English teacher, John Keating (played by Robin Williams) casting a spell on his boys at Welton Preparatory School; of magical scenes and transformations—is seductive. It is difficult to think seriously about DPS . . . until later. The visual experience is so diverting that any thought of resisting it or the possibility of any underlying profundity can be too easily dismissed. DPS is arguably the most significant of all the Hollywood high school films of the 1980s; it is a film of great power that works on several levels. To use Roland Barthes's term, DPS is a plural or "writerly" text, whose meanings are elusive and open to alternative and even contradictory interpretations.

My general orientation to DPS is informed by a phrase from the title of *Resisting Images: Essays on Cinema and History*.[15] "Resisting images" has a double meaning for me. On the one hand, it refers to images that resist our attempts to force a unitary meaning upon them; on the other hand, it refers to our attempts to resist the force of images. The problem then becomes how to develop strategies for reading film that are contrary to the ideological positions constructed in them or that have been overlooked by previous readers. Here, I draw from contemporary literary theory.[16] I find most helpful concepts of plurality and deferral of meaning, which call attention to the ways in which a text works to subvert its apparent meaning, as well as the concept of intertextuality. I give DPS a deconstructive reading which entails the "careful teasing out of warring forces of signification within the text itself."[17] One problem for a critical reading of film is how to address relationships among high and popular culture in a way that allows for a dialogic interaction between texts in different disciplines. Intertextuality is my primary methodological starting point; my reading of DPS is carried out in an aggressively intertextual way. I discuss those aspects of DPS that most delight or provoke me, and I attempt to situate my comments within the movie's narrative, the history of educational ideas, and more general cultural and intellectual history. Without claiming to be an expert in film semiotics, I'm also interested in the rhetorical codes of DPS, in how it works to structure responses in viewers through photography, setting, dialogue, editing, music, and narrative progression.[18]

DPS fits Fredric Jameson's description of the postmodern nostalgia film.[19] But its relationship to postmodernism rests uneasy. Although the narrative unfolds in 1959, DPS is not a film about the 1950s. I

want not to challenge its historicity but to concentrate on what it signifies today. DPS bears markings of the present; it represents distinct
alternative ideological positionings whose conflictual relationship per-
sists at the heart of American education and its culture wars.[20] DPS
addresses some of the most important cultural conflicts of our time—
between self and society, individual and community, self-expression
and institutional constraints; between what Jameson calls freedom
and necessity and what Elizabeth Fox-Genovese calls freedom and
order.[21]

Like most debates on education in the United States—emotional,
polarized discourses—DPS juxtaposes two discourses that are incommensurable: tradition and romanticism. Tradition is epitomized by Mr.
Nolan, the imperious headmaster of Welton. Romanticism is epitomized in the character of John Keating, Welton's maverick English
teacher. With its emphasis on order, authority, discipline, and formalism in education, the film's depiction of tradition reminds us of today's
conservative call for a return to moral absolutism, the Euro-American
canon, and the "basics" in education.[22] With its emphasis on creativity, present lived experience, and self-expression, the depiction of romanticism has many links (unacknowledged in the film) to progressive
education—that branch of progressive education which is devoted to
"self-expression and maximum child growth," resting on a philosophy
of the "concept of Self."[23]

While the fortunes of traditionalism in education ebb and flow
through the decades, its discourses are never far from public debate.
Progressivism in education, on the other hand, must regularly confront exaggerated reports of its premature demise,[24] and even its non-
existence.[25] What DPS brings home forcefully is the sense that progressive education is very much alive by transforming it into
"romanticism." DPS offers another chance to hear the tale within progressive education and thereby recognize the staying power of that
discourse. DPS also offers another chance to renew acquaintance with
the enduring and vital tension between progressivism and traditionalism in American education.

DPS was released in 1989 to popular and critical acclaim. In fact,
its reception can only be called extraordinary. The student audiences
with whom I viewed the film all but gave it a standing ovation. Film
critics broke into superlatives over its depiction of Keating's teaching
and the triumph of romanticism over the totalizing power of Nolan
and tradition. From George F. Will, the critic at *Newsweek*: Keating is

"heroic in his discipline, the purity of his devotion to his vocation, . . . his emulable stance toward life." In the opinion of Stephen Holden, a film critic for the *New York Times*, Keating is "the sort of visionary-rebel teacher that all of us, if we are fortunate, will have encountered at some point in our education." From Robert Seidenberg in *American Film*: "Only the most callous could scoff at [Keating's] and the film's credo: Poetry is rapture. Without it, we are doomed." And from Tom O'Brien in *Commonweal*: "[Keating's] romanticism works. . . . When will someone create a Pulitzer or Nobel prize for the kind of teaching that [Keating] embodies?"[26] The continuing appeal of progressive education is nowhere more evident than in these reviews. It is clear that progressive education still has a firm foothold among young people and liberal intellectuals.

I see DPS with different eyes.

To paraphrase Raymond Williams's claim about texts, no text is a unity. Williams identifies three moments within a text—"dominant," "emergent," and "residual"—each pulling the text in a different direction.[27] Film reviewers have imposed a unity on DPS and simply privileged the most obvious moments in the film. But I don't think DPS is a unity. And it is possible to resist its dominant moments. To put it differently, what we encounter in the reception of DPS is an instance of a film finding its "ideal reader," a reader who agrees implicitly with the author's assumptions and point of view or intention—or what the reader takes to be the author's intention.[28]

If DPS is strongly interrogated, if we resist becoming the "mock" or ideal reader its brilliant images invite us to become and privilege its emergent or residual features, we see more interesting and ambivalent things going on. Keating and romanticism have been too quickly and unreflectively celebrated, and Nolan and tradition have been too quickly and unreflectively dismissed. Keating incarnates not only the genius of the Romantic sensibility, but also its problems. Romantic, progressive, liberationist pedagogy turns out to be no less and perhaps more problematic than the ostensibly reactionary traditional education with which it is contrasted. There are, however, many more layers of meaning in DPS, which make it an exemplary text in the history of American education.

III.

Welton Preparatory School is located in the New England countryside on an idyllic suburban campus far from the "satanic city."[29] Welton is a sheltered enclave, insulated from the complications and distractions of cosmopolis—racial and ethnic conflict, poverty, crime, environmental blight. DPS deliberately ignores the reality of the external world. It excludes all background references to political or public events. There are no African Americans, Latinos, Jews, or other racial or ethnic minorities in this suburb. This is a WASP world—a white Protestant suburb beyond the reach of the carless urban underclass. As the camera admires immaculately tended green fields and chaste, snow-swept lawns, it evokes a nostalgic yearning for a suburbia that existed in a simpler, more innocent time: "a pristine past of Protestant decency . . . , a perfect world of benevolent families and happy children."[30] But DPS says good-bye to the myth of the smiling suburb. In this closed world, the power of teachers and parents is exaggerated, the subjectivity of white middle-class adolescents is tightly focused, conflict over polarized and deeply held educational beliefs reverberates, and an Edenic paradise reveals a malevolent underside.

DPS begins with the symbolic power of ceremony and ritual in perpetuating tradition, order, and patriarchal authority—the lighting of a candle, the "light of knowledge," handed down from the old boys to the new boys, and the procession of banners advances into Welton's main hall. In the next few scenes, a world is created—a world constructed on the four pillars of tradition, honor, discipline, and excellence, representing the putative archaic and static value system of Welton. These words appear on the banners which, accompanied by bagpipes and an orchestrated processional, are ceremoniously carried down the aisle of the chapel. One of the boys, Cameron, carries the first banner, "tradition." In fact, only "tradition" and "discipline" are distinctly visible; "honor" and "excellence" are barely distinguishable, indicating that tradition and discipline are the two most significant virtues to instill in the boys. From the first scenes, tradition is heavily inflected with conservative, even reactionary, meanings and implications. Welton is an intensely focused community, one that forcefully imposes itself on the minds and bodies of the boys, who are programmed to think and behave unquestionably on the basis of its axioms. At Welton the main goal of education is transmission. There is no place for self-expression, lived experience, or independent thinking. We glimpse the boys slogging through a prescribed curriculum: English literature and poetry, math, science, and history—and Latin, *the* subject emblematic of the classical tradition. Welton's teachers rely on unquestioned obedience to authority.

Welton is disciplinary society. Michel Foucault has called our attention to the microtechnologies of discipline, which position not only the body of knowledge but the body itself.[31] Welton's disciplinary practices are inscribed on the body; they manifest themselves in the way the boys walk, sit, and stand. Desexualizing is another method by which Welton constructs the boys' bodies. Welton channels the boys' sexuality into a safe place—sports, and acts *in loco parentis* as a guardian of sexual boundaries. No girls are allowed to enter Welton's grounds; the boys are chaperoned if they leave the grounds. Foucault also reminds us that disciplinary modalities construct docile bodies by means of the *gaze*. Welton insinuates its gaze everywhere into the lives of its students, seeking to displace idiosyncratic values with values defined by Welton. All of Welton's teachers act as wardens, but "super-vision" and enforcement of the rules are in the hands of Nolan, Foucault's Napoleonic character, "the individual who looms over everything with a single gaze which no detail, however minute, can escape."[32] Like the headmasters of the best New England preparatory schools as described by the historian Robert Hampel, Nolan enjoys "untrammeled power" and seems to rule by divine right.[33] Nolan is the ultimate embodiment of the *gaze* that watches, judges, and normalizes all of Welton's inhabitants, teachers as well as students.

The chief end of Welton is not intellectual development. The boys' *habitus,* the gift of their family background, already ensures that they possess the essential cultural capital—the disposition, habits, and skills necessary for academic success. The chief end of Welton is to reinforce and add on to their cultural capital and to keep them on track. Welton's is a metacurriculum that has served the northeastern Protestant upper class very well in terms of Pierre Bourdieu's theory of cultural reproduction. Except in Neil Perry's case, Welton is not a vehicle for social mobility. In a class society characterized by a social hierarchy, the primary function of schooling is the reproduction of that hierarchy; in such a society, education is not necessarily a ticket to opportunity so much as it is a ticket to where you were before (or where your father was before). Following Bourdieu, it can be said of Welton's boys that "the most culturally privileged find their way into institutions capable of reinforcing their advantage."[34]

Welton simultaneously constructs and normalizes the future Harvard man. It is a school whose unyielding commitment to tradition produces graduates who will go on to the Ivy League. This, Nolan proclaims, is why parents send their children to Welton. This is the criterion by which Welton judges itself and its program. What matters is results. Nolan possesses an unshakable belief in Welton's mission, a clear vision of the product of a Welton education, and a ruthlessly instrumental attitude toward the means by which the product is to be achieved. Nolan epitomizes Max Weber's instrumental rationality, which is obsessed with the perfection of the means without ever questioning the ends.[35]

Welton requires that the boys suppress all that is vital, spontaneous, imaginative—in a phrase, all that is adolescent. The boys learn to obey orders and to repress their individuality; Welton knows self-expression only as disorder and transgression. This regime of truth is justified in terms of the boys' good. Like St. Elmo's Preparatory School in *Society's Children: A Study of Ressentiment in the Secondary School,* Welton is preparing its boys to enter the "heavenly city of gold."[36] Thus Welton answers the question posed in this classic: "whether it is more important to enjoy one's adolescence or to surrender it to the anticipation of one's future."[37] And the boys' parents, that is, their fathers, are complicit. (In DPS, as in America generally in the 1950s, fathers carry the sign of "parents.") Welton stands for the perpetuation of WASP hegemony through the education and, one might say, the sacrifice of the sons upon the altar of their fathers' ambitions.

One subtext of DPS is *épater le bourgeois.* As in many Hollywood high school movies of the 1980s that belittle parents (for example, *Ferris Bueller's Day Off, Teachers, Stand and Deliver, The Breakfast Club),* Welton parents are portrayed as foolish, cruel, or uncaring.

The parent-bashing in DPS has an intriguing class bias. The worst-offending parent in DPS is Tom Perry, the parvenu, anxiety-driven lower-middle-class striver who obsessively tries to control Neil's education to secure his future economic success and social status as a physician. Mr. Perry is the self-made man who once stood solidly at the center of American society. His ethic, the old Protestant ethic—work, self-discipline, sacrifice—is that of the post-World War II nouveau middle-class generation, who had forgone living and had denied themselves for the sake of their male children. He finds incomprehensible Neil's "wasting . . . time with this absurd acting business" when he "has opportunities [his father] never even dreamed of," and when Mr. and Mrs. Perry have sacrificed so much for him. Mr. Perry is one of Vance Packard's "status seekers." His is the definitive film portrayal of middle-class angst, the "fear of falling."[38] But no pity is shown. Mr.

Perry's ambition for Neil—Welton, Harvard, medical school—is portrayed as contemptible and heartless.

The Perrys are a wonderfully dysfunctional family. Mr. Perry is a despot. Mrs. Perry is a submissive, mute presence who cannot mediate between her husband and son. The Perrys' spacious home is cold and loveless, a space of sadness, the ultimate site of the loss of self. Thus DPS participates in dethroning the ideal of happy suburban domesticity and traditional family values which was so powerfully promulgated in popular American TV sitcoms of the 1950s like *Father Knows Best* and whose disappearance American conservatives lament today.

IV.

DPS recreates the world of the classic New England boarding school as a site of extreme authority, austere discipline, postponed desire, and bounded rationality. This world, represented by the monumental stone buildings of Welton, is set off by Weir against a very visual passage of time, symbolized by the falling leaves of autumn, the first snowfall, and the geese flying south for the winter. Unlike the geese, who can escape the New England winter, Welton boys must stay and endure the rigors of a world in which the goal of admission to Harvard or Princeton is premier. Into this world comes John Keating, the new English teacher, a former Welton boy. Keating challenges Welton's core values and axiomatic principles. He represents a certain ideological expression of cultural values that is the radical antithesis of Welton's cultural formations. Keating's romantic discourses belong to aesthetic postmodernism: the attempt to expand the aesthetic or poetic to embrace the whole of reality. He is a romantic in a world of realists.

Romanticism is a highly contested site.[39] Keating's version is associated with the enterprises of a select list of romantic poets. Deploying the stirring individualistic language of Whitman, Thoreau, Frost, Tennyson, Wordsworth, and Coleridge, Keating sets the boys in his poetry class off on a quest for self-expression, self-discovery, and self-actualization. (The screenwriter, Schulman, has discovered in the romantics a source of progressive education overlooked even in Lawrence Cremin's *The Transformation of The School.) "Carpe diem*, boys," "seize the day," Keating exhorts his students; "gather ye rosebuds while ye may"; and "make your lives extraordinary." Keating appeals to the boys' repressed poetic nature. His credo is Whitman's: "The powerful play goes on and you may contribute a verse." He calls down Thoreau to inspire the boys to "live deep and suck out all the marrow of life."

Keating's orientation to education is the antithesis of Nolan's. To Nolan, education is preparation *for* life; to Keating, education *is* life. Keating has a different answer to the question of "whether it is more important to enjoy one's adolescence or to surrender it to the anticipation of one's future." Nolan is uncomprehending. Welton boys have the world at their fingertips. Why change anything? Nolan articulates Welton's core belief during a conversation in which he warns Keating about the dangers of unorthodox teaching methods. "Boys are very impressionable," he says, and he lashes out against Keating's notion that the point of education is to think for yourself: "For boys this age? Not on your life. Tradition, John. Discipline. Prepare them for college and the rest will take care of itself." Keating is blissfully indifferent toward this foundational ethic of Welton.

Welton is the traditional school anathematized in progressive education tracts like *The Child-Centered School*: a "place of fears, restraints, and long, weary hours of suppression."[40] The reality principle dominates the lives of its boys. They have had long practice in deferring pleasure, in working hard in the present for remote goals not of their own choosing. These are adolescents who have had their lives predetermined; the days and years have already been inscribed, and they are not the authors. To get to Harvard, the boys have endured years of an arid, regimented, and stultifying education and have paid a price in inhibition, repression, and arrested social development.

Keating taps into what Norman Mailer has called the uniquely American "subterranean river of . . . ferocious, lonely, and romantic desires bubbling just beneath the surface of a self-repressive middle class."[41] He attempts to give the boys some degree of personal control over their own bodies and feelings. He awakens their dormant desires and fills them with new energy and spirit. In violation of Welton's rules, the boys decide to resuscitate Keating's long-banned Dead Poets Society. The boys' newfound sense of freedom and adventure is exquisitely visually portrayed in the scene where they flee Welton and its wardens to find the Indian cave. In this scene, with the night fog rising, Weir evokes a sense of an earlier, more natural time, a time unencumbered by tradition or discipline. The boys, their identities concealed under hooded jackets, run through the mist. Their path is not a direct route, and they must weave carefully around the trees and down the hills on their way to confront the unknown. This scene conveys the bold path the boys must take to free themselves from the grasp of tradition. This is a brilliant representation of youth's own image of itself in flight from a decadent and oppressive society.

The boys find in the cave a space of freedom and a moratorium denied them at Welton. They are free to shed tradition, discipline, and their Welton identity. Here, there are no rules to follow; there is no surveillance. Their creativity and individuality can be freely expressed. They can take up Keating's challenge—to experience life, find their unique voice, contribute their verse, assert their authentic self, or engage in self-refashioning. The boys revel in the new freedom available to them. The cave scenes reverberate with echoes of Bakhtin's account of "carnival."[42] The boys transgressively smoke, rebuke their parents, and profane the voice of authority and the sacred discourses of Welton. They discover new possibilities for self-expression in music, dance, and poetry. They sing, dance, smoke pipes, bang a tom-tom, recite poetry, and attempt to woo girls with poetry. The images are masterfully packaged and hard to resist.

Keating has introduced the boys to a new world. But then they are left to their own devices to reconcile new and old, freedom and necessity. Keating's teachings attempt to subvert Welton's hegemonic maintenance of oppressive relations of power, one of which is between parent and child. The romantic dreams inspired by Keating and the path dictated by Neil's father, vying with Keating for his son's attention, deference, and respect, are at war within Neil's soul and eventually lead to his suicide and Keating's downfall. (Of Keating's effect on his boys, Foucault's comment is apt: "People know what they do, . . . but what they don't know is what what they do does."[43]) Nolan blames Keating for inflaming Neil's imagination and subverting Welton's necessary discipline and proven values. He mounts a campaign to chasten the boys, contain the spread of infection, and rid Welton of Keating, the agent of infection.

In scenes reminiscent of McCarthyism and the reactionary political climate of pervasive conformity and blacklisting in the 1950s, the boys are forced by Nolan, on threat of expulsion, to sign confessions denouncing Keating. This is the penultimate scene of DPS. Its last scenes are a showdown between Nolan and Keating and Keating's boys. Nolan takes over Keating's poetry class and orders the boys to "turn to the realists." In effect, Nolan tries to turn back the clock, to take the boys back to the beginning—to a time before Keating. But the boys have changed. As Keating is leaving, one by one, the boys, his disciples, Knox, Meeks, Pitts, led by Todd Anderson, who had been the most introverted of the boys, erupt. The boys stomp on top of their desks and salute Keating, their dismissed hero, "Captain, my Captain." Nolan, whirling around like a puppet on a string, screams for order. The boys are heedless. Nolan orders Keating to leave. Keating complies but has the last word. Smiling enigmatically, he says "Thank you, boys. Thank you." The film ends with a shot of the boys, now most of the class except for the unheroic, philistine Cameron, posing astride the tops of their desks. The credits roll. The audience applauds.

V.

Up to this point, DPS appears to be a film with a straightforward agenda: to demonize Nolan and portray the discourse of tradition as a totally negative force, perpetuating ignorance, hindering creativity, and crushing the spirit; and to celebrate Keating and the counterdiscourse of romanticism. But the ending is strange. What does it mean? What do the boys mean by standing atop their desks? What does Keating mean by "Thank you, boys"? What happens when the boys come down from their desks? DPS ends in such ambiguity that any meaning is possible. The ending is an example of Douglas Sirk's "unhappy happy ending," which "encourages the audience to think further, even after the curtain goes down."[44]

Weir, who has among his credits *The Year of Living Dangerously* and *Picnic at Hanging Rock,* is a deeply intentional director. The ending of DPS may be ambiguous, but it is not irresolute. As the credits roll, the bagpipes play a mournful tune, signaling a retreat from romance. This is Weir the ironist, finally grown weary of Keating and the pedagogy of romantic individualism. In retrospect, the film's strongest moments have always been ironic. But the brilliance of the images and the acting holds spectators captive, unable to critically explore exactly what pedagogical statements about Keating and romanticism are being made. Certainly, DPS repudiates Nolan and the grand narrative of tradition in education. But what about Keating and the romantic narrative of individual liberation and self-expression? DPS invites our admiration and then our sympathy for Keating and the boys. To accept the invitation, however, is to forfeit further reflection. As an example of a progressive liberationist pedagogy, DPS is hopelessly compromised; Keating's teachings and the Romantic narrative of individual liberation and of the free, self-fashioning adolescent are wickedly subverted.

Any notion of the liberation of the individual is always first about the construction of a particular notion of the individual. Keating assumes the strong postmodernist view of the social construction of the self: Richard Rorty's or Stephen Greenblatt's freely self-creating individual. To Keating, the boys possess an essential poetic nature that, once freed from the dry bones of Welton's tradition, can achieve creativity and self-fulfillment. But this turns out to be an illusion. When we view DPS again, what actually happens in the crucial scenes in the cave? How do Keating's boys carry out his injunction to "contribute a verse" and "suck out all the marrow of life"? The boys' self-expression in poetry, music, and dance is banal and trite. The cave scenes belong to Charlie (Charles Dalton). To refashion himself as more virile and carnal, the hormonally overloaded but inhibited Charlie assumes the name "Nuwanda" and daubs his face and chest with war paint (lipstick) to look like a (movie) Indian. It's fun. It's exciting. It may even be therapeutic. But it's a bogus individualism, a desperate craving for attention. This is not quite liberating one's authentic self but finding an already inscripted form of self, the self as a "recognition seeking, commodified spectacle."[45] In the end, to borrow from Frank Lentricchia's critique of Greenblatt's notion of self-fashioning, the boys settle for a "holiday from reality, a safely sealed place reserved for the expression of aesthetic anarchy, a long weekend that defuses the radical implications of their unhappiness."[46]

The pedagogic project of individual liberation depicted in DPS is shortsighted. Keating may have an inspirational vision of a liberatory education, but he cannot translate his vision in any practical manner to effect change at Welton. Keating never moves beyond slogans and exhortations to a critique of Welton's dominant structures or ideology, nor does he lead the boys into any structural or elaborated understanding of Welton's system of oppression. Keating's teachings prescribe a formula that medicates the audience into accepting the possibility of school reform solely through individual effort. DPS valorizes the realm of the personal. It denies that a collective project might have any relation to school reform. The boys' resistance is largely confined within the privacy of the cave or consists of isolated acts by individuals. This is resistance without political insight, and thus it does not threaten Welton's hegemonic hold on the boys.

Why does the audience applaud? DPS represents an ideal of liberatory education that provides pleasure and appeals to the audience's desires. (Americans, we might say, with Michael Wood, "are vulnerable to glamorous pleas for the self in the way the French are vulnerable to invocations of logic, or the English to appeals to fair play."[47]) DPS privatizes institutional and structural problems and attempts to solve them through heroic individual action. This is romantic illusion—the illusion of individuals creating their own freedom through their own individual activity. It is an illusion that the revolt against Nolan can be won by one teacher and a handful of adolescents who never attempt to gain allies or contest the basic hegemonic discourses, structures, and hierarchies of authority which oppress them and which deny them their individuality and freedom of expression in the first place. DPS leads the audience toward passive acceptance of a vision of a liberatory pedagogy that is completely uncritical and unthreatening to the status quo. That the audience applauds is an example of ideology in Althusser's meaning: the expression of the imaginary relation of individuals to their real conditions of existence. We could argue that the audience's response bears out theories of the Frankfurt School about movies as the opium of the people or, to change the metaphor, the placebo of the people.

"You will learn to think for yourself," Keating admonishes the boys. There is a striking contradiction, however, between Keating's discourses on free thinking, what he actually practices, and what the boys actually practice. Keating never extends his critique of Welton's poetry curriculum to include an interrogation of the Euro-American romantic poetry canon itself. Keating has as uncritical a view of romanticism as Nolan has of tradition. Neither examines the legacy he wants to transmit. Keating's status as a member of Welton's faculty authorizes him to create officiating discourses. It is Keating who contextualizes the poetry of the romantics to induce "radical" readings. It is Keating who legitimizes the romantic narrative of individual emancipation. Yet his interpretation of Wordsworth, Coleridge, Whitman, Thoreau et al., is susceptible to other interpretations. Keating never introduces the boys to any alternative ways of thinking about the romantic poets; he simply initiates them into his own version of the romantics. "Think for yourself" becomes think like Keating. None of the boys develop into independent or critical thinkers. Even Charlie–Nuwanda, the boldest of the boys, says to Keating after the "phone call from God" scene, "I thought you'd like it." The tormented Neil Perry, who exists in the schizophrenic rush of time that Jameson identifies as a central feature of postmodern culture, is too deluded or impetuous an adolescent to be thought of as a critical thinker.

Keating's version of romanticism is synonymous with the expansion of freedom, the liberation of minds, and individual autonomy. But DPS raises the question of whether Keating's practices are exempt from questions of power and imposition. Jennifer Gore's observation about the claims of critical pedagogy, the latest turn of "progressive education," is apposite: "No theory or method or form of pedagogy can ever be innocent; no approach to teaching is *inherently* liberating or free of the effects of power" (my emphasis). [48] There are no inherently liberating or oppressive pedagogical practices. Any practice is co-optable, and any is capable of becoming a source of resistance. The liberatory status of Keating's pedagogical discourses remains a matter for inquiry, not an a priori pronouncement.

Nolan was right; the boys are very impressionable. One could argue that Keating's success as a teacher is due to his understanding of adolescents' emotional needs. The conclusion of DPS can be viewed in terms of the dethroning of one authority, Nolan, but submission to another, Keating. Adolescents in blue blazers with the school crest, school ties, white shirts, gray slacks, and black shoes stomping on desks and hailing Keating as "Captain! My Captain!" is a powerful semiotic message of the vulnerability or susceptibility of adolescents to the power of a charismatic teacher. (Recall Maggie Smith's overwhelming performance in *The Prime of Miss Jean Brodie*.)

Keating's romantic pedagogy finally dissolves into a hedonistic pedagogy of pleasure, selfishness, and self-absorption.[49] Thus DPS depicts that new cultural factor which emerged in the United States in the 1950s—narcissism. The late Christopher Lasch's *The Culture of Narcissism: American Life in an Age of Diminishing Expectations* is a profoundly unsettling attempt to explore the implications.[50]

VI.

The point is conformity. Even though the herd may go "that's bad" . . . Swim against the stream, . . . be extraordinary.

John Keating

The [mass] media give substance to and thus intensify narcissistic dreams of fame and glory, encourage the common man to identify himself with the stars and to hate the "herd," and make it more and more difficult for him to accept the banality of everyday existence.

Christopher Lasch

Juxtaposed, these quotations resonate with reciprocal relations. The two texts, *Dead Poets Society* and *The Culture of Narcissism,* complement and help define one another.

Welton is the epitome of conformity to the past and to tradition. Keating's call to "seize the day" and "make your lives extraordinary" signals a movement away from tradition and into an exciting, unknown future. All of Keating's discourses embody romantic ideals, which inform his boys' revolt against tradition and the banality of everyday existence. DPS is "the media [giving] substance to" and intensifying "narcissistic dreams of fame and glory." Neil's dream of fame and glory and his inability to accept the "banality of everyday existence" lead to his suicide. Nuwanda's (Charlie's) quest for fame and glory lead to his expulsion from Welton. Their acts are made to seem heroic and in keeping with Keating's philosophy of *carpe diem.* Lasch encourages a different perspective: "The preoccupation with self-fulfillment represents unseemly self-absorption, romanticism run rampant . . . [a] dead end of narcissistic preoccupation with the self."[51]

Yes, Keating's boys defiantly stand up to Nolan. But after the boys step down from their desks, what message will they have extracted from Keating's teachings? The boys may have gained a greater appreciation of some romantic poets, but to what enlightened political or social actions will this lead them? Keating's discourses play into the hands of the culture of narcissism and the construction of an individual subjectivity that Jameson calls a characteristic of the consumer society of our time: the decentered subject who experiences time not as a continuum (past, present, future) but as a disconnected series of perpetual presents. There is little at the conclusion of the film to indication that the lessons taught in Keating's classroom will have any lasting effects on his students. In fact it is safe to assume that the 1959 graduating class of Welton will move on to become the lawyers, bankers, doctors, and stockbrokers of the 1980s with nothing more than a distant memory of one lost comrade from Welton and the recurring whisper of the Captain: *"Carpe diem,* boys! Seize the day!"

VII.

DPS ends in such ambiguity, however, that all meaning is put in jeopardy and any meaning is possible. It even becomes possible to say that the final scene is not the defining moment.

Michael Wood observes that popular movies "take up wishes, dreads, and preoccupations that are loosely . . . scattered about ordinary life" and "allow them a quick masked passage across our consciousness." They "permit us to look without looking at things we can neither face fully nor entirely disavow."[52] Take the "social drama" depicted in DPS.[53] This should be moved from the periphery to the center of our attention. A few scenes "permit us to look without looking at things we can neither face fully nor entirely disavow." They involve the suburban public high school where Chris is a cheerleader for the football team and the property of Chet Danbury, the star of the team, and whom Knox courts danger, even death, to pursue. Weir's construction of the sexually mobile Chris is provocative, but I want to foreground the depiction of the cultural and class conflict among white middle-class adolescents.

Let's juxtapose the scenes in the cave with those at the party at Chet's spacious house. These provide some of the most telling images in DPS. The images of divided spaces are superimposed upon each other in such a way as to shock us into new recognitions. White suburbia may look classless, but there is no common white middle-class culture. There is a clearly demarcated class line, a strict segregation of class cultures. Between the boys from Welton and the boys from the public high school, there is nothing in common. The Welton boys seem innocent and unworldly. They owe something to tradition and discipline. They recite poetry. They share cookies and raisins. They smoke pipes, ogle a Playboy-type poster. Now recall the party at Chet's house. Knox, in pursuit of his dream girl, Chris, enters the space of Chet and his pals. Chet's house is their "cave," where Chet and his pals are free to express themselves. But these boys are scarier than the Welton boys. At Chet's party, we glimpse an abyss of disorder, anger, and aggression. (The film's visual coding of the boys at Chet's party—the facial and corporeal expressions and the barbarian horned helmets—reinforces this interpretation.) There are no poetry readings here, no cookies and raisins, just sex and booze and incipient violence. (Chet to Knox: "Next time I see you, you die.") Chet's pals seem to have acquired neither discipline nor a sense of tradition. They are even estranged from language; they butt heads. These adolescents possess what Lasch calls "a void within" and "boundless repressed rage." On Saturday nights they attempt "to beat sluggish flesh to life" by chugging vodka and beer chasers. To quote David James, from a different but relevant discussion, these scenes "detail the grievances, the psychic hopelessness and rage of that group which was excluded from all the post-sixties social reform rhetoric: white, heterosexual, lower-middle-class males."[54]

The images of the boys at Chet's house reflect a state of discontent among white male adolescents in suburbia that is in some ways as sobering as the discontent of youth in the inner city. Adolescents like Chet and his friends are wasted. Not knowing what to do with them, they are warehoused in high schools. The deindustrialization of America and the disappearance of many middle-level white-collar subprofessional jobs may engender resentments and desires that can easily be oriented toward redemption through a strong leader. The Hobbesian potential of adolescents like Chet needs to be approached as by Paul Goodman in *Growing Up Absurd* (1956) or by Joan Didion more recently—with empathy as well as terror—for full comprehension.[55] Although DPS presents Americans with a worry that only briefly sees the light of day, we might be wise to begin preparing for it now.

So Nolan has been defied. But this is not the end of the story. The unruliness of public school boys and the narcissism of private school boys inevitably calls forth a conservative counter-reformation; the Nolans of America are only temporarily defeated. Capitalizing on popular sentiment and discontent, conservatives who urge a return to tradition, discipline, absolutist moral values, and the "basics" in education have reasserted themselves more aggressively than before, while educational progressives are largely on the defensive. This brings us to the issue of what Lawrence Grossberg calls the "politics of pedagogy" and the "pedagogy of politics."[56] In their commitment to any position they believe to be liberatory and anti-authoritarian, progressives force the legitimate need for "tradition, discipline" to find conservative outlets. They seem to have limited comprehension of the appeal of tradition and discipline at the present historical juncture and are thus implicated in the success of the conservative restoration. Some progressives, however, are beginning to acknowledge other possibilities. According to influential critical theorist Henry A. Giroux, a traditional respect for standards, discipline, civic virtue, and family values must become an essential ingredient of any radical educational project that seeks to compete with conservatives for the public mind.[57]

VIII.

The present educational situation . . . confronts us with the age–long conflict: Society? . . . Self ? . . . Which shall orient educational reconstruction? . . . If neither one alone, how shall the two be reconciled? . . . Corresponding

to these two conflicting concepts of orientation are two others of method. . . .
Conformity? . . . Self–expression?

Harold Rugg and Ann Shumaker

This was written more than seventy years ago and remains unimpugnable; the school remains the site of some of the central cultural issues of *fin-de-siècle* America.

In the history of ideas, it seems that a fairly small fund of essential attitudes, if not ideas, is repeated time and again—variations on the same note.[58] Americans seem to be locked into a spiral of intellectual history in which educational philosophies alternate as the inadequacies of each become apparent. Two responses illuminate the different sides of the problem. One response, Nolan's, is that tradition must be preserved and passed on. It is something precious, the cement that binds society, that links one generation to another, that provides stability to our lives. Any attack on tradition is an unmitigated disaster. The other response, Keating's, is that the dissolution of tradition is emancipatory, that at bottom tradition is only constraint which stifles individual creativity and hinders human possibilities. In DPS we're forced to choose between these opposing, polarized pedagogical worlds. We seem to be constantly trying to reconcile contradictory sets of values or to redress an imbalance between hierarchy and equality, self and society, self-expression and conformity, and freedom and order, without ever arriving at a stable equilibrium that satisfies anyone for very long. One might well take this venerable and ongoing spiral to be one of the master themes of educational thought in the United States.[59] DPS brings up the conflict again, a conflict most educationists nowadays seem to be reluctant to address at all.

While I hope my interpretation of DPS has contributed something to our understanding of the history of American education after World War II, its contribution, finally, is not in identifying "truths," though certainly it may do that, but in provoking thought and conversation. I don't presume to give *the* meaning of DPS for understanding recent American educational history, but I do suggest some of its possible meanings. Given the problematic nature of "meaning" in this postmodern age, this is about all we can hope for, but it may be enough to continue the conversation about movies after the movie is over.

Postscript. By the conventions of the genre, I believe I am now obliged to offer a positive program accompanied by some appropriate hortatory injunctions.

I would like to see a dialogue between historians of education and film. As Joyce Appleby, Lynn Hunt, and Margaret Jacob argue, historians cannot be isolationist. Historians cannot quarantine their texts—or other texts.[60] The classifications of academic disciplines cannot stop us from drawing upon philosophy, literary theory, or film. I would like historians of education to welcome film as text. To treat film seriously does not mean sacrificing pleasure; there is pleasure in taking film seriously. As Bill Nichols observes, the pleasure of critical inquiry into film is like the pleasure one gets from taking an exhilarating journey: "The possibility that we will bring back knowledge of value . . . makes the journey not only exhilarating but essential."[61]

The integration of film into our research, practice, and discourse can only broaden and deepen our histories and invigorate our classroom teaching strategies. In the first place, treating film as text in history raises questions about the epistemological status of history—its constructed and rhetorical aspect—that should be of concern to all historians of education. In the second place, we must be concerned because film occupies a privileged space in our culture. Films, with written histories, as Rosenstone argues, are the chief carriers of historical messages in our culture. It may even be that our historical memory seems now to be determined primarily by film imagery. For example, where not too long ago when the subject was education, we might have expected from a reputable journal of opinion a reference to, say, John Dewey, today it's a reference to a film. Thus, the cover of *New Republic*, 17 June 1996, headlining a review of a half-dozen books on the urgent need to reform public secondary education, shouts "Stand and Deliver." In the third place, as teachers, we must talk to students, and their parents, whose access to educational discourse, if not whose life, in important respects, is dominated by the image industry.

The issue, I want to repeat, is not a competition over whether film or written text is the better medium for making meaning from the remains of the past. Film does not replace written history but stands alongside it. Film expands our repertoire of alternative descriptions about the world of education. Of course a film is not a book. An image is not a word. Film cannot do what a book does. But conversely, a book cannot do what a film does. To cite Rosenstone again, the "past did not just mean—it sounded and looked and moved as well."[62] Films can potentially carry ideas and information with more power than the written word, and more effectively than the written word. Thus, some school films capture the daily life, the personal relationships, the lived encounters of classrooms, in ways our written histories do not, cannot do. They reveal things that we historians cannot see (or choose not to see) or cannot see as well, or see but not tell as well. Films like *Teachers, Stand and Deliver, Fast Times at Ridgemont High, Ferris Bueller's Day Off,* and *The Breakfast Club* provide encounters with teachers, parents, and adolescents and a thick description of high schools that histories of education cannot even approximate. We have not begun to exploit the possibilities of film. There is a rich archive waiting for historians of education to explore in film.[63]

Worlds are made, not simply found. Can only written discourse assume the value of "text"? Is written history a privileged form of access to the "real"? Pierre Sorlin, among others, has criticized impoverished conceptions of the real that omit the reality of what is imagined. Bourdieu has also stressed the importance of imagination in the construction of social reality. As Hayden White argues, both film and written history are constructions: "It is only the medium that differs, not the way in which messages are produced."[64] Of course, I do not regard films as independent statements regarding the past. Film must be supplemented by written histories as well as other texts and accompanied by critical commentary. Movies have no immunities. Like any other form of representation, they still must answer to us and to our historical criticism. Finally, as Richard Rorty puts it, it is not so much the form of discourse that is critical—written, oral, or visual—but the willingness to invent stories, tell stories, and keep the conversation going. The risk? Too many words, after all.

Notes

1   Robert A. Rosenstone, *Revisioning History: Film and the Construction of a New Past* (Princeton, 1995), p. 4.

2   Entry to the enormous literature might start with Thomas Docherty, ed., *Postmodernism: A Reader* (New York, 1993); Hal Foster, ed., *The Anti-Aesthetic: Essays in Postmodern Culture* (Seattle, 1983); E. Ann Kaplan, ed., *Postmodernism and Its Discontents* (London, 1988); and Pauline M. Rosenau, *Post–Modernism and the Social Sciences* (Princeton, 1992).

3   "Answering the Question: What Is Postmodernism?" in Docherty, p. 43.

4   Rosenau, *Post–Modernism and the Social Sciences*, pp. xiv, 35–36.

5   Richard W. Fox and T. J. Jackson Lears, eds., *The Power of Culture: Critical Essays in American History* (Chicago, 1993), pp. 1–3; Aletta Biersack, "Local Knowledge, Local History: Geertz and Beyond," ch. 3, in Lynn Hunt, ed., *The New Cultural History* (Berkeley, 1989); Peter Burke, *History and Social Theory* (Ithaca, N.Y., 1992), pp. 118–125.

6   John Storey, *An Introductory Guide to Cultural Theory and Popular Culture* (Athens, Ga., 1993), pp. 15–18, 156–158.

7   Robert Stam, "Mikhail Bakhtin and Left Cultural Critique," in Kaplan, *Postmodernism and Its Discontents,* pp. 132–133; Rosenau, *Post-Modernism and the Social Sciences,* pp. 35–36.

8   Warren Susman, *Culture as History: The Transformation of American Society in the Twentieth Century* (New York, 1984).

9   *The Clothing of Clio: A Study of the Representation of History in Nineteenth-Century Britain and France* (Cambridge, England, 1984).

10   E.g., Robert Sklar and Charles Musser, eds., *Resisting Images: Essays on Cinema and History* (Philadelphia, 1989); John E. O'Connor, ed., *Image as Artifact: The Historical Analysis of Film and Television* (Malabar, Fla., 1990); Phillip Rollins, ed., *Hollywood as Historian: American Film in Cultural Context* (Lexington, Ky., 1983); Douglas Kellner and Michael Ryan, *Camera Politica: The Politics and Ideology of Contemporary Hollywood Film* (Bloomington, Ind., 1988); Robert B. Toplin, *History by Hollywood: The Use and Abuse of the American Past* (Baltimore, 1996).

11   E.g., *American Historical Review*, 93 (1988): 1173–1227 with articles by Rosenstone, O'Connor, Toplin, David Herlihy, and Hayden White. Even earlier, in the mid-1970s, Lawrence A. Cremin was urging historians to study "configurations" of education which would significantly include radio, TV, and film. *Traditions of American Education* (New York, 1977), pp. 105–106.

And see *American Education: The Metropolitan Experience, 1876–1980* (New York, 1988), pp. 331–337.

12   Quoted in Daniel J. Walkowitz, "Telling the Story," *Perspectives: Newsletter of the American Historical Association*, 31 (1993): 1.

13   Robert A. Rosenstone, "Film Reviews," *American Historical Review*, 94 (1989): 1031; and 97 (1992): 1138.

14   Robert B. Toplin, "The Filmmaker as Historian," *American Historical Review*, 93 (1988): 1219.

15   Sklar and Musser, *Resisting Images*, p. 5.

16   Terry Eagleton, *Literary Theory: An Introduction* (Minneapolis, 1983); Raman Selden, *A Reader's Guide to Contemporary Literary Theory* (Brighton, England, 1985); Dominick LaCapra, *History and Criticism* (London, 1985).

17   Barbara Johnson, *The Critical Difference: Essays in the Contemporary Rhetoric of Reading* (Baltimore, 1980), p. 5

18   J. Dudley Andrew, *Concepts in Film Theory* (Oxford, England, 1984); Charles Metz, *Film Language: A Semiotics of the Cinema* (Chicago, 1974).

19   "Postmodernism and Consumer Society," in Foster, *The Anti-Aesthetic*, pp. 116–118.

20   James D. Hunter, *The Culture Wars: The Struggle to Define America* (New York, 1991).

21   Elizabeth Fox-Genovese, "Literary Criticism and the Politics of the New Historicism," in H. Aram Veeser, ed., *The New Historicism* (New York, 1989), p. 220.

22   E.g., William Bennett, "To Reclaim a Legacy," *American Education*, 21 (1985): 4–15.

23   Diane Ravitch, *The Troubled Crusade: American Education, 1945–1980* (New York, 1983), p. 50.

24   Lawrence A. Cremin, *The Transformation of the School: Progressivism in American Education, 1876–1957* (New York, 1961).

25   Herbert M. Kliebard, *The Struggle for the American Curriculum* (London, 1986), p. xi.

26   *Newsweek* (3 July 1989): 74; *New York Times* (13 August 1989): 25; *American Film*, 14 (1989): 57; *Commonweal* (16 June 1989): 372.

27   Storey, *An Introductory Guide to Cultural Theory and Popular Culture*, p. 14.

28   Walker Gibson, "Authors, Speakers, Readers, and Mock Readers," in Jane P. Tompkins, ed., *Reader–Response Criticism: From Formalism to Post-*

Structuralism (Baltimore, 1980); Janet Staiger, *Interpreting Films: Studies in the Historical Reception of American Cinema* (Princeton, 1992), chs. 1–3.

29   Fred H. Matthews, "Flight from the Satanic City: The American Mainstream and the Rejection of Cosmopolitanism," *Cahiers de récherche sociologique,* 15 (1990): 27–51.

30   Lauren Langman, "From Pathos to Panic: American Character Meets the Future," in Phillip Wexler, ed., *Critical Theory Now* (London, 1991), p. 221.

31   Michel Foucault, "Body/Power," in Colin Gordon, ed., *Michel Foucault: Power/Knowledge* (New York, 1980), pp. 57–58.

32   Foucault, *Discipline and Punish: The Birth of the Prison* (New York, 1977), p. 217.

33   *The Last Little Citadel* (Boston, 1986), p. 32.

34   Pierre Bourdieu, "Cultural Reproduction and Social Reproduction," in Jerome Karabel and A. H. Halsey, eds., *Power and Ideology in Education* (New York, 1973), p. 497.

35   Rex Gibson, *Critical Theory and Education* (London, 1986), pp. 6ff.

36   Carl Nordstrom, Edgar Z. Friedenberg, and Hilary A. Gold, *Society's Children: A Study of Ressentiment in the Secondary School* (New York, 1967), p. 121.

37   Ibid., p. 56.

38   Vance Packard, *The Status Seekers* (New York, 1959), p. 8; Barbara Ehrenreich, *The Fear of Falling: The Inner Life of the Middle Class* (New York, 1989), p. 15.

39   Charles Biskin, *The Historicity of Romantic Discourse* (New York, 1988); Jerome McGann, *The Romantic Ideology* (New York, 1983); Nicholas Y. Riasonovsky, *The Emergence of Romanticism* (New York, 1992).

40   Harold Rugg and Ann Shumaker, eds., *The Child-Centered School: An Appraisal of the New Education* (New York, 1928), p. 4.

41   Quoted in Jon P. Klancher, "English Romanticism and Cultural Production," in Veeser, *The New Historicism*, p. 85.

42   Stam, "Mikhail Bakhtin and Left Cultural Critique," pp. 134–137.

43   Quoted in Richard Jones, "Educational Practices and Scientific Knowledge," in Stephen J. Ball, ed., *Foucault and Education* (London, 1990), p. 93.

44   Quoted in Thomas Schatz, *Hollywood Genres* (Philadelphia, 1981), p. 249.

45   Anne Friedberg, *Window Shopping: Cinema and the Postmodern* (Berkeley, 1993), pp. 168–169, 174.

46   "Foucault's Legacy: A New Historicism," in Veeser, *The New Historicism*, p. 241.

47   *America in the Movies* (New York, 1975), p. 36.

48   Jennifer M. Gore, "Enticing Challenges: An Introduction to Foucault and Educational Discourses," in Rebecca A. Martusewicz and William M. Reynolds, eds., *Inside Out: Contemporary Critical Perspectives in Education* (New York, 1994), pp. 13, 115–116.

49   Peter McLaren, "Critical Pedagogy: Constructing an Arch of Social Dreaming and a Doorway to Hope," in L. Erin and D. MacLennan, eds., *Sociology of Education in Canada* (Toronto, 1994), pp. 157–159.

50   New York, 1978.

51   *The Culture of Narcissism*, p. xv.

52   *America in the Movies*, pp. 162–163, 192.

53   A term coined by the British anthropologist Victor Turner to describe local or small-scale social conflict that reveals latent tensions in the society at large. Cited in Peter Burke, *History and Social Theory* (Ithaca, N.Y., 1992), p. 40.

54   David E. James, "Poetry/Punk/Production: Some Recent Writing in L.A.," in Kaplan, *Postmodernism and Its Discontents*, p. 167.

55   Paul Goodman, *Growing Up Absurd* (New York, 1956); Joan Didion, "Trouble in Lakewood," *New Yorker* (26 July 1993): 46–65; Bernard Lefkowitz, *Our Guys: The Glen Ridge Rape and the Secret Life of the Perfect Suburb* (Berkeley, 1997).

56   "Pedagogy in the Present: Politics, Postmodernity and the Popular," in Henry A. Giroux and Roger I. Simon, eds., *Popular Culture, Schooling and Everyday Life* (New York, 1989), p. 91.

57   "Crisis and Possibilities in Public Education," *Issues in Education*, 2 (1984): 1–10.

58   Roland A. Stromberg, "Some Models Used by Intellectual Historians," *American Historical Review*, 80 (1975): 564.

59   Indeed, of American social thought in general, as William McClay points out in *The Masterless: Self and Society in Modern America* (Chapel Hill, 1994).

60   *Telling the Truth About History* (New York, 1994).

61   *Ideology and the Image: Social Representation in the Cinema and Other Media* (Bloomington, Ind., 1981), p. 8.

62   Rosenstone, *Revisioning History: Film and the Construction of a New Past*, pp. 236–237.

63   Judith P. Robertson, Faculty of Education, University of Ottawa, Canada, has mapped some of its dimensions in several papers she generously shared with me. Their scope is broader than their titles indicate: "Screenplay Pedagogy and the Interpretation of Unexamined Knowledge in Preservice Teaching";

and "Fantasy's Confines: Popular Culture and the Education of the Female Primary School Teacher."

64   "Historiography and Historiophoty," *American Historical Review*, 93 (1988): 1193–1194.

Part II

Chapter 7

In the Name of the Prevention of Neurosis: Psychoanalysis and Education in Europe, 1905–1938

> The historical importance of a theory is not restricted to what was originally in the mind of its author. It also consists of extensions, adjunctions, interpretations, and distortions to which it is submitted, and to reactions that result from the impact of the theory and its distortions.
>
> Henri F. Ellenberger

I.

It has been said that we all live in the shadow of Freud. There can be little question regarding the enormous popularity of Freudian ideas in America; the United States has been far more receptive to psychoanalysis than any other nation. Psychoanalysis has had a pervasive influence on American life. American culture in all its manifestations, including its everyday vocabulary, has been deeply affected by psychoanalysis as a way of understanding the human condition. Freudian ideas are a major part of the interpretive perspective of most Americans; in this sense we are all Freudians now.

The historian Nathan G. Hale, Jr. has amply documented the impact of Freud and psychoanalysis on American life and culture in the twentieth century.[1] Given its influence in the United States, it is puzzling that historians of American education have neglected the impact of Freud and psychoanalysis on education.[2]

This study began as a straightforward historical inquiry into the connection between psychoanalysis and the permissivist aspects of American progressive education. My hunch was that psychoanalytic theory provided a major underpinning for the child-centered, permissivist thrust in American progressive education, and from there entered into American educational discourse more pervasively. My original plan was to first investigate the link between psychoanalysis and education in its European setting (this would be brief, I thought), and then move on to the American phase of the investigation. As I burrowed into the archives, the European phase of my study began to take on more importance. My research disclosed a close and surprisingly direct connection between psychoanalytic theory and education in Europe and revealed a hitherto largely unknown chapter, not only in the history of psychoanalysis but in the history of progressive education and the history of education more generally.

The connection between psychoanalysis and education dates back to Vienna in the first decade of the twentieth century, to Freud's *Three Essays on the Theory of Sexuality,* and to the discussions of the fledgling Vienna Psychoanalytic Society. Freud and his early circle were fascinated by the meliorative potential of a new education informed by psychoanalysis, what Freud called a "princely education along psychoanalytic lines." But it was in the 1920s, under the leadership of the newest branch of psychoanalysis, child analysis, that a movement to create a psychoanalytic pedagogy emerged in Vienna. Psychoanalytic pedagogy had as its goal the prevention of neurosis. For almost a generation before its demise in the late 1930s, psychoanalytic pedagogy enjoyed great favor among the psychoanalytic community. To anticipate one of my findings, many of the principles and practices involved in the application of psychoanalysis to education were to become familiar in American progressive education as well as in the mental hygiene movement in education, though with little knowledge of their origin. For several reasons, then, the history of the rise and fall of the movement to create a psychoanalytic pedagogy is too important to be allowed to fade into oblivion.

There are two different, somewhat contradictory sides to Freud. One side is Freud the liberator. Freud once claimed that psychoanalysis "stands in opposition to everything that is conventional, well-established and generally accepted."[3] Freud, observes Peter Gay, "was a moral liberator."[4] But there is another, darker, side to Freud, one more pessimistic and controlling, that deserves equal acknowledgment. This is the Freud who confronted humanity with harsh truths: civilization imposes sacrifices; life is hard and unremitting; blows are inevitable; we are all scarred. There is no way out of our predicament: "The ego of man is not master in its own house."[5] This is the Freud of the mid–1920s and 1930s who teaches that childhood is no golden age of innocence and happiness but a time of extraordinarily intense sexual and aggressive feelings, and that children cannot simply be let free without adult guidance and discipline. Usually one side of Freud—the liberating side in the case of education and child rearing—is emphasized at the expense of the other. The result has been a distorted emphasis on partial aspects of Freudian theory; the rest are ignored or denied.

Some critical phases in the evolution of Freudian theory may be followed in the vicissitudes of the movement to create a psychoanalytic pedagogy in Europe. If earlier developments in theory helped give birth to the movement to create a psychoanalytic pedagogy, later developments in theory helped to hasten its demise—a point of no small historical significance, as we shall see.[6]

A cautionary note may be permitted here. Since this study is inextricably bound to the history of the development of Freud's thought, it is well to keep in mind the difficulty of obtaining a coherent picture of the whole of Freud's work—a massive product that went through an enormously complex evolution over some fifty years of his working life.

The tie between psychoanalysis and education can best be explored in its native habitat—central Europe. What did the pioneers of psychoanalysis have to say about education?

II.

The genesis of psychoanalytic pedagogy can be directly traced to Freud's *Three Essays on the Theory of Sexuality*.[7] Freud notes that the child has sexual instincts and activities from the first: "It comes into the world with them." But the child's sexual instincts must undergo a highly complicated development. Freud located the causative factors of neurosis in disturbances in the child's sexual development. But were these disturbances due essentially to innate constitution or to experience, that is, education? In *Three Essays* Freud leaned toward constitution. But he hedged, leaving room "for the modifying effects of accidental events." And, he added, if "accidental events" do count, "we shall be in . . . closer harmony with psychoanalytic research if we give a place of preference . . . to the experiences of early childhood."[8]

With its theories of infantile sexuality, developmental stages, and, especially, the significance of early childhood experiences, the *Three Essays* seemed to lay the groundwork for a new pedagogy of early childhood. In these early years, Freud stressed the role of parents in mental illness. In 1909, at a meeting of the Vienna Psychoanalytic Society, he observed that mental illness "is often only the echoing voice of parents and educators."[9] Freud's thinking suggested that parents and educators harmed children by a too strict upbringing, which led to repression of sexual instinct, the chief factor in the development of symptoms. The repressed instinct is withdrawn from conscious influence, but it becomes more potent for that.[10] One aim of psychoanalysis was to allow the patient to express feelings that had been repressed. Treatment would "replace repression by healthy suppression" and facilitate "sublimation, the deflection of instinct to more social ends"—an important new concept that first appears in *Three Essays*.[11] Since the decisive repression takes place in childhood, the remedy seemed obvious—a freer, more lenient, or more permissive upbringing. Nevertheless, in these early attempts to apply psychoanalytic findings to education and child rearing, the priority went to sex education.[12] Still, in making recommendations, Freud was inclined to caution. In general, he advised, it was better to delay offering direct proposals until more was known.

In 1909, Freud published the first account of the analysis of a child, "A Phobia in a Five-Year-Old Boy," the famous Little Hans case.[13] This case confirmed Freud's speculations regarding the importance of early childhood, the existence of infantile sexuality, the role of parents in the etiology of neurosis, and the therapeutic effects of sexual enlightenment. Freud also explicitly raised the issue of permissiveness versus strictness in upbringing. Freud was critical of education. In bringing up children, Freud noted, adults aim to train a model child, paying little attention to whether such a course of development is for the child's good. Now Freud voiced a liberationist credo: "Hitherto education has set itself the task of controlling, or it would often be more proper to say, of suppressing the instincts. The results have been by no means gratifying." Suppose, Freud continues:

> that we substitute another task for this one, and aim instead at making the individual capable of becoming a civilized and useful member of society with the least possible sacrifice of his own [instinctual] activity; in that case the information gained by psychoanalysis upon the origin of pathogenic complexes and upon the nucleus of every nervous affection can claim with justice that it deserves to be regarded by educators as an invaluable guide in their conduct toward children.[14]

By 1910, then, Freud had arrived at a set of hypotheses regarding the etiology of the neuroses that rested, uneasily, on two pillars: disposition or innate constitution and experience or education. In theory,

Freud may have been convinced that "disposition and experience are linked up in an indissoluble aetiological unity." In practice, however, the emphasis was on childhood experiences. If the experiences of early childhood were basic, then early childhood was a strategic time for intervention. But on the question of what sort of education was best—strict or lenient—Freud continued to waver. The Little Hans case concludes with a plea for more freedom for the child, for indulgence of the child's instinctual life. But soon Freud was warning against the dangers of indulgence. In 1911, in a famous paper on "two principles of mental functioning" (the "reality principle" and the "pleasure principle"), Freud succinctly defined education as "an incitement to the conquest of the pleasure principle, and to its replacement by the reality principle."[15] A few years later, however, in 1913, during the course of a general review of the status of psychoanalysis, Freud tilted once more toward indulgence. He noted that when adults become familiar with the findings of psychoanalysis, "they will refrain from any attempt at forcibly suppressing the children's instinctual impulses."[16] Education, Freud advised, should "scrupulously refrain from burying these precious springs of action, and should restrict itself to encouraging the processes [sublimation] by which these energies are led along safe paths." He concluded: "Whatever we can expect in the way of prophylaxis against neurosis in the individual lies in the hands of a psychoanalytically enlightened education."[17]

In the meantime, other psychoanalysts in Freud's early circle had become deeply interested in the problems of education. The application of psychoanalysis to the upbringing and education of children was a staple of the discussions of the Vienna Psychoanalytic Society. Some of the pioneers in the psychoanalytic movement were publishing for a lay audience on the subject of education.[18] In 1913, Otto Rank and Hanns Sachs, in *The Significance of Psychoanalysis for the Mental Sciences,* summarized the mainstream position of Freudians so far as education was concerned. On the negative side, they warned against imposing a too-demanding suppression of instinct: "So far as possible, one should leave the child alone, with as complete withholding of direct injurious influences as possible, and inhibit him as little as possible in his natural development."[19] On the positive side, they advocated sexual education. In the period before World War I, then, the essential ingredients of a psychoanalytic pedagogy were already present. Nevertheless, the fusion of psychoanalysis and education had to wait for the postwar period and the emergence of a new branch of applied psychoanalysis—child analysis.

The emergence of child psychoanalysis was almost exclusively the work of a small group of analysts, most of them women, many of them former nursery or elementary school teachers: Hermine von Hug-Hellmuth, Berta Bornstein, and Anna Freud in Vienna; Alice Balint in Budapest; Steff Bornstein in Prague; and Ada Mueller-Braunschweig and Melanie Klein in Berlin. They were encouraged by a small group of men: Siegfried Bernfeld, Willi Hoffer, and August Aichhorn in Vienna; Sandor Ferenczi in Budapest; and Karl Abraham in Berlin.[20] The child analysts served as a bridge between psychoanalysis and education. It was with the child analysts that the movement to create a psychoanalytic pedagogy began.

III.

In the period after World War I, everywhere in Europe there seemed to be a new interest in the child: child rearing, children's problems, the mental life of the child. The child was becoming a social issue. Parents and teachers were expecting expert advice on the rearing and education of children. The first generation of psychoanalysts, however, was slow to respond. Freud and the circle of psychoanalysts around him were not eager to pursue child analysis; they were not able to work with children.[21] The field was left to a group with first-hand experience with children—the teaching profession. Former teachers became the first child analysts. As early as 1911, Hug-Hellmuth, the first woman to become a member of the Vienna Psychoanalytic Society, was experimenting with a form of psychoanalytic treatment combining education and play therapy for emotionally disturbed children.[22] With her death in 1924, it fell largely to Anna Freud in central Europe and to Melanie Klein in London to create child analysis as a branch of psychoanalysis. It was Anna Freud and the Vienna-Prague-Budapest circle of child analysts who subsequently attempted to combine psychoanalysis and education into a psychoanalytic pedagogy for children that, by preventing neurosis, might do away with the need for treatment.

In Vienna in the postwar period, the mood among those concerned with education was one of optimism and receptivity to educational innovation. Educational reform was in the air. The war had administered a profound shock to comfortable dogmas. The redrawing of frontiers was not enough. Only the reconstruction of humanity itself, through a "new education," could prevent further catastrophe.[23] Progressive education was everywhere gaining enthusiastic converts. It was the time of New Ideals in Education, the New Education Fellowship, the League of Resolute School Reformers, *Doctrine Nouvelle*, and *Die Nieue Erziehung*. Armed with their new insights into the working of the psyche and encouraged by liberal trends in politics, the child analysts thought they were on the threshold of a new era. Many Viennese young people were swept up in the enthusiasm for the "new education" and went into the teaching profession. Anna Freud and Willi Hoffer saw in these schoolteachers promising material from which to create not so much a corps of child analysts as a corps of psychoanalytic pedagogues.[24]

As a service of child experts, child analysts could reach only a few children. But the child analysts seemed to be in a strategic position to do more. If psychological problems were due to nurture, to faulty education—rather than to nature, heredity, or constitution—then potentially, through a new education, neuroses might be ameliorated or even prevented *en masse*. What visions were opened up! The Little Hans case was exemplary. Child analysis, Anna Freud declared in 1926, "furnishes a transition to a sphere of application which, as many think, should in the future be one of the most important for psychoanalysis: to pedagogics, or the science of upbringing and education."[25]

The child analysts were carried away by the idea of a new education informed by psychoanalytic principles. An elite group of schoolteachers would be recruited, given training, and persuaded to undergo analysis, and then they would return to the schools as a revolutionary vanguard. At the Vienna Psychoanalytic Society in the mid-1920s, Anna Freud, Hoffer, and August Aichhorn gave special courses and lectures and organized discussion groups for teachers. A small number of schoolteachers were introduced to psychoanalytic theories in Anna Freud's seminars on child analysis, beginning in 1926–1927. Besides the lectures, courses, and seminars, especially important in diffusing psychoanalytic views of pedagogy among educationists was the inauguration of *Zeitschrift für Psychoanalytische Pädagogik,* or *Journal of Psychoanalytic Pedagogy,* in 1926 under the psychoanalysts Heinrich Meng and Ernst Schneider. In 1931, Hoffer organized a formal, three-year training course in psychoanalytic pedagogy, "Lehrgang für Psychoanalytische Pädagogen," at the Vienna Psychoanalytic Institute.[26]

The first issue of the *Zeitschrift für Psychoanalytische Pädagogik* announced as its aim to lay the foundation of a psychoanalytic pedagogy that would extirpate neurosis from human life.[27] The psychoanalyst Heinz Hartmann recalls a time when preventing neurosis was considered the heart of the psychoanalytic contribution to education.[28] But the prevention of neurosis through a new education was not just a utopian dogma of child analysts. Even Freud was swept up in the enthusiasm. "None of the applications of psychoanalysis," he wrote in 1925, "has excited so many hopes, and none consequently has attracted so many capable workers, as its use in the theory and practice of education."[29] In 1928, Freud speculated that a treatment that combined analytic influence with educational measures could bring about two things at once—the removal of neurotic symptoms, and the reversal of any change for the worse that might already have begun.[30]

IV.

"Freud himself," writes Willi Hoffer, "encouraged us to think not only of cure but of how to minimize or prevent the 'traumatic effects of education on children.'"[31] As we have seen, the earliest conclusions drawn for education by the analysts called for more freedom and indulgence for the child and emphasized the faults of parents and teachers and the cost of repressing a child's instincts. Then in 1923, in *The Ego and the Id,* Freud reemphasized the superego's harsh and punitive nature. Freud's point was that psychoanalysts were obliged to do battle with the superego and work to *moderate* its demands.[32] But it was easy to jump to the conclusion that the less superego the better. The psychoanalyst Franz Alexander in Berlin confidently proclaimed: "The dissolution of the superego is and will continue to be the task of all future psychoanalytic therapy."[33] It was this notion of the superego as the root of all evil that helped to inspire the child analysts' utopian hope of preventing neurosis through a permissive education. Through the 1920s on the continent, repression and the tyranny of a too strict superego—the "echoing voice of parents and teachers"—were the factors considered to contribute most to psychopathology. Psychoanalytic writings of the decade stressed the faults of parents and teachers, who were seen as overly strict, rigid, traumatizing. Ferenczi used to say, "There are no bad children. There are only bad parents."[34] To Wilhelm Reich, the family was the "emotional Achilles' heel of society." Reich looked forward to the time when every family would have its own psychoanalyst, a "doctor of souls."[35]

The new psychoanalytic pedagogy had as its main platform the liberation of the child's instinctual drives and the abolition of repression. In a sense, the child analysts were restating in psychoanalytic terms a hoary theory of progressive education going back to Rousseau, Pestolozzi, and Froebel, while connecting with contemporary progressive education. Indeed, some child analysts used the terms "progressive education" and "psychoanalytic education" interchangeably. Rudolf Ekstein, a former schoolteacher in Vienna who joined the movement to create a psychoanalytic pedagogy, called the new education the child analysts were advocating "progressive education," and described it thus: "Progressive education was seen as the liberation of the instincts . . . as favoring *laissez-faire*, with a minimum of intervention on the part of educators and parents."[36] Anna Freud was one of those caught up in the enthusiasm.

Anna Freud, the youngest of Freud's six children, came into child psychoanalysis after having taught for five years in a primary school in Vienna. Beginning in 1923, with the discovery of Freud's cancer, she became her father's spokesperson and heir apparent as leader of the psychoanalytic movement. With Hug-Hellmuth's death in 1924 and Melanie Klein's move from Berlin to London in 1926, she quickly assumed leadership in child analysis on the continent.[37] It was she who in 1929 most explicitly attempted to define the relationship between child psychoanalysis and education.[38]

Anna Freud pinned her hopes on permissiveness in education. She referred to the "definite danger arising from education," meaning the demands of the adult world, and the prohibitions imposed on children. Too often, she continued, parents secure obedience by threatening children with punishment. But what happens to the child's shrewdness and originality? The "originality of the child, together with a great deal of his energy and talents, is sacrificed to being 'good.'"[39] Obviously, she observed, "to bring up 'good' children is not without its dangers."[40] Whenever psychoanalysis has come into contact with pedagogy, she continued, it has always stressed the dangers arising from education: "The analyst would rather risk the chance of children being somewhat uncontrolled in the end instead of forcing on them from the outset a crippling of their individuality." In fact, "the question remains unanswered as to what would happen if the adults around a child refrained from interfering in any way."[41] The apogee of permissiveness in education is reached in Fritz Wittels, *The Liberation of the Child,* a book whose title can stand as the slogan of the new psychoanalytic pedagogy.[42]

V.

Psychoanalytic pedagogy referred, in the main, to early education within the family circle. In the 1920s a handful of psychoanalysts in Europe—Siegfried Bernfeld, Lili Roubiczek-Peller, Anna Freud, and Dorothy Burlingham in Vienna; and Vera Schmidt in Moscow—working independently, at different times, in different places, and with various degrees of eclecticism, actually attempted to demonstrate the practical corollaries of psychoanalytic doctrine for the education of children in school settings.[43] These experiments in psychoanalytic pedagogy are too important to be relegated to the archival dustbin.

The Kinderheim ("Children's Home") Baumgarten was the first experiment to apply psychoanalytic principles to education. In the fall of 1919, Siegfried Bernfeld, a young socialist, Zionist, and leader in the Jewish youth movement in Vienna, deeply immersed in psychoanalysis, opened the Kinderheim Baumgarten, a coeducational residential school for Jewish refugee children displaced by the war. The school, five cottages in a former army barracks on the outskirts of Vienna, was established under the auspices of the Austrian branch of the Joint Distribution Committee for Relief of Jewish War Sufferers (later renamed the American Joint Distribution Committee).[44] The Kinderheim opened with almost 300 children and adolescents, who ranged in age from three to sixteen, with Bernfeld as director. Of course, Bernfeld was concerned with the children's optimal emotional development. But he also hoped to develop the kind of character and personality that would prepare these children for life in a socialist, Zionist state in Palestine.

Bernfeld and his colleagues at the Kinderheim were especially influenced by Freud in their approach to the psychosexual problems of the children. They tried to help the children therapeutically, through a permissive milieu, rather than control the children through restraint, punishment, or coercion. The children's psychological problems were explored, not suppressed. In his fascinating account of the experiment, Bernfeld described the children as being at first selfish and always complaining, distrustful of adults, brutal toward those younger than themselves, and habitually lying and stealing. In a specific reference to their sexual behavior, Bernfeld described many of the children as lacking in anal inhibitions, with the adolescent boys frequently indulging in masturbation, especially mutual masturbation.[45]

During the first few months of its existence, the Kinderheim Baumgarten was chaotic. There were no rules. The children were free from all restraints; they received no punishments. The results were apparently as unanticipated then as they now seem predictable. The youngsters fought, broke furniture, destroyed plates and utensils; the buildings of the Kinderheim were quickly covered with graffiti. But Bernfeld encouraged the children and adolescents to speak and write freely and to express their grievances and desires, and what soon emerged was a form of student self-government in a family atmosphere. There was a general legislature—or meeting of the whole body of the Kinderheim, presided over by a small elected board—which formulated the rules and regulations. There was a student court, which dealt with disciplinary offenses. The oldest boys were organized into a sort of monitor squad to help police the Kinderheim. Most of the children responded positively. In Bernfeld's words, the youngsters began to sublimate their anal and sadomasochistic tendencies, diverting them toward higher, more social ends.[46]

The abandonment of discipline and compulsion in the Kinderheim implied a compensatory emphasis on the children's own interests. At first, Bernfeld's idea was to offer no formal instruction at all. It soon became clear that this policy was impractical or imprudent. Many of the teachers wanted more formal instruction, the Joint Distribution Committee demanded it, and the Austrian authorities prescribed it. The teachers, anyway, were encouraged to develop their own courses. Unfortunately, there is no account of precisely what subjects were taught. Bernfeld mentions math, history, civics, and Bible-reading. We know that there was a Montessori-type kindergarten for the youngest children and that youngsters were encouraged to participate in activities like gardening, handiwork, sewing, and bookbinding. And we also know that the adolescents took formal classes or participated in interest groups gathered around an adult, as well as in peer-led clubs, which usually met once a week to read books, discuss politics and social issues, or study Hebrew. Bernfeld hoped that the Kinderheim would become a model for other residential schools for special children in Austria. It was not to be. The Kinderheim was short-lived, remaining open for only about nine months in all. Bernfeld fell seriously ill in December of 1919. Owing to his illness and to insuperable problems with the Joint Distribution Committee and with some of the teaching staff, for whom the permissive atmosphere was anathema, the experiment was terminated on 15 April 1920.[47]

In 1922, Lili Roubiczek-Peller, with the assistance of four other young women—part of that pioneer group of young Viennese teachers attracted to the "new education"—founded the Haus der Kinder, a Montessori school in a working-class district of Vienna.[48] Peller, who before undergoing Montessori training in London had studied psychology under Karl Bühler at the University of Vienna, soon came under the influence of the charismatic Bernfeld and became interested in psychoanalysis. Since both Freud and Montessori emphasized the critical importance of early childhood, it seemed feasible to Peller and her coworkers to attempt a synthesis of the two. With the psychoanalysts, Peller believed that "permissiveness should be the keynote of early education." She wanted to allow children the free expression of their instincts. At the Haus der Kinder, prohibitions and restrictions were minimal; punishments were forbidden on principle. Like the Montessorians, Peller was concerned with the child's moral and social education. The infant's social education was to be steered by "transference"—a powerful leverage of attachment to the teacher—as well as by the "reality" factors inherent in the Montessori didactic apparatus and in the group life of the school.[49]

The Haus der Kinder began with twenty–five children—boys and girls between the ages of two and four—and quickly gained a reputation. By 1928 the school had enrolled fifty children, aged 2 ½ to ten, and had moved into a handsome new building designed by architect Franz Schuster of the Bauhaus. By that time most of the teachers at the Haus der Kinder, as well as Peller, were attending Anna Freud's seminars in child analysis and other courses at the Vienna Psychoanalytic Institute. Subsequently most of them enrolled in Hoffer's special training course for teachers at the institute. Montessori, ever possessive of her "method," was enraged by Peller's interest in psychoanalysis and withdrew her blessing from the Haus der Kinder. In any event, Peller had become more interested in child analysis than pedagogy. In February, 1934, as the Nazi darkness descended on the continent, Peller and her husband, Sigmund, a physician, emigrated to Palestine, but the Haus der Kinder continued until the Nazis closed it in 1938.[50]

In 1927, Anna Freud, along with child analyst Dorothy Burlingham, collaborated in the establishment of a nursery school for children.[51] There were about twenty children enrolled in the school. Many of them were in analysis, as were many of their parents who intended to become analysts themselves. The teachers—Erik Erikson and Peter Blos, two fledgling child analysts, soon joined by Erikson's wife, Joan—were given full freedom to organize the curriculum and teach it any way they chose. Erikson's biographer, Robert Coles, describes the school. The children were encouraged to share in planning the day's activities and choosing the subject matter. Blos and Erikson "wanted the children to feel free, that is, unafraid of school, and in many respects their own masters." There were no formal classes. But the children were introduced to science, history, geography, and English, Blos's specialties. Artistic self-expression—drawing, painting, and poetry—was also emphasized. The result, says Coles, was "what could be called a progressive school, similar in some respects to some American experimental schools."[52] The school closed in 1933, as Blos and the Eriksons emigrated to the United States.

The experiments in applied psychoanalysis are not of a piece; they have their different emphases and degrees of psychoanalytic orthodoxy. In a place by itself in the history of psychoanalytic pedagogy is the experiment undertaken by psychoanalyst Vera Schmidt in Moscow.

In Russia in the early 1920s, psychoanalysis was for a time held in favor by the state. In the summer of 1921, Schmidt was given permission by Dr. Ivan Ermakov, director of the State Institute of Neuropsychology in Moscow and the leader of the psychoanalytic movement in Russia, to organize a residential school for infants, to be run exclusively on psychoanalytic principles.[53] The Moscow Children's Home and Psychological Laboratory, as it was called, began with thirty young children, boys and girls aged one to five, from families that had been torn apart by the revolution. The children were divided into three groups: there were six children aged one to 1 ½, nine children aged two to three, and fifteen children aged three to five. There were four women teachers, or "directresses," for each group.

The teachers refrained as much as possible from interfering with the children's spontaneous process of development. The children's instinctual manifestations were permitted free expression. It was not until the end of the second year and only "at certain intervals" that children were put on the toilet. And even then the children were never forced to attend to their needs in precisely this manner. The attitude of the teachers toward the children's excretory processes was, in principle anyway, entirely casual. Our method, writes Schmidt, "seems likely to save children from the severe traumatic experiences usually connected with sphincter control."[54] No moral judgments were made regarding the children's sexual activities. Masturbation was not condemned. Children were free to satisfy their sexual curiosity among themselves. Nudity was the rule in warm weather. Children's questions about sexual matters received clear, truthful answers. Punishments of any kind on the part of the teachers were forbidden. There was no praise or blame, but neither was there overt display of love or affection. Since there was no need on the children's part for secrecy or shyness, Schmidt writes, teachers had every opportunity to observe the sexual development of the children step by step. By such means, Schmidt hoped to learn whether the various phases of infantile sexuality postulated by Freud arise spontaneously and then disappear without any educational influence. However, "when necessary," the child was aided progressively to conquer the "pleasure principle" and replace it with the "reality principle."[55]

The Moscow Children's Home never found the going easy. Even for Moscow in the early 1920s the experiment was radical. In April 1922, after a public outcry and a series of investigations having to do with accusations that the Children's Home was encouraging sexual precociousness, the Institute of Neuropsychology withdrew its support. Subsequently, the Children's Home was saved by the joint effort of a group of workers—miners, in fact—and the newly organized Russian Psychoanalytic Society. But now the experiment, renamed the International Solidarity Children's Home, was reduced to twelve children—five boys and seven girls, ages three to five—of whom only four remained from the original group.[56] Schmidt reported on the experiment in the winter of 1923 in a series of talks to the psychoanalytic community in Vienna and Berlin. She spoke of favorable results in the children's sexual and personality development. She also remarked on the unsettling effect of the experiment on the emotional lives of the teachers who had not been psychoanalyzed.[57] (Similar results had been observed by Bernfeld at the Kinderheim Baumgarten.)

Schmidt was forced to terminate the experiment in 1929, as psychoanalysis went out of favor with the Russian authorities. At about that time, Wilhelm Reich met Schmidt in Moscow. He was very disappointed to learn that Schmidt had encouraged the children to learn to control their instincts. But on the whole he was favorably impressed. Schmidt's experiment, he wrote, "was the first attempt in the history of education to give practical content to the theory of infantile sexuality."[58] In a brief, tantalizing reference written in 1929, Anna Freud

observed that Schmidt's experiment was short-lived and that the question of the relative influence of predisposition and education, "except
in the case of one child," remained unsolved.[59]

VI.

The demise in the 1930s of the movement to create a psychoanalytic
pedagogy was almost as sudden and rapid as its efflorescence in the
1920s. Anna Freud and her circle had at one time believed that they
were ushering in a historical epoch; it was only a historical moment.
By the early 1930s, among the child analysts and the psychoanalytic
pedagogues the mood had begun to shift from optimism to pessimism—a shift that in psychoanalytic terms was overdetermined. There
were many problems—some having to do with theory, some with the
relationship between theory and practice, some with professional status and identity, and some with politics. For example, many members
of the older generation of psychoanalysts never accepted child analysis as legitimate and looked on its practitioners with suspicion, if not
contempt.[60] Instances of cooperation between child analysts and teachers remained few and far between. The movement to create a psychoanalytic pedagogy was confined to a small circle of enthusiasts and
scarcely affected the public-school sector or rank-and-file teachers. The
Central European group of child analysts around Anna Freud, who
had led the effort to create a psychoanalytic pedagogy, rarely made
any direct effort to cooperate with or propagate their views among
progressives in education.[61] The Lehrgang für Psychoanalytische
Padagogen was a major effort on the part of the movement to break
out of its isolation, but this reached relatively few teachers. Then,
those who were recruited from teaching to be trained at Vienna, and
who were supposed to become the vanguard of psychoanalytic pedagogy and bear it to the schools, instead of returning to the schools,
preferred, like Lili Roubiczek, to stay and become child analysts.[62]

Most significant, there was growing evidence of a huge lacuna between principle and practice, through which many a theory, and many
a child, could fall. Take the key area of sexual enlightenment. It was
clear by the late 1920s that this innovation was not delivering the
hoped-for results. Erik Erikson warned in 1930 that sexual enlightenment of children, through the simple process of imparting information, was no panacea. It applies, he said, too much to the child's
intellect, but does not connect enough with the child's unconscious

fantasies and is therefore of little use. The "formation of anxieties, fantasies, and unconscious theories continues," Erikson said, regardless of sexual enlightenment.[63] Freud himself became increasingly disillusioned with what had at one time been the major plank of his liberating pedagogy. In one of his last works, Freud declared of sexual education that "the prophylactic effect of this liberal measure has been greatly overestimated." We come to see, he said, that children make no use of the new knowledge that has been presented to them. "For a long time after they have been given sexual enlightenment they behave like primitive races who have had Christianity thrust upon them and who continue to worship their old idols in secret."[64]

Nor did disillusion strike only at this plank of psychoanalytic pedagogy. The experiments in psychoanalytic pedagogy at the Kinderheim Baumgarten, the Haus der Kinder, and the Moscow Children's Home and Psychological Laboratory may have been short-lived and inconclusive, but the first-hand experience of a generation of effort in education and child rearing by the analysts, their friends, and their patients provided an across-the-board corrective to the utopian hopes of a psychoanalytic pedagogy that would prevent neurosis.

Over and over again it appeared that even with the most enlightened pedagogical attitudes and practices the same problems and difficulties made themselves manifest. Willi Hoffer speaks with authority on this subject. The psychoanalysts attempted to turn the course of upbringing and education toward abolishing repression and giving way to the child's instinctual drives. Sexual curiosity was satisfied, and information about sex was willingly given. Masturbation was unrestricted, and parents' naked bodies were revealed to their children's sight. Expressions of jealousy, hate, and discontent never met with disapproval. In general, "there was a tendency to avoid any form of prohibition."[65] It was thought, Hoffer says, that if the child's development was left to itself it would automatically follow the course of Freud's psychosexual stages. Thumb sucking, pleasure in dirt, smearing, exhibitionism, scopophilia, and masturbation were expected to give way step by step to the normal processes of the latency period. When children reached school age, they would settle down to normal intellectual and social activities, less hampered by repression and more inclined to sublimation.

To the surprise of those who advocated it, Hoffer continues, psychoanalytically based education did not yield satisfactory results. Children from an "enlightened environment" had been spared overly strict prohibitions and traumatic restrictions. Yet many cases of character disturbance and behavior disorder in children brought up along these lines became known. In comparison with children reared in the conventional way, these children appeared less inhibited, "but they were often less curious about the more complicated world of objects, they had no perseverance, and they easily relapsed into daydreaming." They clung to many infantile habits. Thus the changes expected during the latency period did not occur. Normal school life put a great strain on these children; they were extremely intolerant of the demands of adults. These children, Hoffer concludes, "showed an unexpected degree of irritability, a tendency to obsessions and depression, and . . . anxiety." When these children reached the period of latency, "psychoanalysis had to be called in to deal with the threatened deterioration of character."[66]

In the end, the child psychoanalysts had to accept the pessimistic conclusions to which personal experience as well as educational experiment increasingly led. This brings us finally to Freud's new theoretical formulations, which in retrospect help explain why things went wrong in practice.

VII.

The psychoanalytic pedagogy that emerged in Europe in the 1920s was for the most part composed of strands from theories formulated by Freud prior to World War I, a partial selection at that, emphasizing the liberationist aspect of his work. But Freud's concepts were seldom static, enunciated in finished, final form; they changed and developed during the course of almost half a century of work. By 1926 Freud had made thorough revisions in the psychoanalytic edifice. One effect of Freud's new theoretical speculations was a pronounced shift in emphasis from the role of the environment in the etiology of neuroses to the role of the instincts and their vicissitudes. By the late 1920s, Freud had come around to the view that little could be done to mitigate the force of infantile conflict. The child lives in a world of frustration, goaded by unappeasable desires and envies. Conflict and hence anxiety are bound up with growth. Childhood neurosis is not the exception but the rule; it is unavoidable.[67] In *Civilization and Its Discontents* (1930), Freud clarified his position. If civilization was to survive, the instincts must be repressed. Repression, restraint, and social controls serve necessary functions. We exchange happiness, that is, instinctual satisfaction, for security: "Civilization has been attained through the renunciation of instinctual satisfaction." The superego, said Freud, far from being an anachronism, "represents the ethical standards of mankind."[68]

There may be an ebb and flow to Freud's thoughts, but from at least the mid-1920s Freud's thinking developed in a direction that was stoic, even pessimistic, and certainly antiliberationist.[69] Freud's newer formulations concerning the psychology of anxiety and of the aggressive drives clearly showed that gratification of the instincts cannot lead to mental health. "Where id was," Freud declared, "there ego shall be."[70] In 1933, in *New Introductory Lectures on Psychoanalysis*, Freud returned, for the last time, to the theme of the possible role of education as a prophylaxis against neurosis and concluded that the problems involved were insurmountable. Let us make ourselves clear, Freud wrote, as to what the first task of education is: "The child must learn to control his instincts . . . education must inhibit, forbid and suppress." But psychoanalysis teaches that precisely this suppression of the instincts involves the risk of neurotic illness. Thus, education has to find its way "between the Scylla of noninterference and the Charybdis of frustration." An optimum must be discovered that will enable education to achieve the most and damage the least.[71]

By the early 1930s all those concerned with psychoanalytic pedagogy had begun to realize that it was impossible to rear children nonjudgmentally. They were beginning to appreciate the fact that parents and teachers had to play an active role in curbing the strength of the instinctual drives. Finally, there was the belated acknowledgment that the prevention of neurosis could no longer be a realistic goal of pedagogy. Anna Freud made this point clear in *The Ego and the Mechanisms of Defense* (1939): "Mental distress has to be accepted as a normal by-product of the child's dependency, his exposure to frustrations, and the inevitable strains and stresses of development." The emergence of neurotic conflicts is the price paid for the complexity of the human personality: "The hope of extirpating neurosis from human life is . . . illusory."[72]

The last great conference of child analysts and psychoanalytic pedagogues before the final curtain descended on an epoch and before the diaspora of the child analysts from the continent was held in Budapest in May 1937. At this Four Countries Conference the major topic for discussion was "A Review of Psychoanalytic Pedagogy." Present were many of the child analysts from Italy, Germany, Hungary, Austria,

France, and Czechoslovakia who had not yet fled into exile, including Anna Freud, Dorothy Burlingham, Alice Balint, Berta and Steff Bornstein, Greta Bibring, and Sophie Morgenstern. There were revisionist papers by Burlingham, Steff Bornstein, Balint, and Anna Freud. It fell to Anna Freud to read the epitaph for the movement: "After years of intensive work by some of the best psychoanalytical research workers, we are certain only that there still exists no practicable psychoanalytical pedagogy."[73] In March 1938, Austria was invaded by the Nazis. The Vienna Psychoanalytic Society was disbanded; the Lehrgang für Psychoanalytische Padagogen gave its last courses in the winter of 1937–1938.[74] The last issue of the *Zeitschrift für Psychoanalytische Padagogik,* containing the articles from the Budapest conference, came out in the winter of 1938. Freud and his daughter Anna fled to England that June. He died in London on 23 September 1939.

For many years, nothing more was heard about the movement to create a psychoanalytic pedagogy in Europe. The child psychoanalysts who were involved in the movement—most of them now in the United States—wrote about education in the 1940s and 1950s, mostly criticisms of American progressive education for its overindulgence of children, and its lack of structure and limits, that is, its misuse or misinterpretation of Freudian concepts. They carefully detached psychoanalysis from permissive attitudes and practices in child rearing and education. Then in 1965 Anna Freud published *Normality and Pathology in Children.* In the introductory section, a significant cultural document, Miss Freud summarized the history of the efforts to achieve a psychoanalytic education for children.[75] Psychoanalysts took the observations they made in their offices with neurotic adult patients and began to apply their knowledge to the upbringing and education of children. Analysis of adult patients left no doubt about the detrimental influence of many parental attitudes and actions, such as dishonesty in sexual matters, overstrictness, and punishments. It seemed a feasible task to remove some of these dangers from the next generation of children by enlightening parents and educators and by altering the conditions of upbringing, thus creating "a psychoanalytic education serving the prevention of neurosis." Anna Freud took note of the great hope that was involved in all this: "In the unceasing search for pathogenic agents and preventative measures, it seemed always the latest analytic discovery which promised a better solution of the problem." She also noted the great disappointment: "In spite of many partial advances, psychoanalytic education did not succeed in becoming the preventive measure that it had set out to be. The children who grew up under its influence were not free from anxiety or from conflicts, and therefore not less exposed to neurotic or other mental illnesses." She concluded that this need not have come as a surprise "if optimism and enthusiasm for preventive work had not triumphed with some persons over the strict application of psychoanalytic tenets." There is "no wholesale prevention of neurosis."[76]

VIII.

Investigation of the interconnection between psychoanalytic theory, the movement to create a psychoanalytic pedagogy, and American progressive education will be a difficult but fascinating subject. There has never been a psychoanalytic movement in American education as such. Psychoanalytic ideas have filtered into American progressive education, then into American education more generally, in an indirect way for the most part through the mental hygiene movement.[77] In the meantime, I think this study makes at least two contributions to the history of education. One, it preserves an important episode in the history of psychoanalytic thought and makes it a part of the history of educational ideas, particularly the history of progressive education. Two, it may have something important to tell us about the present educational situation in America.

History, John Lukacs reminds us, does not teach us what to expect or what to do, but it does suggest what is not likely to happen, what not to expect, what not to do. Perhaps in this sense we can learn something from the movement to create a psychoanalytic pedagogy.

In the United States, permissiveness in child rearing and in education has often been justified in the name of prevention of neuroses; that is, in the name of "mental hygiene" or "mental health." The history of the movement to create a psychoanalytic pedagogy cuts sharply against this persuasion. It offers an unsettling critique of permissiveness in education; the school's role in the prevention of neurosis or in other grandiose psychological missions, may be in need of serious reappraisal. The movement to create a psychoanalytic pedagogy is a reminder of the limitations imposed on us by our nature, of the inevitability of psychic conflict, of the irreconcilable antagonism inherent in the human condition, and of the basic tensions of human existence: between instinctual happiness and socializing repression, between the contrary claims of freedom and authority, self-expression and regulation of impulse.

The foundational myth of twentieth-century American progressive education, where children are concerned, is one of unlimited optimism. As viewed at least by the middle-class, well–educated sector of American society, the child is a *tabula rasa*, a creature of infinite potentialities that can be educed by a tractable environment. And American progressivism is characterized by its almost unbounded faith in the possibility of controlling or manipulating the environment. Any defects that subsequently appear are due to the ignorance or malice of parents or teachers, who mar what would otherwise be a perfect, or at least well-adjusted, human being. Alexis de Tocqueville, writing in 1835, was impressed by the prevalence in the United States of what he called the "idea of the indefinite perfectibility of man." Francis Keppel, more than a century later, observed that American education rests on two assumptions from which all else derives: "The idea that man is potentially good and that this good can be brought about by education." The American educational system "renews each day its faith in this principle of the perfectibility of man."[78] The idea of human perfectibility, still widely if implicitly shared, is far too simplistic on the one hand and far too idealized on the other. Like Freud, some Americans know better. F. Scott Fitzgerald ends his greatest work this way. "Gatsby believed in the green light, the orgastic future that year by year recedes before us. It eluded us then, but that's no matter—tomorrow we will run faster, stretch out our arms farther. . . . And one fine morning—So we beat on, boats against the current, borne back ceaselessly into the past." If Americans would give up the tendency to think of human perfectibility and of education in such idealized terms, then a step toward demystification would be taken, and a step away from demoralization as well.

Notes

1   Nathan G. Hale, Jr., *Freud and the Americans: The Beginnings of Psycho-analysis in the United States, 1876–1917* (New York, 1971); *The Rise and Crisis of Psychoanalysis in the United States,1917–1985* (New York, 1995).

2   E.g., Lawrence A. Cremin, *The Transformation of the School: Progressiv-ism in American Education, 1876–1957* (New York, 1961), pp. 207–210; and Fred Kerlinger, "The Origins of the Doctrine of Permissiveness in Educa-tion," *Progressive Education*, 33 (1954): 161–165.

3   "Psychoanalysis and Telepathy," James Strachey, ed., *The Standard Edition of the Complete Psychological Works of Sigmund Freud* (London, 1953–1964) vol. 18, p. 178. Hereafter referred to as S.E.

4   *Freud, Jews and Other Germans* (New York, 1978), pp. 66–69. See also Paul Roazen, *Freud: Political and Social Thought* (New York, 1968), pp. 247–248, 252ff.; and Philip Rieff, *Freud: The Mind of the Moralist* (New York, 1961), pp. 163ff.

5   "A Difficulty in the Path of Psychoanalysis" (1917), S.E. 17, p. 143.

6   Nathan Hale, Jr. and Fred Matthews were generous in their comments on early versions of this essay as well as on my subsequent work on the mental hygiene movement and the medicalization of American education.

7   *Three Essays on the Theory of Sexuality* (1905), trans. and ed. by James Strachey (New York, 1962). There is a summary in Freud's "Five Lectures on Psychoanalysis" (1910), S.E. 11, pp. 42–48.

8   *Three Essays on the Theory of Sexuality,* pp. 71–72, 145–146.

9   "Fragment of an Analysis of a Case of Hysteria" (1905), S.E. 7, p. 18.

10 "Repression" (1915). In Joan Riviere, ed., *Collected Papers of Sigmund Freud*, IV, pp. 87, 92–93.

11 pp. 143–144.

12 "The Sexual Enlightenment of Children" (1907), S.E. 9, pp. 136–137. See also Discussion of 12 May 1900, and the meeting of 15 December 1909, in Herman Nunberg and Ernst Federn, eds., *Minutes of the Vienna Psychoana-lytical Society* (New York, 1962–1975), vol. II, pp. 236, 353–364.

13 "The Little Hans Case" (1909), S.E. 10, pp. 143–149.

14 Ibid., pp. 146–147.

15 "Formulations on the Two Principles of Mental Functioning" (1911), S.E. 21, p. 224; "Introduction" to Oskar Pfister's *The Psychoanalytic Method* (1913), S.E. 12, p. 331.

16   It seems self-evident that the "educator" or "parent" to whom Freud refers is the mother, though she is never mentioned as such.

17   Ibid., p. 190.

18   E.g., Alfred Adler, "The Child's Need for Tenderness," *Imago*, 1 (1912): 95–96; Carl Jung, "The Association Method," *American Journal of Psychology*, 21 (1910): 246–251; Ernest Jones, "Psychoanalysis and Education," *Journal of Educational Psychology*, 1 (1910): 497–520; and Oskar Pfister, *Die psychoanalytische Method* (Zurich, 1913), trans. into English as *Psychoanalysis in the Service of Education* (London, 1922). There was so much interest in education among Freudians that in 1923 the German psychologist William Stern published a *Protest-Pamphlet* against enthusiastic followers of Freud who were recommending the psychoanalysis of children as the general foundation of education reforms. Stern, *Psychology of Early Childhood*, 2nd ed. (New York, 1930), pp. 31–32.

19   New York, 1916, p. 121.

20   See the following by Anna Freud: "Child Analysis as a Sub-Specialty of Psychoanalysis," *International Journal of Psychoanalysis*, 53 (1972): 152; "A Short History of Child Analysis," *Psychoanalytic Study of the Child*, 21 (1966): 7–8.

21   Even Freud was skeptical: "If mankind had been able to learn from a direct observation of children," wrote Freud in 1920, in the preface to the fourth edition of *Three Essays on the Theory of Sexuality*, "these three essays could have remained unwritten," p. xviii. See also Ernest Jones, *The Life and Works of Sigmund Freud* (New York, 1955), vol. I, pp. 11, 260–261.

22   *International Journal of Psychoanalysis*, 6 (1925): 106.

23   Robert Dottrens, *The New Education in Austria* (New York, 1930), p. 202.

24   Rudolf Ekstein and Rocco L. Motta, eds., "Psychoanalysis and Education—An Historical Account," in *From Learning for Love to Love of Learning* (New York, 1969), p. 8.

25   "The Theory of Children's Analysis," *International Journal of Psychoanalysis*, 8 (1927): 65.

26   *International Journal of Psychoanalysis*, 20 (1939): 212; Anna Freud, "Willi Hoffer, M.D., Ph.D.," *Psychoanalytic Study of the Child*, 23 (1968): 7–8; Rudolf Ekstein, "Willi Hoffer's Contribution to Teaching and Education," *Reiss-Davis Clinic Bulletin*, 5 (1968): 4–10.

27   Ernst Schneider, "Geltingsbereich der Psychoanalyse für die Padagogik," *Zeitschrift für Psychoanalytische Padagogik*, 1 (1926–27): 2–6.

28   Heinz Hartmann, *Ego Psychology and the Problem of Adaptation* (1939), trans. by David Rapaport (New York, 1958), pp. 12–13.

29   "Introduction" to August Aichhorn's *Wayward Youth* (1925), S.E. 19, p. 273.

30 Freud went on to speculate that it might be the destiny of psychoanalysis to train "a band of helpers for combating the neuroses of civilization, . . . 'a new kind of Salvation Army.'" "The Question of Lay Analysis" (1928), S.E. 20, p. 249.

31 "Psychoanalytic Education," *Psychoanalytic Study of the Child,* 1 (1945): 299.

32 *The Ego and the Id* (1923), trans. by Joan Riviere, revised and ed. by James Strachey (New York, 1960), pp. 18, 24–25.

33 "A Metapsychological Description of the Process of Cure" (1925), in *The Scope of Psychoanalysis, 1921–1961: Selected Papers* (New York, 1961), p. 223.

34 Quoted in Maurice R. Green, ed., *Interpersonal Psychoanalysis: The Selected Papers of Clara M. Thompson* (New York, 1964), p. 74.

35 *The Sexual Revolution,* trans. by Therese Pol (New York, 1970), p. xiv.

36 Ibid.

37 Paul Roazen, *Freud and His Followers* (New York, 1975), pp. 436ff. See also Robert Coles, "The Achievement of Anna Freud," *Massachusetts Review,* 7 (1966): 203–220.

38 *Einfurung in die Psychoanalyse für Padagogen.* Published first in England in 1931 as *Introduction to Psychoanalysis for Teachers,* and then in the United States in 1935 as *Psychoanalysis for Teachers and Parents.* The following discussion is from the 1931 edition.

39 *Introduction to Psychoanalysis for Teachers,* p. 39.

40 Ibid., pp. 45–46.

41 Ibid., pp. 76–77.

42 The "fundamental idea," Wittels proclaimed, "is leave your children to themselves. Do not educate them, for you cannot educate them." *The Liberation of the Child,* trans. by Eden and Cedar Paul (New York, 1927), p. 242.

43 Outside the scope of this chapter are Susan Isaacs's Malting House School, A. S. Neill's Summerhill, and Margaret Naumberg's Walden School. They are well known and there is a copious literature on all three.

44 Siegfried Bernfeld, *Kinderheim Baumgarten* (Berlin, 1921). There are brief descriptions of the Kinderheim in Willi Hoffer, "Siegfried Bernfeld and Jerubbaal," Publications of the Leo Baeck Institute, *Yearbook,* 10 (1965), pp. 159–166. See also Peter Paret's Introduction to Bernfeld's *Sisyphus, or the Limits of Education,* trans. by Frederic Lilge (Berkeley, 1973).

45 Bernfeld, *Kinderheim Baumgarten,* pp. 30, 74.

46 Ibid., p. 74.

47   The final blow-up is described by Hoffer in "Siegfried Bernfeld and Jerubbaal," pp. 165–166.

48   The following is based largely on information from Emma Plank's eulogy, "In Memory of Lili Peller" (17 December 1966), mimeo copy in my possession. Also: Emma N. Plank, "Reflections on the Revival of the Montessori Method," *Journal of Nursery Education*, 17 (1961–1962): 131.

49   Peller published three articles describing the experiment in the *Zeitschrift für Psychoanalytische Pädagogik* in 1929, 1932, and 1933. Two of her articles published later, in English, are: "Incentives to Development and Means of Early Education," *Psychoanalytic Study of the Child*, 2 (1946): 397–415; and "The School's Role in Promoting Sublimation," *Psychoanalytic Study of the Child*, 12 (1956): 437–449.

50   The ethos of the Haus der Kinder has been expressed by a former pupil. On learning of Peller's death, he wrote to Emma Plank: "You all laid the foundation in me, as in the other children, for our attitude towards life. You educated us with the hope that we would grow up to be honest people, who could grasp the spirit of Internationalism, understand democracy, and carry the banner and propagate the responsibility for others and for an ideal socialism." Plank, "In Memory of Lili Peller," p. 10.

51   Robert Coles, *Erik H. Erikson: The Growth of His Work* (Boston, 1970), pp. 16–20.

52   Ibid., p. 20. An American psychoanalyst who trained in Vienna in the 1930s makes an almost identical observation. He refers to the school as "the nearest thing to the American progressive schools" with which he was familiar. Edward Liss, "The Vicissitudes of a Hybrid," *Journal of the American Academy of Child Psychiatry*, 3 (1964): 765.

53   Vera Schmidt, "Education Psychoanalytique en Russie Sovietique," *Partisans*, 46 (1969): 58–71. There is a brief account in *International Journal of Psychoanalysis*, 5 (1924): 258–266.

54   Schmidt, "Education Psychoanalytique en Russie Sovietique," p. 66.

55   Ibid., pp. 69–70.

56   *International Journal of Psychoanalysis*, 5 (1924): 259.

57   "Education Psychoanalytique en Russie Sovietique," p. 70.

58   *The Sexual Revolution*, pp. 259–260.

59   *Psychoanalysis for Teachers*, pp. 79–80.

60   "Child analysis did not have the triumphant career we had envisaged for it," Anna Freud sadly observed. "The analyst of adults remained more or less aloof from child analysis, almost as if it were an inferior type of professional occupation." "Child-Analysis as a Sub-Specialty of Psychoanalysis," *International Journal of Psychoanalysis*, 53 (1972): 153.

61   I'm aware of only one direct effort to build a bridge to educational progressives. This was at the Fifth International New Education Fellowship Conference, at Elsinore, Denmark, in August 1929. William Boyd, ed., *Towards a New Education* (New York, 1930).

62   Fritz Redl, *When We Deal with Children* (New York, 1969), pp. 147–149.

63   "Psychoanalysis and the Future of Education," *Psychoanalytic Quarterly*, 4 (1935): 50–68.

64   "Analysis Terminable and Interminable" (1937), S.E. 23, pp. 223–224.

65   Hoffer, "Psychoanalytic Education," p. 301.

66   Ibid., pp. 302–303. See also Dorothy Burlingham, "Problems Confronting the Psychoanalytic Educator," in *Psychoanalytic Studies of the Sighted and the Blind* (New York, 1972), pp. 76–78.

67   "An Outline of Psychoanalysis" (1940), pp. 41–42.

68   "An Autobiographical Study," p. 59.

69   "The Future of an Illusion" (1927), S.E. 21.

70   "Civilization and Its Discontents" (1928), S.E. 21, p. 145.

71   *New Introductory Lectures*, pp. 149, 150.

72   *The Ego and the Mechanisms of Defense,* pp. 54ff.; "Psychoanalysis and Education," *Psychoanalytic Study of the Child*, 9 (1954): 14–15.

73   Quoted in Michael Balint, "Ego Strength, Ego-Education and Learning" (1938), in *Primary Love and Psychoanalytic Technique* (London, 1952), p. 197. There is a brief account of the symposium in *International Journal of Psychoanalysis,* 19 (1938): 170–171.

74   In all, the teacher training course at the Vienna Psychoanalytic Institute had been attended by some 180 teachers; the number of analyzed teachers had reached more than forty. "Report of the International Training Commission," *International Journal of Psychoanalysis*, 20 (1939): 212–213.

75   New York, 1965, pp. 4–8.

76   Erik Erikson provides an interesting sidelight: "In psychoanalytic circles we have witnessed a little private history of tentative child training systems dedicated to instinct indulgence, or to the avoidance of anxiety in our children. We know that not infrequently a new system of 'scientific' superstitions has resulted." *Childhood and Society*, 2nd ed., rev. and enlarged (New York, 1963), p. 414.

77   I treat various aspects of this subject in Chapters 8–11 below.

78   *The Necessary Revolution in American Education* (New York, 1966), p. 11. See also Henry J. Perkinson, *The Imperfect Panacea: American Faith*

in Education, 1865–1965 (New York, 1968); and Sanford W. Reitman, *The Educational Messiah Complex: American Faith in the Culturally Redemptive Power of Schooling* (Sacramento, Ca., 1992).

Chapter 8

The Mental Hygiene Movement, the Commonwealth Fund, and Education, 1921–1933: "Every School a Clinic"

This gift, . . . , is absolute, . . . , to do something for the welfare of mankind.

Anna V. Harkness

I.

The school's responsibility for the mental health of children is a powerful theme in the American educational experience of the twentieth century. Some sub-themes can be identified. The child's personality, not his or her intelligence or character, is the essence of the human being; the experiences of childhood are of critical importance; the school is the strategic agency to detect, ameliorate, and prevent maladjustment. In the construction of this model of education, the mental hygiene movement played the leading role. For an education based on mental hygiene principles to be accepted by educators and parents, there first had to be a change in the American cultural consciousness. The main conduit for the dissemination of the mental hygiene view of education was the Commonwealth Fund.

Until the emergence of the federal government in the 1950s as a major source of funding, private foundations played a dominant role in fostering educational innovation. It is well known that the Carnegie Foundation, the Russell Sage Foundation, the Rockefeller Foundation's General Education Board, and the Ford Foundation's Fund for the Advancement of Education have been extremely active in the field of public education. Not so well known, but perhaps as influential as any of the above, was the Commonwealth Fund. No history of the mental hygiene movement, the child guidance movement, child psychiatry, psychiatric social work, or the transformation of the school in America in the twentieth century would be complete without reference to the Commonwealth Fund. In the 1920s the Fund was the main link between the mental hygiene movement and public education. From 1920 into the 1930s the *raison d'être* of the Fund was to strengthen that link.[1] This chapter, centering on the Fund, is the first part of a broader investigation of the mental hygiene movement and the medicalization of American education.

II.

The mental hygiene movement was another expression of the concern for child welfare, faith in science, impulse toward organization, and unbounded optimism that characterized reform movements of the progressive era. The beginnings of the mental hygiene movement can be dated from 1908–1909 and the organization first of the Connecticut Society for Mental Hygiene and then of the National Committee for Mental Hygiene (NCMH) in 1910. An early concern of the NCMH was to ameliorate the treatment and conditions of institutionalized adult mental defectives and the mentally disordered.[2] By the outbreak of World War I, the mental hygiene movement had changed from this initial reform effort, becoming a crusade for prevention and thus involving work with children and ultimately the school. The optimism, not to say utopianism, that animated the mental hygiene movement was supplied by the new dynamic psychiatry of Adolf Meyer, to which was added elements of John B. Watson's Behaviorism and psychoanalytic theory contributed by American exegetes of Freud like the psychiatrist William Alanson White.

Dr. Adolf Meyer is an extraordinary figure in the history of psychiatry and the mental hygiene movement. When William James wrote that "the power of certain individuals to affect . . . others is to me almost the all in all of social change," he might have had Adolf Meyer in mind. Meyer was at the hub of a wheel of influence connecting psychiatry, child guidance, psychiatric social work, the mental hygiene movement, and education. It was Meyer, at the turn of the century the country's most prominent psychiatrist, who not only provided the key term "mental hygiene" but did more than anyone else to steer the NCMH into the field of prevention.

In a series of articles between 1906 and 1909, Meyer gave American psychiatry a new orientation.[3] In the mid-1890s he had begun to work out his notion of dynamic psychiatry or "eclectic psychiatry of the whole person." By 1906 Meyer was ready to offer his formulation of the etiology of dementia praecox, then the most dreaded of mental illnesses. Meyer rejected Emil Kraepelin's definition of dementia praecox as organic and irreversible and, borrowing from Watson's behaviorist psychology, redefined it in terms of defective adaptation, deterioration of habits, and faulty ways of meeting life's problems. People suffering from dementia praecox had failed to adjust to the circumstances, tests, and stresses of life. Meyer identified some danger signs of incipient mental illness: evasiveness, seclusiveness, drifting away from concrete interests, daydreaming, refusing to cope with reality, and other "substitutive" forms of behavior (what the psychiatrist August Hoch subsequently was to label the "shut–in personality"). Meyer's proposed therapy or cure was re-education in better or more efficient ways of adapting to life.

Because dementia praecox was considered not so much a disease but a form of faulty social adaptation, new vistas were opened up. One implication drawn by Meyer was that many forms of mental illness were preventable—in fact, "much more easily prevented than cured." Childhood, when habits were very largely established, was the critical point of intervention. If childhood was the critical period, then family and school were the obvious points of attack. Meyer had little to say about the family, but much to say about that other social agency greatly affecting children, the school. As early as 1908 he was complaining that the line between "pedagogue and psychopathologist," between teacher and psychiatrist, was too sharply drawn. The school was the place to detect early manifestations of potential mental illness like seclusiveness and daydreaming. Meyer singled out the shy and quiet child—the kind of child whom teachers typically considered the ideal, the "good" child—as a problem, a potential candidate for mental illness. "Teachers," Meyers advised, "should get over the notion that only the bad pupil needs attention." The "so-called good pupil is very much more likely to be endangered by mental disease and nervous states than the frankly and outspokenly bad and happy-go-lucky child." The children affected, Meyer continued, "are the very ones whom a former generation might have looked upon as model children." Meyer urged teachers to go beyond labeling children who misbehaved as "lazy" or "bad," and in need of punishment, but to consider them a "problem" that could be remedied by scientific understanding of the causes of their behavior.[4]

Meyer inveighed against "abstract studies" and "cramming the pupil with the subjects of the conventional curriculum," which encouraged students to "withdraw from straightforward and wholesome activity" into "seclusion or flights of imagination." Meyer was especially concerned about the pathogenicity of the school through induction of stress. He assigned to failure special etiological significance, and he warned that "reality" should not be made too harsh or too difficult, lest children escape into a world of fantasy and daydreams. Here, Meyer sounds like John Dewey: education should be practical, active, and social. Meyer called for more emphasis on doing, less on knowing: "If the school gave more opportunity for doing things, and doing things successfully, then mere dreams of doing things would be less tempting."[5] Extrapolations from psychoanalysis reinforced Meyer's prescriptions.

Thanks to the work of the historian Nathan Hale, Jr., among other historians who could be cited, the influence of Freud and psychoanalysis on American life and culture is now taken for granted. But Freud's influence on the theory and practice of American education has yet to be sufficiently measured. The subject will be a difficult one; psychoanalysis has filtered into education in a roundabout way and in a severely attenuated form, and psychoanalytic concepts and terminology are rare in the pedagogical literature. The tendency in America, Freud predicted, would be to welcome his theories and water them down with equal enthusiasm. He was not to be disappointed. Freudian concepts were used to supplement and bolster Meyer's dynamic psychiatry. Psychiatric progressives and adherents of psychoanalysis like William Alanson White, James J. Putnam, Thomas W. Salmon, and Smith Ely Jeliffe domesticated psychoanalysis by sloughing off its pessimistic, biologically oriented side, while taking from Freud what suited their own more optimistic, environmentalist, reformist inclinations.[6] The prime example is White, a tireless advocate and interpreter of Freud and psychoanalysis to psychiatry and the mental hygiene movement. Mental illness did not strike out of the blue; there was an "incubation period." Childhood was the critical time. In White's oft-cited phrase: "childhood was the golden period for mental hygiene." The inferences to be drawn were obvious: with proper child rearing and educational practices, psychological maladjustment and all forms of mental illness could be prevented. Home and school were the obvious points of attack in any program of prevention. But to hygienists, the home seemed to offer the least encouragement. They were convinced that the school was the most practical place to work for results. "Practically all the hopeful points of attack" Salmon declared in 1916, "exist in early childhood, and if the psychiatrists are to take up such work, they must be permitted to enter the schools."[7] This was only wishful thinking until the founding of the Commonwealth Fund in 1918.

III.

The Commonwealth Fund was not only endowed with a great deal of money by the standards of the day but endowed open-endedly. Mrs. Anna V. Harkness's initial bequest, about $10 million, was unbounded; her mandate was "to do something for the welfare of mankind." The Fund began life under its first general director Max Farrand, on leave from his position as professor of history at Yale, with no special priorities. But the Fund needed to make a big impact quickly. It was being swamped with applications for small grants, and Farrand was worried that the Fund's money would be frittered away without accomplishing any large purposes. The Fund's president, Edward Harkness, Mrs. Harkness's son, agreed. He urged Farrand to get on with the task of carving out a special niche. Finally, in 1920 Farrand and the Fund found what they were looking for. Farrand resolved to focus all the Fund's efforts on child welfare and "preventive work with children" as the most promising field for its endeavors, and within this larger field on the prevention of juvenile delinquency.[8] Delinquency seemed a promising field, but the subject was so large and complex that the difficulty was to find the best method of attack.

While Meyer and the National Committee for Mental Hygiene had lots of ideas about preventive work with children, it was desperate for financial support. The NCMH had already applied to the Commonwealth Fund in 1919 and had been the recipient of the Fund's largest award that year, $10,000. In November 1920, the Fund invited Thomas Salmon, the NCMH medical director, to submit a program for possible funding. Salmon responded quickly with a lengthy proposal for a program aimed at the prevention of juvenile delinquency.[9] The Fund responded with a call for a conference to be held at Lakewood, New Jersey, on 30 January 1921, to discuss Salmon's proposal. Among the participants were Dr. William Healy of Boston's

Judge Baker Foundation; Dr. Bernard Glueck, director of the New York School of Social Work; Professor Henry C. Morrison of the School of Education at the University of Chicago, as well as Dr. Salmon and the Fund's Farrand.

The conference adopted Salmon's entire plan and rationale and urged speedy implementation. The final report of the conference is worth summarizing. The conferees announced that enough was now known about the causes of delinquency to focus on methods of prevention, and "the first steps in prevention must deal with incipient conduct disorders of childhood." Indeed, "the importance of centering all constructive work in childhood could not be over-emphasized: the adult is what the child was." Adverse social conditions and their impact on delinquency were declared outside the scope of the conference. The conferees decided to focus on the public school. They explained that "lack of knowledge by teachers and school authorities of existing information regarding disorders of conduct results in many instances in the actual causation of delinquency through mismanagement of incipient disorders . . . and, to a much greater extent, in failure to carry out preventive measures in an environment presenting many favorable opportunities." The conferees recommended that schools greatly extend their activities with reference to conduct disorders and, as a first step toward this end, that "a systematic attempt be made . . . to inform teachers, students in the field of education, and school authorities of the present scientific conception of disorders of conduct and their treatment."[10]

The Fund took no immediate initiative. But in the summer of 1921, just when it seemed likely that the Laura Spelman Rockefeller Memorial Foundation was about to enter (and preempt) the general field of child welfare, the Fund acted. In July, Farrand resigned as general director to return to Yale. Barry C. Smith, a former social worker, was appointed to succeed him. On 9 November 1921 the Fund adopted a five year Program for the Prevention of Delinquency.[11]

This program became one of the most influential of its kind ever attempted in the United States, and it needs to be described in some detail. Its stated general objectives were demonstration of the value of psychiatric study and treatment of "difficult, pre-delinquent, or problem children"; the nationwide promotion of the "visiting teacher" or school social worker; and the dissemination among educators and the general public of the new, scientific methods of studying, treating, and preventing behavior problems in children. For working purposes, the program was organized into four divisions: I, the National Committee for Mental Hygiene; II, the New York School of Social Work; III, the Public Education Association of New York City; IV, the Joint Committee on Methods of Preventing Delinquency.[12] Divisions III and IV are the most relevant for us.

Division III: Public Education Association of New York City (PEA). The PEA was assigned the task of carrying out the largest phase of the program: the national demonstration by visiting teachers. A specially organized National Committee on Visiting Teachers was established under the auspices of the PEA, placed under the direct supervision of the psychiatric social workers Howard Nudd and Jane Culbert, and assigned the task of placing thirty visiting teachers in public schools in thirty different communities around the country, for three-year demonstration periods. The Fund was to pay two-thirds of the salaries of these teachers, and the demonstration periods were to be staggered so as to end in 1927, when the program was slated to end.

Why the emphasis on the visiting teacher? Barry Smith raised this question rhetorically. His answer has echoed through the decades. Smith explained that the Commonwealth Fund had first considered traditional techniques for preventing delinquency such as improved housing and organized recreation, but rejected them as impractical and decided to concentrate its efforts "only at certain strategic points"— the most vital being the public school. "Practically all children," Smith pointed out, "are for a shorter or longer period in our schools. The public school, coming into close contact with the lives of over twenty million young boys, girls, and adolescents, is—or should be—our greatest social welfare agency." Schoolteachers, he continued, provided they were aware of it, had unequaled opportunities to observe the first signs of undesirable tendencies on the part of the child. Any child who was tending in any way toward delinquency invariably indicated that something was amiss by his or her conduct, work, or attitude. "The public school teachers of the nation," Smith concluded, "if they can be socialized, can accomplish more to prevent delinquency than all the social workers together." But Smith disclaimed any intention of adding to the teacher's burden. This was where the visiting teachers or school social workers came into the picture. They were to work with "problem children" until the public school teachers of the nation became "socialized."[13]

Division IV: The Joint Committee on Methods of Preventing Delinquency. The Commonwealth Fund established the Joint Committee to coordinate its various enterprises in the fields of mental hygiene, to evaluate the program, and to educate the public in the mental hygiene point of view so as to gradually "change the attitude of thinking people." The Commonwealth Fund, Smith explained, "does not expect to reform the world. The definite measurable results of the program may even be difficult to ascertain." But, he concluded, "if the program shall succeed in ever so small a degree in demonstrating the value of new methods of approach, and in pointing the way to what may be accomplished with the individual by the basing of adequate treatment upon adequate knowledge, the effort will have been worthwhile."[14]

IV.

By 1924 the National Committee on Visiting Teachers had thirty demonstrations in operation. Thanks to the Fund, the visiting teacher was introduced to rural areas such as Boone County, Missouri, and Huron County, Ohio, and to towns such as Chisholm, Minnesota; Hutchinson, Kansas; Pocatello, Idaho; Bluefield, West Virginia.[15] During the summers of 1927–1929, the staff of the program's National Committee on Visiting Teachers introduced pioneer courses on mental hygiene and the behavioral problems of children to teachers and teachers in training at Harvard University, George Peabody College for Teachers, the University of Washington, the University of Kansas, the University of North Carolina, Western Reserve University, Michigan State Normal School, as well as the University of Alabama, the University of California, Minnesota University, the University of Missouri, Wyoming University, and New York University.[16] But visiting teachers and courses for teachers were not high on the list of the Commonwealth Fund's priorities. The Fund's highest priority was the public's education. The Fund's Annual Report for 1932 referred to a period when "all the educational and social agencies of the community needed to be educated simultaneously in the principles and practices of mental hygiene." The philosophy, aims, and methods of the Program for the Prevention of Delinquency were to be disseminated as widely as possible, in order that the community "may develop a consciousness regarding the value of mental hygiene." This was from the beginning one of the main responsibilities of each division of the program; by 1924 it had become the major thrust of the entire program. It was the responsibility of the Joint Committee to coordinate all educative efforts. In 1927 the Joint Committee was replaced by a more professional Division of Publications, which became the main conduit for the dissemination of mental hygiene in American education through the 1920s and the 1930s. The promotional activities of the Division of Publications were extraordinary in scope: monthly newsletters, reprints of articles, a service to inquirers, a speakers' bureau, lectures to any group that asked, as well as personal contacts.[17] The Division of Publications became the most consequential division of the Program for the Prevention of Delinquency.

V.

Through the 1920s and into the 1930s the Program for the Prevention of Delinquency carried out the implications of policy formulated in 1921. There was a definite change in emphasis, but this had been implicit from the beginning; the focus was narrowed to the school and the teacher. One of the most striking things about the program is how masterfully it wove together the implications of the new psychiatry and mental hygiene for education.

A major difficulty in studying the mental hygiene movement in education is the difficulty of finding a program that can be considered authoritative or representative. The Program for the Prevention of Delinquency helps us get at the strategic core of the movement's efforts at school reform. The program was made up almost entirely of elements at hand in the decade before World War I. We need to reconstruct this cognitive package. If this could be accomplished, it would help define the intellectual and cultural outlook of an entire period. What follows is an attempt to provide a thread, like Ariadne's, through the labyrinth.

In his Annual Report for 1926, Smith stated that the understanding and treatment of personality difficulties of children offered the possibility not only of preventing delinquency but of preventing mental illness in general—that early detection of symptoms could eliminate conflicts or cure habits likely to lead to "unhappiness, inefficiency, and failure in adult life." But for prevention to succeed, it was necessary to reach the child at home or at school, to reach the parent or teacher. Of course, the program was concerned with educating parents. But the program was convinced that the school, not the home, was the most promising site for preventive work.

Implicit, and sometimes explicit, in the program's literature, was what might be called a doctrine of parent blaming; parents were to blame for all the problems of children. Parent blaming entered the American cultural consciousness through many channels; Christopher Lasch has documented some of them in *Haven in a Heartless World: The Family Besieged* (1977), but none had more impact than the mental hygiene movement. The NCMH's Thomas Salmon once commented that it was hard for him to think of the home as any kind of beneficent institution.[18] The social work educators Porter R. Lee and Marion Kenworthy in their influential textbook, *Mental Hygiene and Social Work,* proclaimed that at the age of five or six the child may be described as a "symptom-complex of his parental handling."[19] The faults of parents were many. The "most consummate skill" was needed to rear children properly.[20] This was a skill that parents not only did not possess but were scarcely aware they needed to possess. Hygienists launched an effort to educate parents. Unfortunately, parents couldn't be required to take courses or forced to obtain a degree before having children. To hygienists the public school, thanks to compulsory attendance laws, surpassed the home and parents by far in its potential for preventive work with children.

If the schools were to live up to their potential, there was much that had to be done, especially in the enlightenment of teachers. Hygienists accused teachers of concentrating exclusively on intellect and knowledge; they were ignorant of the child's emotional life. Echoing Adolf Meyer, hygienists ranked failure and nonpromotion as foremost among school experiences that violated the principles of mental hygiene and sinned against children's personality development. A refrain running through the program's literature was that the school would have to abolish failure.[21] In any event, the intellectual side was no longer that important. The school would have to deemphasize its traditional academic fare and provide experiences that would enhance the child's personality and emotional life. "By itself alone," according to one staff member, Howard Nudd, "the intellectual appeal is inadequate in the training of personality. Positive feelings and habits must be constantly nurtured or corrected, as the case may be, in the entire daily life of the child."[22]

Teachers would have to be educated about mental hygiene. To hygienists, teachers were ignorant not only of the personality development of the child but of how their own personalities powerfully affected children. Even the subtlest things about the teacher were important, such as "attitude, gesture, tone of voice." But the most important attribute of a teacher, Dr. Bernard Glueck explained, was understanding the personality of the individual child. Glueck urged teachers to go beyond overt behavior to get to know the child's personality makeup. The teacher had to provide a freer, more relaxed classroom climate that would encourage the child to "show himself for what he is" and not "deceive" for the sake of good discipline.[23] No child should be able to escape the teacher's *gaze*, Michel Foucault's evocative term.

Hygienists required the teacher to become an expert on normality and a vast area of deviations from the standard. Hygienist's greatly enlarged the scope of the classroom teacher's responsibility to include the "early detection of the child out of adjustment," and the "early detection of inabilities, instabilities, and dissatisfactions."[24] And hardly any child was immune from maladjustment. It was not only children who overtly misbehaved in class who were "out of adjustment"; the quiet, timid, or shy child and the "overconformer"—Meyer's so-called "good" child—were "problems" as well. A staff member, Dr. Ralph Truitt, identified seclusiveness, shyness, laziness, fearfulness, and quarrelsomeness as potential "signs of a disease process." The child *may* outgrow these traits, Truitt warned, but might not.[25] Howard Nudd described the types of problem children the visiting teacher dealt with: "the precocious and gifted, the irritable, the worried, the violent tempered, the repressed, . . . and the indescribable, who are always in need of counsel."[26] Schools seemed to be filled with problem children.[27] The burden of responsibility for surveillance, detection, and treatment fell on the school and the teacher. What finally emerges from the literature of the Program for the Prevention of Delinquency is an agenda for the medicalization of American education: every student a "problem" or patient, every teacher a therapist, the class period a therapeutic hour, and "every school a clinic."[28]

VI.

The Commonwealth Fund launched its Program for the Prevention of Delinquency in 1921 and for all practical purposes terminated the program in 1933. During its relatively short life the program left a lasting imprint on child psychiatry, child guidance, and psychiatric social work. The program also left an enduring legacy to American education. In this concluding section, I venture an appraisal of that legacy.

From 1921 to 1933, the Commonwealth Fund gave priority to furthering the mental hygiene movement in the public schools. So far as the Fund's impact on education, there are facts and figures regarding numbers of visiting teachers and child guidance clinics. But figures cannot get at the problem of influence. There was no attempt to apply principles of mental hygiene directly in the schools or to educate parents and teachers in the "mental hygiene point of view" until the NCMH and the Commonwealth Fund launched the Program for the Prevention of Delinquency. The point is the program's role as architect and disseminator of a medical or therapeutic ideal of education.

The main objective of the mental hygiene movement was to develop the consciousness of the community with regard to mental hygiene and to make the "mental hygiene point of view" the guiding principle of American public education. I think it is clear that the Fund had some success in "diffusing through the entire field of education . . . a firmer knowledge of mental hygiene and its application," and that it also achieved some success in disseminating the mental hygiene point of view, to a broader public of parents, professionals, and other influential people, which facilitated acceptance by schools and teachers. Still, this is hard to document quantitatively. The nature of influence is more subtle than figures can suggest. As I elaborate elsewhere in this book, the way to track the diffusion of the mental hygiene point of view is through language, vocabulary, and rhetoric.[29] The mental hygiene movement in education changed the way Americans think and talk about education. Americans routinely think and speak about education in terms of its language of discourse, even when they don't know that this is what they are in fact doing. It is here, in the area of developing the "consciousness of the community" regarding the value of the mental hygiene point of view of education is the place to look for the legacy of the Program for the Prevention of Delinquency.

VII.

Revisionist interpretations of the helping professions by historians David Rothman, John Burnham, and Anthony Platt, among others, depend on a "social control" model and are skeptical of do gooders. [30] This study of the Commonwealth Fund makes me lean somewhat toward their camp. Of course, if a therapeutic milieu could be created in schools, frustration and resentment would be prevented or reduced and with it a potential source of hostility to the social order. The hygienist ideal of adjustment or what Michel Foucault calls "normalization" instantiates the essential conservatism of the mental hygiene movement. But there is something else involved. The issue raised by the program lies in some ironic reflections on the limits of "doing good." While what follows is written from a viewpoint somewhat skeptical of the effects of the mental hygiene movement and the Commonwealth Fund, it should not be read as imputing either conscious class interest or bad faith to the advocates of mental hygiene, who appear to have been sincerely convinced that the diffusion of their beliefs would have enormous social benefit.

Altruism is as real a motive as self-interest. Suppose we grant the altruism of the Commonwealth Fund—that the Fund was trying to do something for the welfare of children, trying to "do good." But the irony is that the Fund didn't really know what it was doing. The Program for the Prevention of Delinquency rested on a shaky knowledge base; in fact it rested on hardly any empirically verifiable knowledge at all.

In an article published in 1915, William Healy and Augusta Bronner describe a long-term project for the education and treatment of juvenile delinquents. They admit that their project was complex and difficult, but they assured readers that it was worth the effort: "We are told that in Heaven there is much rejoicing over even one delinquent saved."[31] In 1927, Barry Smith, in a wrap-up of the accomplishments of the program, states that it was "more successful than had been anticipated," and that "much has been learned as to the technique of applying the principles of mental hygiene to the individual child." There is "ample evidence" that the work has been "well done and that sound results have been secured."[32] As a matter of fact, Smith was concerned with the inadequacy of the research and evaluation he was receiving from the Program's various divisions. The outstanding need, Smith warned, was for research "so that the scientific basis of [our] work may become more accurate and definite."

There are some figures on the number of "problem children" treated in the program, most of them successfully "adjusted," we are told. I can accept this. Even if only a small percentage of children were saved from juvenile delinquency or from the crippling effects of introversion, shyness, or constant failure, it would be to the program's credit. But here is an irony: if some children were saved, it would seem to involve luck, intuition, the passage of time, or practical forms of social intervention rather than any special psychiatric "science" or professional expertise. The Fund was loaded with money and looking for a project; it rushed into the embrace of the NCMH. It launched the Program for the Prevention of Delinquency with a minimum of research and a maximum of publicity. For more than a decade, the Fund devoted a large share of its appropriations to the furtherance of the mental hygiene movement in the public schools. And why not? The Program for the Prevention of Delinquency was a product of expert opinion in psychiatry and medicine. The Fund stepped into an uncharted field and erected there a major construction. Who could have known how flimsy its theoretical foundation, with the benefit of hindsight, would turn out to be?

The general field of psychiatry, on which the program was based, has come in for its share of critical attention as an autonomous medical specialty in recent years. But the Commonwealth Fund's own literature provides a record of progressive disillusionment and finally a trenchant critique of the Program for the Prevention of Delinquency. From the beginning, Barry Smith's and the Fund's position was that the Program would have to be made scientifically unassailable. As it turned out, the Fund could never obtain the critical evaluation it sought. Take the visiting teacher project: it was "difficult to record in black and white the methods followed by visiting teachers; it is even harder to evaluate the results they have obtained."[33] As regards the child guidance clinics, the results with individual children "were hard to measure." As late as 1933, there was still "no methodology for evaluating results."[34] Finally, in 1940, Helen L. Witmer's *Psychiatric Clinics for Children* appeared, a volume commissioned by the Fund. Witmer explicitly questioned the basic theoretical assumptions underlying the child guidance and mental hygiene movements and implicitly questioned the viability of the Program for the Prevention of Delinquency. The potential psychotic, she said, cannot be identified in childhood. Consequently, "it would seem that the prevention of mental illness must be abandoned as a primary objective of child psychiatry." So far as the prevention of delinquency was concerned, social, economic, and legal factors were so central that this goal "would seem to be an even less tenable aim" than the prevention of mental illness.[35]

The Commonwealth Fund stayed with the Program for the Prevention of Delinquency for twelve years, got out, and then drew a veil over its involvel   in the program and in the mental hygiene movement in educati   then, the mental hygiene movement in education no longer needed the Commonwealth Fund; the "socialization" of the nation's schoolteachers went on without it. In the 1930s, the Commonwealth Fund left it to the Progressive Education Association and the Rockefeller Foundation's General Education Board to carry on the work of socializing public school teachers, that is, indoctrinating teachers in the mental hygiene point of view. In 1937, Barry Smith, still the general director of the Fund, with the recent partnership between the Progressive Education Association and the General Education Board clearly in mind, poured scorn on "poorly planned and illconceived efforts to introduce mental hygiene into various school systems under varying plans."[36] By then, the Fund's priorities had shifted from mental hygiene and the identification and treatment of problem children in the schools to medical research and medical education.

Notes

1   Besides the explicit references, which I have tried to keep to a minimum, this chapter is based on the following archival sources: Annual Reports of the Commonwealth Fund, 1919–1937; Minute Book of the Fund's Joint Committee on Methods of Preventing Delinquency, 1922–1927; and the Fund's Staff Newsletter, 1922–1927; all in the Archives of the Commonwealth Fund, Rockefeller Archive Center, Sleepy Hollow, New York; and the Thomas W. Salmon Papers at the Archives of Cornell–New York Hospital, New York City.

2   Barbara Sicherman, *The Quest for Mental Health in America, 1880–1917* (Ann Arbor, 1971); and Norman Dain, *Clifford W. Beers, Advocate for the Insane* (Pittsburgh, 1980).

3   Theodore Lidz, "Adolph Meyer and the Development of American Psychiatry," *American Journal of Psychiatry*, 123 (1966): 320–332; William Alanson White, "The Origin and First Twenty-Five Years of the Mental Hygiene Movement," *Science*, 52 (25 July 1930).

4   "What Do Histories of Cases of Insanity Teach Us Concerning Preventive Mental Hygiene During the Years of School Life?" *Psychological Clinic*, 2 (15 June 1908): 95.

5   Ibid., pp. 242–245. See also Meyer's "Modern Conceptions of Mental Disease," in H. S. Jennings, ed., *Suggestions of Modern Science Concerning Education* (New York, 1917).

6   Nathan G. Hale, Jr., *Freud and the Americans: The Beginnings of Psychoanalysis in the United States, 1876–1917* (New York, 1971), and *The Rise and Crisis of Psychoanalysis in the United States: Freud and the Americans, 1917–1985* (New York, 1995). See also John Chynoweth Burnham, *Psychoanalysis and American Medicine, 1894–1918* (New York, 1967), and Fred H. Matthews, "The Americanization of Sigmund Freud: Adaptations of Psychoanalysis Before 1917," *Journal of American Studies*, 1 (1967): 39–62.

7   Quoted in Sicherman, *The Quest for Mental Health in America*, p. 280.

8   *Commonwealth Fund, Annual Report, 1920*; Commonwealth Fund, *The Commonwealth Fund: A Historical Sketch, 1918–1962* (New York, 1963), pp. 1–4; A. McGehee Harvey and Susan L. Abrams, *"For The Welfare of Mankind": The Commonwealth Fund and American Medicine* (Baltimore, 1986), chs. 1–3; and Margo Horn, *Before It's Too Late: The Child Guidance Movement in the United States, 1922–1945* (Philadelphia, 1989), chs. 1–2.

9   Earl D. Bond, *Thomas W. Salmon: Psychiatrist* (New York, 1950), pp. 188ff.

10   Commonwealth Fund, *Annual Report, 1921*; Bernard Glueck, "Thomas W. Salmon and The Child Guidance Movement," *Journal of Juvenile Research,* 13 (1929): 79–89.

11   Commonwealth Fund, *Annual Report, 1922*, pp. 8–25. The program is also described in Barry C. Smith, "The Commonwealth Fund Program for the Prevention of Delinquency," *Proceedings, National Conference of Social Work, 1922*, pp. 168–174.

12   McGehee and Abrams, *For the Welfare of Mankind*, ch. 3; Horn, *Before It's Too Late*, chs. 3–4.

13   Commonwealth Fund, *Annual Report, 1922*, pp. 21–23.

14   Ibid., p. 25; *Proceedings, National Conference of Social Work, 1922*, p. 174.

15   Lois Meredith French, *Psychiatric Social Work* (New York, 1956), pp. 63–66. The term "visiting teacher" was replaced in 1941 by the more accurate term, "school social worker."

16   Commonwealth Fund, *Annual Report, 1928*, p. 58. At Western Reserve University there was a seminar described as "intensive study of several types of problem children, such as the dull, normal, superior, emotionally unstable, neglected, and socially maladjusted." W. Carson Ryan, "The Preparation of Teachers for Dealing with Behavior Problem Children," *School and Society*, 28 (18 August 1928): 210.

17   Commonwealth Fund, *Annual Report, 1926*.

18   Quoted in Bond, *Thomas W. Salmon, Psychiatrist*, p. 218.

19   New York, 1929, p. 65.

20   Miriam Van Waters, *Parents on Probation* (New York, 1927).

21   *Annual Report, 1923*, p. 14.

22   Howard W. Nudd, "Social Work Enters the School," *Survey*, 54 (1925): 32–34; and "The Purpose and Scope of Visiting Teacher Work," in Mary B. Sayles, ed., *Problem Children in School* (New York, 1927).

23   As William Healy explains, the primary question is not "What does the child learn in school?" but rather, "How does the child feel because of school?" William Healy and Augusta Bronner, "How Does the School Produce or Prevent Delinquency?" *Journal of Educational Sociology*, 6 (1933): 470; Ralph P. Truitt, "Barriers to Mental Hygiene: Teachers," *Proceedings, National Conference of Social Work, 1925*, pp. 426–430.

24   Commonwealth Fund, *Annual Report, 1929*, p. 60.

25   "Community Child Guidance Clinics," in Ralph T. Pruitt, ed., *The Child Guid-ance Clinic and the Community* (New York, 1933), p. 13.

26   "The Purpose and Scope of Visiting Teacher Work," p. 258. Edwin K. Wickman's study *Children's Behavior and Teachers' Attitudes* (New York, 1928), sponsored by the Fund, is a classic.

27   A study by the program's Minneapolis Child Guidance Clinic estimated that 39 percent of the children in the city's public elementary schools needed psychiatric treatment. Merle E. Haggerty, "The Incidence of Undesirable Be-havior in Public School Children," *Journal of Educational Research*, 12 (1925): 102–122.

28   Elizabeth L. Woods, "The School and Delinquency: Every School a Clinic," National Conference of Social Work, *Proceedings*, 1929, pp. 213–221.

29   Chapter 11, "The Medicalization of American Education: The Social History of an Idea."

30   Willard Gaylin et al., *Doing Good: The Limits of Benevolence* (New York, 1978); David J. Rothman, *Conscience and Convenience: The Asylum and its Alternatives in Progressive America* (Boston,1980); John C. Burnham, "The New Psychology: From Narcissism to Social Control," in John Braeman et al., *Change and Continuity in Twentieth Century America* (Columbus, Ohio, 1968), pp. 396–398; Anthony M. Platt, *The Child-Savers:The Inven-tion of Delinquency* (Chicago, 1969).

31   "An Outline for the Institutional Education and Treatment of Young Offend-ers," *Journal of Educational Psychology*, 6 (1915): 316.

32   Commonwealth Fund, *Annual Report, 1927,* p. 43.

33   Mabel Brown Ellis, *The Visiting Teacher in Rochester* (New York, 1925), p. 132.

34   Commonwealth Fund, *Annual Report, 1933*, pp. 60–61.

35   Helen L. Witmer, *Psychiatric Clinics for Children* (New York, 1940), ch. 10, especially pp. 257–259, 273ff.

36   Commonwealth Fund, *Annual Report*, p. 7.

Chapter 9

Changing Conceptions of the American College and University, 1920–1940: The Mental Hygiene Movement and the "Essentials of an Education"

One of the extraordinary fallacies of the present system of education is the assumption that the emotional and mental characteristics of the cultivated person can be developed merely by instruction in the Classics.

Stewart Paton

I.

This chapter depicts a little-known episode in the history of American higher education: the attempt by the mental hygiene movement to gain a foothold in the colleges and universities. The initial objective of psychiatrists who led the movement was to persuade colleges and universities to establish a psychiatric service for students with problems of "adjustment." Once this service was established, their objective became more ambitious—to disseminate the "mental hygiene point of view" throughout American higher education, to make students' emotional and personality development the guiding principle of colleges and universities, and to become the moral tutors of America's college students. A group of rather obscure or only vaguely known psychiatrist–educational reformers were instrumental in obtaining psychiatric or mental health services for college and university students, and their conception of higher education is as provocative and perhaps fresher than that of better-known figures in college and university reform such as Alexander Meiklejohn, Irving Babbitt, or Robert Hutchins.

Because of the nature of its subject matter, this essay enters into historiographical debates about reform movements, the helping professions in general, and psychiatry in particular. It also touches on some broader phenomena: the analyses by Philip Rieff, Christopher Lasch, and Fred Matthews, among others, of a more general cultural development in this century, the infiltration of psychiatric authority and psychiatric categories of thought, discourse, and value into all aspects of American life.[1] To do justice to the mental hygiene movement in higher education would require an interprofessional history of psychiatry, psychology, social work, organized philanthropy, and higher education as well as the mental hygiene movement itself. Now the problem is to provide enough information to make the subject intelligible without telling readers more than they want to know.

II.

Turn-of-the-century progressivism was the matrix from which the mental hygiene movement emerged. The mental hygiene movement was part of a many-faceted effort to come to grips with life in the new urban-industrial society that characterized the progressive era. The National Committee for Mental Hygiene (NCMH), the organizational spearhead of the mental hygiene movement, was established in 1910. While many prominent laypeople took part in the founding and early years of the NCMH, a group of psychiatric progressives, including Drs. August Hoch, C. Macfie Campbell, Thomas W. Salmon, Stewart Paton, Frankwood E. Williams, and William Alanson White, and led by Adolf Meyer, provided the movement's leadership.[2]

Inspired by advances in public health, especially the campaign against tuberculosis, hygienists were eager to launch an aggressive campaign against mental illness. But the NCMH began in a modest, even desultory way. Funds were difficult to obtain, and the general therapeutic pessimism regarding the mentally ill, characteristic of American psychiatry and medicine in the late nineteenth and early twentieth century, was hard to combat. By the 1920s, however, under its first medical director, Thomas Salmon, the scope of the NCMH had grown considerably, expanding from a concern with insanity and mental deficiency to the prevention, in White's words, of "all forms of social maladjustment and even unhappiness," and extending well beyond the confines of the hospital and the mental asylum to all agencies having to do with individual and social welfare. The theoretical basis for the imperialism of the mental hygiene movement in the 1920s was formulated in the period before World War I out of such diverse sources as Meyer's "dynamic psychiatry of the whole person" and psychoanalytic concepts extrapolated from Freud—though a domesticated Freud, to be sure. Its hopes rested on a new conception of mental illness, which placed the emphasis on disorders of personality rather than heredity or organic injury.

According to the hygienists, mental illness was not a disease of the brain or nervous system but a personality maladjustment caused by the stresses of life.[3] Disorders of personality were responsible not only for individual suffering but for social problems like delinquency, crime, dependency, and industrial unrest. And—*the* fundamental working assumption of the mental hygiene movement—personality was basically malleable.[4] Belief in the malleability of personality made the hygienists optimistic regarding the treatment and cure of mental illness, inspired their belief in prevention through "mental hygiene," and led them to the schools and then to the colleges and universities.

At first, hygienists proclaimed that childhood was the critical period for personality development and that the strategic institution for mental hygiene was the public school. The hygienists' therapeutic imperialism, cautious at first, gradually grew stronger. By the early 1920s, the same principles of mental hygiene were considered as valid for young adults in colleges or universities as for children in grade school or adolescents in high school.

Hygienists' experiences during World War I were crucial in this change in focus. The psychiatrists' experience with so-called "shell shock" provided convincing evidence for the role of personality disorders in mental illness. Specifically, their experience in treating shell shock confirmed the hygienists' belief in the psychological nature of mental illness. Psychological disorders might have their roots in childhood, but maladjustment could arise from precipitating events much later and, more important, could be ameliorated or even cured in adulthood. The psychiatrists' well-publicized successes in the treatment of shell shock created an atmosphere in which the mental hygiene movement subsequently thrived.[5]

Salmon's ambition had always been to steer the NCMH into a grandiose mission of preventive mental hygiene. He had been on leave during the war, but he resumed his post as medical director of the NCMH in 1920. Before he resigned in 1922, Salmon planned the Commonwealth Fund's momentous "Program for the Prevention of Delinquency," which launched the child guidance movement, greatly stimulated the development of psychiatric social work, and disseminated the principles of mental hygiene into the public schools.[6] In the meantime, first under Salmon and then under his successor, Dr. Frankwood E. Williams, the mental hygiene movement made even more rapid progress in colleges and universities.

III.

The pioneer college mental hygiene service was started in 1910 at Princeton University by Dr. Stewart Paton. As a lecturer in neurobiology, Paton, a psychiatrist, informally used his office as a mental hygiene clinic to help students with problems of adjustment.[7] Although his "conferences" were popular with students, he was at first unable to convince his psychiatrist colleagues that there was a field for useful work on the nation's campuses. By 1915 Paton had won over a small group of fellow psychiatrists and NCMH activists, including Salmon, Williams, and Campbell; but the war intervened before they or the NCMH could pursue the matter. The real drive for mental hygiene at colleges began in earnest after the war, when a connection with colleges and universities became a high priority of the NCMH.

The psychiatrists' experience in treating war neuroses had proved that even with adults, timely psychiatric intervention might prevent more serious mental illness. But prosaic concerns of self-interest were also involved in the project to establish mental hygiene in colleges and universities. The status of the profession of psychiatry was still marginal in the early 1920s; psychiatry as a distinct scientific specialty was not yet even completely accepted in schools of medicine.[8] Psychiatrists were anxious to enhance their stature in the academic community. The prestige of a university or college connection would help legitimatize both psychiatry and mental hygiene in a way that a connection with asylums, courts, the penal system, or industry could not. In addition, if mental hygiene and psychiatry were to gain widespread public acceptance—another goal of the mental hygiene movement—it would be necessary to reach young people in college.[9] Finally, and perhaps most important, many psychiatrists had come out of their war service determined to avoid the problems of the insane and the mentally deficient, which had been their preoccupation before the war. They preferred to deal with functional disorders, that is, general problems of psychological maladjustment. They were joined by younger psychiatrists who came of age during the war years, were disinclined to pursue their profession in hospitals or asylums or with veterans suffering from neurosis, and preferred the new child guidance clinics, private practice, or practice at a college or university.[10]

In the early 1920s, mental hygiene services were established at a handful of colleges almost simultaneously by a cadre of psychiatrists influenced or actively recruited by Paton, Salmon, and the NCMH. The pioneers were Drs. Harry Kerns at West Point, Karl Menninger at Washburn College, Arthur Ruggles at Dartmouth, Angus Morrison at the University of Minnesota, Austen Fox Riggs at Vassar, and S. Kinnear Smith and Eva Reid at the University of California, Berkeley. The postwar expansion of college and university student services provided an opening for them. Ruggles, Riggs, and Menninger, for example, were able to become situated in recently established student personnel bureaus.[11] Kerns, Morrison, Smith, Reid, and Paton found niches in recently established student health services.[12] In 1925, Ruggles, who had left Dartmouth in 1923 to become superintendent of Butler Hospital in Providence, Rhode Island, was persuaded to take a leave of absence for a year to inaugurate a mental hygiene service at Yale's Department of University Health.[13] One year later, Yale took center stage in the mental hygiene movement in American higher education.

The NCMH, prodded by Williams, had been active in the 1920s in securing a handful of psychiatrists to lecture or practice at colleges and universities. The NCMH published a journal, *Mental Hygiene,* and a monthly *Bulletin* by means of which psychiatrists could keep in regular contact with each other. Nevertheless, after an initial flurry of enthusiasm, interest in mental hygiene in higher education seemed to be waning.

One obstacle to progress was confusion about where exactly in the college or university the psychiatrist should be located. Should he or she be located in the personnel bureau, the department of student health, the department of psychology, the hospital, or the medical school? This issue was a thorny one, bedeviling the NCMH throughout the 1920s. If integrating mental hygiene into campus life was the goal, it would seem logical that the psychiatrist be attached to a student personnel bureau. But personnel bureaus were largely dominated by psychologists, whom most psychiatrists viewed with antipathy as

narrowly trained practitioners focusing on a minor part of the psyche—
intelligence—and ignoring the most important part—the emotions or
personality. Also, the psychologists were increasingly becoming their
professional rivals in therapy.[14]

Psychiatrists interested in practicing in colleges and universities
wished to avoid as far as possible any association with psychologists;
they desired as close an association with medicine as possible, identifying "mental hygiene" as a medical specialty. Logically, this meant
affiliation with the medical school or hospital. But these were isolated
from campus life. That left the physician-dominated student health
service as the preferred location. This became the official NCMH position. Nevertheless, some psychiatrists advocated the personnel bureau, while college and university administrators did not care if there
was a controversy about location, so long as the job got done. A model
mental hygiene service might settle the matter.

Williams had for years been urging the Commonwealth Fund to
extend its interest in promoting mental hygiene in the public schools
to include higher education. Now Williams turned to Yale, a bastion of
the mental hygiene movement since the founding of the NCMH.[15]
Clifford Beers, the author of the inspirational *A Mind That Found
Itself* (1908)—the text that inspired the mental hygiene movement—
was an alumnus of Yale, and from the beginning, the NCMH enjoyed
the support of what Beers called his "Yale group," which included
Arthur Twining Hadley, Yale's president. In 1921, the NCMH gained
an invaluable addition to the group when James R. Angell became
president of Yale, succeeding Hadley. Angell, a longtime member of
the NCMH, was elected its vice–president in 1924 and subsequently
became active in its affairs. Angell had personally intervened to get
Ruggles to come to Yale to inaugurate the mental hygiene service
there, and he had also secured a small subvention from the General
Education Board, $15,000 a year for five years, to help establish a
department of psychiatry in the Yale School of Medicine.[16] Williams
brought Angell, Beers, and Barry Smith of the Commonwealth Fund
together to discuss the possibility of having the Fund subsidize a project
in mental hygiene at Yale. When the Commonwealth Fund agreed to
support generously the proposed department of psychiatry and a mental
hygiene project, Williams was able to secure the cooperation of Dean
Milton C. Winternitz on behalf of the conservative Yale School of
Medicine.[17]

In the fall of 1926 a $250,000, five-year demonstration in mental
hygiene was launched at Yale. The project involved the establishment

of a Division of Student Hygiene within a Department of Mental Hygiene and Psychiatry, fully integrated into the School of Medicine but housed in and associated with Department of University Health. Incorporating the team concept in mental hygiene exemplified in the Commonwealth Fund's child guidance clinics, the project included provision for four psychiatrists, two psychiatric social workers, and one psychologist. The team was to be headed by Paton, now retired from Princeton.[18] The goal of the project was to establish a department of psychiatry in the School of Medicine at Yale, to lay the foundation of a permanent mental hygiene service for students at Yale, and to stimulate the development of a mental hygiene service at other colleges and universities.

Yale, the "guide and mentor for scores of inland colleges," was finally in the hygienist camp. Now the NCMH looked forward confidently to further and more rapid conquests. In fact, by 1930, about twenty colleges and universities were employing a psychiatrist full-time, part-time, or as a consultant for mental hygiene work with students. Though relatively few, these institutions were both influential and geographically diverse, including, by 1930, not only Yale, Princeton, Dartmouth, Vassar, Washburn College, West Point, the University of Minnesota, and the University of California, but also Harvard, Smith, Brown, Wellesley, Mount Holyoke, the University of Vermont, the University of Colorado, Northwestern University, the University of Michigan, and the University of Chicago.[19]

IV.

"As a general rule," the sociologist Robert C. Angell observed in 1928, "undergraduate life is pleasurable, even at times gay."[20] Not according to the hygienists. To the hygienists, carefree college days were a myth. Colleges and universities were crowded with "casualties," victims or potential victims of mental illness, with more students suffering from mental disorders than anyone realized. Not even "geniuses or . . . Phi Beta Kappas" were immune.[21] In the early 1920s the hygienists conducted questionnaire surveys of students to demonstrate the need for mental hygiene.[22] Dr. Vivian V. Anderson, then the associate medical director of NCMH, concluded that ten to fifteen percent of all college students required psychiatric help.[23] Shortly thereafter, however, the hygienists began to take a different line, that serious mental illness or full-fledged neurosis was not the real concern of college mental hygienists. Their concern was with minor personality disorders, the problems of adjustment that occur in otherwise healthy people during late adolescence. That the hygienists made the problems of late adolescence one of their key theoretical justifications is an interesting development.

The hygienists needed a theory to help explain or justify their activities on the campus, since reference to students as "wrecks" and "casualties" had limited utility. Hygienists found what they needed in G. Stanley Hall's conception of adolescence. Hall had defined adolescence as a special phase of the life cycle at the turn of the century in his monumental *Adolescence*.[24] By the time of World War I, however, Hall's ideas had fallen into neglect. In the early 1920s, the hygienists revived Hall's view of adolescence as a formative period and added to it the period of "late" adolescence, when "personality was still plastic" and "the repressing forces have not yet become too despotic."[25] Now hygienists could depict the college years as a more propitious time for mental hygiene than the grade school years. Young people in college were even more vulnerable than children, because they were away from home and the supervision of parents.

Hygienists stressed that the college years were a time of grave danger. Adolescents entering college faced "all the common problems of adolescent growth and social adjustment . . . feelings of inferiority, feelings of guilt, unhealthy attachments to members of the family, many confusions over matters of sex, unhealthy attitudes toward questions of authority, fears of various sorts."[26] The inevitable problems of adolescence were exacerbated by stresses and strains unique to the college experience: loneliness, adapting to newfound freedom, coping with unsettling ideas, meeting the college's academic standards, adjusting to college society.

Without help, students floundered. Their difficulties surfaced in symptoms of all sorts: physical complaints, social maladjustment, mood swings, and scholastic or disciplinary problems.[27] The college hygienists took all students' complaints seriously; every complaint was a "problem." Psychiatrists, said Williams, had learned through hard experience not to belittle minor or "absurdly simple" cases, which, if neglected, might turn into something serious indeed.[28] Another reason hygienists took all complaints seriously was that the hygienists' model of normal personality and mental health was maximalist or perfectionist: perfect "happiness" and perfect "efficiency," with all deviations from the model viewed as symptomatic.[29] For example, at Vassar, in the five years from 1923 to 1927, 187 students sought Riggs's help on their own or were referred to him by college authorities. Riggs lists the complaints. They are as inclusive as life itself: "discouragement, depression, living on a poor schedule or none at all, below par physically, bored, dissatisfied, pain of a love affair, infringement of rules, fear, too dependent, homesickness, acute grief, low cultural interests, narrow interests, poor work, cheating, lack of purpose, talk of suicide, sex difficulties, difficult home life, fear of mental disorder, carrying too heavy an academic schedule, working long hours, religious difficulties, financial strain, sleep-walking, nightmares, and stammering." Menninger describes some of the students he treated at Washburn College: the dean refers a student for over-cutting; another student is referred because he participated in an auto theft; a student comes to Menninger to learn why he misplaces his belongings (hat, gloves, watch, bicycle, saxophone); a student is reported for bragging about her sexual exploits; a student comes to find out why others snub her; a sorority refers a student who refuses to attend parties. Menninger treated them all.

The hygienists' goal of preventing mental illness required that they reach all students. This could not be achieved by waiting for students to show up at the mental hygiene service. Dr. Milton Harrington, Ruggles's successor at Dartmouth, urged that students be divided into small sections with a junior faculty member assigned as a counselor to each section. The faculty counselor would follow each student in his section through the four years of college and be responsible to the "mental hygiene officer," the psychiatrist.[30] However, most hygienists favored more practical and less expensive methods of reaching students. A popular technique was the informal small-group discussion. For example, during the winter of 1926–1927, psychiatrists on Yale's mental hygiene service held nightly "smokers" with small groups of freshmen. Informal discussions were held before an open fire. Personal questions were encouraged. The psychiatrists made themselves available for consultation afterward. However, only a relative handful of students could be reached this way. The most efficient way to reach students seemed to be through courses in mental hygiene.

As early as 1922, Menninger was offering a course in mental hygiene at Washburn. Dartmouth, Vassar, Brown, the University of Minnesota, and George Washington University followed within a few years. In 1927, Yale introduced a course in mental hygiene as an elective for sophomores and upperclassmen. Some hygienists preferred courses based upon psychology and mental hygiene, taught with the aid of textbooks and formal lectures. Other hygienists preferred to lecture informally on the emotional and social problems confronting students, for example, mental mechanisms, the instinctual life, healthy and un-healthy modes of adjusting to life, and the new view of mental illness. The hygienists who taught courses in mental hygiene invariably re-quired their students to write an end-of-term autobiography or "psy-chiatric life history," followed up by a personal conference.[31] Probably all hygienists would agree that their main educational/therapeutic task lay in the field of sex education.[32] Several were more ambitious. Karl Menninger provided students with a five-point guide to mental health: (1) set up as an ideal the facing of reality; (2) cultivate social contacts and social ideals; (3) recognize neurotic evasions and take opportuni-ties for sublimation; (4) learn to recognize the evidence of mental pathology in others; and (5) "assume that the unhappy are always wrong."[33] Austen Riggs taught a ten–point program, which included the following: do not hurry; do not worry; do not procrastinate; lead a balanced life; shun the New England conscience; and accept life as it is. Yale's Dr. E. Van Norman Emery conceived of his course in mental hygiene as a "molding force," "a re-creation of the person-ality."[34]

Successful pursuit of the goal of prevention required that the hy-gienists try to influence students' mental health not only directly, through personal consultation or courses in mental hygiene, but indirectly, through reform of the whole college and university milieu, especially its disciplinary procedures. One of the key objectives of the hygienists was to medicalize or psychologize behavior, that is, to transform all student transgressions into medical issues, to influence college and university authorities to take the "mental hygiene point of view" to-ward the sins and failings of college students. The hygienists sought— through campus-wide lectures, personal contacts, and informal meet-ings with small groups of administrators and faculty members (and their wives)—to give presidents, deans, personnel officers, and the faculty the new view of students' discipline problems. According to hygienists, any disciplinary problem should be viewed as a symptom. A student with a problem should be treated as sick or maladjusted, in need of treatment rather than punishment.[35] The important thing was to search for causes. The hygienists agreed that parents were usually to blame for the psychological problems of college students.[36]

The mental hygiene point of view toward discipline problems was part of a more comprehensive hygienist conception of the college and university. In hygienist writings three themes were salient: one, a scorn for intellectualism in general; two, a more specific critique of intellectualism in higher education; three, a demand that the university or college deemphasize intellectual concerns and become an institution nurturing the whole person. The hygienists' underlying assumption was close to that held by reform-minded academics like Irving Babbitt, Paul Shorey, Alexander Meiklejohn, and Robert Hutchins—that colleges should provide a liberal education that would prepare students for life. The hygienists gave this ancient ideal an interesting twist. The writings of Frankwood E. Williams and Stewart Paton were especially influential among hygienists.[37] Here is Williams. We have all been to college, and just look at us. Our intellects have been developed, but "there is not one of us but has his psychic scars" from this period. In the colleges we were stuffed with information, when "it is our emotions we stumble over." We graduate from college, some of us even cum laude, suffering from "feelings of inferiority, feelings of guilt and a variety of problems of sex." There were "battalions" of college graduates of sound physique and high IQ who were handicapped emotionally and burdened with unhealthy personality traits like introversion, overconscientiousness, oversensitivity, and excessive ratiocination, which contributed to the world's supply of "college educated wrecks and mediocrities." At present, according to Williams, no American college or university was preparing students for life.[38] Paton, more eclectic in his psychiatry, nevertheless came to the same conclusion as Williams, then went further to propose a new conception of higher education for the twentieth century.

Paton, an elder statesman of psychiatry, devoted a good part of his professional life to writing about mental hygiene and education. His influence on the mental hygiene movement in higher education was profound; only Williams, perhaps, exceeded it among psychiatrists in colleges and universities. First, Paton extended Williams's critique of higher education. As the saying goes, said Paton, physicians bury their failures. But the "academic conception of education" is responsible for more failures than all the doctors put together—failures in living. For the failures of life are products of that education. The colleges and universities cram students' minds with information but fail to provide students with self-knowledge. Thus, the colleges and universities do not provide the "essentials of an education," to use a phrase from the title of one of Paton's articles, which was much quoted in the 1920s. Like Williams, Paton reproached the colleges and universities for their exaggerated emphasis on development of the intellect and acquisition of knowledge. Years are devoted to the study of the minds of past generations and to the acquisition of knowledge. That has constituted an "education." But the test of education is "preparation for life." And little of this kind of academic knowledge is actually helpful in preparing for life. What knowledge is of most worth in preparing for life? Paton's answer: "Know thyself."

"One of the extraordinary fallacies of the present system of education," Paton argued, "is the assumption that the emotional or mental characteristics of the cultivated person can be developed merely by instruction in the Classics." A knowledge of mathematics, Greek, or chemistry does not imply possession of the knowledge necessary for "intelligent direction of the emotional life," or for "success in living." It is the emotions, not any lack of intelligence, that leads people to believe in "witchcraft, demonology, Christian Science, patent medicines, and the vagaries of Bolshevism." The problem, Paton concluded, is lack of knowledge of ourselves. Paton saw in the colleges and universities an opportunity to create a new kind of person and a new ethic that would save civilization. Only psychiatry provided the essentials of an education: "knowledge of the real driving forces of human behavior," the "instinctive life," and the "deep emotional undercurrents shaping the personality."[39] The Socratic injunction "Know thyself" was at last to be fulfilled, not through the arts and sciences, nor through philosophy and history, but through psychiatry and mental hygiene.

V.

With the resignation of Williams as medical director of NCMH in 1930 and the onset of the Depression, the hygienists' drive to gain a foothold in the colleges and universities slackened. Then, under the leadership of Yale's Dr. Clement Fry, the movement again picked up momentum. Interest in mental hygiene at colleges and universities in the pre-World War II period peaked at the National Conference on College Hygiene held in Washington, D.C., in the winter of 1936.[40] By then, the NCMH could look back on some substantial accomplishments. A survey of more than 865 collegiate institutions gave impressive evidence of the development of a "mental hygiene consciousness." Of the 479 institutions that responded, 45 percent indicated interest in establishing a mental hygiene service, 93.5 percent thought attention to mental hygiene important for college students, and 41 percent were actually offering some kind of formal mental hygiene services.[41] At most of the colleges and universities, the mental hygiene work was undertaken by psychologists or other personnel specialists, but at 43 institutions it was the responsibility of a psychiatrist. Another survey in 1939–1940 found that 75 major colleges and universities were offering courses in mental hygiene, approximately three times as many as in 1930.[42]

There is an irony in these surveys detailing progress in mental hygiene. As late as 1936, college and university psychiatrists were taking a hard line toward psychology. Although the hygienists may have wished to disseminate mental hygiene as widely as possible, they also wished to keep mental hygiene the exclusive preserve of medicine and psychiatry. In this they failed. It was never their intention to enhance the prestige or increase the number of psychological counselors or other nonmedical mental health professionals. But, having taken as their province the everyday problems of life, the psychiatrists' claim to exclusive rights to mental hygiene was hardly defensible.[43] By 1940, most of the mental hygiene work on campuses was in fact being performed by psychologists. On the other hand, by then the mental hygiene point of view had deeply penetrated psychological counseling. In the military terminology so dear to them, the hygienists lost the battle but won the war.

The real influence of the mental hygiene movement in higher education, however, cannot be stated quantitatively. Its goal was to alter attitudes and to influence life so that, in Meyer's words, "what is medicine today will become mere common sense tomorrow or at least with the next generation."[44] In this, the mental hygiene movement also enjoyed some success, as can be documented in the area of student discipline, where the hygienists did not have to wait a generation to make their ideas accepted as common sense.

Once upon a time, students who broke rules were punished.[45] By the mid-1920s in some progressive colleges and universities, such students were instead diagnosed as psychologically maladjusted and referred to the psychiatrist for treatment. Thanks to the mental hygiene movement, Vassar's president Henry McCracken observed in 1925, he now had a better understanding of why students got into trouble. In the old days students caught stealing, lying, or cheating were accused of "badness, naughtiness, moral depravity," and "disregarding the high ideals of the college." We expelled those students, he continued, more or less publicly. Now, he said, "we retain them and cooperate with the psychiatrist to bring them back again to normality."[46] In the 1930s, the mental hygiene point of view dominated student counseling at the University of Minnesota, the country's acknowledged leader in that field. Students in trouble were dealt with as "problems of maladjustment," and the "harsh certitudes of arbitrary authority [had] given way to a program of adjustment guided by scientific principle." Dean Edmund G. Williamson called it the "Minnesota point of view."[47]

VI.

Revisionist historical interpretations of reform movements of the progressive era view "doing good" as a mask for manipulation and social control.[48] Critics of psychiatry and the mental health professions like David Rothman and Christopher Lasch, among others, suggest that psychiatry can be best understood not as an autonomous scientific discipline but as an ideology; a "normalizing" mechanism, in Michel Foucault's term. This study provides some evidence on behalf of those with a skeptical view of psychiatry and mental hygiene. The college and university psychiatrists were concerned with social control. However, they were opposed to social control through coercion by laws or prohibitive regulations. They were committed to the psychological process of social control—the outcome of healthy personality development. But the hygienists' agenda for higher education went far beyond a concern for wholesome personality development to incorporate, as we have seen, a guide for living, an orientation to life. The campus psychiatrists aspired to be the moral tutors of youth. They were prescribing not so much a program for preventing "nervousness" as for producing a new cultural type, suitable for a post-Victorian era. As George K. Pratt, Williams's successor in 1931 as medical director of the NCMH, put it, with reference to the psychiatrist: "His is a task formerly relegated to the priest or pastor, to teacher and philosopher."[49] That the psychiatrist fulfill this task was a matter of great urgency.

The 1920s were a time of rejection of old moralities; an "assault on Victorianism," to use Stanley Coben's apt phrase;[50] profound disillusionment with America's political leadership, a legacy of the Wilsonian era; and loss of confidence in democracy.[51] In the immediate postwar years, many hygienists were convinced that the fate of America, of democracy, of civilization itself rested in the hands of young people at college. Hygienists invariably referred to college students as a select group, an intellectual elite, the "best men." College students were in the impressionable years. Would they provide the "wise, sane, constructive leadership" the nation so urgently required? Would they turn out to be "safe" and "dependable" if only their intellect was developed and not their emotions?[52] How could one ensure that their talents and energies would be directed toward responsible values and behavior? The hygienists stepped forward as the guides and mentors of the country's future leaders. If the college and university faculties would not provide youth with the "essentials of an education," or until they did, the psychiatrists would have to do it.

VII.

The hopes and dreams of the prewar progressive movement in America lived on in the 1920s in the mental hygiene movement. The hygienists were convinced that education provided the cure for every ill, the key to war and peace and even to the preservation of democracy itself. It was a quintessentially conservative approach to social reform, yet it had utopian appeal. There was no need to engage in political struggles or change the structure of society in order to bring a new world into being. Only human psychology had to be changed; the ultimate battle to determine the fate of democracy was to be fought out in the colleges and universities. "I switched from psychiatry to education," Paton reminisced, "as it seemed to me that unless students were educated in humane ways of living there would be no way of checking the spread of emotional and mental disturbances that are the greatest existing menace to democracy."[53] Convictions like these help explain why so many psychiatrists devoted so much time and energy to nurturing the psychological well-being of a very small sector of society.

It is tempting to be condescending toward the college and university hygienists with their self–image as saviors of civilization, their sermonettes on the prevention of mental illness, their cheery five- or ten-step programs for mental hygiene, their disregard of social and economic conditions as having anything to do with life, mental health, and happiness. It's even possible to be cynical. Karl Menninger recalled that when he started out in private practice (in 1919) he had to go out and look for patients; Washburn College was one of the places he looked. Fifty years later, he observed that all psychiatrists were busy.[54] Part of the reason was that psychiatrists had successfully promoted themselves and their services. College students, their spouses, and later their children, were the hygienists' future clients. However, to stress professional self-interest would be unfair; the campaign to make psychiatric or mental hygiene services an integral part of the university and college was undertaken from generous as well as self-interested motives. Mental disorder seemed to be ubiquitous, taking a terrible toll in individual misery. Vulnerable adolescents in colleges and universities might be fortified or immunized against mental illness. In former times religion might have provided solace, or the faculty might have provided support and guidance. The hygienists took it upon themselves to fill the void.

Still, most college and university faculties in the period before World War II thought that the responsibility of colleges and universities for students' psychological adjustment and personality development should be minimal. In fact, most faculty members were antagonistic to the mental hygiene point of view. They were concerned with what Laurence Veysey calls, in *The Emergence of the American University* (1965), "utility" and "research," not the "well-rounded man." They were concerned with matters of intellect, not personality, and they found the mental hygiene point of view subversive of their values. The hygienists, for their part, anathematized the faculty.[55] In 1928, a survey of mental hygiene programs in higher education found that nearly all the colleges' hygienists identified the faculty as "the greatest hindrance to the success of the mental hygiene program."[56] At Yale, the hygienists had to fight a general feeling among faculty that hygienists were coddling students and that students' problems were simply growing pains. According to the faculty, willpower, perseverance, and intestinal fortitude were adequate tools for handling any problems, and students who couldn't shape up were "weak and immature and should not survive" in college.[57]

The hygienists were acutely sensitive to accusations of coddling, of fostering in students a sense of continuing dependence, of perpetuating an outmoded *in loco parentis* educational philosophy. Hygienists protested that they had no wish to "turn our universities into sanitoria" or into "a haven from the more strenuous life."[58] This would be harmful, they said, and directly opposed to the requirements of mental hygiene. However, hygienists argued, colleges and universities could not escape responsibility for the personality development of their students. The young men and women were there, and they were not solely "minds" but "whole persons"; their personality development *had* to be a concern of the college. By the late 1920s, this view was accepted by prestigious college administrators like presidents McCracken of Vassar, Angell of Yale, and Lotus B. Coffman of the University of Minnesota. The colleges and universities could not ignore personality. Where the emotions were concerned, students could not be left to sink or swim. The colleges and universities had to be concerned with their student's psychological well-being. Psychological maladjustment was a personal disaster and a social waste, besides adversely affecting the student's academic achievement.[59]

By and large, the college and university psychiatrists were elitist. Some may have been anti-intellectual. All were convinced of the one-sidedness of American higher education. The so-called humanities, the hygienists claimed, left out everything truly humane—knowledge of the self, of human nature, of the emotions, of personality. College and university faculty gave only lip service to the ideal of a liberal education; the education of the "whole person." The mental hygiene movement in higher education may be seen as trying to encourage colleges and universities to realize that ideal. To depreciate intellect and privilege "personality," however, reenforced what Marcia Synnott in *The Half-Opened Door: Discrimination and Admissions at Yale, Harvard, and Princeton, 1900–1970* (1979), calls the "club system," and made it easier for the Ivy League to justify student admissions on other than academic criteria. Criteria of "personality" could even operate as a cloak or subterfuge for ethnic, racial, or religious prejudice. On the other hand, at the great state universities like the University of Minnesota, which were increasingly becoming a destination for poor young people and the children of immigrants, the mental hygiene movement may have served egalitarian ends—a means to help first-generation students adjust better to college life and get more out of the college experience.

One of the more interesting issues posed by the hygienists was this: where does the college's responsibility toward the student's psychological adjustment begin, and where does it end? How much responsibility should the college assume for the development of students' personality? The stage was thus set in the 1920s and 1930s for a fuller discussion of the affective outcomes of education and the responsibility of colleges and universities in the sphere of emotional or personality development of students beyond the provision of mental hygiene services. However, between hygienists and faculties, psychiatrists and professors, there was never much communication; no debate ever took place between them. The idea that colleges and universities are institutions with a special obligation for the personality development of students remains a potent one, always being rediscovered, but with little accretion of historical awareness.

Finally, the subject of mental hygiene is one of continuing relevance. Mental hygiene is no dead end in the history of thought—no phrenology. The NCMH and the mental hygiene movement *qua* movement are no more. But the "mental hygiene point of view"—its values, concepts, and language of discourse—is simply taken for granted today, as part of cultural common sense. The role of the mental hygiene movement in American colleges and universities deserves the most careful historical investigation, as does the role of the colleges and universities in the diffusion of the mental hygiene point of view.

Notes

1 Philip Rieff, *The Triumph of the Therapeutic: Uses of Faith After Freud* (New York, 1966); Christopher Lasch, *The Culture of Narcissism: American Life in an Age of Diminishing Expectations* (New York, 1978); Fred H. Matthews, "In Defense of Common Sense: Mental Hygiene as Ideology and Mentality in Twentieth-Century America," *Prospects*, 2 (1979): 459–516.

2 For the beginnings and early years of the mental hygiene movement, see Norman Dain, *Clifford W. Beers: Advocate for the Insane* (Pittsburgh, 1980); and Barbara Sicherman, *The Quest for Mental Health in America, 1880–1917* (Ann Arbor, 1971).

3 Adolf Meyer, "Modern Conceptions of Mental Disease," in Herbert S. Jennings, ed., *Suggestions of Modern Science Concerning Education* (New York, 1917); C. Macfie Campbell, *A Present–Day Conception of Mental Disorders* (Cambridge, Mass., 1924), and *Destiny and Disease in Mental Disorders* (London, 1935). See also William Alanson White, *Twentieth Century Psychiatry* (New York, 1936).

4 George K. Pratt, *Your Mind and You: Mental Health* (New York, 1924); Ernest R. Groves and Phyllis Blanchard, *Introduction to Mental Hygiene* (New York, 1930); and William Burnham, *The Normal Mind* (New York, 1924).

5 Thomas W. Salmon, "War Neuroses and Their Lesson," *New York Medical Journal*, 109 (1919): 933–936; "Notes and Comments," *Mental Hygiene*, 2 (1918): 480–481; Dain, *Clifford W. Beers*, chs. 13–15. In general, see Nathan G. Hale, Jr., *The Rise and Crisis of Psychoanalysis in the United States: Freud and the Americans, 1917–1985* (New York, 1995), ch. 1.

6 See Chapter 8, "The Mental Hygiene Movement, the Commonwealth Fund, and Education, 1921–1933: 'Every School a Clinic.'"

7 Clarence B. Farrar, "I Remember Stewart Paton," *American Journal of Psychiatry*, 117 (1960): 161–162; Adolf Meyer, "Stewart Paton, M.D.," *Journal of Nervous and Mental Disease*, 95 (1942): 518–520.

8 William C. Menninger, *Psychiatry in a Troubled World* (New York, 1948), pp. 5–6, 340–341.

9 Clarence M. Hincks, "Public Education and Mental Hygiene," in Frankwood E. Williams, ed., *Proceedings of the First International Congress on Mental Hygiene* (New York, 1932), vol. I, p. 577.

10 As Salmon put it, psychiatrists preferred to treat "minor and relatively insignificant departures from health, where there is opportunity for prevention and early treatment." Quoted in F. L. Wells, "The Status of 'Clinical' Psychology," *Mental Hygiene*, 6 (1922): 418.

11   For Dartmouth, see Arthur H. Ruggles, "College Mental Hygiene Problems," *Mental Hygiene*, 9 (1925): 263. For Vassar, see Henry N. McCracken, "Mental Hygiene in the College Curriculum," *Mental Hygiene*, 9 (1925): 473–477; and Austen Fox Riggs and William B. Terhune, "The Mental Hygiene of College Women," *Mental Hygiene,* 12 (1928): 559–562.

12   For West Point, see Harry N. Kerns, "Cadet Problems," *Mental Hygiene*, 7 (1923): 688–696. For the University of Minnesota, see Angus W. Morrison and Harold S. Diehl, "Some Studies in Mental Hygiene Needs of Freshman University Students," *Journal of the American Medical Association,* 83 (1924): 1666–1672; for the University of California, see Sydney K. Smith, "Psychiatry and University Men," *Mental Hygiene,* 7 (1928): 38–47.

13   "Notes," *Mental Hygiene Bulletin*, 3 (October 1925): 1, 3.

14   William Healy, "Psychiatry, Psychology, Psychiatrists, Psychologists," *Mental Hygiene*, 6 (1922): 248–256; Thomas V. Moore, "A Century of Psychology in Relation to American Psychiatry," in *One Hundred Years of American Psychiatry* (New York, 1950), pp. 472–474.

15   Based on unpublished material in "Yale University-Department of Mental Hygiene," File 701, in the Commonwealth Fund Archives, Rockefeller Archive Center, Sleepy Hollow, New York.

16   "Psychiatry at Yale," *American Journal of Psychiatry*, 5 (1925): 323–325; George Wilson Pierson, *Yale: College and University, 1921–1937* (New Haven, 1955), pp. 516–517.

17   Frankwood E. Williams to James R. Angell (12 June 1925), in Yale University-Department of Mental Hygiene, File 701, Commonwealth Fund Archives.

18   Clement C. Fry and Edna Rostow, *Mental Hygiene in College* (New York, 1942), pp. xii–xiii.

19   Winifred Richmond, "Mental Hygiene in the College," *Journal of the American Medical Association*, 93 (1929): 1937.

20   *The Campus: A Study of Contemporary Undergraduate Life in the American University* (New York, 1928), p. 6.

21   "Mental Hygiene and the College Student Twenty Years After," *Mental Hygiene*, 5 (1921): 736–740; Earl D. Bond, "To a Graduating Class of Geniuses," *Mental Hygiene*, 13 (1929): 520–528.

22   Stanley Cobb, "A Report on a Brief Neuropsychiatric Examination of 1,141 Students," *Journal of Industrial Hygiene*, 3 (1922): 309–315; Smiley Blanton, "A Mental Hygiene Program for Colleges," *Mental Hygiene*, 9 (1925): 479.

23   Vivian V. Anderson, "Psychiatry in College," *Mental Hygiene*, 13 (1929): 372.

24   *Adolescence: Its Psychology* (New York, 1905), vol. I, pp. xiii–xviii. And see Joseph Kett, *Rites of Passage: Adolescence in America, 1970 to the Present* (New York, 1977), pp. 217–221.

25 C. Macfie Campbell, "The Responsibilities of the University in Promoting Mental Hygiene," *Mental Hygiene*, 3 (1919): 205; Arthur H. Ruggles, "College Mental Hygiene Problems," *Mental Hygiene*, 9 (1925): 262.

26 Fry and Rostow, *Mental Hygiene in College*, pp. 6–9, 14–15, 32–33; Frankwood E. Williams, "Mental Hygiene and the College Student," *Mental Hygiene*, 9 (1925): 225–227; Sidney L. Pressey, "The College and Adolescent Needs," in *Research Adventures in University Teaching* (Bloomington, Ind., 1927), pp. 81–85.

27 Riggs and Terhune, "The Mental Hygiene of College Women," pp. 561–565; Karl Menninger, *The Human Mind* (New York, 1930), pp. 406–407, and "Adaptation Difficulties in College Students," *Mental Hygiene*, 11 (1927): 519–523.

28 Williams, "Mental Hygiene and the College Student," p. 222.

29 Ibid; and Arthur H. Ruggles, "The College Student and Mental Hygiene," *Progressive Education*, 7 (1930): 282, 284–285.

30 Milton A. Harrington, "A College Mental Hygiene Department," *Survey*, 59 (15 January 1928): 510–512; Vivian V. Anderson, *Psychiatry in Education* (New York, 1932), p. 37.

31 E.g., Blanton, "A Mental Hygiene Program for Colleges," p. 484; Harry A. Steckel, "Outline of a Comprehensive Course in Mental Hygiene," *Psychiatric Quarterly*, 2 (1928): 342–324; Menninger, *The Human Mind*, p. 432.

32 Fry and Rostow, *Mental Hygiene in College*, p. 160.

33 Ibid., p. 407.

34 "The Content and the Method of Instructing College Students in Mental Hygiene," *Mental Hygiene*, 17 (1933): 596–597.

35 Smith, "Psychiatry and University Men," p. 44; Williams, "Mental Hygiene and the College Student," p. 245; Kimball Young, "Mental Hygiene and Personality Guidance in College," *Mental Hygiene*, 9 (1925): 490; Menninger, *The Human Mind*, pp. 425–428.

36 Frankwood E. Williams, "Finding a Way in Mental Hygiene," *Mental Hygiene*, 14 (1930): 225–237. See also Ruggles, "College Mental Hygiene Problems," p. 81. Vassar's dean rapidly assimilated the mental hygiene point of view. Where students' problems were concerned, she explained, "two-to-one, a neurotic mother or father is at the root of the difficulty." C. Mildred Thompson, "The Value of Mental Hygiene in the College," *Mental Hygiene*, 9 (1927): 235.

37 Williams's *Adolescence: Studies in Mental Hygiene* (New York, 1930), brings together many of his papers on mental hygiene. Many of Paton's speeches and articles of the immediate postwar period are collected in two books: *Education in War and Peace* (New York, 1921), and *Signs of Sanity and the Principles of Mental Hygiene* (New York, 1922).

38   Williams, *Adolescence: Studies in Mental Hygiene* chs. 3–4. Williams, "Mental Hygiene and the College Student," *Mental Hygiene*, 5 (1921): 268; George K. Pratt, *Your Mind and You* (New York, 1924), ch. 5, "Intellect and Emotions."

39   "The Essentials of an Education," *Mental Hygiene*, 4 (1920): 268–280.

40   Theophile Raphael, "Mental Hygiene Services for Colleges and Universities," *Mental Hygiene*, 21 (1937): 559–574.

41   Ibid., pp. 559–560.

42   Harold W. Bernard, "College Mental Hygiene: A Decade of Growth," *Mental Hygiene*, 22 (1940): 413–417.

43   John C. Burnham, "The Struggles Between Physicians and Paramedical Personnel in American Psychiatry, 1917–1941," *Journal of the History of Medicine and Allied Sciences*, 29 (1974): 93–107.

44   "The 'Complaint' as the Center of Genetic-Dynamic Teaching in Psychiatry," *New England Journal of Medicine*, 199 (1928): 360.

45   "When it comes to matters of discipline, the dean must . . . be punitive." Lois Kimball Matthews, *The Dean of Women* (New York, 1915), p. 28.

46   "Mental Hygiene in the College Curriculum," *Mental Hygiene*, 9 (1925): 475.

47   James Gray, *The University of Minnesota, 1851–1951* (Minneapolis, 1951), pp. 359–360. See also *Higher Education for American Democracy: A Report of the President's Commission on Higher Education* (Washington, D.C., 1947), pp. 53–54, 65–66.

48   David J. Rothman, *Conscience and Convenience: The Asylum and Its Alternatives in Progressive America* (Boston, 1980), Part IV; John C. Burnham, "The New Psychology: From Narcissism to Social Control," in John Braeman et al., *Change and Continuity in Twentieth-Century America: The 1920s* (Columbus, Ohio, 1968), pp. 394–398; Willard Gaylin et al., *Doing Good: The Limits of Benevolence* (New York, 1978).

49   Pratt, *Your Mind and You,* pp. 54–55. Now, according to Angell, religion was becoming passé, and "thousands of students do not know a single professor in any but a professional way." *The Campus*, p. 64. See, in general, Paula S. Fass, *The Beautiful and the Damned: American Youth in the Twenties* (New York, 1979).

50   Stanley Coben, "The Assault on Victorianism in Twentieth Century America," *American Quarterly*, 27 (1975): 604–625; and Daniel Walker Howe, ed., *Victorian America* (Philadelphia, 1976). In general, see Coben, *Rebellion Against Victorianism: The Impetus for Cultural Change in 1920s America* (New York, 1991).

51   Everywhere, proclaimed a widely read hygienist, there was "doubt in regard to democracy, . . . pessimism in regard to civilization, hopelessness in regard to

the lack of intelligence in . . . the people, and hope only in the superior few."
Burnham, *The Normal Mind*, p. 685.

52   Arthur H. Ruggles, *Mental Hygiene: Past, Present, and Future* (Baltimore, 1934), pp. 103–104; Williams, "Mental Hygiene and the College Student," 229–230.

53   Paton, *Education in War and Peace*, p. 5; Farrar, "I Remember Stewart Paton," p. 162.

54   Lucy Freeman, ed., *Sparks: By Karl Menninger* (New York, 1973), pp. xxi, 255.

55   Donald Slesinger, "Professor vs. Psychiatrist," *Survey*, 59 (1928): 761–763.

56   Richmond, "Mental Hygiene in the College," p. 1936.

57   Fry and Rostow, *Mental Hygiene in College*, p. 4.

58   Ibid., p. 19; Angus Morrison, "A Further Discussion of College Mental Hygiene," *Mental Hygiene*, 12 (1928): 53; Ruggles, "The College Student and Mental Hygiene," p. 281.

59   Angell, "Mental Hygiene in the College and University," *Mental Hygiene Bulletin*, 7 (1929): 2, 4–5, 8; and "Mental Hygiene and Education," in Williams, *Proceedings of the First International Conference on Mental Hygiene*, 1, 788–793. See also, Gray, *University of Minnesota, 1851–1951*, pp. 282–285, 360.

Chapter 10

The Mental Hygiene Movement, "Personality," and the Making of Twentieth-Century American Education

Studies in the history of ideas are needed that will deepen our understanding of the development of key notions about education, both in the philosophical tradition and educational theorizing . . . and of the changing emphasis in the institutions contributing to and responsible for the education of children.

Lee J. Cronbach and Patrick Suppes

I.

In 1969, the National Academy of Education issued a call for studies in the history of ideas that would deepen our understanding of the development of "key notions" of American education.[1] The call, a commendable one, came out at the wrong time, just when intellectual history had begun to fall into disfavor with historians of education, and social history was beginning to dominate the historiography of education. This essay is a belated response to the Academy's call and another chapter in my exploration of the mental hygiene movement and the medicalization of American education.

Some years ago I began, seriatim, a program of research in three related areas: first, the impact of psychoanalysis on American education; then, the more general impact of psychiatry on American education; and finally, closely related to the first two, but more comprehensive, the impact of the mental hygiene movement on American education. I discovered a fascinating subject which has not been explored in sufficient detail and which opened a new avenue to under-standing the development of modern American education.

Few intellectual and social movements have had so deep and per-suasive an influence on the theory and practice of American educa-tion as the mental hygiene movement. It has substantially altered our ways of talking and thinking about American education, and it has provided the inspiration and driving force for one of the most far-reaching yet little understood educational innovations of the twentieth century, what I call the "medicalization" of American education. I mean by this metaphor the infiltration of psychiatric norms, concepts, and categories of discourse—the "mental hygiene point of view"—into vir-tually all aspects of American education in the twentieth century. In this chapter I emphasize the idea of the school's responsibility for children's personality development.

The school's responsibility for personality development is one of the key ideas of American education. By the late 1940s this idea was firmly entrenched in the literature of powerful professional educational organizations like the National Education Association, the American Council on Education, and the Educational Policies Commission. In 1950, the Mid-Century White House Conference on Children and Youth took as its motto "For Every Child a Healthy Personality" and ratified the idea that the school is primarily an institution for develop-ing the personality.

The key word is "personality." As Raymond Williams has observed, from the viewpoint of the cultural historian, the emergence of a piv-otal word, whether a new coinage or an old word invested with signifi-cantly different meaning, is invariably a marker of far-reaching changes in society and culture; when language changes, the world changes. Changes in language ultimately redefine the way we conceive our-selves, our world, and our relationship to the world.[2] So it was with "personality." To paraphrase Virginia Woolf's provocative declaration, sometime around World War I, our notion of human character changed.

It is difficult to unravel the exact meaning of the term "personality." Historically, the word dates back at least to the fourteenth century. Personality development was a central concern and conscious goal of the Italian Renaissance, harking back to a much older Greek ideal of harmonious balance of personality. But the modern idea of personal-ity emerged in the early twentieth century and came into its own only in the period after World War I. By 1930, according to the psycholo-gist Gordon W. Allport, interest in personality had reached "astonishing proportions." In 1934, in the *Encyclopedia of the Social Sciences,* Edward Sapir distinguished five broad meanings of the term "personality." He observed that "it is the peculiarly psychiatric conception of personality . . . which is most difficult to assimilate but important to stress." It is the psychiatric conception of personality with which we are concerned here.

The hygienist conception of personality has its roots in turn-of-the-century psychiatry. To progressive psychiatrists, the culturally constructed, protean, and morally ambiguous "personality," as distinguished from "character," with its moralistic and relatively fixed overtones, was the most essential component of human nature and therefore the most vital aspect of the psychiatrist's and ultimately the educator's realm. Thus the phrase "development of personality" has a special meaning in hygienist discourse. It is used by hygienists in a particular way to bind together certain meanings or a certain field of meanings, a certain way of looking at children and schooling. It serves as shorthand notation for a cluster of systematically related assumptions, concepts, and values concerning childhood, family, and school, which includes the following essential elements: Personality is the defining aspect of the self. Maladjustments of personality are the cause of individual mental disorders and social problems of all sorts. Childhood is the critical period in the development of personality. The school is the vehicle for preventing, or detecting, treating, and curing—that is, "adjusting"—problems in children's personality development. And finally, children's personality development must take priority over any other educational objective. What is ultimately involved in this idea is a reorientation of American education amounting to a transformation of the school—a shift from an "intellectual-moral" discourse of education whose key words are character, will, and individual responsibility to a therapeutic discourse of education which privileges the vocabulary of personality, psychological adjustment, and maladjustment, views children's behavior problems as symptoms, and which conceives of the school as a kind of psychiatric clinic.

The mental hygiene movement has provided an orientation, a language of discourse, and a body of conceptions that have become part of our common sense about American education and which mediate all aspects of education. The successful dissemination of the "mental hygiene point of view" marks a fundamental linguistic and rhetorical shift in the history of American culture. Hygienist discourse created, as Auden said of Freud and psychoanalytic discourse, a climate of opinion that affects many who have never heard of the books, articles, authors, and organizations that initiated and articulated the educational reorientation I shall be describing below. The subject matter of this essay thus intersects with one of the more crucial shifts in American culture in the twentieth century, identified by Warren Susman as a shift from a "culture of character" to a "culture of personality."[3] The idea of the school's responsibility for personality development is so much a part of our ordinary common sense about education that few are aware of how radical and far-reaching its implications and ramifications are, extending to virtually every facet of education from curriculum to grading and promotion practices to methods of teaching to notions of authority, achievement, and discipline. Yet the impact of the mental hygiene movement on American education has until recently remained largely unacknowledged and unexplored.

The idea of the school's responsibility for the development of personality crucially implicates the other part of the Academy's call—historical investigation into the changing emphases in the institutions contributing to and responsible for the education of children. The idea of the school's responsibility for children's personality development has these corollaries: parents are the child's natural enemy, to blame for all the problems of children; the family is an incubator for maladjustment; the school and the teacher must counterbalance, or if need be, supplant, the parents and the family. The transfer to the school and teacher of responsibilities formerly belonging to parents and the family (and other social agencies) is one of the major themes of twentieth–century American education.

In this chapter I call attention to sources for a history of American education that do not yet figure in historical accounts. Though it is not its chief purpose, this chapter may also provide some insight into our present educational concerns. The endeavor of the mental hygiene movement to define and to realize a "kingdom of good adjustment" in the public school casts a long shadow over the present. The question to ask is: How has it happened that we have come to expect the school, as if it were somehow omnipotent, to assume responsibility for the development of children's personality?

II.

Turn-of-the-century child-saving movements of the Progressive Era constitute the general matrix within which the mental hygiene movement originated. Prominent among the laypeople who took part in the founding of the National Committee for Mental Hygiene (NCMH), the spearhead of the mental hygiene movement, were William James, Julia Lathrop, Charles W. Eliot, and Clifford Beers. Its early leaders were a small group of progressive psychiatrists, including Drs. August Hoch, C. Macfie Campbell, Thomas W. Salmon, and William Alanson White, and led by Adolf Meyer, then the country's foremost psychiatrist.[4] The earliest objectives of the NCMH were limited: to investigate and publicize the problems of the mentally ill and to improve their conditions and treatment. By the 1920s, however, the objective of the NCMH had broadened into a crusade for the prevention of mental illness and "all forms of social maladjustment and even unhappiness," extending far beyond the hospital and the mental asylum to include all agencies having to do with individual and social welfare, particularly the school.

The theoretical base of the mental hygiene movement was eclectic, largely comprised of Meyer's dynamic psychiatry and psychoanalytic concepts extrapolated from Freud; psychoanalysis was the catalyst, but in an attenuated and diluted form.[5] Freudian concepts were used to supplement Meyer's dynamic psychiatry, and psychiatric progressives led by William Alanson White domesticated psychoanalysis by sloughing off its biologically oriented side and keeping what suited their own reformist and environmentalist tendencies. The crusading zeal which characterized the mental hygiene movement rested on a new conception of mental illness, which placed the emphasis on personality and for all practical purposes chose to ignore or disregard organic causes or heredity. As the psychiatrist and hygienist C. Macfie Campbell put it: "Personality moved front and center . . . in the modern conception of mental disorder."[6] This was crucial. Mental illness was a personality disorder; it referred to problems of the personality confronting the stresses of life and therefore was amenable to treatment and even prevention. And personality was no mystery; its secrets were known. The emotions were the essential core of personality, the "most determining aspect of mental life." Childhood was the "conditioning period of personality." And the fundamental working assumption of the mental hygiene movement was that personality was malleable as wax. This belief underlay the hygienists' optimism and faith in prevention, and it led them to the school.

The hygienist reformulation of the role of personality in mental disorders had significance far beyond prevention of mental illness. New vistas opened up for understanding dependency, delinquency, crime, and other forms of deviant behavior. All could be interpreted as "symptoms" of underlying personality maladjustment. To correct the basic factors causing the symptoms would be to strike at the roots of many social problems. Everything pointed back to faulty personality development, which had its roots in childhood. If childhood experiences were critical in the etiology of maladjustment, childhood was also, in William Alanson White's phrase, the "golden period for mental hygiene." On this all hygienists agreed. The implications were clear. Why leave personality development to chance or the vagaries of life when the means were at hand to shape or guide the personality in the making? Even before World War I, psychiatrists had their eye on the school. In the fight against mental illness, declared NCMH's medical director, Thomas Salmon, "practically all the hopeful points of attack exist in childhood." If they were to win the fight, "psychiatrists must be permitted to enter the schools."[7] In the prewar period such sentiments were largely pious hopes. But the psychiatrists' therapeutic imperialism gradually grew stronger.

In 1917, when the United States entered the war, the NCMH concentrated its efforts on organizing the psychiatric service for the armed forces. The psychiatrists' success in treating "shell shock" seemed to confirm Meyer's theories about the role of personality in mental disorder. Salmon explained that the psychological basis of the war neuroses—as of neuroses in civil life—was the individual's incapacity for making adjustments; the fault was in the make-up of the personality. Victims of shell shock suffered from a predisposition to maladjustment, a residue of childhood experiences. Obviously, maladjustments could arise from stressful events in adult life and could be ameliorated or even cured then. But psychotherapy with adults was slow, difficult, and an inefficient use of a psychiatrist's time. Another lesson driven home for the hygienists by the war was that prevention was the only feasible approach to the problem of mental illness.[8]

In the postwar period many hygienists envisioned a kind of psychiatric end-of-days: mental illness extirpated, asylums and hospitals emptied, unhappiness abolished. It seemed possible: the knowledge was available; only the means were lacking. For some years, Salmon's ambition had been to steer the NCMH into a program of mental hygiene, maximally conceived, with the focus on children and the school, but the NCMH lacked the necessary financial resources.

After having been on leave during the war, Salmon resumed his post as medical director in 1920 and pushed the NCMH into an alliance with the newly created Commonwealth Fund (CF). In early 1921 he proposed a joint NCMH-CF project aimed at the prevention of juvenile delinquency. His proposal was accepted and quickly acted upon. In December 1921 the Commonwealth Fund launched its Program for the Prevention of Delinquency. This program provided the main financial support for NCMH in the 1920s and was the dynamic core of the mental hygiene movement. Under the direction of NCMH psychiatrists, the program launched the child guidance movement, greatly encouraged the development of child psychiatry and psychiatric social work, and was at the forefront of the mental hygiene movement in education.[9] In the 1920s and into the 1930s the Program for the Prevention of Delinquency was the main link between the mental hygiene movement and education.

III.

The hygienists' goal was to surround the child with what the French historian Jacques Donzelot calls a "tutelary complex" or an infrastructure of prevention.[10] The visiting teacher or school social worker (for the early identification of children with minor personality problems) and the child guidance clinic (with its psychiatrists, psychiatric social workers, and psychologists for the treatment of "problem" children) were important components of the network. In the interest of prevention, however, it was critical to reach children before they became problems. That left parents and the school.

Given the hygienist emphasis on the importance of childhood, we would expect that the primary site for preventive efforts should have been parents, not the school. In fact, hygienists turned their attention to parents only to give them short shrift. One of the hygienists' main themes during the 1920s was parent blaming. Parents were the weakest link in the preventive network. Like some latter-day Rousseauians, hygienists assumed that everything is good as it comes from the hands of the creator; everything degenerates in the hands of the parents. Hygienists made a direct causal connection: the parents' treatment of children was the chief pathogenic factor in later personality maladjustment.[11] The seeds of maladjustment were sown in childhood. Few children escaped the home unscathed. "Be it ever so humble" observed Salmon, "there is no place that isn't better than home." Salmon called for the establishment of "parentorium" for the treatment of par-

ents. Marion Kenworthy, a child psychiatrist on the staff of the Bureau of Child Guidance—the flagship of the Program's child guidance
clinics—explained that by the time a child was five or six, "we may
describe the child as a symptom-complex of his parental handling."
The dictum "for every problem child a problem parent" was generally
accepted. The faults of parents were many. In her suggestively titled
book, *Parents on Probation* (1928), the psychiatric social worker
Miriam Van Waters, who was on the program's staff, listed "Nineteen
Ways of Being a Bad Parent."[12]

Parents were not so much deliberately bad as ignorant of and un-
trained for their highly demanding responsibilities. William Alanson
White cautioned that the most consummate skill was needed to rear
children properly. This was a skill which few parents possessed, and
which they were scarcely aware they needed to possess in the first
place. Dr. Frankwood E. Williams, Salmon's successor as medical director of the NCMH, refers to "innocent but dangerous parents" and
"idealistic but infected homes."[13] The hygienists identified parents as a
primary target for reeducation. Through the Program for the Prevention of Delinquency, the NCMH advocated and demonstrated parent
education and published much literature aimed at parents. But parent
education had one major drawback—people could not be compelled to
take courses or to obtain a degree in mental hygiene before having
children. To the hygienists, the problem of reaching the parents was
perplexing, if not intractable. They turned to the public school and to
the teacher to accomplish everything that parents had bungled.

It was not that hygienists thought teachers were any less rigid or
more enlightened than parents, but teachers seemed more accessible;
and thanks to compulsory education, the school provided a huge captive audience. All children had to attend school; thus the school had
jurisdiction over them during the formative years. Dr. Ralph Truitt,
head of the NCMH division on child guidance clinics, spoke for the
hygienists: "If we are going to prevent delinquency, insanity, and general inadequacy, the school should be the focus of our attack."[14] Social
workers, the chief intermediaries between the psychiatrists and the
schools in the 1920s and 1930s, were even more emphatic. Jane
Culbert, president of the National Association of Visiting Teachers, in
an address in 1923 to National Conference of Social Work, pointed
out that the public school stood as the country's "greatest child welfare agency." The school, she declared, "has come to be recognized as
the logical place from which to work for the prevention of delinquency

and other social problems." Culbert exhorted her colleagues "to push into the schools" and eliminate the need for social work at the source. Given the schools' potential for reaching the greater part of the juvenile population, it was little wonder that leaders of the mental hygiene movement were dazzled by the prospect of the school as clinic. Their mood was captured by a social work educator, Jessie Taft: "The only practical and effective way to increase the mental health of the nation is through its schools. Homes are too inaccessible. Only the school has the time of the child and the power to do the job." It is for us who represent mental hygiene and its applications, Taft continued, "to help the school and the teacher see that their vital responsibility is for an education which shall mean the personality adjustment of the child." Taft was transfixed by the thought of "someone young, unformed, unmarred, with whom mental health was as possible of attainment as physical health." Why spend one's life trying to make over a bad job, she concluded, "when children are at hand to be guided into the kingdom of good adjustment"?[15]

For the public school to become the kingdom of good adjustment required not merely some minor reforms but a radical shift in the school's and the teacher's orientation. Education, proclaimed William Alanson White, "has been . . . too much confined to teaching. It needs to be developed as a scheme for assisting and guiding the developing personality." This was fundamental. To redefine education as a process for assisting and guiding the developing personality became the hygienist project, the central plank of the mental hygiene movement in education.

IV.

Belief in the malleability of personality directed the hygienists' attention to the environment of the school; everything had an impact on personality. The transformation of the public school into the kingdom of good adjustment could be achieved only by psychologizing the total milieu, by converting every aspect of school life into psychiatric phenomena and putting all school procedures to the test—seeing whether they passed psychiatric muster. This meant, first, the eradication, so far as possible, of all sources of stress in school.

When hygienists viewed the public school, they saw not the benign, uplifting little red schoolhouse of folklore, but a place of anxiety, stress, and repression, a psychologically harmful milieu responsible for untold

cases of emotional disorder, juvenile delinquency, and crime. Here
was a radical departure from traditional views of the school. For example, it was an implicit assumption of the once reigning moral-intellectual tradition of education that if the school provoked stress or
frustration, this was ultimately beneficial to the child: adversity developed character; it trained or strengthened the will.[16] Hygienists spoke
a different language. They ignored the vocabulary of character and
will, while insisting that stress was the source of serious and potentially lasting psychological harm. From this hygienist perspective, there
was no special target group of children in school: all schoolchildren
were at risk; "every child was a problem child." Hygienists identified
four main sources of stress in the school: (1) grading and promotion,
(2) the subject-centered curriculum, (3) methods of discipline and classroom management, and (4) the training, attitude, and personality of
the teacher.

Failure in school was singled out as a cardinal sin against mental
health. Failure led to feelings of inferiority, then to "undesirable defense mechanisms" like withdrawal or to "compensations" like truancy and delinquency. On the other hand, success bred confidence
and a positive management of reality. "Failure, regardless of whether
'deserved' in the older moralistic sense," declared Clark University's
William Burnham, an influential popularizer of mental hygiene, would
have to be eliminated and replaced by success. The school's responsibility, "is to see to it that every child at some time, in some way, in
some subject, achieves a marked success."[17] Hygienists turned their
attention to the subject-centered curriculum as the ubiquitous source
of failure. Moreover, the school's emphasis on the acquisition of knowledge, on academic content and achievement, was antisocial, starved
the emotions, and led to a compulsive striving that left the personality
scarred. C. Macfie Campbell observed that the child brings the "whole
self" into a classroom. The school, Campbell said, could not disclaim
responsibility for the personality. Hygienists urged that children's
achievement in subject matter be deemphasized and that teachers pay
more attention to their personality development.

Classroom discipline was the other cardinal offense against personality. In the matter of discipline, what the hygienists required of the
school was that the new scientific concepts and theories that psychiatrists were beginning to apply to the understanding and treatment of
delinquents and criminals be applied to the misbehavior of students in
the classroom. Hygienists urged that misbehavior in school be rede-

fined or reconceptualized as a medical problem; misbehavior was a symptom that required psychological intervention or treatment, rather than a sin calling for punishment. The student who broke rules, defied orders, and otherwise misbehaved was not willfully bad or malicious and in need of discipline or punishment, but sick or maladjusted—a problem to be "understood" or diagnosed, then treated.

Here is another striking reversal of traditional notions. It was once thought that the child had aggressive impulses which needed to be curbed, through self-control if possible, or by threat of punishment if necessary. Now those aggressive impulses were seen as dangerous only if suppressed and harmless if expressed: too much self-control was dangerous; the discharge of emotions was healthy. Thus in another radical break from tradition, hygienists redefined aggression in the classroom as hardly a problem at all; repression was the problem. To hygienists, introversion, inhibition, shyness, too much suppression of feelings, and excessive self-control were more serious problems than aggressive behavior and overt violation of rules. Hygienist theory held that the shy, quiet, introverted student who caused no trouble for the teacher in class was the real "problem child," more in need of help than the aggressively misbehaving student, because the eventual price of repressed aggression might be neurosis and, even more serious, mental illness. Hygienists called upon teachers to be more sympathetic to or tolerant of aggressive behavior in the classroom, assuring them that "sublimation" or "catharsis" would provide a happy ending, that in a therapeutic environment all classroom discipline problems would disappear and students' personalities would be freed to develop in wholesome directions. Hygienists were not oblivious of the imperatives of discipline or classroom management, but they were convinced they were offering teachers a more scientific and more effective way to control students' behavior than punishment and the threat of punishment: the psychiatric management of students' emotional "needs."

The critical link between hygienist principle and hygienic classroom practice was the teacher. The mental hygiene movement enormously extended the teacher's field of operation, providing the profession of education with a new ideal: the teacher as therapist. Hygienist discussions of the teacher-therapist's responsibilities are implicitly grounded in the Freudian mechanisms of "transference" and "identification." Teachers had to provide favorable conditions for transference as well as opportunities for identification with models of wholesome personality adjustment. Hygienist theory held that the child perceives the classroom situation as approximating the situation in the family; the teacher becomes the surrogate of the parent. Hygienists pointed out that when children enter school, they greet teachers with essentially the same feelings and attitudes they have toward their own parents. This gives the teacher a favorable opportunity to correct faulty patterns of personality development formed during the earliest parent-child relationship.

V.

To transform the schools into the "kingdom of good adjustment" was not so easy as the hygienists first thought. Teachers were no paragons of mental health. It didn't take long for the hygienists to realize that teachers were as bad as parents. Edwin K. Wickman's *Children's Behavior and Teachers' Attitudes*, a classic in the literature, reveals how far teachers had to go to meet standards of mental hygiene. Hygienists complained that teachers, like parents, were moralistic, domineering, and punitive, thus forcing children to conceal their true feelings and emotions, and exacerbating problems of personality development originating in the home. Teachers were also ignorant of advances in psychiatry. The most important thing, Dr. Bernard Glueck of the program's staff explained, was for teachers to get to know the individual child. To know the child, the teacher had to go beyond overt behavior. Glueck urged the teacher to take an active interest in the child's fears, fantasies, dreams, and feelings about and relations with parents and siblings. He elaborated: "Is the child free and natural . . . or awkward and strained? . . . How does he take his successes and failures? . . . How much do I know about his daydreams?" The teacher's relation to the student was to become a relation of surveillance, inscribed, to paraphrase Foucault, at the heart of the practice of teaching. It signified a displacement of the parents as the principle agent of socialization; the teacher-child relationship was to supersede the parent-child relationship. This is what the psychologist and hygienist Percival Symonds apparently had in mind when he flatly explained of the school's assuming responsibility for the adjustment of personality that it "provides for the transfer to the school, in part, of the last remnant of child training that has been the exclusive prerogative of the home."[18]

In the meantime, there were external developments that greatly facilitated the mental hygiene movement in education. In the pre-World

War I period, as the mental hygiene movement was broadening its purview to include the whole child, professional educators were also broadening their concept of education. They frequently depicted parents as failing, children at risk, and subject-centered schools as anachronistic. Changing social conditions, they frequently observed, had thrust upon the public schools the care of the whole child. Even before 1917, then, there was a tendency for the school to appropriate more and more functions of the family. By 1917, the school was already assuming responsibilities in health, nutrition, and recreation and was becoming, in Lawrence Cremin's apposite phrase, a legatee institution. All these tendencies were accentuated by the mental hygiene movement. The main thrust of the mental hygiene movement in education was captured by William I. and Dorothy S. Thomas in their study *The Child in America* (1928). "The school," they observe, "is taking over from the court, the clinic, and other social agencies a large share of that responsibility which the increasing helplessness of the family had thrust upon them." At present, they continue, "the sentiment that the school is the logical place from which to work for the prevention of social problems has taken the form of a demand that the school shall take over the responsibility for the 'whole child,' . . . the development of his whole personality." This, at any rate, is the tendency, they add, though not so explicitly expressed.[19]

VI.

The goal of the mental hygiene movement was to disseminate the mental hygiene point of view and its application through the entire field of public education. Hygienists devised a long-term program to reach a broader public of opinion leaders, including parents and professionals, who would facilitate the schools' acceptance of the mental hygiene viewpoint. The main conduit throughout the 1920s was the Commonwealth Fund Program for the Prevention of Delinquency. I describe these efforts in detail elsewhere in this volume. Suffice it to say here that the program's advocacy and promotion of the mental hygiene movement was extraordinary in its scope and vigor. The philosophy, aims, and exemplary methods of the program were to be disseminated as extensively as possible, in order that, as Barry Smith of the Commonwealth Fund declared, parents, professionals, and the general community "may develop a consciousness regarding the value of mental hygiene." Some irrefutable evidence of how successful the

NCMH was in the 1920s in bringing the "mental hygiene point of view" and its language of discourse into the consciousness of all groups concerned with education and child welfare can be found in the reports of the 1930 White House Conference on Child Health and Protection.[20] It would be hard to exaggerate the importance of this conference. It legitimized and greatly accelerated the acceptance of the mental hygiene point of view of parents, children, and schooling among cultural and intellectual elites as well as the helping professions and parent-education groups. By 1933, when the Commonwealth Fund terminated the Program for the Prevention of Delinquency, the mental hygiene movement in education had taken on a life of its own; there was little left for the program to do.

By the mid-1930s, the notion of the school's responsibility for the personality development of children began to filter into books for teachers and teachers in training. In the 1930s and 1940s the mental hygiene point of view was firmly entrenched in the literature of the Progressive Education Association (PEA); in the 1930s the PEA replaced the Commonwealth Fund's Program for the Prevention of Delinquency as the main channel for the dissemination of the mental hygiene point of view in education.[21] In the late 1930s and 1940s, mental hygiene concepts and rhetoric began to figure prominently in publications of the National Education Association, the American Council on Education, the Association for Supervision and Curriculum Development, and the Educational Policies Commission. The climax of the NCMH's efforts to make personality development the guiding principle of American education was reached in 1950, at the great Mid-Century White House Conference on Children and Youth. As noted earlier, the conference adopted the slogan "For Every Child a Healthy Personality." "The school," the conference declared, "must assume the primary responsibility for the healthy development of the whole personality of each child."[22]

The 1950 White House Conference marks a significant moment in the history of American education. Without controversy or debate, its deliberations established the mental hygiene point of view as a new sphere of educational orthodoxy. The conference indicated the emergence of a new national consensus, at least among the educated, progressive middle class, that development of personality had become an explicit and legitimate goal of American schooling—a given, no longer problematic. There was no need to translate or spell out in great detail all the implications for grading and promotion, for curriculum, for teaching methods, or for discipline. The conference could assume a large and receptive audience which understood the language of discourse. If, with Foucault, we consider discourse as the object or the result of a struggle for power, then the conference signaled a shift in the power relationships in American educational thought: the intellectual-moral paradigm of education had been displaced from its long established position of dominance.

The Commonwealth Fund began to phase out the Program for the Prevention of Delinquency and its support of the NCMH in the 1930s. In the 1940s, the NCMH was almost moribund; by 1950, it was finished. But by then, so far as American education was concerned, neither the program nor the NCMH was needed. The movement that the NCMH had started and steered through four decades had developed a momentum of its own. The medicalization of American education went forward without it. By the 1950s, hygienist concepts and language of discourse had become an idiom of parents and teachers, part of the lore of all those concerned with child rearing and education, and in Fred Matthews's phrase, the "common sense of ideology and mentality" in twentieth-century America.[23]

VII.

Most contemporary historians of psychiatry and the helping professions, as previously remarked, are deeply suspicious of "doing good." They perceive psychiatry as a mask for social control.[24] Foucault teaches us that psychiatry can be best understood if treated not as a medical or scientific discipline but as a mechanism of "normalization."[25] The mental hygiene movement in education provides evidence for a more ironic interpretation of do-gooders and the helping professions. To broaden the definition of maladjustment to include all sorts of behavior and personality traits previously thought normal, trivial, or evanescent—for example, shyness—is to broaden the definition of deviancy, and to open up more areas of hitherto private life to surveillance and thus to control. The child's feelings; the child's hopes, fears, and dreams became objects of inquiry, solicitude, and "treatment." The hygienist-teacher's *gaze* objectifies children, making them more amenable to surveillance, discipline, and control. But a reminder of the historical context is appropriate here.

The 1920s were a period of deep divisiveness in American life, a time of xenophobia and nativism.[26] The hygienists' new understanding of the malleability of personality opened up exhilarating possibilities for a more effective, scientific, socially progressive control of behavior, the outcome of wholesome personality development. "We need not accept personality as we find it," explained Dr. Stanley Davies, a psychiatrist and prominent hygienist, "personality may be consciously improved and better adapted to social needs. . . . This is social progress." Here was a form of social control without coercion by laws, rules, and legal prohibitions; the ideal of personality adjustment bespeaks the essential concern of the hygienists. The well-adjusted personality was happy, efficient, productive, and above all social. The ideal of mental health, declared William Alanson White, is "the all-round, through and through personality, and that personality is the social personality." The social personality served a self-evident need in the 1920s.

It would not be fair, however, to ignore the altruism of the hygienists, their generous impulses, their intention to do good, a legacy of the child-saving movements of the progressive era. Maladjustment seemed to be ubiquitous, afflicting the nation like a modern plague, an individual tragedy and a social problem of vast, if unspecified, dimensions. Hygienists were convinced that prevention of mental illness was feasible: the scientific knowledge was available; it only had to be applied. But the ignorance and ineptitude of parents stood in the way. Finally, the hygienist assault on parents and the hygienist conception of the school as an agency for children's personality development speaks not just to meliorist hopes but to utopian dreams. Hygienists blamed the parents and then turned to the school to usher children into the "kingdom of good adjustment." We should not underestimate the appeal of utopian thinking. In fact, where the mental hygiene movement is concerned, the appeal to utopian or messianic thinking is all-important. It helps explain the enthusiasm and energy with which hygienists sought to establish the idea of the schools' responsibility for children's personality development—as well as the hygienists' indifference to the need for research to validate their faith in the school as an agency for personality development. The mental hygiene conception of education was transmitted to the public and to educators as an inspirational doctrine; where there is faith, there is no need for proof.

What did the mental hygiene movement have to offer to the education profession? Professionals were not immune to the temptations of empire building, but perhaps the most decisive factors that made educators receptive to the mental hygiene point of view were the imperatives of compulsory education and the concomitant phenomenon of school failure and school dropout.[27] The mental hygiene movement pointed to a solution of the problem—what sort of schooling was appropriate under conditions of universal education? A critical context is intelligence testing in the period after World War I, with its dramatic and well-publicized findings about how scarce a resource intelligence seemed to be in the general population. In this light, what with compulsory attendance laws, the traditional academic fare seemed irrelevant, even undemocratic. The connection between failure, nonpromotion, and leaving school early—between dropping out of school and the twin evils of waste and inefficiency—forced educators to seek alternatives to the traditional subject-centered education. The vocational education movement proved attractive for a time, but the mental hygiene movement ultimately provided educators with a more appealing alternative. With personality development as the fundamental test of the educational program, they were able to deemphasize subject matter and unite medical science with efficiency to promise a happier and more productive life for all children.[28]

Progressives, as the historian David Rothman observes, gave "remarkable primacy to the idea of the State as parent." This chapter amply documents Rothman's observation. The school, an agency of the State, has gradually taken on more and more responsibility for the care of the young, with a consequent dimunition of parental responsibilities.[29] Soon enough, the "kingdom of good adjustment" began to display some deficiencies. It is ironic that hygienists seemed never to consider how destabilizing the mental hygiene point of view could be. Teachers were encouraged to believe that it was in their power to preserve the coming generations from maladjustment or neurosis or to heal the afflicted. Thus, in the name of children's personality development and mental health, teachers were required to hold standards in suspension and give up their systems of rewards and punishments, while providing opportunities for the expression of the component of aggressiveness in children's personality. At the same time hygienist notions about there being "no such thing as a bad child" absolved children who misbehaved of accountability for their actions, made teachers feel guilty and personally responsible for children's misbehavior in class, and for a long time led to a conspiracy of silence regarding the existence of such problems. Schools and teachers were left ill-prepared to cope with students' defiance, disruptiveness, and violence.

In the meantime, teachers could not ignore the fact that they were still supposed to achieve certain academic objectives and to maintain discipline. They were confused and overburdened with conflicting messages. By 1932 Adolf Meyer was having second thoughts about the incursion of mental hygiene into the school. "We must," he said, "look to the school to attend to things that it can do." Then: "I am very skeptical about the wisdom of introducing too much pathology into the school. . . . We have to cultivate in the school interest in the things which are of the school and for the school."[30] Few were willing to listen to Meyer's warnings then or later. By 1932 the NCMH had passed from the scene, and the Commonwealth Fund had washed its hands of the mental hygiene movement and the public schools. The public schools have been left to bear the burden of responsibility for the personality development of children and at the same time fend off criticism by those with short memories who accuse them of usurping or undermining parents.

What final observations can we make about the mental hygiene movement, personality, and the making of twentieth-century American education?

This essay was primarily intended as an exercise in intellectual puzzle-solving, not an exercise in contemporary problem-solving. Still, I think historians have an obligation to contribute to an understanding of the present as well as to make some sense of the past. A major concern of American educators and school reformers has to do with declining academic skills and achievement and deteriorating discipline. A popular remedy is to take a tough line, as exemplified by the calls for "excellence," a return to the "basics," accountability, minimum competency testing, and codes of discipline backed up by sanctions like failure or nonpromotion. Another remedy is to call upon the school to divest itself of its legatee functions. But education in the United States is distinguished by the broad, almost unlimited responsibilities placed on the school and the teachers. This emphasis is unlikely to recede in the future. The clock cannot be turned back on changes in family, social, or economic life. So school reformers may find themselves in for a surprise; to neglect history does not mean to escape its influence. No diagnosis, and thus no remedy, for the problems of American education will get very far if it neglects the body of ideas bequeathed by the mental hygiene movement and now part of our common sense. The school's responsibility for personality development remains an unexamined assumption underlying educational discourse. If this idea were to be placed on the table and made an explicit object of scrutiny, it would be possible to open up for public debate the whole question of the relative responsibilities of parents, schools, and other agencies in the education of the "whole" child.

Notes

1   Lee J. Cronbach and Patrick Suppes, eds., *Research for Tomorrow's Schools: Disciplined Inquiry for Education* (London, 1969), p. 259.

2   Raymond Williams, *Keywords: A Vocabulary of Culture and Society* (London, 1983), pp. 20–22. And see Richard Rorty, "The Contingency of Language," *Contingency, Irony, and Solidarity* (Cambridge, England, 1989).

3   "'Personality' and the Making of Twentieth-Century Culture," in John Higham and Paul K. Conkin, eds., *New Directions in American Intellectual History* (Baltimore, 1979), pp. 212–226. See also Christopher Lasch, *Haven in a Heartless World: The Family Besieged* (New York, 1977), ch. 4, "Culture and Personality," and *The Culture of Narcissism: American Life in an Age of Diminishing Expectations* (New York, 1979). For background, see Edward B. McClellan, *Schools and the Shaping of Character: Moral Education in America, 1907–Present* (Bloomington, Ind., 1991).

4   For the beginning and early years of the movement, see Norman Dain, *Clifford W. Beers, Advocate for the Insane* (Pittsburgh, 1980); Barbara Sicherman, *The Quest for Mental Health in America, 1880–1917* (Ann Arbor, 1967), chs. 5–6; and Fred H. Matthews, "In Defense of Common Sense: Mental Hygiene as Ideology and Mentality in Twentieth-Century America," *Prospects*, 2 (1979): 467–480.

5   Nathan G. Hale, Jr., *Freud and the Americans: The Beginnings of Psychoanalysis in the United States, 1876–1917* (New York, 1971), ch. XII; Fred H. Matthews, "The Americanization of Sigmund Freud: Adaptations of Psychoanalysis Before 1917," *Journal of American Studies*, 1 (1967): 39–62; David Shakow and David Rappaport, *The Influence of Freud on American Psychology* (New York, 1964); and John Chynoweth Burnham, *Psychoanalysis and American Medicine, 1894–1918* (New York, 1967).

6   *A Present-Day Conception of Mental Disorders* (Cambridge, Mass., 1924), p. 38.

7   Quoted in Sicherman, *The Quest for Mental Health in America*, p. 180.

8   Thomas W. Salmon, "War Neuroses and Their Lesson," *New York Medical Journal*, 109 (1919): 933–996; "Notes and Comments," *Mental Hygiene*, 2 (1918): 480–481. In general, see Nathan G. Hale, Jr., *The Rise and Crisis of Psychoanalysis in the United States: Freud and the Americans, 1917–1985* (New York, 1995), ch. 1, "The Great War: A Human Laboratory."

9   See Chapter 8, "The Mental Hygiene Movement, The Commonwealth Fund, and Education, 1921–1933: 'Every School a Clinic.'"

10 Jacques Donzelot, *The Policing of Families*, trans. by Robert Hurley (New York, 1979), pp. 96ff.

11 "There are sick children, . . . misunderstood children, children from miserable homes, and children seeking satisfactions in mistaken ways; but a deliberately 'bad' child is an impossibility. . . . The problems of the child . . . point directly back to the adults surrounding the child." Clara Bassett, *Mental Hygiene and the Public School* (New York, 1933), pp. 9–10.

12 Miriam Van Waters, *Parents on Probation* (New York, 1928), ch. 4.

13 "Finding a Way in Mental Hygiene," *Mental Hygiene*, 14 (1930): 246–247. Blaming the parent entered the American cultural mainstream through various channels. Lasch, *Haven in a Heartless World*, ch. 2 and *passim*; and *The Culture of Narcissism*, ch. 7.

14 Ralph P. Truitt, "Mental Hygiene and the Public School," *Mental Hygiene*, 11 (1927): 270.

15 Quoted in Virginia P. Robinson, *Jessie Taft, Therapist and Social Work Educator* (Philadelphia, 1962), p. 63. Jane Culbert,"The Public School as a Factor in the Training of the Socially Handicapped Child," and M. Edith Campbell, "The Strategic Position of the School in Programs of Social Work," National Conference of Social Work, *Proceedings*, 1923, pp. 93, 362ff.

16 McClellan, *Schools and the Shaping of Character*, chs. 1–2, 4.

17 "Success and Failure as Conditions of Mental Health," *Mental Hygiene* 3 (1919): 387–397.

18 Percival Symonds, *Mental Hygiene of the School Child* (New York, 1934), p. ix; and "Mental Hygiene in the Classroom: Historical Perspective," *Journal of Social Issues*, 15 (1959): 1–6.

19 New York, 1928, p. 234.

20 White House Conference, 1930, *Addresses and Abstracts of Committee Reports* (Washington, D.C., 1931). See also Chapter 11 in this volume.

21 Burton Fowler, president of the PEA from 1931 to 1933, observed: "It might astonish Clifford Beers to know that the Progressive Education Movement owes more to mental hygiene than to any other source, with the possible exception of the philosophy of John Dewey. Mr. Beers and his associates have taught us . . . to realize that all of our educational experiences are conditioned by the fundamental necessity of well-adjusted personality." In Wilbur H. Cross, ed., *Twenty-Five Years After: Sidelights on the Mental Hygiene Movement and Its Founder* (New York, 1934), pp. 146–147.

22 Edward A. Richards, ed., *Proceedings of the Mid-Century White House Conference on Children and Youth* (Raleigh, N.C., 1950), pp. 175, 176. See also Helen Leland and Ruth Kotinsky, eds., *Personality in the Making: The Fact-Finding Report of the Mid-Century White House Conference on Children and Youth* (New York, 1952), chs. 1, 4, and 11. In general, see Wesley Allinsmith and George W. Goethals, *The Role of the School in Mental Health* (New York, 1962).

23   Satirized in novels, in movies, and on the stage. E.g., Maggie: "Guido, do you know what a teacher's job is? . . . A teacher's job—no, a teacher's sacred obligation—is to repair the trauma that children have incurred at home." Max Shulman, *Rally Round the Flag, Boys* (New York, 1957), p. 7. Or recall the "Officer Krupke" number from Leonard Bernstein's *West Side Story* (1957), or the guidance counselor in Robert Mulligan's film, *Up the Down Staircase* (1967). In general, see Fred H. Matthews, "In Defense of Common Sense: Mental Hygiene as Ideology and Mentality in Twentieth-Century America," *Prospects*, 2 (1979): 459–516.

24   E.g., Willard Gaylin et al., *Doing Good:The Limits of Benevolence* (New York, 1978); David J. Rothman, *Conscience and Convenience: The Asylum and its Alternatives in Progressive America* (Boston, 1980); John C. Burnham, "The New Psychology: From Narcissism to Social Control," in John Braeman et al., *Change and Continuity in Twentieth–Century America* (Columbus, Ohio, 1968).

25   *Discipline and Punish: The Birth of the Prison*, trans. by Alan Sheridan (New York, 1977).

26   Stanley Coben, "The Assault on Victorianism in the Twentieth Century," *American Quarterly*, 27 (1975): 604–625. Daniel Walker Howe, ed., *Victorian America* (Philadelphia, 1976); and Coben, *Rebellion Against Victorianism: The Impetus for Cultural Change in 1920s America* (New York, 1991).

27   Leonard P. Ayres, *Laggards in Our Schools* (New York, 1909), is the classic work.

28   The mental hygiene point of view also enabled school professionals to place the onus of blame for children's problems in school on the parents or the home and family situation. David W. Swift, *Ideology and Change in the Public Schools: Latent Functions of Progressive Education* (Columbus, Ohio, 1971).

29   David J. Rothman, "The State as Parent: Social Policy in the Progressive Era," in Gaylin, p. 39; Kenneth Keniston and the Carnegie Council on Children, *All Our Children: The American Family Under Pressure* (New York, 1977).

30   *American Journal of Orthopsychiatry*, 2 (1932): 228–229.

Chapter 11

The Medicalization of American Education: The Social History of an Idea

> The goal of medicine is peculiarly the goal of making itself unnecessary; of influencing life so that what is medicine today will become mere common sense tomorrow.
>
> Adolph Meyer

I.

Few intellectual and social movements of the twentieth century have had so deep and pervasive an influence on the theory and practice of American education as mental hygiene. The mental hygiene movement has radically changed our ways of thinking and speaking about education: curriculum, grading, classroom management, and teaching methods, as well as the nature of the person to be educated. It was the inspiration and the driving force behind one of the most radical and far-reaching, yet least understood, educational innovations of the twentieth century, what I call the medicalization of American education: the infiltration of psychiatric, psychoanalytic, and therapeutic norms, concepts, and language of discourse—the "mental hygiene point of view"—into virtually all aspects of American schooling, and into all aspects of American culture in the twentieth century.[1]

The term "mental hygiene point of view" is a shorthand notation for a cohesive set of ideas that includes the following essential elements: personality is the most basic component of the self; psychological maladjustment is the cause of mental illness and social problems of all sorts; childhood is the critical period for the later emergence of psychological disorders; the family is the seedbed of neurosis; the school is the strategic agency for preventing or identifying and treating problems in children's psychological development; and finally, the psychological adjustment of children must take priority over any other educational objective. What is ultimately involved in the medicalization of American education is a transformation in the idea of the school, a reordering of education on new principles.

The radical nature of the medicalization of education is to be gauged not only by what it includes but by what it implicitly or explicitly repudiates or excludes. The medicalization of education takes on its full meaning when it is considered in relation to the traditional or classical and formerly hegemonic paradigm of education, an intellectual-moral paradigm of education, in which the core objective is children's character development and the proximate objectives are to strengthen the will and develop the intellect. It is this paradigm of education which the mental hygiene movement opposed and whose hegemony it sought to undermine and overthrow and, in my view, eventually did overthrow.

As I noted earlier, the mental hygiene movement has left a lasting imprint on American education. It has altered our way of perceiving education, providing an orientation, a language of discourse, and a body of ideas which have become a part of our common sense about education. It clearly needs much more attention by historians of education. My purpose in this essay, the last of a series on the subject, for now anyway, is to spur further research. In addition, I offer this essay as a novel contribution to the social history of ideas. I am particularly concerned with the idea diffusion process, with the problem of how and in what form ideas about education circulate in society and become influential, and of how to estimate their influence (a subject that I have addressed in this book in a different but complementary context, that having to do with the progressive education movement), a subject historians of education need to reflect upon more seriously than we usually do.

II.

The National Committee for Mental Hygiene (NCMH), the organizational spearpoint for the mental hygiene movement, has its roots in progressive era reform movements. Though exact figures as to the dimensions of the problem were hard to ascertain, NCMH leadership—the psychiatrists C. Macfie Campbell, Thomas W. Salmon, and William Alanson White, among others, and led by Adolf Meyer, head of the Phipps Psychiatric Clinic—considered mental illness the most serious social evil of the time, exacting an appalling cost in individual suffering and exacerbating many of the nation's social problems. Inspired by advances in the field of public health, especially the campaign against tuberculosis, hygienists were eager to launch an aggressive campaign for the prevention of mental illness. But funding was difficult to attract, and the general therapeutic pessimism regarding the mentally ill was hard to combat. The early activities of the NCMH were modest and essentially meliorist. By the early 1920s, the goal of the NCMH had broadened into a crusade for the prevention of all forms of maladjustment, extending far beyond the hospital and the mental asylum to encompass the courts, prisons, industry, and the school.

Although notably eclectic, two strands of thought stand out as comprising the theoretical basis for the optimism that characterized the mental hygiene movement in the 1920s: Adolf Meyers's dynamic psychiatry, and psychoanalytic concepts extrapolated from Freud, though a domesticated and watered-down psychoanalysis.[2]

The hygienists' hopes rested on a new approach to the etiology of mental illness which minimized or disregarded the then-prevalent hereditarian and biomedical emphasis of traditional American psychiatry. The new psychiatry held that mental illness was not a mysterious disease—an untreatable organic disorder—but a disorder of the personality confronting the stresses of life.[3] This was crucial. Some other key assumptions follow: Mental illness did not strike suddenly but developed insidiously, according to definite psychological principles. Childhood was the conditioning period of personality. The emotions were the essential core of personality and the most determining aspect of mental life, more decisive than intellect or will. Behavior was motivated by the search for gratification of emotional or inner "needs." Maladjustment and mental illness resulted from the frustration or too harsh suppression of "needs," leading to repression, the scourge of mental health and personality development. Repressed emotions would surface later in serious problems of all sorts. But long before the onset of serious mental illness, it was possible to spot symptoms of psychiatric trouble. Meyer identified the early danger signs of future mental disorder—personality traits like seclusiveness or introversion, which could be treated and cured if detected early enough or, better yet, prevented. And prevention was feasible because—here we come to the core belief of the mental hygiene movement—personality was basically malleable.[4]

The reformulation of mental disorder had implications far beyond prevention of mental illness. New vistas opened up for understanding, treating, or preventing not only mental illness but dependency, delinquency, crime, and other social problems. These could be understood not as separate problems but as one problem with different manifestations; all were symptoms of underlying psychological maladjustment. The implications were enormous. To correct the basic factors causing the symptoms would be to strike at the root of all social problems. The pieces for a mental hygiene movement with a focus on children and the school were almost in place.[5] Even before World War I, progressive psychiatrists—Meyer, C. Macfie Campbell, William Healy, John MacCurdy, and L. Pierce Clark, among others—were calling attention to the public school system as a fertile and untouched field for mental hygiene.[6] There is "no more hopeful avenue of approach to many of the . . . social problems of today than through the school," declared Campbell.[7] In the fight against mental illness, declared NCMH's medical director, Thomas Salmon, practically all the promising points of attack exist in childhood. If they were to win the fight, "psychiatrists . . . must be permitted to enter the schools."[8] Such declarations were futile sermonizing until the founding of the Commonwealth Fund in 1919.

III.

In the postwar period the NCMH and the mental hygiene movement entered a completely new phase. Salmon had been on leave to the army during the war; when he resumed his post as NCMH's medical director in 1919, he steered the NCMH into a partnership with the Commonwealth Fund and into a broad mission of mental hygiene focused on children and the schools. In 1921, Salmon proposed that the newly-organized Fund, flush with money and looking for a project, do something in the area of the prevention of delinquency. Under the guidance of the NCMH, the Fund launched its Program for the Prevention of Delinquency, which hugely spurred the development of child guidance, child psychiatry, and psychiatric social work, and became the driving force behind the mental hygiene movement in education.[9]

The Program for the Prevention of Delinquency was in fact only nominally concerned with preventing delinquency. Salmon conceived, and the Commonwealth Fund put into effect, a plan that from its inception was much farther reaching than its title indicates. The program's earliest stated objective may have been to provide psychiatric services for "predelinquent" children, with the child guidance clinic as the strategic agency for intervention. But hygienists quickly concluded that by the time children came to the attention of social workers and psychiatrists, it was too late. In the interests of prevention it was critical to reach children before they became problems. That implied reaching parents and the school.

For a time, parents became a primary target for hygienist reeducation. The program encouraged, demonstrated, and disseminated parent education in mental hygiene. Nevertheless, parent education had a serious drawback: no one could be compelled to take parent education courses or to obtain a degree in mental hygiene before having children.[10] The school, then, had to become the strategic agency in the fight against mental illness. The reason is obvious: compulsory attendance laws. The school took children in their critical formative years; all children were compelled to attend school. Salmon declared: "Practically all children are for a shorter or longer period in our schools. The public school, coming into close contact with the lives of over twenty million young boys, girls, and adolescents, is or should be our greatest social welfare agency."[11] The ultimate goal of the mental hygiene movement in education was stated succinctly by program staff member, Elizabeth Woods: "every school a clinic."[12] For the school to become general headquarters for preventive psychiatry or applied mental hygiene required not merely reform but something altogether new—the medicalization of education.

Hygienists were confident that psychiatry had isolated a specific environmental factor—stress—as the chief precipitating cause of psychological disorders; the personality buckled under stress. They singled out the school as a uniquely stressful and psychologically pathogenic milieu where "worry, confusion, mental strain, and nervousness" reigned. From this perspective there was no special group of problem children; all children were at risk, and all had to be saved. Hygienists targeted four particular sources of stress in school: (1) failure and nonpromotion; (2) the curriculum which was centered on academic subject matter; (3) classroom management and disciplinary procedures; and (4) the teacher's own personality and training.

Failure in school was a cardinal offense against mental health. Failure led to feelings of inferiority and behavior problems like truancy or juvenile delinquency, or, worse, to withdrawal and the "development of an unsocial attitude."[13] Success, by contrast, led to confidence, a sense of self-worth, and a positive attitude toward life. Hygienists pointed out that the school's emphasis on subject matter under conditions of compulsory education made a large number of failures inevitable. How was failure to be eliminated or minimized? How could all children achieve success? The remedy seemed obvious—deemphasize the academic subject-matter curriculum. In any event, hygienists believed that the subject-centered curriculum rested on outdated rationalistic assumptions about the role of intellect in mental life. Hygienists invariably depicted the curriculum in pejorative terms: "rigid curriculum," "mere acquisition of knowledge." They condemned that curriculum as a procrustean bed, resulting in behavior problems of all sorts: "The reason for misfit children is a misfit curriculum."[14] Hygienists made few concrete proposals for reforming the curriculum. They simply urged the school to pay less attention to subject matter and count itself successful if it enhanced the child's psychological development.

Classroom disciplinary procedures were another grave offense against mental health. If the school was to be transformed into a therapeutic environment, traditional ideas about discipline would have to be discarded. What hygienists insisted upon was this: for the school to redefine all children's classroom behavior problems as psychological problems, that is, for badness to be redefined as sickness, misbehavior as maladjustment, sin as symptom.[15] What hygienists sought was for the concepts and theories that progressive psychiatrists were then applying to the treatment and rehabilitation of delinquents and criminals to be applied by teachers to the misbehavior of children in the classroom. If the real revolution, as John Adams said of the American Revolution, was in the mind and heart, then what the hygienists attempted to accomplish was revolutionary. To go from labeling misbehavior "bad" or "naughty" to labeling misbehavior a "symptom" is to bring psychiatric norms into an entirely new domain and was a revolutionary extension of the psychiatrist's province.

In another startling departure from traditional views, the mental hygiene perspective entailed a complete change in attitude toward aggression. To hygienists, children's aggression was hardly a problem at all. Aggressive behavior was healthier than introverted behavior—in fact, the real problem was the introverted child. To hygienists, the shy, quiet child who caused no trouble for the teacher was the more serious problem and more in need of help than the aggressively misbehaving child, because the price of suppressed aggressiveness, the price of "goodness," might be neurosis. From the perspective of hygienist theory, the kind of children whom a former generation of teachers had looked upon as good children were "shut-in" or repressed children who had to be freed from inhibitions, drawn out of their shells.

Radical ideas, if repeated long enough, lose their force. Soon it requires an effort to remember how radical they once were. Teachers, who once upon a time only made demands of children—to show respect, to work hard—and who were more or less oblivious of children's "needs," now had to learn that children had needs that had to be respected, and that children's misbehavior was the inevitable result of frustrating those needs. Thus, the mental hygiene movement sought to persuade teachers to give a green light to the component of aggressiveness in children's personality, trusting that "sublimation" or "catharsis" would provide a happy ending. Hygienists promised an end to discipline problems and a gain in teachers' prestige the day the mental hygiene point of view ruled the classroom.

Hygienists envisioned a school that would provide a form of prophylaxis or immunity against mental illness. In pursuit of this goal, they called upon the schools to make considerations of mental hygiene paramount in all its operations. They placed the major burden of responsibility on the teacher. The mental hygiene movement provided American education with a new model: the teacher as therapist. The teacher-therapist was expected to be an expert in children's mental hygiene, to interpret behavior problems as symptoms of maladjustment, and to go beyond overt behavior to get to know children's dreams, secret hopes and fears, and inquire into their relations with parents and siblings. As Foucault might put it, inspection would function ceaselessly.

The teacher-therapist was expected to foster the psychological adjustment of all students, the quiet, shy, or withdrawn as well as, or more than, the aggressive. Hygienists called for a radical change in the way teachers were recruited and educated. Teacher training institutions were called upon to screen prospective teachers on the basis

of their psychological adjustment and train them in a scientific understanding of children's personality.[16]

Such, briefly sketched, are the essential components of the
medicalization of American education. By way of summary, we may
say that the hygienists formulated a therapeutic model of schooling:
every child a problem; every teacher a therapist; the general ambience
of the class period that of a therapeutic hour; and every school a
clinic. It is tempting to apply to the hygienist's conception of the school-
child T. S. Eliot's memorable line, "a patient etherized upon a table."

IV.

Of course the NCMH and the Commonwealth Fund sought to increase
the number of psychiatrists, psychologists, social workers, and child
guidance counselors in the schools. But this was a peripheral concern. The hygienists' ultimate goal was something more fundamental
and lasting: to persuade the teaching profession to change its view of
education—its methods, its goals, its values, its notion of what problems were important and unimportant and what to emphasize and
deemphasize. The hygienists' goal was not to tell teachers concretely
what or how to teach but, as Philip Jackson and Sara B. Kieslar make
clear in their discussion of educational innovation generally, "to alter
the practitioner's view of reality," confident that a change in the
teacher's view of reality would be carried over ultimately into the classroom.[17] Hygienists were well aware that deeply rooted educational
traditions stood in their way. Their conception of education was radical: educationists and parents had traditionally given the highest priority to character, good behavior, and academic achievement while
neglecting the psychological or emotional needs of children. To overcome resistance from teachers and parents, hygienists adopted a long-
term strategy of educating an audience of community leaders, middle-
class parents, and professionals who would facilitate the acceptance
of mental hygiene by the general public, school officials, and teachers.
The hygienists' main instrument in this educative war against mental
illness was the Commonwealth Fund's Program for the Prevention of
Delinquency.

Herbert Croly, describing reformers of the progressive era, refers
to their "faith in education [and] the Subsidized Word." Reformers, he
observed, "propose to evangelize the individual by the reading of books
and by the expenditure of money and words."[18] Thanks to the Com-

monwealth Fund, hygienists were able to launch a campaign to evangelize leaders of public opinion through the "subsidized word." The program adopted several strategies. In the first place, the visiting teacher served indirectly as a change agent in the schools. Then, in the late 1920s, the program launched a promotional plan directly among teachers and teachers in training through summer sessions in a score of carefully selected schools and colleges of education. Next, the program started its own publishing house, issuing a monthly newsletter and press releases; it also established a reference and bibliographic service and a speakers' bureau. At the same time, the program launched a deliberate, systematic effort to reach a carefully classified list of leaders of public opinion, including "leaders in education, teachers and professors in schools, colleges and universities, physicians, social workers, judges, probation officers, writers, editors." Finally, it disseminated a vast literature aimed at public opinion more generally. The program kept exact records. Between 1922 and 1926, staff members delivered 2,345 talks and 120 formal lectures and published 83 articles. As of 1926, 98,359 free books and pamphlets describing various aspects of the Program were distributed, including 15,922 copies of Howard Nudd's pamphlet "The Visiting Teacher," 13,869 copies of Bernard Glueck's article "Some Extra-Curricular Problems of the Classroom," and 11,762 copies of Mary B. Sayles's *The Problem Child in School*. By 1926 the program's publications were being used in courses in 80 schools of education and in college and university courses in psychology, social work, and child study.[19]

How effective was the strategy? The above figures are suggestive. But the real influence of the mental hygiene movement cannot be demonstrated numerically; the process of diffusion of an idea hardly lends itself to quantitative treatment. The goal of the mental hygiene movement in education was, in Adolf Meyer's words, to reorder the "common sense" of the community in terms of psychiatric principles, to influence life "so that what is medicine today will become mere common sense tomorrow." On this level, I believe the success of the mental hygiene movement is impressive indeed. How can we document its success? Admittedly, there is the vexing problem of evidence. But there is more evidence than might be supposed, though so far we have not been able to see it for lack of an appropriate approach or theoretical framework. As I point out in several essays in this book, I find in the linguistic turn the approach to influence and change in education most satisfactory to me.

Briefly, the critical datum is language, and use of language. It is not just that language is used to communicate but that language communicates more than we think. Language, as John G. A. Pocock discerns, is historically conditioned and in turn is itself a historical agent.[20] Fundamental linguistic shifts mark a reformulated sense of who we are, how we relate to the world, how we define "reality." Once individuals accept a certain vocabulary, they are drawn into a community of discourse, an epistemic community sharing a special language and by virtue of this fact sharing a common value system and agreeing on the proper perspective for the construction of reality.[21] To put this another way, one proposed earlier by the sociologist C. Wright Mills, the use of language enables us to locate a writer or speaker among political and social coordinates by ascertaining what key words his or her functioning vocabulary contains.[22] The implications are far-reaching; language constitutes an invaluable source of evidence for the diffusion and adoption of hygienist ideas. The means the mental hygiene movement used and the field on which it fought were not legalistic or bureaucratic but linguistic; the stakes for which it fought were control of the language of educational discourse. The mental hygiene movement created a new vocabulary, a new language with which to think, write, and speak about education. Once we know the language, or language system, then we can track where, when, how, and by whom its key words are employed. It is here, in the cumulative process of the sedimentation of language, that we can trace the diffusion of hygienist ideas and the influence of the mental hygiene movement in American education.

The NCMH and the Program for the Prevention of Delinquency launched their educative war in the early 1920s. A handful of psychologists like Arnold Gesell, Lewis M. Terman, and J. Wallace Wallin—students of Clark University's William H. Burnham, an early recruit of the mental hygiene movement—became important publicists and advocates for mental hygiene.[23] The mental hygiene movement found its most zealous and dedicated allies in the social work profession. Leading social workers such as Jane Culbert, Edith Campbell, and Jessie Taft aggressively espoused the mental hygiene view of the school.[24] Gradually, the hygienist language of discourse filtered into the consciousness of influential publics; ways of comprehending education were changed. Within less than a decade, the mental hygiene point of view, hygienist concepts and language, and the hygienist view of parents, children, and education were in the ascendancy.

A turning point in the history of the mental hygiene movement and in the history of American education was the White House Conference on Child Health and Protection of 1930. The conference provides convincing evidence that the diffusion process had taken a giant step forward. This was the largest conference on child welfare ever held in the United States to that time. It provided hygienists with a national forum; it was dominated by the hygienist view of children, parents, and schools; and it introduced into the national scene a whole new language of discourse. Here is a sample of that language disseminated by the conference:

> The problem child has become the problems of the child.
>
> Truancy and other behavior disorders are symptoms of school dissatisfaction—the child is not having his fundamental needs met.
>
> We live by what we feel rather than what we know, so the primary question is not what does the child learn in school, but how does the child feel because of school.
>
> Failure in school is a frequent source of children's problems; nothing fails like failure.
>
> The teacher must change her emphasis from the subject taught to the person taught.
>
> The school and the child may conflict but these conflicts will disappear as the teacher interests herself less and less in what the child did, and more and more in why he did it.
>
> The school must take full cognizance of the child's emotional needs.
>
> The school must get to know the twenty-four hours a day and three hundred and sixty-five days a year of the individual child. Only then can it meet the needs of the child.
>
> The school is far more than merely a dispenser of academic education. . . . the school must be viewed as primarily an experiment in life adjustment for the child.[25]

We recognize in these passages language, rhetoric, and concepts which have become so much the common sense of American educational discourse today that it is hard to remember how novel they once were or where they came from. It is this language of discourse and these concepts, that in the late 1930s and 1940s begin to saturate American education.

The NCMH established ties with the National Education Association in 1924, but these were loose and were never pursued aggressively. The key strategic objective of the NCMH was to coopt the Progressive Education Association (PEA), which proved an easy conquest. Hygienists published in the PEA's journal, *Progressive Education,* as early as 1926.[26] Personal contacts were established at the First International Congress on Mental Hygiene held in Washington, D.C., in May 1930, and at the White House Conference on Child Health and Protection later that year. Relations between the NCMH and the PEA became even closer in the 1930s. Prominent hygienists like the psychiatrists Edward Liss and Frankwood Williams, Salmon's successor as NCMH's medical director, were active in progressive education in the 1930s. Meanwhile, progressives in education like Carleton Washburn, Elizabeth Irwin, W. Carson Ryan, Jr., Vivian T. Thayer, Carolyn Zachry, and Lawrence K. Frank became advocates of the mental hygiene view of education. By the late 1930s the mental hygiene point of view was firmly entrenched in the PEA; hygienist conceptions, rhetoric, and vocabulary had become part of the linguistic currency of progressive education.[27] The PEA's various commissions, with their innumerable publications, conferences, and workshops, became the main conduit for dissemination of the mental hygiene point of view among parents and teachers throughout the 1930s.

We can identify other layers of the diffusion process. For example, hygienists sought to reach prospective teachers directly by encouraging teacher training institutions to offer courses in mental hygiene; in fact, the Program for the Prevention of Delinquency sponsored and financed a score of summer courses for teachers in diverse colleges and universities around the country in 1927 and 1928.[28] But hygienists had more success with the written word. The program began to publish pamphlets for teachers in the early 1920s. In the late 1920s, the mental hygiene point of view began to filter into textbooks for teachers in training in a thin trickle; this trickle slowly and steadily gained force in the early 1930s.[29] The sensitive antennae of publishing houses saw which way the trend was moving. In the late 1930s and early 1940s almost a score of textbooks on mental hygiene and education appeared. They bore the imprimatur of some of the most respected publishing houses of the day: Pitman; Longmans, Green; McGraw-Hill; Farrar-Rinehart; Houghton-Mifflin; Macmillan; D. Appleton; and Ronald Press. Their authors were professors of education affiliated with colleges and universities that were geographically diverse and had large teacher training components: Teachers College, Columbia University; City College of New York; University of Southern California; Northwestern University; University of Texas; Massachusetts State Teachers College; and Stanford University. Here are some authors and titles: Percival Symonds, *The Mental Hygiene of the School Child* (1934); W. Carson Ryan, *Mental Health Through Education* (1938); Harry Rivlin, *Educating for Adjustment: The Classroom Applications of Mental Hygiene* (1936); Lawrence A. Averill, *Mental Hygiene for the Classroom Teacher* (1939); Norman Fenton, *Mental Hygiene in School Practice* (1943); Ernest W. Tiegs and Barney Katz, *Mental Hygiene in Education* (1941); Paul A. Witty and Charles Skinner, eds., *Mental Hygiene in Modern Education* (1939); Mandel Sherman, *Mental Hygiene and Education* (1938); Daniel Prescott, *Emotion and the Educative Process* (1938); C. R. Myers, *Towards Mental Hygiene in School* (1939); Lester D. Crow and Alice V. Crow, *Mental Hygiene in School and Home Life* (1942); and Norma E. Cutts and Nicholas Mosely, *Practical School Discipline from the Standpoint of Mental Hygiene* (1941).

These textbooks are a vital source of data.[30] They provide evidence that the mental hygiene point of view was becoming an insistent theme in American educational thought. They embody prevailing notions of mental hygiene and reveal which hygienist beliefs were being disseminated and in what specific vocabulary these beliefs were embedded, and they displaced or dislodged traditional texts in teacher education. Taken together, they reflect a new way of conceiving of education. A new era is revealed in just a sentence in a textbook by Norman Fenton, a Stanford University professor of education: "Children's misbehavior . . . is an outward expression of an inward condition of mental ill-health as truly as a chill or a fever is a manifestation of physical disease."[31] A new climate of opinion is revealed by the language in which another professor of education, Daniel Prescott, formulates a rhetorical question: "The issue must be made clear. Is it more important that children develop adjusted, integrated personalities, or that they fulfill some other traditional academic objectives?"[32] Finally, these textbooks functioned as a national communication network for dissemination of the mental hygiene point of view among aspiring entrants to the profession of education, initiating future professors of education as well as future classroom teachers and school administrators. By the late 1930s mental hygiene conceptions and rhetoric begin to appear in publications sponsored by powerful professional education organizations like the National Education Association, the Educational Policies Commission, and the American Council on Education.[33] Hygienist rhetoric was employed to explain and justify progressive innovations like the "activity program" and the "core curriculum."[34] By the late 1930s the tests and measurement branch of the educational establishment were creating instruments to measure the efficiency of (and to legitimize) the school's concern with the psychological adjustment and mental health of children.[35]

The culmination of the NCMH's efforts to medicalize American education was, as I say above, the 1950 Mid-Century White House Conference on Children and Youth, a milestone in the history of American education. When the conference adopted as its slogan "For Every Child a Healthy Personality," it ratified the hygienists' notion that the school is basically an institution for developing children's personality.[36] This conference did not break new ground or chart a new course for the future of American education. Its importance lies in the fact that it signified the emergence of a national consensus regarding the school's responsibility for the psychological adjustment of children. The conference marked a shift in power relationships in American educational thought: the displacement of the moral-intellectual paradigm from its long dominance. By putting the imprimatur of the White House on the mental hygiene point of view, the conference encouraged laggards among educationists to acquiesce in the idea that the school must assume the responsibility for psychological adjustment and placed those who did not acquiesce on the defensive; moreover, it helped initiate a new generation of parents and teachers into the mental hygiene discourse.[37]

The Commonwealth Fund ended the Program for Prevention of Delinquency in 1933. In 1950, the NCMH passed quietly from the scene. By then, neither one was needed. The school reform movement that the NCMH had started and then, with the Commonwealth Fund, steered through the 1920s had developed a momentum of its own. The medicalization of American education continued without them. By the late 1950s, less than forty years after the NCMH and the Commonwealth Fund had launched their educative war—and much sooner than the fifty years Paul Mort considered the minimum amount of time for the diffusion of educational innovation—psychiatric values, concepts, and language of discourse and the mental hygiene point of view had been incorporated into educational ideology and had become the common sense and common language of educationists and part of the lore of all those concerned with children and education.[38] The mental hygiene point of view, at least for educated middle-class

Americans, had become part of the common stock of knowledge, a language and set of doctrines that had deeply penetrated the *Zeitgeist*, the "conceptual small change of the mass media."[39]

V.

How can we explain the energy, enthusiasm, and zeal with which hygienists sought to bring about the medicalization of the school? It goes without saying that the mental hygiene movement was concerned with social control. The key hygienist term, "adjustment," implies that social control was an essential aspect of the mental hygiene movement. But it would be simplistic to leave it at that. The incentive and motive for the mental hygiene movement, like that of most social movements, were provided by an urgent, concrete, and objective problem situation.[40] Mental illness was a social problem of vast, if hard to specify, dimensions. And then there were the children—from the mental hygiene point of view, "every child . . . a problem child."[41] Many of these children were slated to join the ranks of the mentally ill or the social misfits if action wasn't taken. When the psychiatrist looks at schoolchildren, declared Frankwood Williams, "he sees a young army from which will be recruited in the future the victims of mental disease, the vocational misfits, the individuals who swell the divorce statistics, . . . the inmates of reformatories and prisons, the partially adjusted, . . . and in the minority—a small number of children who will be healthy, well-adjusted adults."[42] Hygienists had the solution, thanks to the new psychiatry. Hygienists were confident that they were in possession of the requisite scientific knowledge; it had only to be applied. No new institutions had to be created. The most effective place of intervention in the child's life was the school. The school would heal the maladjusted while fortifying the personality of all children, thus providing a form of inoculation against mental illness.[43]

The hygienist faith in psychiatric science, like the faith in science of many reform movements in the progressive era, was real. It helped give the mental hygiene movement utopian appeal. Hygienists envisioned a society free of problems; a society in which war and even unhappiness were eliminated, thanks to the new knowledge of human nature vouchsafed by psychiatry and mental hygiene. Indeed, the mental hygiene movement took on aspects of a quasi-religious phenomenon; the truths of psychiatry were a surer foundation for the new era than the truths of the Bible. The mental hygiene movement "has revealed to many a revolutionary point of view," in the words of Dr. Ralph Truitt, a program official and member of the hygienist inner circle. The "thrill of this has made them expect miracles."[44] A popular textbook on mental hygiene published in 1930 captures the dominant mood. Referring to the failed hopes of Versailles, the authors write of the progressives' disillusionment with social reform and social crusading: "Into the province of lost hope [mental hygiene] entered as a new promise."[45] The role of the school was to fulfill the promise. As the psychiatric social worker Jessie Taft put it, in that insistent note of religiosity in which many hygienists' phrased their hopes for the future, the schools' mission was to usher children into the "kingdom of good adjustment."[46] In a more vaticinal style, Dr. E. Stanley Abbott, another hygienist, proclaimed that "when every home and school has learned to apply mental hygiene, and when all agencies are administered in conformity with the laws of mental hygiene, then we shall have reached the millennium." Guided by the experts in mental hygiene, the school would be the headquarters of the "new kingdom," an educational utopia in psychiatric terms.

In fact, where the mental hygiene movement is concerned, the appeal to utopian thinking is all-important and helps explain some otherwise puzzling phenomena. For example, one of the remarkable aspects of the mental hygiene movement in education is that its project and the whole diffusion process went forward from start to finish with scarcely any research. Few seemed to think it necessary to ask for evidence that a "mental hygiene" existed, that mental hygiene could prevent mental illness, or that the school was the best place to apply mental hygiene. Hygienists were swept up in a therapeutic fervor. Hygienist literature is remarkably optimistic about the malleability of personality and the possibility of preventing mental illness, and equally pessimistic about children's vulnerability to mental illness. Of course, both the optimism in the first case and the pessimism in the second may have been exaggerated for strategic reasons: to publicize the problem, attract attention, gain members, aggrandize the helping professions. But rhetoric had consequences beyond what the enthusiastic advocates of mental hygiene may have intended. From the start, Barry Smith of the Commonwealth Fund was concerned about the shaky theoretical foundation upon which the Fund's juvenile delinquency prevention program was erected and what results it was achieving. Throughout the 1920s, he pleaded for research. But the NCMH was convinced that its educational reconstruction program rested on psychiatric science; research was unnecessary and none was forthcoming.

Histories of psychiatry and the helping professions have not been kind to the scientific claims of psychiatry. Nor does all the critical attention come from revisionist historians or those who can be identified as antipsychiatry; some of it comes from people who are sympathetic. In fact, there were warnings from psychiatrists and hygienists themselves from time to time in the 1920s about mental hygiene "propaganda" and the need for more research into the etiology of personality disorders. By 1932 Adolf Meyer felt called upon to warn social workers against their frequent proposal that teachers were in a good position to detect and treat early signs of personality maladjustment: "We must look to the school to attend to things that it can do. I am very skeptical," he continued, "about the wisdom of introducing too much pathology into the school. We have to cultivate in school interest in the things which are of the school and for the school."[47] By then the mental hygiene point of view had attained for many of its advocates the status of a paradigmatic assumption; their commitment was so passionate, fundamental, and tenacious that they were impervious to warnings or to evidence that might modify or falsify it. The diffusion of the mental hygiene point of view of education finally bears out Matthew Miles's axiom that educational innovations are almost never installed on their merits: "In the absence of evaluatory evidence, substitute bases for judgment are used, such as educational ideology, sentiment, or persuasive claims by advocates or salesmen."[48]

While not primarily intended to function as a guide to America's current educational situation, this study may have some implications for present debates about school reform. Therapeutic concepts of education command passionate loyalty in the profession and remain firmly entrenched in the public's thinking. Of course, words like "mental hygiene" and "mental health" are rarely attached to them; they function as largely tacit convictions—a fact that attests to their deep-rooted nature. So long as therapeutic concepts of education remain unexamined, they pose an unresolved problem for school reform movements.

To mention one or two of the most obvious examples. The drive for excellence in education necessarily involves setting standards of academic achievement, much higher standards than have been in place. Some students, perhaps a large number, will fail to meet those standards. School reform movements have not yet seriously addressed the problem of failure. But the notion of failure as psychologically damaging is deeply embedded in the consciousness of parents as well as the education profession. Will parents be able to tolerate their children's failure? Will public school teachers and administrators be able to fail students? Will they be *allowed* to fail students? Achievement and classroom discipline are closely intertwined. Reform movements have yet to seriously confront the problem of indiscipline in school. That children's misbehavior and even violence in school is a symptom of frustration and unmet "needs," and that it calls for understanding of causes and not discipline, also has a strong hold on the public and the profession. Will educational practitioners be able or allowed to enforce standards of behavior, impose sanctions, prevent students from receiving diplomas, or suspend or even expel students? It may not be so easy to de-medicalize the school. A public debate on the medicalization of American education would seem to be overdue.

Notes

1   Philip Rieff, *The Triumph of the Therapeutic: Uses of Faith After Freud* (New York, 1968), ch. 8; and *Freud: The Mind of the Moralist* (New York, 1959), ch. 10. See also Christopher Lasch, *The Culture of Narcissism: American Life in an Age of Diminishing Expectations* (New York, 1979); Fred H. Matthews, "In Defense of Common Sense: Mental Hygiene as Ideology and Mentality in Twentieth-Century America," *Prospects*, 4 (1979): 459–516; Andrew I. Polsky, *The Rise of the Therapeutic State* (Princeton, 1991). For analogous developments in Canada, see Theresa R. Richardson, *The Century of the Child: The Mental Hygiene Movement and Social Policy in the United States & Canada* (Albany, N. Y., 1989).

2   Nathan G. Hale, Jr., *Freud and the Americans: The Beginnings of Psychoanalysis in the United States, 1876–1917* (New York, 1971); Fred H. Matthews, "The Americanization of Sigmund Freud: Adaptations of Psychoanalysis Before 1917," *Journal of American Studies*, 1 (1967): 39–61.

3   C. Macfie Campbell, *A Present-Day Conception of Mental Disorders* (Cambridge, Mass.,1924), p. 38. See also Adolf Meyer, "Modern Conceptions of Mental Disease," in Herbert S. Jennings et al., *Suggestions of Modern Science Concerning Education* (New York, 1917). In general, see Hale, *Freud and the Americans*, chs. VII and XVI.

4   George K. Pratt, *Your Mind and You: Mental Health* (New York, 1924); William H. Burnham, *The Normal Mind* (New York, 1924); and Ernest R. Groves and Phyllis Blanchard, *Introduction to Mental Hygiene* (New York, 1930).

5   "Childhood: The Golden Period for Mental Hygiene," *Mental Hygiene*, 4 (1920): 266–267. William Alanson White, *The Mental Hygiene of Childhood* (Boston, 1919).

6   For example, Adolf Meyer, "What Do Histories of Cases of Insanity Teach Us Concerning Preventive Mental Hygiene During the Years of School Life?" *Psychological Clinic*, 2 (15 June 1908): 89–101; John T. MacCurdy, "Psychiatric Clinics in the Schools," *American Journal of Public Health*, 18 (1916): 1262–1267; William Healy, "An Outline for the Institutional Education and Treatment of Young Offenders," *Journal of Educational Psychology*, 6 (1915): 301–316.

7   C. Macfie Campbell, "A City School and Its Subnormal Children," *Mental Hygiene*, 2 (1918): 244.

8   Quoted in Barbara Sicherman, *The Quest for Mental Health in America, 1880–1917* (Ann Arbor, 1967), p. 180.

9   Described in Chapter 8 of this volume.

10   Frankwood E. Williams, "Finding a Way in Mental Hygiene," *Mental Hygiene*, 14 (1930): 246–247; and "Every Child: How He Keeps His Mental Health," *Annals of the American Academy of Political and Social Science*, 121 (1925): 181–186. See also Miriam Van Waters, *Parents on Probation* (New York, 1928).

11   Quoted in Commonwealth Fund, *Annual Report, 1922*, p. 21. Or as another staff member of the program pointed out: "The public school represents the most powerful agency in the field of child welfare. It touches practically every child and has jurisdiction over him during the important formative years." Ralph P. Truitt, "Mental Hygiene and the Public School," *Mental Hygiene*, 11 (1927): 261.

12   "The School and Delinquency: Every School a Clinic," National Conference of Social Work, *Proceedings* (1929), pp. 213–221.

13   William H. Burnham, "Success and Failure as Conditions of Mental Health," *Mental Hygiene*, 3 (1919): 387–397.

14   Frankwood E. Williams, "The Significance of Mental Hygiene for the Teacher and the Normal Child," *Proceedings of the National Conference of Social Work* (1921), pp. 359–363.

15   Ethel Cornell, "Mental Hygiene: Its Place in the Classroom," Southern California Society for Mental Hygiene, *Mental Hygiene Bulletin*, 3 (1927): 5; Groves and Blanchard, *Introduction to Mental Hygiene*, pp. 83–84; Ira S. Wile, "Laziness in School Children," *Mental Hygiene*, 6 (1922): 68–82. For the broader context, see Andrew Scull, *Social Order/Mental Disorder* (Berkeley, 1989), especially ch. 3, "From Madness to Mental Illness: Medical Men as Moral Entrepreneurs."

16   Clara Bassett, *The School and Mental Health* (New York, 1931).

17   "Fundamental Research and Education," *Educational Researcher*, 6 (1977): 14.

18   Herbert Croly, *The Promise of American Life* (New York, 1909), pp. 401–402.

19   Commonwealth Fund, *Annual Report*, 1928, pp. 80–81.

20   John G. A. Pocock, *Politics, Language, and Time: Essays on Political Thought and History* (New York, 1971), pp. 23–29, 284ff; and "Working on Ideas in Time," in L. P. Curtis, ed., *The Historian's Workshop* (New York, 1970), pp. 153–165. I treat other facets of the linguistic turn and its relevance to historians of education interested in change in Chapters 4 and 5 of this volume.

21   Burkardt Holzner, *Reality Construction in Society* (Cambridge, Mass., 1968), pp. 69–71; Peter Berger and Thomas Luckman, *The Social Construction of Reality* (New York, 1966).

22   "Language, Logic and Culture," in Irving L. Horowitz, ed., *Power, Politics and People: The Collected Essays of C. Wright Mills* (New York, 1963), pp. 433–434.

23   Arnold Gesell, "Mental Hygiene and the School," *Mental Hygiene*, 3 (1919): 59–64; Lewis M. Terman, *The Hygiene of the School Child* (Boston, 1914), chs. 16–18; J. E. Wallace Wallin, *The Mental Hygiene of the School Child* (Boston, 1914).

24   Jessie Taft, "Mental Hygiene and Social Work," in Frankwood E. Williams, ed., *Social Aspects of Mental Hygiene* (New Haven, 1925). See also Jane Culbert, "The Public School as a Factor in the Training of the Socially Handicapped Child"; M. Edith Campbell, "The Strategic Position of the School in Programs of Social Work," *Proceedings of the National Conference of Social Work* (1923), pp. 98, 362ff; and Anna Black Pratt, "The Relation of the Teacher and the Social Worker," *Annals*, 98 (1921): 90–96.

25   White House Conference on Child Health and Protection, Report of the Committee on the Socially Handicapped—Delinquency, *The Delinquent Child* (New York, 1932), pp. 38–41, 99–133; and Report of the Committee On the School Child, *School Health Program* (New York, 1932), pp. 61–82.

26   In *Progressive Education*, 3 (1926): Frankwood E. Williams, "The Field of Mental Hygiene," pp. 7–13; Esther Loring Richards, "Has Mental Hygiene a Place in the Elementary School?" pp. 31–38; and Isidor Coriat, "The Psychoanalytic Approach to Education," pp. 19–23. In *Progressive Education*, 8 (1931): Fritz Wittels, "Psychoanalysis for Teachers," pp. 238–241. *Progressive Education* also devoted its December 1934 issue to mental hygiene and education.

27   The summary volume of the PEA's Commission on Secondary School Curriculum declares: "It cannot be too strongly stated that considerations of mental hygiene must come to pervade the whole atmosphere of the school." V. T. Thayer, Caroline B. Zachry, and Ruth Kotinsky, *Reorganizing Secondary Education* (New York, 1939), pp. 364–365. See also Lois Hayden Meek, *The Personal-Social Development of Boys and Girls* (New York, 1940); and Caroline B. Zachry, *Emotion and Conduct in Adolescence* (New York, 1940).

28   W. Carson Ryan, "The Preparation of Teachers for Dealing with the Behavior Problems of Children," *School and Society*, 38 (1928): 208–215.

29   Lawrence A. Averill, *The Hygiene of Instruction: A Study of the Mental Hygiene of the School Child* (Boston, 1928); Burnham, *The Normal Mind*.

30   For the role of textbooks in the diffusion of ideology, the following are suggestive: Lee J. Cronbach. ed., *Textbook Materials in Modern Education* (Urbana, Ill., 1955); and C. Wright Mills, "The Professional Ideology of Social Pathologists," in Horowitz, *Power, Politics and People*. In general, see Thomas S. Kuhn, *The Structure of Scientific Revolutions*, 2nd ed. (Chicago, 1970), chs. XI–XII.

31   *Mental Hygiene in School Practice* (Palo Alto, Ca., 1943), p. 242. Cf., William C. Bagley: "The first principle [of school discipline]: coercive measures must be swift, certain and unerring." *School Discipline* (New York, 1914), p. 133.

32   *Emotion and the Educative Process* (Washington, D.C., 1938), p. 137.

33   National Education Association, Department of Elementary School Princi-
      pals, Fifteenth Yearbook, *Personality Adjustment of the Elementary School
      Child* (Washington, D.C., 1936); National Education Association, Depart-
      ment of Supervisors and Directors of Instruction, *Mental Hygiene in the
      Classroom, Thirteenth Yearbook* (Washington, D.C., 1939); Educational
      Policies Commission, *Education for All American Youth* (Washington,
      D.C., 1944), p. 330; Association for Supervision and Curriculum Develop-
      ment, *Fostering Mental Hygiene in Our Schools, 1950 Yearbook* (Washing-
      ton, D.C., 1950).

34   University of the State of New York, *The Activity Program: A Curriculum
      Experiment* (Albany, N.Y., 1941), passim. See also Charles R. Foster, *Men-
      tal Hygiene in New Jersey Schools* (New Brunswick, N.J., 1939).

35   J. Wayne Wrightstone, *Appraisal of Newer Elementary School Practices*
      (New York, 1938); and J. Paul Leonard and Alvin G. Eurich, eds., *An Evalu-
      ation of Modern Education: A Report Sponsored by the Society for Cur-
      riculum Study* (New York, 1942).

36   Edward A. Richards, ed., *Proceedings of the Mid-Century White House
      Conference on Children and Youth* (Raleigh, N.C., 1950), pp. 175, 176.
      See also Helen Leland Witmer and Ruth Kolinsky, eds., *Personality in the
      Making: The Fact-Finding Report of the Mid-Century White House Con-
      ference on Children and Youth* (New York, 1952), especially chs. 1, 4, and
      11.

37   The conference led to another outpouring of textbooks. E.g., Dorothy Rogers,
      Mental Hygiene in Elementary Education (Boston, 1957); Henry C. Lindgren,
      Mental Health in Education (New York, 1954); Nelson B. Henry, ed., *Men-
      tal Health in Modern Education* (Chicago, 1955); Louis Kaplan, *Education
      and Mental Health* (New York, 1959); Fritz Redl and William W. Wattenberg,
      Mental Hygiene in Teaching (New York, 1959); Merl E. Bonney, *Mental
      Health in Education* (Boston, 1960).

38   Wesley Allinsmith and George W. Goethals, *The Role of the School in Men-
      tal Health* (New York, 1962). In the late 1960s one could see hygienist ra-
      tionales for teaching various subjects. E.g., "In the social sciences . . . a
      consideration of the child's mental health is paramount." Paul Brandwein,
      Notes on Teaching the Social Sciences: Concepts and Values (New York,
      1969), p. 11.

39   Matthews,"In Defense of Common Sense: Mental Hygiene as Ideology and
      Mentality in Twentieth-Century America," pp. 459–516.

40   Hans Toch, *The Social Psychology of Social Movements* (New York, 1965),
      pp. 5–7.

41   Aaron J. Rosanoff, "The Problem Child," Southern California Society for
      Mental Hygiene, *Mental Hygiene Bulletin*, 1 (1924): 1.

42   "Community Responsibility in Mental Hygiene," *Mental Hygiene*, 7 (1923):
      497.

43   Smiley Blanton, "Mental Hygiene for College Students," in E. Huddleston, ed., *Problems of College Education* (New York, 1928), p. 303.

44   Ralph P. Truitt, "Community Aspects of Child Guidance," *Mental Hygiene*, 10 (1926): 296.

45   Groves and Blanchard, *Introduction to Mental Hygiene*, pp. 436–437.

46   Quoted in Virginia P. Robinson, *Jessie Taft: Therapist and Social Worker* (Philadelphia, 1962), p. 63; E. Stanley Abbott, "What Is Mental Hygiene?" *American Journal of Psychiatry*, 10 (1924): 284.

47   "Teachers could give only inadequate and biased data such as constituted psychiatric records at the beginning of the century, largely the complaints of the attendants as to the annoyances they were put to by the presence of patients." *American Journal of Orthopsychiatry*, 2 (1932): 229. See also Meyer, "Freedom and Discipline," *Progressive Education*, 5 (1928): 205–210.

48   "Innovation in Education: Some Generalizations," in Matthew B. Miles, ed., *Innovation in Education* (New York, 1964), p. 658.

Lawrence A. Cremin: Lives and Transformations

The essential element of plot in romance is adventure. . . . We may call [the] major adventure, the element that gives literary form to the romance, the quest.

Northrop Frye

One

Lawrence A. Cremin, the most influential American historian of education of the post-World War II era, died suddenly of a heart attack on 4 September 1990. He was sixty-four. His untimely death caught everyone by surprise. There was so much one wanted to know about him, and there are so many questions left unanswered. Cremin never got around to writing a memoir or an autobiography. He gave only a few interviews.[1] Of book reviews, which frequently are revelatory, I can find only one by him, from 1961. The obituaries written by historians of education who knew him best are suited to the occasion: "eulogies which trace the outlines of a life measured in terms of profession, position, and accomplishment," and which observe a certain decorum and privacy.[2] The rest is silence.

Almost a decade has passed since Cremin's death. It's time to break the silence. If everything had gone according to plan this epilogue would have been another homage to Cremin. Instead, it became a reflection on the academic life.[3] As I remark elsewhere in this volume, it is striking how little information exists about the paths that academics choose to follow in the course of their careers. Cremin was not only a historian but also an administrator: president of Teachers College, Columbia University, and then of the Spencer Foundation. There may be some lessons to be learned from Cremin's career about our own professional lives and the historian's vocation.

As this account took on the form of a narrative embedded in a recognizable literary genre—the romance quest—I experienced considerable anxiety. Cremin received many awards, including Bancroft and Pulitzer Prizes for history. Viewed conventionally, his career as a historian was a great success. Nevertheless, in my view of it, although his quest has an honorable ending, as much as I willed it to be otherwise, it is a melancholy one. In the early 1960s with the publication of *The Transformation of the School: Progressivism in American Education, 1876–1957* (1961), winner of the 1962 Bancroft Prize in American History, Cremin was at the pinnacle. At the age of thirty-seven he had achieved the kind of fame no historian of education had enjoyed before. In 1964 he accepted a commission to do the trilogy, *American Education.* After that, Cremin's career as a historian took a downward trajectory. I am way ahead of my story, but I have indicated its principal theme. I am deeply concerned with telling Cremin's story correctly. But I can write only what I remember, what I know, and what I imagine. However problematic this memoir, a conversation has begun.

I should preface what follows by making my relationship with Cremin clear. I'm a former student of Cremin's. I did my professional training in the history of education with him. From the late 1950s to the mid-1960s, Larry (he insisted on being called Larry) was my adviser and friend (though we were never, until almost the end, really friendly). I was his teaching assistant, or "TA," at Teachers College, Columbia University, in the late 1950s. I did my doctoral thesis under him. Upon its completion, he saw to its publication by Teachers College Press. Larry helped secure all of my faculty positions: first at the University of Massachusetts, Amherst; then at Cornell University; and finally at UCLA.

Two

I am going to begin with some personal reminiscences.

After I moved to Los Angeles, I lost touch with Larry for almost two decades. In the 1970s our correspondence was brief and episodic: a letter to Larry in December 1974 congratulating him on his appointment as president of Teachers College, to which he didn't reply; another one from me in June 1981 congratulating him for winning the Pulitzer Prize in history, to which he did reply, briefly. I saw Larry about as frequently: a few days in the fall of 1977, when he came to UCLA as the guest speaker at the Thirty-Fifth Sir John Adams Lecture series; again in the spring of 1979 at a conference on philanthropy and education at the Rockefeller Archive Center, Pocantico Hills, New York; and then in October of 1982, when I gave my presidential address to the History of Education Society (HES) at Teachers College. I never saw Larry again.

Though Larry sent me a copy of every book he published in the 1970s and 1980s, and I sent him a copy of my few publications, he seemed to have nothing to say about my work, nor I about his. Toward the end of 1975, I was invited to do an article on American educational historiography for the bicentennial edition of the *Harvard Educational Review (HER)*. I promised *HER* "The History of the History of American Education, 1900–1976." I wrote to Larry in December 1975 saying that I wished I had the time to interview him and other members of the "old (Ford Foundation Fund for the Advancement of Education) Committee on the Role of Education in American History, especially [Bernard] Bailyn" about their part in what was going on in and around the history of American education during the mid-1950s and early 1960s. But Larry never replied, nor did he acknowledge the article when it appeared in August 1976.

As I remark above, in the mid-1960s, Larry began work on a three-volume history of American education. So in 1981, when Larry won the Pulitzer Prize—it was for *American Education: The National Experience, 1783–1876,* the second volume of the trilogy[4]—I wrote to congratulate him. He replied on 20 April. He thanked me for the note and said about winning the Pulitzer only, "it's a nice surprise." He closed with a hurried "All best." We had no further correspondence until 1988.

Sometime in May 1988, I received a warmly inscribed copy of *American Education: The Metropolitan Experience, 1876–1980,* the final volume of the trilogy.[5] I responded on 20 June with a long letter. I wrote Larry congratulating him on a "terrific accomplishment." The book's "richness of detail and breadth of learning," I said, "give a new dignity and interest to all those forms of education which make up the American educational experience and which have heretofore not been seen as related and interlocking parts of a whole or of a configuration." One implication, I continued, "is that all those who focus exclusively on the school for whatever project they have in mind have a limited vision of the alternative sites for intervention, while overburdening the school." I added the following: "I hope your readers understand that we can enter into the historical record at different points and that we don't have to do history as a consecutive narrative." I then mentioned that I was continuing my research on the mental hygiene movement (the subject of my paper at the Rockefeller Archive Center and my presidential address to the HES), but that now I was thinking of exploring the movement in the context of language and the "discursive landscape of American education." Larry answered promptly on 27 June thanking me for my "gracious note" and adding unexpectedly: "That sounds like fascinating stuff you're working on." He was taken by my "discursive landscape of American education"— he called it "a lovely [his favorite word of praise] phrase." And then came a surprising close: "Take care."

In January 1989, I was invited by *Historical Studies in Education/Revue d'histoire de l'éducation (HSE/RHE)*, the journal of the Canadian History of Education Association, to review *American Education: The Metropolitan Experience*—1,500 words, with "a bit more leeway" as to length. I agreed. But now I was stuck. Easy enough to say that "we don't have to do history as a consecutive narrative," but how does one review a history which precisely illustrates this nice but abstract principle? I was overwhelmed by its length, the density of the material, the lack of a unified narrative line. I griped that *The Metropolitan Experience* was a "monster of a book" and that I was "having difficulty finding the proper voice." After a struggle, I turned in an essay review of about 6,000 words, which was accepted and published in full.[6]

In the meantime, on 31 October 1989, Larry wrote to me from New York to "wonder if [he] might ask a favor." He needed a copy of Frances Littlefield Davenport's doctoral thesis, "The Education of John Dewey" (UCLA, 1946), which we had in our library on microfilm. He said he had embarked on a biography of Dewey and was "having a marvelous time of it." The "only drawback is that the archive is in beautiful downtown Carbondale" [Center for Dewey Studies, Southern Illinois University] and "the nightlife leaves much to be desired." He hoped that the request wouldn't prove burdensome. On 13 November, I wrote Larry to tell him that the thesis was in the mail, that I had glanced through it, and that it appeared to be a competent piece of work; I added, "it will make a few nights in Carbondale pass quicker."

That same fall of 1989, the *History of Education Quarterly (HEQ)*, the journal of the History of Education Society, had carried a "Forum" on *The Metropolitan Experience*, with commentaries by the historians of education Robert L. Church, Michael B. Katz, and Harold Silver, and an uncharacteristically sharp response by Larry.[7] I gathered that the "Forum" must have really stung, so I added, "one would think *HEQ* or someone would give readers some idea of the book's contents before doing their thing." And then: "Is that why your response seemed unusually cross?" With much trepidation, I then informed Larry that I had done a review of *The Metropolitan Experience*, it would be available soon, and he should look for it.

I was concerned because the review was decidedly mixed and ambivalent; I had covered all the criticisms that Church, Silver, and Katz had made of the book, and more, but I began and ended the review on a note of tribute. I described Larry's breadth of knowledge as "staggering." I called *The Metropolitan Experience* "a seminal work." I said it "opens up a prospect on American education that is inexhaustibly suggestive of fruitful avenues of research." I said Larry's discussion of newspapers and magazines, and of radio, television, and motion pictures were all worthy of book-length treatments in themselves. I also described the volume as shapeless and repetitive. I complained that for Larry, "the discipline of education no longer exists as a distinct, bounded field or object of knowledge." I questioned how he could give the natterings of Margaret Mead the status of educational theory. I called Larry's treatment of ideas the least satisfactory part of the volume, especially his treatment of change in education. Then, I pointed out that all the problems of *The Metropolitan Experience* were a function of its ambitions. I said: "One finishes *The Metropolitan Experience* with the feeling that there are more 'transformations' of American education that Cremin will yet write about." I ended the review: "If, as Eugen Weber states, historiographical progress is made not in depth . . . but in breadth—a widening of vision—Professor Cremin has made a seminal contribution to historiographical progress." Somewhat tongue-in-cheek, I asked Larry to "read [the review] backward, starting with the last paragraph, then going to the beginning." With my letter I also sent along a copy of *From the Campus: Perspectives on the School Reform Movement*, a just-published collection of essays by UCLA Graduate School of Education faculty which I had co-edited with Lewis Solmon.

On 20 November 1989, Larry wrote to say that he had received the copy of Davenport's thesis, and that he was "truly grateful for my kindness," and he offered to reimburse me for the costs of Xeroxing and dispatching the manuscript to New York. Meanwhile, he said, it was good to be in touch and he was eager to catch up on my work. He ended the letter: "Take care—and again, my sincere appreciation for your great kindness."

Larry wrote again on 12 January 1990. By now he had read my review of *The Metropolitan Experience*. He called it "a lovely review." He was "grateful for the time and effort that were patently involved"; it "provided a marvelous lift." Referring to the *HEQ* "Forum," he said I was right in my estimate of why he "was less irenic than usual in [his] response to Silver and Church." He continued: "Disagreement troubles me not in the least—it's what makes the world go 'round; but the kind of insistent misunderstanding and misrepresentation that marked the Silver and Church reviews does trouble me, and it was that that I was responding to." Larry went on to thank me for the copy of *From the Campus*. He said I was "a bit kinder to the so-called excellence movement" than he would have been. He disagreed with "the kind of academic fundamentalism that [William] Bennett and [Allan] Bloom propounded." What he liked about the essays in *From the Campus*, Larry graciously added, "was their understanding of the complexity of education and their acceptance of pluralism."

A few weeks later, Larry sent me a copy of *Popular Education and Its Discontents*, his last book.[8] I thought it vintage Larry. I wrote on 5 February to thank him. I said that I thought *Popular Education and Its Discontents* an "essential book" and remarked that there was "no one who can do what you do—that is, to bring the conversation about public education to a higher level, but who can do it in plain language for the teacher and nonspecialist as well as the specialist." Larry replied on 9 February 1990, his last letter to me, expressing gratitude for my kind words about "the little book," and remarking, "'essential' is a lovely word!" He said he was again in my debt and ended: "With warmest personal regard." Larry died on 4 September. How gentle and elegiac his letters seem to me now.

Three

We have to go back in time, to the beginning of my relationship with Larry.

I was Larry's TA while he was writing *The Transformation of the School*. He never asked me to look at a draft or talked much about the book. He once questioned me about the title. Which did I prefer, he asked: *Progressivism in American Education: The Transformation of the School*, or *The Transformation of the School: Progressivism in American Education*?

Finally reading *The Transformation of the School* came as somewhat of a surprise to me because I found so little new in it. *The Transformation* was Larry's lectures in his course in history of American education for which I was a TA. Reread, aloud this time, the preface and conclusion of *The Transformation*. You can hear the cadences of the first and last lectures of a term. It was the reviews that really caught me by surprise. *The Transformation of the School* was widely reviewed in New York City and widely praised. A history of education by a historian at Teachers College was deemed important enough to generate encomiums from the *New York Post*, the *Saturday Review*, the *Reporter*, and the *New York Times*. Fred M. Hechinger, education editor of the *Times*, called *The Transformation of the School* "masterful" and a "fascinating tale," adding, "it is not the least remarkable fact that this sensitive and brilliant history comes from a young professor at Teachers College."[10] In a lengthy review in the *Reporter*, Martin Mayer called *The Transformation of the School* "a major work of educational history by a first class historian," and one of the "distressingly few links between Teachers College and Columbia University, between teacher training and the intellectual community at large."[11]

Historians were almost as enthusiastic. Richard Hart lauded *The Transformation of the School* as the "definitive history of the Progressive Education movement," and "almost a comprehensive history of education in America [and] an excellent example of historical scholarship."[12] The most emphatic praise came from Arthur Mann in the *American Historical Review*. Mann described *The Transformation of the School* as "an important book by a scholar who is practically alone today in trying to break down the parochialism separating the fields of education and history." As for Cremin's achievement, he "is the first historian to take the transformation of the school seriously enough to place it in the context of history." Mann ended his review by calling the book "a major contribution to both the substance and the method of social and intellectual history."[13] Frederick Rudolph called *The Transformation of the School* a "pioneer history of the American school in a period of tremendous change." Rudolph did have some reservations: "All late nineteenth century educational reform does not deserve to be called progressivism." And "Professor Cremin does a disservice to his study by being reluctant to advance a close definition either of the Progressive movement or of progressive education." Still, Rudolph concluded, "this is an important book . . . that social and intellectual historians will have to read."[14] Curiously, *The Transformation of the School* was harshly criticized in education journals: *Educational Theory, Studies in Philosophy of Education*, and even the *History of Education Quarterly*.[15] I put it down to professional jealousy or a narrow-minded conception of the kind of history historians of education should be writing. And Larry won the Bancroft Prize.

When *The Transformation of the School* won the Bancroft Prize, Larry was thirty-seven years old and on top of the world. It was great being a historian of education and a student of Larry's in the 1960s. Writing this now, I am reminded how influential Larry used to be; his "visibility" in the parlance of academe today. I was on the faculty of the School of Education at the University of Massachusetts, working on my doctorate while teaching courses in history of western education and history of American education from the European antecedents to the mid-twentieth century; I was also responsible for supervision of student teaching (high school) in western Massachusetts. When Larry won the Bancroft Prize it gave me the confidence to inform my dean, Albert Purvis, that I would keep History of Western Ed, but that I wanted to concentrate on the post-Civil War period in my courses in history of American education and be relieved of all supervision of student teaching duties. Of course, Dean Purvis said. It was awesome accompanying Larry to meetings of the American Historical Association and the American Educational Research Association. *The Transformation of the School* gave Larry entrée into the world of history's and professional education's elite. At the AHA he seemed to know everybody, including all the famous historians of the day. At the annual conferences of the AERA he was treated like a celebrity. A gibe I recall had to do with 120th Street being "the widest street in the world" because it separated Columbia University from Teachers College. Larry turned 120th Street into a corridor. But Larry's moment didn't last very long.

The Transformation of the School was a milestone in American educational historiography: its romantic mythos played off a conventional metaphor of death and resurrection, set the stage, and became the pivot around which so many subsequent histories of American education explicitly or implicitly were to revolve. It remains an essential context for interpreting every modern history of American education. I think *The Transformation of the School* was the peak of Larry's career as a historian.

In the spring of 1964, Larry was invited by officials of the American Historical Association and the United States Office of Education to prepare a comprehensive history of American education. He eagerly accepted. This was the beginning of the end of Larry's Camelot days.

Four

In order to understand what happened in 1964, I have to retrace some events. In December 1954, president Clarence H. Faust of the Ford Foundation's Fund for the Advancement of Education called a conference of leading American scholars and some of the most distinguished historians of the time—Arthur Schlesinger, Sr., Merle Curti, Richard Storr, Paul H. Buck, Ralph Gabriel, Walter Metzger, and Richard Hofstadter—to explore the possibility of encouraging historical investigation of the role of education in the development of American society. Although by that time the history of American education had long been a special field of study, the conferees were unanimous in their conviction that it had been "shamefully neglected by American historians." The Fund for the Advancement of Education stressed that none of the historians could be described as a "specialist" in history of American education; that is, none was a member of a professional education faculty, although Curti, Metzger, and Hofstadter were deeply interested in the history of American education. The group held a second meeting in May 1956, at which time it became the Committee on the Role of Education in American History. In the spring of 1957, the committee announced that financial assistance was available to faculty members or graduate students in history departments who wished to pursue monograph studies calculated to bring "thorough knowledge of education immediately into the mainstream of historical scholarship and instruction."[16] In the meantime, as we learned from a memoir Richard Storr published in 1976, the committee had in 1956 or early 1957 appointed a subcommittee of junior scholars to advise it, which included the history professor Bernard Bailyn of Harvard University and Lawrence Cremin of Teachers College, Columbia.[17]

In 1960 Bailyn published his famous critique of American educational historiography, *Education in the Forming of American Society: Needs and Opportunities for Study*, a work initiated and sponsored by the Fund. Bailyn, who was formally invited to join the Committee on the Role of Education in American History in 1961, flogged "educational missionaries" like Ellwood P. Cubberley and Paul Monroe, who pioneered the history of education as a special field and wrote the most influential textbooks, chiefly Cubberley's *Public Education in the United States: A Study and Interpretation of American Educational History* (1919). I discuss Bailyn's critique of the Cubberly school of historiography above and it does not have to be repeated here. What has to be repeated is his expansive conception of a new history of education. There were infinite needs and opportunities for study in the history of education, Bailyn argued, if historians were to think of education "not only as a formal pedagogy but as the entire process by which a culture transmits itself across the generations [and] in its elaborate, intricate involvements with the rest of society." Larry, who was formally invited to become a member of the committee in 1961, the same year as Bailyn, reviewed Bailyn's *Education in the Forming of American Society* in the *Mississippi Valley Historical Review*.[18] Larry duplicated Bailyn's denunciation of Cubberley and applauded his new approach to the historiography of American education—"conceiving of education in Platonic terms." Larry praised Bailyn's hypotheses as "original and imaginative, [pointing] to a vast and hitherto inadequately explored literature." Hopefully, Larry concluded, "they will prove sufficiently provocative to set in motion the kind of informed historical scholarship that to date has been all too rare in the field of American education."

In June 1964, Larry was invited to help organize a symposium for the Committee on the Role of Education in American History at which he presented the historiographical essay that was subsequently published as *The Wonderful World of Ellwood Patterson Cubberley: An Essay on the Historiography of American Education* (1965). While acknowledging Cubberley's contributions to professional education, Larry, following Bailyn, observed that a general reinterpretation of Cubberley was much needed. The "anachronism and parochialism of his work require correction, as do its evangelism and its isolation from the mainstream of American historiography." Larry went on to describe his vision of a new general interpretation of the history of American education.

Recall Bailyn's expansive definition of education. Larry defined the scope of history of education even more expansively, suggesting that historians consider "what agencies, formal and informal, have shaped

American thought, character, and sensibility over the years, and what have been the significant relationships between these agencies and the society that has sustained them." That question, he said, would move the historian's concerns "beyond the schools to a host of other institutions that educate: families, churches, libraries, museums, publishers, benevolent societies, youth groups, agricultural fairs, radio networks, military organizations, and research institutes." In addition, Larry argued, a more inclusive history of education would allow for cross-fertilization between the history of education and new fields such as the history of science and the history of communications; would view [that] history in a "broader . . . world context"; and would borrow from the social sciences for its methods. Larry suggested that this approach would allow historians to become bolder in inquiring into "the impact of education, broadly conceived, on the American mind and character," an enterprise, he cautioned, "fraught with methodological difficulty." Nevertheless, he implied, it must be attempted. Cubberley "may well have been correct in his judgment that at least one clue to the genius of American civilization lay in education." "It remains to be seen," Larry concluded, "whether anyone in our own time can portray the relationship more accurately, comprehensively, and imaginatively."[19] To provide that more accurate, comprehensive, and imaginative history of American education was to become Larry's quest.

Soon after he presented his paper on Cubberley, in the spring of 1964, as Larry described it, "there occurred one of those unexpected events that give decisive direction to a person's life and work."[20] W. Stull Holt, secretary of the American Historical Association, asked Larry whether he would be willing to prepare a "comprehensive history of American education" under the joint sponsorship of the Association and the United States Office of Education, for the latter's approaching centenary in 1967. Larry's reply was "enthusiastically affirmative."[21] Subsequently, Holt and the United States Commissioner of Education, Francis Keppel, obtained a "generous grant" for the project from the Carnegie Corporation of New York, then led by John Gardner.

Larry agreed to produce three volumes in seven years. He managed to produce the first volume in six years, and the first two volumes in fifteen years. The entire undertaking, which took him twenty-three years, almost a quarter of a century, to complete, yielded: *American Education: The Colonial Experience, 1607–1783*, published in 1970; *American Education: The National Experience, 1783–1876*, published in 1980; and, finally, *American Education: The Metropolitan Experience, 1876–1980*, which appeared in 1988.

Larry was fond of aphorisms. One aphorism he liked goes something like this (I think he attributed it to Emerson or Oscar Wilde): "The only thing more tragic than a person who does not get his heart's desire, is one who does." The commission must have been Larry's heart's desire. But it was a trap. Larry was trapped by an impossible publishing commitment and his hopelessly unconstrained and unfocused conception of "education."

It turns out that neither Bailyn nor Cremin were all that original. We learn from Storr's really startling memoir that their "new" approach to the history of education, the "seminal idea," was first broached to the Committee on the Role of Education in American History in December 1954 by Arthur Schlesinger, Sr., and then was modified by Storr before being circulated sometime in 1955 to the entire committee. The "seminal idea" seems to have been inspired by de Crèvecoeur's question— What then is the American, this new man?—and had to do with "the role of education in the formation of American character as a conscious work of art." To comprehend American character, now this is Storr modifying Schlesinger, "one must grasp the meaning of the sum total of the . . . influences that have poured in upon Americans to make them what they are." Storr went on: "Education might be defined, objectively, as the sum of those influences or, subjectively, as the reaction of human beings to them, [but] the touchstone of education is the intent to shape intellectual traits."[22] Sometime in late 1955 or early in 1956, Schlesinger complained that Storr "left the definition of education fuzzy." A little later, Storr and Larry sparred over Storr's definition of education. Storr recalls that Larry thought the final report of the committee (1957) "did not leave the distinction between education and other kinds of formative experiences sufficiently clear to show what the historian of education was *not* committed to study" (italics mine). At the time, Storr thought that both his critics, Schlesinger and Larry, agreed with his "generous" definition of education but that they were concerned lest the historian of education bite off more than anybody could chew and Storr dismissed their reservations as "conservative." Writing two decades later, in 1976, Storr admitted that he may have been recommending an approach to "skew research away . . . from conservatism and the regard for established and more readily definable modes of education [that] may have been more important than his memorandum [of 1957] implied."[23]

Five

What had Larry gotten himself into? Why? The rewards in prestige and esteem were obvious enough, perhaps even the financial incentive. But so, to Larry or someone, should have been the potential problems and risks.

One obvious problem was the remarkably expansive definition of education to which Larry was committed: education "as the deliberate, systematic, and sustained effort to transmit or evoke knowledge, attitudes, values, skills, and sensibilities." And despite his expressed concern that the committee's final report was not sufficiently clear to show what the historian of education was *not* committed to study, Larry later expanded his definition even further to include "any effort to transmit, evoke, or *acquire* knowledge, . . . as well as any learning that results from the effort, direct or *indirect*, intended or *unintended*" (my italics). As the historian of education Douglas Sloan put it, Bailyn's and Cremin's definitions of education are so abstract and encompassing that they raise the question: what is educational history and what isn't? Sloan asked: "Where do the educationally significant strands of the total social cultural network begin, interweave, and end? If everything can educate, and if everything affects education, what is educational history about?"[24] Another historian of education, Bruce Hood, expressed concern that "if the history of education is approached from the perspective of socialization or enculturation, the history of education would become the history of civilization."[25]

What historian could live up to the challenge Larry implicitly set for himself in his conclusion to *The Wonderful World of Ellwood Patterson Cubberley*? According to Ellen Lagemann, Larry wrote *American Education* "in the hope that it would long be regarded as the magisterial, definitive work of scholarship . . ." "Magisterial, definitive"? Larry never protected himself with any notion of the provisionality of history. There was never a disclaimer from Larry that what he was doing was a reconnaissance of the field at the behest of the Committee on the Role of History in American Education or of Schlesinger or Storr or Bailyn, which would have made his project, and this is hindsight, less vulnerable to criticism later. Or, with that team behind him did Larry think the project unassailable? Then in 1965, the committee disbanded and everyone involved forgot about Larry and the "new" history of education.[26] After that, Larry was on his own, embarked on a project without limits, without models.

Why was Larry chosen for the project? Why did he think he could do it? The early 1960s were Larry's moment of commanding influence. No American historian of education was held in higher esteem. He was by far the country's preeminent historian of education. But still. Larry's reputation rested on just one book: *The Transformation of the School*. Or, was Larry's invitation to that Committee on the Role of Education in American History symposium an audition for the lead role in the new history of American education? With *The Wonderful World of Ellwood Patterson Cubberley,* did Larry pass the audition with flying colors?

Why three volumes? Why not just one volume which might be finished by 1967, the centennial year of the U.S. Office of Education? Or, if three volumes, why was the assignment not distributed among three different historians, each taking responsibility for a different period? Why did Larry take on all three volumes? Even senior historians rarely try anything so immoderate, something on so grand a scale as a three-volume "comprehensive history" of anything. Who, if anyone, was advising Larry?

Why did anyone think Larry could do it? Why did Larry think he could do it? Of course, Larry knew a lot, more than anyone, about the history of American education from the colonial beginnings and its antecedents in the Old World to the present. He had been teaching it for years, and he was a co-author (with R. Freeman Butts) of the comprehensive *A History of Education in American Culture* (1953). But he was no specialist in any subject or chronological period but the "common school" movement of the mid-nineteenth century and the progressive movement in education in the twentieth century, and what he knew best was schools and the history of education with a small "e." Larry's forte was the good story with a strong narrative line epitomized in *The Transformation of the School*, or the "little book" exemplified by *Popular Education and Its Discontents*. It's bewildering to consider. Did Larry, after he finished *The Transformation of the School*, ask himself, "What do I do next?" It is a well-known fact that Larry was a compulsive worker who didn't believe in vacations. But the history of progressive education was still very much unexplored territory. Was *American Education*, the project, simply a career move? An offer Larry couldn't refuse? The opportunity of a lifetime? After *The Transformation of the School* won the Bancroft Prize, did Larry aspire to be more than just a historian of education and a university professor? Did Larry become enamored of the culture of laurels?

Obviously, these are rhetorical questions, whose answers are, in my opinion at this point, in the affirmative.

Six

American Education: The Colonial Experience, 1607–1783 finally came out in 1970. If Larry or anyone had any second thoughts about the project, they must have been excised when the reviews began to appear. There were positive reviews by Arthur G. Powell and Theodore Sizer, both then at the Harvard University Graduate School of Education—Sizer was its dean[27]—as well as by Merle Borrowman, then dean of the School of Education at the University of California, Berkeley.[28] The reviews by historians and specialists in colonial history must have given Larry special satisfaction. They were all he could have hoped for—a historian's dream come true. "No other history of early American education," said Robert Middlekauff (who would himself win the Bancroft Prize in 1971), "begins to approach Lawrence A. Cremin's study in breadth of knowledge, in imaginative definition of the problems of colonial educational history, or in insight in discussing them." Middlekauff goes on to say that "much in Cremin's method, his research and his conclusions, is fresh and original." Cremin "confronts in a major way . . . the relationship of education to society. . . . His achievement is especially important for American social history as well as for the history of American education." Middlekauff finished by calling *The Colonial Experience* a "detached reconstruction of the history of early American education—massive in research, monumental in range, and penetrating in assessments."[29] Jack P. Greene exclaimed that Larry's inclusive conception of education "is broad enough to have enabled him to produce the most comprehensive study ever published of seventeenth and eighteenth century Anglo-American culture." Greene concluded that the volume was "tightly integrated and lucidly written," a "major work of synthesis and analysis" and "a necessary starting point for all subsequent studies of the first two centuries of American education."[30] John Demos also registered his admiration for *The Colonial Experience*: "There is no way to fault the erudition, the thoroughness, and the sheer sweep of it all. Simply, to have mastered such a huge range of historical materials is a major personal *tour de force*." Then, in a foreshadowing of the reviews of volumes II and III of *American Education,* Demos went on to voice several problems with *The Colonial Experience*. For one: "If earlier historians have defined education too narrowly, Cremin has tried to encompass too much." Cremin "ends by claiming for 'education' virtually the entire range of cultural history. The result is frankly bewildering." And then: "It is ironic but true . . . that Cremin begins from a set of 'revisionist' premises, and proceeds to write in the manner of an earlier generation of historians." But Demos was hopeful that in subsequent volumes Cremin "will be able to sharpen his view of the subject, break free from the old conventions of structure and style, and adopt a more vigorously analytic posture towards his evidence." If so, Demos concluded, "we may yet have the definitive history of American education that he—and perhaps *only* he—is qualified to write."[31]

A few years after the publication of *The Colonial Experience*, in 1974, Larry was elected president of Teachers College. Looking back now, it is clear that Larry should have quit the project then, with *The Colonial Experience* as his legacy to his and Bailyn's "new" history of education and those reviews as a gift to his sponsors. The right time would have been 1974.

I think Larry wanted to be president of Teachers College more than he wanted anything. There was still *American Education*, but now he was embarked on a new career. His working life was no longer dedicated to history. Once Larry became president of Teachers College, his priorities had to change. *American Education* no longer had much relation to his primary professional interests and responsibilities and less to his time. Besides his administrative duties—governance, policy planning, curricula reform, recruiting, mentoring, and monitoring faculty—there were responsibilities for fundraising, public functions, and so forth. Larry was now a full-time administrator and a part-time historian. And Larry was never at rest. In the 1970s he lectured at Harvard, Stanford, the University of London, and the University of Wisconsin, among others. He gave two lecture series in the mid-1970s which were subsequently published as *Public Education* (1976) and *Traditions of American Education* (1977). When he came to UCLA to deliver the John Adams Lecture in 1976, he spent three full days in Los Angeles. He led a delegation of American educators that visited the People's Republic of China during the summer of 1978. He served on the Board of Directors of a half dozen major organizations. He worked on *American Education* whenever he had a spare moment.

Then in the early 1970s, as Larry was working on Volume II of *American Education*, the radical revisionist movement in American educational historiography exploded. Radical revisionism couldn't have come at a worse time for Larry. He didn't have very long to enjoy his status as president of Teachers College and the country's premier historian of education.

Historians of education hardly had a chance to assimilate the significance of Bailyn's and Larry's new history of education when radical revisionism erupted, a development I discuss at greater length elsewhere in the book. The radical revisionists broke with Larry's liberal-consensus view of America and of American educational development, which they perceived as a homogenizing and mystifying history, a history willfully blind to struggle, conflict, and the betrayal of democratic ideals. But radical revisionists went further, into a raw critique of America and American liberalism and a confrontational, in-your-face rhetorical style.

The radical revisionists challenged everything Larry stood for, not only his commitment to liberalism in politics and his progressive emplotment of educational historiography but to civility in discourse. The field of history of American education that he had struggled so mightily to revive in the 1950s was going down around him. Some historians of education, and I was one of them (I was on the Board of Directors of the History of Education Society in the late seventies), were convinced the radical revisionists were trying to take over the History of Education Society and *History of Education Quarterly*.[32]

The conflict over radical revisionism was splitting apart the entire history of education community in the United States (and in Canada). Larry seemed to be unaware of the stakes involved. He could have elevated the controversy over radical revisionism from the level of politics and power to the level of historiography. The radical revisionists had raised questions about schooling that could not be ignored. Larry could have seized the opportunity to undertake a reappraisal of progressive historiography of education, or radical revisionist scholarship, or even a rethinking of *American Education*. He did none of these things. Whether he was preoccupied with being president of Teachers College or whether it was his abhorrence of conflict, Larry remained passive, aloof. For a long time, he did nothing.

Finally, in the late 1970s, Larry realized that something had to be done. Larry never offered his own judgment on the controversy. He chose Diane Ravitch, a disciple, for the assignment; she became his spokesperson in the revisionist affair. Larry saw to it that her famous, or infamous, "The Revisionists Revised: Studies in the Historiography of American Education" (1977) was published by the National Academy of Education, of which he was one of the founders and a former president. "The Revisionists Revised" helped alter the intellectual climate. It stopped the momentum of radical revisionism and created a space for reflection. Thanks to Ravitch, everyone interested learned that there was an alternative version of the history of American education: Larry's version. Ravitch paid a price in vilification by the radical revisionists.[33] Larry paid a price, too. In part because of his refusal to publically engage the radical revisionist controversy, Larry's status as the reigning historian of American education eroded.

Seven

American Education: The National Experience, 1783–1876 finally came out in 1980. It took too long; it was too late in coming. Its historical moment had passed. A new generation of historians had come on the scene. Historiographical fashions change. Larry had no time to keep up with historiography. As the 1960s passed into the 1970s, and the 1970s passed into the 1980s, the questions and "problematics" Larry posed in the early 1960s, which then seemed fresh and promising, could not survive the passage of time. The day of the American-centered, grand narrative occupying the literary space Northrop Frye designated *romance* was over.[34] Didn't Larry remember (he used it frequently in his lectures) Carl Becker's admonition that each generation writes its own history? *American Education* was conceived and meant for a different time. The historiographical mainstream had moved on, but Larry was never willing to change course. Larry was convinced he was on the right course. If the reviews of *The Colonial Experience* were a dream come true, then the reviews of *The National Experience* were a nightmare. They ranged from the dismissive to a critical but balanced middle ground.

Larry was always afraid of being pegged as a latter-day Ellwood P. Cubberley. He prefaced *The National Eperience* with the advice that he had "tried steadfastly to avoid the related sins of Whiggishness and anachronism." In the *American Historical Review*, Michael Katz dismissed *The National Experience*:

> Cremin does not set his history within any systematic exposition of American social and economic development. . . . His book reads as though the work of a generation of social historians on his period barely exists.[35]

Cremin "presents his story as the emergence of a liberal and liberating tradition." From reading this book, Katz continued, "one would have little hint of the violence, poverty, corruption, and racism that marked the late nineteenth and early twentieth century America." Katz concludes, "thus Whiggism and anachronism are avoided." The Bennington College historian Rush Welter's review of *The National Experience* in *Teachers College Record*, no less, must have felt like a knife in the ribs. Welter starts out with praise: "There is no doubting the scope of Cremin's research, the seriousness of his purpose, or the significance of his achievement." He goes on: "As many reviewers of the first volume noted, [Cremin's] history will undoubtedly dominate inquiry in the field for many years to come, just as Ellwood P. Cubberley's work dominated it previously." It is clearly a major study, Welter continued, "one that makes room for a whole range of contemporary scholarship and incorporates it into a definitive account of the American experience conceived as an educational quest." Then, a twist of the knife: "But it is also a monument to that quest, one strikingly similar to the Cubberley-inspired volumes that Cremin has sought to repudiate, and one that seems to me to warrant a similar fate." There was more. Welter described *The National Experience* as "at bottom, establishment history . . . Whig history." Welter added: "Cremin largely ignores questions of pedagogical practice and pays scant attention to pedagogical theory."[36]

Larry must have looked forward to validation at least in the *New York Times*. If Welter's review in *Teachers College Record* wasn't enough, now came the cruelest blow—a harsh review in the *Times* by the historian Kenneth S. Lynn of Johns Hopkins University. Lynn began by praising *The Transformation of the School* as "one of the freshest, most beautifully focused books on the history of education that has ever been published." Then the blows. Cremin, Lynn said, was himself "transformed" by Bernard Bailyn's *Education in the Forming of American Society*; Cremin became Bailyn's "disciple." Cremin's review of *Education in the Forming of American Society*, Lynn declared, was "more than a rave; it testified to a conversion experience." Thenceforth, "Mr. Cremin was no longer his own man, he was another man's disciple." Then:

> It would be a pleasure to say that volume two was worth waiting for, but such
> is not the case. Instead, it confirms the suspicion engendered by volume one
> that Mr. Cremin is engaged in an impossible task. . . . One of the many

unfortunate consequences of [Cremin's] quixotic effort at comprehensiveness is that neither the child nor the schoolhouse receives adequate attention, and another is that the book is so incoherent as to be almost unreadable.[37]

Lynn ended:

In his next volume, Mr. Cremin will presumably attempt to embrace radio and television and all the other educational components of 20th-century American civilization. At the slowing rate at which he is turning out his history, we can look for volume three about the year 2000.[38]

Daniel Howe's review in *History of Education Quarterly* displayed some balance, analyzing the merits of *The National Experience* as well as its flaws. Howe praised *The National Experience* as a "magisterial work and its publication . . . a major event in the field." He referred to its "extraordinary breadth" and called it "magnificent in scope." Cremin's volume, Howe said, "comes closer to being a comprehensive textbook of American cultural history during the first century of independence than anything else we have." Its "massive bibliography will be of lasting benefit to scholars." On the other hand, Howe observed, "the breadth of Cremin's conception entails sacrifice." If there is more on the intellectual and social context, there is too little on the schools and colleges themselves; it is "more valuable as a general cultural history . . . than it is as a history of education, conventionally defined." Howe went on to say that Cremin avoids theories of social change in the book. It is ironic, he continued, that a historian who recognizes the importance of theories for educators should make so little use of them in his own work. Nevertheless, Howe found *The National Experience* "an impressive accomplishment." "If it is not altogether satisfying as a history of education," Howe observed in his penultimate assessment of the work, "it is an indispensable prolegomena to any future one."[39]

That *The National Experience* won the Pulitzer Prize must indeed have come as a "nice surprise" to Larry and provided a measure of solace and even reaffirmation.

But there was still one more volume to go. Howe concluded his review:

Cremin has another volume in his set to produce, and some of the problems pointed out can be remedied there. Unfortunately, the difficulty of his task increases with each volume, for his subject becomes ever vaster and more complex as it moves through time. One cannot withhold admiration from so ambitious an enterprise as this.[40]

That was a very generous sentiment. But I think one could admire an enterprise so ambitious and still think that for Larry to continue with volume III was a mistake. Then again a moment came, another opportunity to say, enough. Larry resigned as president of Teachers College in 1984 and in May 1985 accepted a position as president of the Spencer Foundation. That was the moment. Where were his sponsors, the American Historical Association, the U.S. Office of Education, the Carnegie Corporation? Where were his closest friends and colleagues? Did they ever say: "Larry, you were supposed to finish *American Education* in seven years. It's going on twenty years and you're still not finished. You've won a Pulitzer. That's enough"? Probably not. I'm sure Larry wasn't pressured to finish the project; he chose to finish it. *American Education: The Metropolitan Experience, 1876–1980* came out in 1988. The reviews, as implied in his letter to me of 20 November 1989 referring to the *History of Education Quarterly* "Forum," baffled and frustrated Larry.

In the *American Historical Review,* Laurence Veysey began by saying of *American Education* that it "has unveiled itself in splendid isolation from most scholarship in the field." Cremin's definition of education was so broad "that schooling itself had to be nearly left out." *The Metropolitan Experience* was the best of the three volumes, Veysey conceded, but "has no real bite." The main thrust of the book is "celebration of diversity," but Cremin's "avoidance of all sharp-edged notions of conflict makes his story seem unreal." Veysey claimed that Larry was deeply influenced by Daniel J. Boorstin but "Cremin lacks Boorstin's grace." Veysey ends: "Those seeking a broad account of American culture in the last century, . . . would do better to read Boorstin."[41] In the *Journal of American History,* Thomas James of Brown University gave *The Metropolitan Experience* a more sympathetic review. He noted that Larry handled his "capacious conception of education with extraordinary skill and breadth of learning." He called *The Metropolitan Experience* a "virtuoso performance everywhere alive with intellectual interest." It will be difficult, James wrote, "to imagine anyone attempting to understand the history of American education without attending closely to Cremin's work, not only to disagree with him, as will be inevitable given his consensual and idealistic frame of reference, but also to grasp the centrality of education in this nation's quest for cultural self-definition."[42] Neil Sutherland of the University of British Columbia, Vancouver, gently reproved the strain of American exceptionalism running through *The Metropolitan Ex-*

perience. He found Cremin's portrait of New York City a salutary antidote to much of what appears about the city in popular culture. But, since it plays down those elements that might contribute to a darker view of it, "we see New York not as it has been so much as how it should have been," and so, Sutherland continues, "for much of the views of America in the book as a whole." Nevertheless, *The Metropolitan Experience* is a "major book" which enables us "to see the world in a different way." Sutherland concludes by calling *The Metropolitan Experience* "the culmination of a great work, an outstanding historical accomplishment," and "the final installment of an exemplary work of liberal humanism."[43]

Eight

In my review of Larry's *Popular Education and Its Discontents,* I make the point that history is written for some particular audience, some particular community of discourse, and that the reception of a history is determined by, in Hans Robert Jauss's evocative term, that audience's "horizon of expectations." From this perspective, misreadings occur when there is no fit or a poor fit between a history and the horizon of expectations of its audience.[44] Jauss helps us to better understand the reception of Larry's work: its early canonization and its later fall from grace. In Larry's case, there was a bad fit, too great a distance, between *American Education,* volumes II and III anyway, and its reviewers' horizon of expectations.

American Education is emplotted in the genre of romance—not that of irony, satire, or tragedy. Larry could not conceal his belief that America was in the midst of an extraordinary experiment in educating the populace of a vast, heterogeneous, pluralistic society. Larry does "celebrate." His work is optimistic and full of hope. Larry had no use for gloomy reflections on the state of the nation or the state of American education; no use for what he called "the neo-Marxian literature of alienation." Larry believed completely in the idea of American progress. A constant in Larry's thinking was his unwavering belief in what Jurgen Herbst calls his "American *Paideia*"; America's special destiny and its unique mission in the world. And Larry had a boundless faith in the power of popular education. In 1975, he described the alienation and disenchantment with the public schools as a "passing aberration." "A renaissance is coming," Larry predicted.

In the late 1950s and 1960s the romance genre in historiography was still credible. By 1980, what reviewers of *American Education* preferred, expected, as the only appropriate emplotment for the representation of the past was the rhetorical mode of irony, satire, or tragedy. But there was something else on the reviewers' horizon of expectations. What every reviewer seemed to expect and seemed to want, even to demand, of Lawrence A. Cremin of Teachers College, Columbia, myself included, was a history of American *education*, not a history of American *culture*. And here was Larry writing a kind of anti-history of education. And he was not open to trial and revision. Larry would never make a midcourse concession. This was a major source of so much of the querulous frustration that comes out in so many of the reviews. But I feel there was something else, something more personal, some personal animus. I cannot recall reviews by the community of historians so mean-spirited about so distinguished a colleague.

It may be that, as one of his obituarists, Diane Ravitch, maintains, Larry wrote to please himself and was indifferent to what others thought. But historians don't write to please themselves. And Harper & Row didn't publish *American Education* to please Larry. With the one exception I know of—the *HEQ* "Forum"—Larry never bothered to respond to critics (nor, so far as I know, did anyone answer for him). But he must have been deeply wounded by the reviews of volumes II and III of *American Education*. Anyone who is wondering what might have been the repressed content of Larry's feelings about his reviewers has only to turn to the "President's Comments" in the *Spencer Foundation Annual Report, 1990*, his last report. In the context of some observations about the shortcomings of peer review, Larry delivered himself of these poignant sentences:

> Individuals who disagree on substantive, methodological, or ideological questions can easily transform those disagreements into criticisms of quality. . . . Then, beyond that, one must watch out for the kind of "killer" review one sees from time to time in the book review sections of newspapers, or in theater or music columns—the kind of review that manages to be meanly destructive without being even minimally informative. Good reviewing demands qualities of character and sensibility as well as depth of expertise—the capacity to savor excellence without envy.[45]

What finally is there to say? Much, hopefully, from others who knew Larry. In the meantime, Michael Kammen's observation in "Vanitas and the Historian's Vocation" holds up well as a means of making some sense of Larry's career as a historian, post–*Transformation of the School*:

Ambition may often result in a form of self-imprisonment, with psychological consequences that I cannot begin to fathom . . . Our chosen vocation can become a compulsion, a form of entrapment.[46]

I think there was something in Larry's character, some great personal ambition, some vanitas, that motivated him to undertake *American Education*, to which he devoted a quarter of a century. But I think there was also something valiant, even heroic in Larry's character. I am reminded of Alasdair MacIntyre's observation that "the unity of human life is the unity of a narrative quest."[47] The quest is also, as Northrop Frye reminds us, the archetypal theme of romance. The "romance quest" theme runs thoughout Larry's histories and also says something about Larry and his dedication to finishing *American Education*. Quests sometimes fail, are frustrated, even abandoned. But in the romance quest there is also a strong emphasis on the success or completeness of the hero's achievement. To provide that more accurate, comprehensive, and imaginative history of American education he promised in *The Wonderful World of Ellwood Patterson Cubberley* became Larry's quest. This was not to be his achievement. Somewhere along the long and winding road he traveled as a historian, Larry must have asked himself whether *American Education*, the project, his quest, was worth the effort. Although Larry freely chose how to lead his professional life, I wonder if he ever had any regrets for not having dedicated himself entirely to history (or to administration). Or did he think it was all "misunderstanding and misrepresentation"? My guess is that Larry, like a character in the romantic histories he wrote, never lost hope in the possibility of ultimate triumph and redemption. No matter. If *American Education* started out as vanitas, it became a moral obligation. To complete *American Education* was Larry's achievement. He honored the project. Now Larry was at peace with himself. He was free to turn his attention to John Dewey, the school, and the history of education. Larry's best work may still have been ahead of him.

Notes

1 So far as I know, just two: Lynn Olson, "History: A Lamp to Light the Present," *Education Week* (16 March 1988), pp. 5, 20; and Paul L. Houts, "A Conversation with Lawrence A. Cremin," *National Elementary Principal*, 54 (1975): 23–35.

2 Ellen Condliffe Lagemann and Patricia Albjerg Graham, "Lawrence A. Cremin: A Biographical Memoir," *Teachers College Record*, 96 (1994): 102–113; Diane Ravitch, "Lawrence A. Cremin," *American Scholar*, 61 (1992): 83–89. See also John Calam, "Lawrence A. Cremin, 1925–1990," *Historical Studies in Education/Revue d'histoire de l'éducation*, 2 (1990): 175–176. The quote is from Peter S. Hawkins, "Stitches in Time," *Yale Review*, 83 (1997): 13.

3 Michael Kammen, "Vanitas and the Historian's Vocation," *Reviews in American History*, 10 (1982): 1, 27; and Patricia Nelson Limerick, "Turnerians All: The Dream of a Helpful History in an Intelligible World," *American Historical Review*, 100 (1995): 697–716.

4 New York, 1980.

5 New York, 1988.

6 *Historical Studies in Education/Revue d'histoire de l'éducation*, 1 (1989): 307–326.

7 "The Metropolitan Experience in American Education," *History of Education Quarterly*, 29 (1989): 419–446.

8 New York, 1989.

9 New York, 1961.

10 *New York Times Book Review*, 9 July 1961, sec. VIII, p. 3.

11 *The Reporter*, 8 June 1961, pp. 39–40.

12 *American Quarterly*, 14 (1962): 99–100.

13 *American Historical Review*, 47 (1961): 156–157.

14 *Mississippi Valley Historical Review*, 48 (1961): 549–551.

15 Paul Nash, "The Strange Death of Progressive Education," *Educational Theory*, 14 (1964): 64–75; Myron Lieberman, "The Transformation of the School," *Studies in Philosophy and Education*, 2 (1962): 68–70; J. J. Chambliss, "Review," *History of Education Quarterly*, 3 (1963): 43–52. In recent years I have come to have my own reservations about *The Transformation of the School*. See Chapters 4 and 5.

16 Committee on the Role of Education in American History, *Education and American History* (New York, 1965).

17 Richard J. Storr, "The Role of Education in American History: A Memorandum for the Committee Advising the Fund for the Advancement of Education in Regard to This Subject," *Harvard Educational Review*, 46 (1976): 334.

18 47 (1961): 678–679.

19 *The Wonderful World of Ellwood Patterson Cubberley: An Essay on the Historiography of American Education* (New York, 1965), p. 52.

20 *American Education: The Colonial Experience, 1607–1783* (New York, 1970), p. xii.

21 Ibid.

22 Storr, "The Role of Education in American History," p. 332.

23 Ibid., p. 334.

24 "Historiography and the Historian of Education," in Fred N. Kerlinger, ed., *Review of Research in Education*, 1 (1973): 259.

25 Hood adds: "What the historian of education taking this broader approach does not seem to realize is that he has interpreted himself out of a job." "The Historian of Education: Some Notes on his Role," *History of Education Quarterly*, 9 (1969): 373.

26 Bailyn's involvement in the history of education was a brief flirtation, over when he contributed "Education as a Discipline: Some Historical Notes" to John Walton and James L. Kuethe, eds., *The Discipline of Education* (Madison, 1963). In Bailyn's presidential address to the American Historical Association in 1982, "The Challenge of Modern Historiography," there is no mention of the "new" history of education or any history of education or of Larry. *American Historical Review*, 87 (1982): 1–24.

27 *Harvard Educational Review*, 41 (1971): 250–255; *Saturday Review*, 20 March 1971, pp. 50–51.

28 *Teachers College Record*, 73 (1971): 117–120.

29 *Journal of American History*, 58 (1971): 432–434.

30 *Reviews in American History*, 2 (1973): 183–187.

31 *Commonweal*, 94 (1971): 145–146.

32 For a different take on this period and these events see Harvey J. Graff's reminiscence, "Towards 2000: Poverty and Progress in the History of Education," *Historical Studies in Education/Revue d'histoire de l'éducation*, 7 (1991): 191–210.

33   "The Revisionists Revised: Studies in the Historiography of American Educa-
      tion" was subsequently expanded and published as *The Revisionists Revised:
      A Critique of the Radical Attack on the Schools* (New York, 1978). Michael
      Katz answered in "An Apology for American Educational History," *Harvard
      Educational Review*, 49 (1979): 256–266. I discuss the radical revisionist
      controversy in Chapter 2 of this volume.

34   Dorothy Ross, "Grand Narrative in American Historical Writing: From Ro-
      mance to Uncertainty," *American Historical Review*, 100 (1995): 651–677.

35   *American Historical Review*, 86 (1981): 205–206.

36   *Teachers College Record*, 35 (1981): 702–704.

37   *New York Times Book Review*, 25 January 1981, p. 23.

38   Ibid. Lynn advised that "in lieu of completing *American Education*, Mr. Cremin
      . . . immediately return to writing more manageable books of the sort he
      offered us 20 years ago."

39   "The History of Education as Cultural History," *History of Education Quar-
      terly*, 22 (1982): 205–214. See also Marvin Lazerson, "Lawrence Cremin's
      Democracy in America," *Reviews in American History*, 9 (1981): 382–386,
      and David Tyack and Theodore Mitchell's review in *American Journal of
      Education* (1982): 175–181.

40   "The History of Education as Cultural History," p. 214.

41   *American Historical Review*, 95 (1990): 285. Larry did need a model. He
      may have borrowed two of his titles from Boorstin: *The Americans: The
      Colonial Experience* (New York, 1958), and *The Americans: The National
      Experience* (New York, 1965).

42   *Journal of American History*, 75 (1989): 1340.

43   *Educational Studies* (1990): 318. And see Jurgen Herbst's more fully devel-
      oped critique, "Cremin's American *Paideia*," *American Scholar*, 61 (1991):
      128–140.

44   *Historical Studies in Education/Revue d'histoire de l'éducation*, 4 (1992):
      144–145.

45   Spencer Foundation, *Annual Report, 1990*, p. 9.

46   Michael Kammen, "Vanitas and the Historian's Vocation," *Reviews in Ameri-
      can History*, 10 (1982): 11.

47   *After Virtue: A Study in Moral Theory* (Notre Dame, Ind., 1981), p. 219.

Select Bibliography

Andrew, J. Dudley. *Concepts of Film Theory* (Oxford, England, 1984).

Angelo, Richard. "Myth, Educational Theory, and the Figurative Imagination." *Philosophy of Education, Proceedings* (1978).

————. "Ironies of the Romance and the Romance with Irony: Some Notes on Stylization in the Historiography of American Education Since 1960." *Educational Theory*, 40 (1990).

Ankersmit, Frank, and Hans Kellner, eds. *A New Philosophy of History* (Chicago, 1995).

Appleby, Joyce, Lynn Hunt, and Margaret Jacob. *Telling the Truth About History* (New York, 1994).

Attridge, Derek, Geoff Bennington, and Robert Young, eds. *Post-structuralism and the Question of History* (Cambridge, England, 1987).

Austin, J. L. *How to Do Things with Words* (Oxford, England, 1962).

Bailyn, Bernard. *Education in the Forming of American Society: Needs and Opportunities for Study* (Chapel Hill, 1960).

Ball, Stephen J., ed. *Foucault and Education* (London, 1990).

Barthes, Roland. "The Discourse of History" (1967). In Michael Lane, ed., *Structuralism: A Reader* (London, 1970).

Berkhofer, Robert F., Jr. *Beyond the Great Story: History as Text and Discourse* (Cambridge, Mass., 1995).

Bouwsma, William J. "Intellectual History in the 1980s: From History of Ideas to History of Meaning." *Journal of Interdisciplinary History*, 12 (1981).

Boyer, Paul. *Urban Masses and Moral Order in America, 1820–1920* (Cambridge, Mass., 1978).

Breisach, Ernst. *Historiography: Ancient, Medieval, and Modern,* 2nd ed. (Chicago, 1994).

Bruner, Jerome. *Actual Minds, Possible Worlds* (Cambridge, Mass., 1986).

Buck, Paul H., Clarence Faust, Richard Hofstadter, Arthur Schlesinger, Sr., and Richard J. Storr. *The Role of Education in American History* (New York, 1957).

Buenker, John D., John C. Burnham, and Robert M. Crunden. *Progressivism* (Cambridge, Mass., 1977).

Burke, Peter. *History and Social Theory* (Ithaca, N.Y., 1992).

————, ed. *New Perspectives on Historical Writing* (Cambridge, England, 1991).

Burstyn, Joan. "History as Image: Changing the Lens." *History of Education Quarterly,* 27 (1987).

Canary, Robert, and Henry Kozicki. *The Writing of History: Literary Form and Historical Understanding* (Madison, 1978).

Carpenter, Ronald H. *History as Rhetoric: Style, Narrative and Persuasion* (Columbia, S.C., 1995).

Carrard, Philippe. *Poetics of the New History: French Historical Discourse from Braudel to Chartier* (Baltimore, 1992).

Caws, Peter. *Structuralism: The Art of the Intelligible* (London, 1990).

Chartier, Roger. *Cultural History: Between Practices and Representations* (London, 1988).

————. *On the Edge of the Cliff: History, Language, and Practices* (Baltimore, 1997).

Church, Robert L., Michael B. Katz, Harold Silver, and Lawrence A. Cremin. "The Metropolitan Experience in American Education." *History of Education Quarterly,* 29 (1989).

Coben, Stanley. *Rebellion Against Victorianism: The Impetus for Cultural Change in 1920s America* (New York, 1991).

Cohen, Sol. Review of *American Education: The Metropolitan Experience, 1876–1980*, by Lawrence A. Cremin. *Historical Studies in Education/Revue d'histoire de l'éducation*, 1 (1989).

————. "The Triumph of the Therapeutic." *History of Education Quarterly*, 30 (1990).

————. Review of *Popular Education and Its Discontents*, by Lawrence A. Cremin. *Historical Studies in Education/Revue d'histoire de l'éducation*, 4 (1992).

———— and Marc Depaepe, eds. "History of Education in the Postmodern Era." *Paedagogica Historica*, 32 (1996).

Committee on the Role of Education in American History. *Education and American History* (New York, 1965).

Conkin, Paul K., and Roland R. Stromberg. *Heritage and Challenge: The History and Theory of History* (Arlington Heights, Va., 1989).

Cremin, Lawrence A. *The Transformation of the School: Progressivism in American Education, 1876–1956* (New York, 1961).

————. *The Wonderful World of Ellwood Patterson Cubberley: An Essay on the Historiography of American Education* (New York, 1965).

————. *Traditions of American Education* (New York, 1977).

————. *American Education: The Metropolitan Experience, 1876–1980* (New York, 1988).

————. *Popular Education and Its Discontents* (New York, 1990).

Cuban, Larry. "Reforming Again, Again, and Again." *Educational Researcher*, 19 (1990).

Cubberley, Ellwood P. *Public Education in the United States: A Study and Interpretation of American Educational History* (Boston, 1919).

Culler, Jonathan. *The Pursuit of Signs: Semiotics, Literature, Deconstruction* (Ithaca, N.Y., 1981).

Cunningham, Peter. "Educational History and Educational Change: The Past Decade of English Historiography." *History of Education Quarterly*, 29 (1989).

Curti, Merle. *The Social Ideas of American Educators* (Paterson, N.J., 1959).

Darnton, Robert. "Intellectual and Cultural History." In Michael Kammen, ed., *The Past Before Us: Contemporary Historical Writing in the United States* (Ithaca, N.Y., 1980).

Davis, Natalie Zemon. *Fiction in the Archives* (Cambridge, England, 1987).

De Certeau, Michel. *The Writing of History* (New York, 1988).

Depaepe, Marc. "History of Education Anno 1992." *History of Education*, 22 (1993).

————. "Demythologizing the Educational Past: An Endless Task in the History of Education." *Historical Studies in Education/Revue d'histoire de l'éducation*, 9 (1997).

De Saussure, Ferdinand. *Course in General Linguistics*, trans. by Roy Harris. (London, 1983).

Docherty, Thomas, ed. *Postmodernism: A Reader* (New York, 1993).

Donzelot, Jacques. *The Policing of Families,* trans. by Robert Hurley. (New York, 1979).

Eagleton, Terry. *Literary Theory: An Introduction* (Minneapolis, 1983).

Eco, Umberto. *The Limits of Interpretation* (Bloomington, Ind., 1994).

Escolano, Agustín. "Postmodernity or High Modernity? Emerging Approaches in the History of Education." *Paedagogica Historica*, 32 (1996).

Fairclough, Norman. *Discourse and Social Change* (Cambridge, England, 1994).

Fass, Paula S. *Outside In: Minorities and the Transformation of American Education* (New York, 1989).

Fish, Stanley. *Is There a Text in This Class? The Authority of Interpretive Communities* (Cambridge, Mass., 1980).

Foster, Hal, ed. *The Anti-Aesthetic: Essays in Postmodern Culture* (Seattle, 1983).

Foucault, Michel. *Discipline and Punish: The Birth of the Prison* (New York, 1977).

Fox, Richard Wightman, and T. J. Jackson Lears, eds. *The Power of Culture: Critical Essays in American History* (Chicago, 1993).

Frye, Northrop. *Anatomy of Criticism: Four Essays* (Princeton, 1957).

Gardiner, Juliet, ed. *What Is History Today?* (London, 1988).

Geertz, Clifford. *The Interpretation of Culture: Selected Essays* (New York, 1973).

Gibson, Walker. "Authors, Speakers, and Mock Readers." In Jane P. Tompkins, ed., *Reader-Response Criticism: From Formalism to Post-Structuralism* (Baltimore, 1980).

Giroux, Henry A., and Roger I. Simon, eds. *Popular Culture, Schooling, and Everyday Life* (New York, 1989).

Goodman, Nelson. *Ways of Worldmaking* (Indianapolis, 1978).

Gordon, Colin, ed. *Michel Foucault: Power/Knowledge.* (New York, 1980).

Gordon, Peter, and Richard Szreter, eds., *History of Education: The Making of a Discipline* (London, 1989)

Graff, Harvey J. "Towards 2000: Poverty and Progress in the History of Education." *Historical Studies in Education/Revue d'histoire de l'éducation,* 3 (1991).

Grob, Gerald. *Mental Illness and American Society, 1876–1940* (Princeton, 1983).

Gubrium, Jaber F., and James A. Holstein. *The New Language of Qualitative Method* (New York, 1997).

Hale, Nathan G., Jr. *Freud and the Americans: The Beginnings of Psychoanalysis in the United States, 1876–1917* (New York, 1971).

————. *The Rise and Crisis of Psychoanalysis in the United States: Freud and the Americans, 1917–1985* (New York, 1995).

Harari, Josué V., ed. *Textual Strategies: Perspectives in Post-Structuralist Criticism* (Ithaca, N.Y., 1979).

Harlan, David. *The Degradation of American History* (Chicago, 1997).

Harland, Richard. *Superstructuralism: The Philosophy of Structuralism and Post-Structuralism* (London, 1987).

Herbst, Jurgen. "Beyond the Debate Over Revisionism." *History of Education Quarterly*, 20 (1980).

————. "Cremin's American *Paideia*." *American Scholar*, 60 (1991).

————. "Toward a Theory of Progressive Education?" *History of Education Quarterly*, 37 (1997).

Higham, John, and Paul K. Conkin, eds. *New Directions in American Intellectual History* (Baltimore, 1979).

Holub, Robert C. *Reception Theory: A Critical Introduction* (London, 1984).

Hollinger, David A. *In the American Province: Studies in the History and Historiography of Ideas* (Baltimore, 1985).

Howe, Daniel. "The History of Education as Cultural History." *History of Education Quarterly*, 22 (1982).

————, ed. *Victorian America* (Philadelphia, 1976).

Hunt, Lynn, ed. *The New Cultural History* (Berkeley, 1989).

Hutcheon, Linda. *A Poetics of Postmodernism: History, Theory, Fiction* (New York, 1988).

Ingleby, David, ed. *Critical Psychiatry: The Politics of Mental Health* (New York, 1981).

Jackson, James R. de Jager. *Historical Criticism and the Meaning of Texts* (London, 1989).

Jarausch, Konrad H. "The Old 'New History of Education': A German Reconsideration." *History of Education Quarterly*, 26 (1986).

Jay, Martin. "Should Intellectual History Take a Linguistic Turn?" In Dominick LaCapra and Steven L. Kaplan, eds., *Modern European Intellectual History: Reappraisals and New Perspectives* (Ithaca, N.Y., 1982).

Jenkins, Keith. *Re-Thinking History* (London, 1991).

Johnson, Barbara. *The Critical Difference: Essays in the Contemporary Rhetoric of Reading* (Baltimore, 1980).

Kaestle, Carl F. "Recent Methodological Developments in the History of American Education." In Richard M. Jaeger, ed., *Complementary Methods for Research in Education* (Washington, D.C., 1986).

―――. "Standards of Evidence in Historical Research: How Do We Know When We Know?" *History of Education Quarterly*, 32 (1992).

Kammen, Michael. "Vanitas and the Historian's Vocation." *Reviews in American History*, 10 (1982).

―――. *Selvages and Biases: The Fabric of History in American Culture* (Ithaca, N.Y., 1987).

Kaplan, E. Ann, ed. *Postmodernism and Its Discontents: Theories, Practices* (New York, 1988).

Katz, Michael B. *The Irony of Early School Reform: Educational Innovation in Mid-Nineteenth Century Massachusetts* (Cambridge, Mass., 1968).

―――. "An Apology for American Educational History." *Harvard Educational Review*, 49 (1979).

―――. *Reconstructing American Education* (Cambridge, Mass., 1987).

Kellner, Hans. *Language and Historical Representation: Getting the Story Crooked* (Madison, 1989).

Kett, Joseph. "On Revisionism." *History of Education Quarterly*, 19 (1979).

Kliebard, Herbert M. *The Struggle for the American Curriculum, 1893–1958* (New York, 1987).

Kloppenberg, James T. "Objectivity and Historicism: A Century of American Historical Writing." *American Historical Review*, 94 (1989).

Kozicki, Henry, ed. *Developments in Modern Historiography* (New York, 1993).

Kramer, Lloyd S. "Literature, Criticism, and Historical Imagination: The Literary Challenge of Hayden White and Dominick LaCapra." In Lynn Hunt, ed., *The New Cultural History* (Berkeley, 1989).

Kuhn, Thomas S. *The Structure of Scientific Revolutions*, 2nd ed. (Chicago, 1970).

LaCapra, Dominick. *Rethinking Intellectual History: Texts, Contexts, Language* (Ithaca, N.Y., 1982).

————, and Steven L. Kaplan, eds. *Modern European Intellectual History: Reappraisals and New Perspectives* (Ithaca, N.Y., 1982).

Lagemann, Ellen Condliffe, and Patricia Albjerg Graham. "Lawrence A. Cremin: A Biographical Memoir." *Teachers College Record*, 96 (1994).

Lasch, Christopher. *Haven in a Heartless World: The Family Besieged*. (New York, 1977).

Lazerson, Marvin. "Lawrence Cremin's Democracy in America." *Reviews in American History*, 9 (1981).

Lears, T. J. Jackson. *No Place of Grace: Antimodernism and the Transformation of American Culture, 1880–1920* (Chicago, 1983).

Limerick, Patricia Nelson. "Turnerians All: The Dream of a Helpful History in An Intelligible World." *American Historical Review*, 100 (1995).

Lowe, Roy. "Postmodernity and Historians of Education: A View from Britain." *Paedagogica Historica*, 32 (1996).

Lowenthal, David. *The Past is a Foreign Country* (Cambridge, Mass., 1985).

MacIntyre, Alasdair. *After Virtue: A Study in Moral Theory* (Notre Dame, Ind., 1984).

Martusewicz, Rebecca A., and William M. Reynolds, eds. *Inside/Out: Contemporary Critical Perspectives in Education* (New York, 1994).

Matthews, Fred H. "The Americanization of Sigmund Freud: Adaptations of Psychoanalysis Before 1917." *Journal of American Studies*, 1 (1967).

————. "In Defense of Common Sense: Mental Hygiene as Ideology and Mentality in Twentieth-Century America." *Prospects*, 2 (1979).

McClellan, Edward B. *Schools and the Shaping of Character: Moral Education in America, 1607-Present* (Bloomington, Ind., 1991).

Megill, Allan. "Recounting the Past: Description, Explanation and Narrative in Historiography." *American Historical Review*, 94 (1989).

Middlekauff, Robert. Review of Lawrence A. Cremin, *American Education: The Colonial Experience, 1607–1783* (New York, 1970). *Journal of American History*, 58 (1971).

Molho, Anthony, and Gordon S. Wood, eds., *Imagined Histories: American Historians Interpret the Past* (Princeton, 1998).

Nichols, Bill. *Ideology and the Image: Social Representation in the Cinema and Other Media* (Bloomington, Ind., 1981).

Norris, Christopher. *Deconstruction: Theory and Practice* (London, 1982).

Novick, Peter. *That Noble Dream: The "Objectivity Question" and the American Historical Profession* (Cambridge, England, 1988).

Pagden, Anthony. "The Linguistic Turn and Intellectual History." *Journal of the History of Ideas*, 49 (1988).

Palmer, Bryan D. *Descent into Discourse: The Reification of Language and the Writing of Social History* (Philadelphia, 1990).

Platt, Anthony M. *The Child Savers: The Invention of Delinquency* (Chicago, 1974).

Pocock, John G. A. *Politics, Language and Time: Essays on Political Thought and History* (New York, 1971).

———. "Intellectual History." In Juliet Gardiner, ed., *What Is History Today?* (London, 1988).

Polsky, Andrew J. *The Rise of the Therapeutic State* (Princeton, 1991).

Porter, Theodore M. *Trust in Numbers: The Pursuit of Objectivity in Science and Public Life.* (Princeton, 1995).

Poster, Mark. *Cultural History and Postmodernity* (New York, 1997).

Rabb, Theodore K., and Robert I. Rotberg, eds. *The New History: The 1980s and Beyond* (Princeton, 1982).

Ravitch, Diane. *The Revisionists Revised: A Critique of the Radical Attack on the Schools* (New York, 1978).

————. *The Troubled Crusade: American Education, 1945–1980* (New York, 1983).

————. "Lawrence A. Cremin." *American Scholar*, 61 (1992).

————, and Maris A. Vinovskis, eds. *Learning from the Past: What History Teaches Us About School Reform* (Baltimore, 1995).

Reitman, Sanford W. *The Educational Messiah Complex: American Faith in the Culturally Redemptive Power of Schooling* (Sacramento, Ca., 1992).

Richardson, Theresa R. *The Century of the Child: the Mental Hygiene Movement & Social Policy in the United States and Canada* (Albany, N.Y., 1989).

Ricouer, Paul. *From Text to Action* (London, 1991).

Rieff, Philip. *The Triumph of the Therapeutic: Uses of Faith After Freud* (New York, 1966).

Rodgers, Daniel T. "In Search of Progressivism." *Reviews in American History*, 10 (1982).

Röhrs, Hermann, and Volker Lenhart, eds. *Progressive Education Across the Continents* (Frankfurt am Main, 1995).

Rorty, Richard. *Contingency, Irony, and Solidarity* (Cambridge, England, 1989).

Rosenau, Pauline M. *Post-Modernism and the Social Sciences: Insights, Inroads, and Intrusions.* (Princeton, 1992).

Rosenstone, Robert A. *Revisioning History: Film and the Construction of a New Past* (Princeton, 1995).

————. *Visions of the Past: The Challenge of Film to Our Idea of History* (Cambridge, Mass., 1995).

Ross, Dorothy. "Grand Narrative in American Historical Writing: From Romance to Uncertainty." *American Historical Review*, 100 (1995).

Rothman, David J. "The State as Parent: Social Policy in the Progressive Era." In Willard Gaylin et al., eds., *Doing Good: The Limits of Benevolence* (New York, 1978).

————. *Conscience and Convenience: The Asylum and its Alternatives in Progressive America* (Boston, 1980).

Rury, John L."*Transformation* in Perspective: Lawrence Cremin's *Transformation of the School.*" *History of Education Quarterly*, 31 (1991).

Sarup, Madan, *An Introductory Guide to Post-Structuralism and Postmodernism* (Athens, Ga., 1989).

Scott, Joan Wallach. *Gender and the Politics of History* (New York, 1988).

Selden, Raman. *A Reader's Guide to Contemporary Literary Theory* (Brighton, England, 1985).

Seller, Maxine Schwartz. "Boundaries, Bridges, and the History of Education." *History of Education Quarterly*, 31 (1991).

Skinner, Quentin, ed. *The Return of Grand Theory in the Human Sciences* (Cambridge, England, 1985).

Sklar, Robert, and Charles Musser, eds. *Resisting Images: Essays on Cinema and History* (Philadelphia, 1989).

Smith, Wilson. "The New Historian of American Education." *Harvard Educational Review*, 31 (1961).

Sobchack, Vivian, ed. *The Persistence of History: Cinema, Television, and the Modern Event* (New York, 1996).

Southgate, Beverly. *History: What and Why? Ancient, Modern, and Postmodern Perspectives* (New York, 1996).

Storey, John. *An Introductory Guide to Cultural Theory and Popular Culture* (Athens, Ga., 1993).

Storr, Richard J. "The Role of Education in American History: A Memorandum for the Committee Advising the Fund for the Advancement of Education in Regard to This Subject." *Harvard Educational Review*, 46 (1976).

Stromberg, Roland A. "Some Models Used by Intellectual Historians." *American Historical Review*, 80 (1975).

Suleiman, Susan R., and Inge Crosman, eds. *The Reader in the Text: Essays on Audience and Interpretation* (Princeton, 1980).

Susman, Warren I. "History and the American Intellectual: Uses of a Usable Past." *American Quarterly*, 16 (1964).

————. "'Personality' and the Making of Twentieth-Century Culture." In John Higham and Paul K. Conkin, eds., *New Directions in American Intellectual History* (Baltimore, 1979).

————. *Culture as History: The Transformation of American Society in the Twentieth Century* (New York, 1984).

Sutherland, Neil. Review of *American Education: The Metropolitan Experience, 1876–1980,* by Lawrence A. Cremin. *Educational Studies*, 21 (1990).

Taylor, Charles. *Human Agency and Language. Philosophical Papers I* (Cambridge, England, 1985).

Taylor, William, ed. *Metaphors of Education* (London, 1984).

Toews, John E. "Intellectual History After the Linguistic Turn." *American Historical Review*, 92 (1987).

Tompkins, Jane P., ed. *Reader-Response Criticism: From Formalism to Post-Structuralism* (Baltimore, 1980).

Tyack, David B. *The One Best System: A History of American Urban Education* (Cambridge, Mass., 1974).

————, and Elisabeth Hansot. "Using Photographs as Evidence of Gender Practice in Schools." In *Learning Together: A History of Coeducation in American Schools* (New Haven, 1990).

————, and William Tobin. "The 'Grammar' of Schooling: Why Has It Been So Hard to Change?" *American Educational Research Journal*, 31 (1994).

————, and Larry Cuban. *Tinkering Toward Utopia: A Century of Public School Reform* (Cambridge, Mass., 1995).

Veeser, H. Aram, ed. *The New Historicism* (New York, 1989).

Veyne, Paul. *Writing History: Essay on Epistemology* (Middletown, Conn., 1984).

Wagoner, Jennings L., Jr. "Historical Revisionism, Educational Theory, and an American *Paideia*." *History of Education Quarterly*, 18 (1978).

White, Hayden. *Tropics of Discourse: Essays in Cultural Criticism* (Baltimore, 1978).

————. *The Content of the Form: Narrative Discourse and Historical Representation* (Baltimore, 1987).

Wilson, J. Donald. "The New Diversity in Canadian Educational History." *Acadiensis*, 19 (1990).

Wood, Gordon S. "Intellectual History and the Social Sciences." In John Higham and Paul K. Conkin, eds., *New Directions in American Intellectual History* (Baltimore, 1979).

Yogev, Abraham, ed. "Educational Reform in International Perspective." *International Perspectives on Education and Society*, 4 (1994).

Index

COUNTERPOINTS

Studies in the Postmodern Theory of Education

General Editors
Joe L. Kincheloe & Shirley R. Steinberg

Counterpoints publishes the most compelling and imaginative books being written in education today. Grounded on the theoretical advances in criticalism, feminism and postmodernism in the last two decades of the twentieth century, Counterpoints engages the meaning of these innovations in various forms of educational expression. Committed to the proposition that theoretical literature should be accessible to a variety of audiences, the series insists that its authors avoid esoteric and jargonistic languages that transform educational scholarship into an elite discourse for the initiated. Scholarly work matters only to the degree it affects consciousness and practice at multiple sites. Counterpoints' editorial policy is based on these principles and the ability of scholars to break new ground, to open new conversations, to go where educators have never gone before.

For additional information about this series or for the submission of manuscripts, please contact:

> Joe L. Kincheloe & Shirley R. Steinberg
> 637 West Foster Avenue
> State College, PA 16801